Computer-Aided Design of User Interfaces III

AF181559

Sponsors

Official CADUI WWW site: http://www.isys.ucl.ac.be/bchi/cadui

Université de Valenciennes et du Hainaut-Cambrésis
http://www.univ-valenciennes.fr/

Laboratoire d'Automatique, de Mécanique et d'Informatique, industrielles et Humaines (LAMIH)
http://www.univ-valenciennes.fr/LAMIH/

Institut des Sciences et Techniques de Valenciennes
http://www.univ-valenciennes.fr/ISTV/

Région Nord-Pas de Calais
http://www.cr-npdc.fr/

Ville de Valenciennes
http://www.ville-valenciennes.fr

The XIML Forum
http://www.ximl.org/

Ministère de la Recherche
http://www.recherche.gouv.fr/

Centre National de la Recherche Scientifique (CNRS)
http://www.cnrs.fr

Institut National de Recherche en Automatique et en Informatique (INRIA) http://www.inria.fr

Association Francophone d'Interaction Homme-Machine (AFIHM) http://www.afihm.org

ACM Belgian SIGCHI Chapter (BelCHI)
http://www.belchi.be

Institut d'Administration et de Gestion
http://www.iag.ucl.ac.be/

Université catholique de Louvain
http://www.ucl.ac.be

COMPUTER-AIDED DESIGN OF USER INTERFACES III

Proceedings of the Fourth International Conference on
Computer-Aided Design of User Interfaces
15-17 May 2002, Valenciennes, France

edited by

Christophe Kolski
Université de Valenciennes et du Hainaut-Cambrésis,
Valenciennes, France

and

Jean Vanderdonckt
Université catholique de Louvain,
Louvain-la-Neuve, Belgium

SPRINGER-SCIENCE+BUSINESS MEDIA, B.V.

A C.I.P. Catalogue record for this book is available from the Library of Congress.

ISBN 978-94-010-3915-4 ISBN 978-94-010-0421-3 (eBook)
DOI 10.1007/978-94-010-0421-3

Printed on acid-free paper

All Rights Reserved
© 2002 Springer Science+Business Media Dordrecht
Originally published by Kluwer Academic Publishers in 2002
Softcover reprint of the hardcover 1st edition 2002

No part of this work may be reproduced, stored in a retrieval system, or transmitted in any form or by any means, electronic, mechanical, photocopying, microfilming, recording or otherwise, without written permission from the Publisher, with the exception of any material supplied specifically for the purpose of being entered and executed on a acomputer system, for exclusive use by the purchaser of the work.

TABLE OF CONTENTS

Invited speakers

1. Computer-Aided Design of User Interfaces by Example 1
   H. Lieberman
2. Foundations for a Theory of Contextors 13
   J. Coutaz and G. Rey
3. WSXL: A Web Services Language
   for Integrating End-User Experience 35
   D. Chamberlain, A. Diaz, D. Gisolfi, R. Konuru, J. Lucassen,
   J. Macnaught, S. Maes, R. Merrick, D. Mundel, TV Raman,
   S. Ramaswamy, T. Schaeck, R. Thompson, and Ch. Wiecha

Specification of User Interfaces

4. From Formal Specifications to Secure Implementations 51
   F. Jambon
5. Just-UI : A User Interface Specification Model 63
   P.J. Molina, S. Meliá, and O. Pastor
6. DTS-Edit : an Interactive Development Environment for
   Structured Dialog Applications 75
   F. Depaulis, S. Maiano, and G. Texier

Task Scenarios: Elicitation and Derivation

7. Automatically Eliciting Task Models from Written Task Narratives 83
   M. Brasser and K. Vander Linden
8. From Usage Scenarios to User Interface Elements in a Few Steps 91
   H. Kaindl and R. Jezek
9. Exploring Design Heuristics for User Interface Derivation
   from Task and Domain Models 103
   C. Pribeanu and J. Vanderdonckt

Model-Based Approaches

10. A User Modeling Design Tool Based on a Cognitive
    Architecture for Comparing Interfaces 111
    F.R. Ritter, D. Van Rooy, and R. St. Amant
11. A Model-Guided and Task-Based Approach to User Interface
    Design Centered in a Unified Interaction and Architectural Model ... 119
    C.V. Serey Guerrero and B. Lula Jr.
12. Using User Interface Models in Design 131
    H. Trætteberg

User Interfaces for Multiple Contexts of Use

13. One Model, Many Interfaces 143
F. Paternò and C. Santoro

14. Combining Handcrafting and Automatic Generation of User-Interfaces for Pervasive Devices 155
L.D. Bergman, G. Banavar, D. Soroker, and J. Sussman

15. Concepts for Generating Multi-User Interfaces Including Graphical Editors 167
A. Brandl

Domain-Oriented Model-Based Approaches

16. DIGBE : Online Model-Based Design Automation 179
R. Penner and E. Steinmetz

17. Meeting Activity Theory through Task-Based and User-Oriented Development of User Interfaces 193
Ch. Stary

18. Model-Based Interactive Prototyping of Highly Interactive Applications 205
D. Navarre, Ph. Palanque, and R. Bastide

Innovative Model-Based Approaches

19. Modeling Style of Work as an Aid to the Design and Evaluation of Interactive Systems 217
J. Wu, T.C.N. Graham, K. Everitt, D. Blostein, and E. Lank

20. An Online Multimedia System for Learning to Design User Interfaces 229
E. Furtado, V. Furtado, K. Sousa, and A. Belchior

21. UML and Interactive Systems, Another Step Forward 243
J.R. Ruault

UIML- and XML-Based User Interfaces

22. Building Multi-Platform User Interfaces with UIML 255
M.F. Ali, M.A. Pérez-Quiñones, M. Abrams, and E. Shell

23. Development of an UIML Renderer for Different Target Languages 267
C. Binnig and A. Schmidt

24. Generic Interface Descriptions using XML 275
K. Richter

User Interface Migration: Forward and Backward

25. Specifying User Interfaces for Runtime Modal Independent Migration ... 283
K. Luyten, T. Van Laerhoven, K. Coninx, and F. Van Reeth
26. Reverse Engineering Interaction Plans for Legacy Interface Migration ... 295
E. Stroulia and R.V. Kapoor
27. Recovering Alternative Presentation Models of a Web Page with VAQUITA ... 311
L. Bouillon, J. Vanderdonckt, and N. Souchon

Usability Engineering and the Web

28. Evidence-Based Usability Engineering ... 323
E. Metzker and H. Reiterer
29. A Framework and a Language for Usability Automatic Evaluation of Web Sites by Static Analysis of HTML Source Code ... 337
A. Beirekdar, J. Vanderdonckt, and M. Noirhomme-Fraiture
30. First Steps Towards Task-Related Web User Interfaces ... 349
B. Bomsdorf

Agent-Based User Interfaces

31. Cooperative Agents Design in a Technological Watch Context ... 357
L. Jonnequin, E. Adam, Ch. Kolski, and R. Mandiau
32. A Multi-Agent Approach to Cooperative Work ... 367
J.C. Routier and P. Mathieu
33. Agent Oriented Specification of Interactive Systems: Basic Principles and Industrial Case Study ... 381
F. Cartegnie, H. Ezzedine, and Ch. Kolski

PROGRAMME COMMITTEE MEMBERS

Mourad Abed, Univ. de Valenciennes et du Hainaut-Cambrésis, France
Demosthenes Akoumianakis, ICS-FORTH, Greece
Ghassan Al-Qaimari, RMIT University, Australia
Thomas Baudel, ILOG, France
Alain Derycke, Université des Sciences et Technologies de Lille, France
Houcine Ezzedine, Univ. de Valenciennes et du Hainaut-Cambrésis, France
Jean-Daniel Fekete, Ecole des Mines de Nantes, France
Peter Forbrig, University of Rostock, Germany
Elizabeth Furtado, University of Fortaleza, Brazil
Patrick Girard, LISI/ENSMA, France
Emmanuelle Grislin-Le Strugeon, Université de Valenciennes et du Hainaut-Cambrésis, France
Peter Johnson, University of Bath, UK
Christophe Kolski, Univ. de Valenciennes et du Hainaut-Cambrésis, France
Henri Lieberman, MIT, USA
Frank Lonczewski, BetaResearch, Germany
Claude Machgeels, Université Libre de Bruxelles, Belgium
Mark Maybury, The MITRE Corp., USA
Faouzi Moussa, ENSI Tunis, Tunisia
Jocelyne Nanard, Université de Montpellier, France
Philippe Palanque, Université Paul Sabatier, France
Fabio Paternò, ISTI-CNR, Italy
Norman Paton, University of Manchester, UK
Angel Puerta, RedWhale Software Corp., USA
Anthony Savidis, ICS-FORTH, Greece
Dominique Scapin, INRIA, France
Egbert Schlungbaum, University of Rostock, Germany
Robert St. Amant, North Carolina State University, USA
Constantine Stephanidis, ICS-FORTH, Greece
Eleni Stroulia, University of Alberta, Canada
Pedro Szekely, University of Southern California, USA
Jean Vanderdonckt, Université catholique de Louvain, Belgium
Charles Wiecha, IBM T.J. Watson Research Centre, USA

CONFERENCE ADDITIONAL REVIEWERS

Emmanuel Adam, Univ. de Valenciennes et du Hainaut-Cambrésis, France
Ayman Ammoura, University of Alberta, Canada
Rémi Bastide, LIHS, Université Toulouse 1, France
Pablo Figueroa, University of Alberta, Canada
Murielle Florins, Université catholique de Louvain, Belgium
Nick Graham, Queen's University, Canada
Tony Griffiths, University of Manchester, UK
Maurine Hatch, University of Alberta, Canada
Quentin Limbourg, Université catholique de Louvain, Belgium
Céline Mariage, Université catholique de Louvain, Belgium
Panos Markopoulos, Technische Univ. Eindhoven, The Netherlands
André Péninou, IUT Blagnac, France
Paulo Pinheiro da Silva, University of Manchester, UK
Chris Roast, Sheffield Hallam University, UK
Carmen Santoro, ISTI-CNR, Italy
Yiqiao Wang, University of Alberta, Canada

Chapter 1

COMPUTER-AIDED DESIGN OF USER INTERFACES BY EXAMPLE

Henry Lieberman
Media Laboratory, Massachusetts Institute of Technology (MIT), 20 Ames St. 320 G Cambridge, MA 02139 (USA)
E-mail: lieber@media.mit.edu – URL: http://lieber.www.media.mit.edu/people/lieber/
Tel.: +1-617-253-0315 – Fax: +1-617-253-6215

Abstract A promising approach to Computer-Aided Design of User Interfaces (CADUI) is *Programming by Example*, where an interface designer demonstrates the behavior of an interface by presenting concrete examples and demonstrating how the system should behave on those examples. It lets the user interface designer "play end-user", simulating what an end-user would see and do. A software agent records the steps of the user interface and generalizes a program that can be used in analogous situations in the future. The popular genre of so-called Interface Builders can be seen as a "poor-man's" Programming by Example. It is now time to extend such systems so that behavior as well as appearance can be specified by example.

Keywords: Computer-aided design, Interface builders, Machine learning, Programming by demonstration, Programming by example, Software agents.

1. CAD/CAM AND USER INTERFACE DESIGN

The goal of Computer-aided Design of User Interfaces (CADUI) is to enlist the computer to aid an interface designer in constructing an interactive interface to be eventually used by an end-user. This point of view is by analogy to Computer-Aided Design and Computer-Aided Manufacturing (CAD or CAD/CAM). CAD traditionally refers to tools to visualize, describe, edit and test manufactured artifacts, which are now an indispensable part of all manufacturing and production processes.

Computer-Aided Design systems are successful in manufacturing because they replace the specifications of numerical parameters, a task difficult

C. Kolski and J. Vanderdonckt (eds.), Computer-Aided Design of User Interfaces III, 1–12.
© 2002 *Kluwer Academic Publishers.*

for humans to perform reliably, with the visualization and editing of visual representations of virtual objects, which is much more natural for humans to perform. Computer-Aided Design systems can be successful in user interface design because they replace specification of programming language constructs, which are difficult for humans to perform reliably, with the visualization and editing of visual representations of virtual interfaces, which are more natural for humans to perform (Fig. 1).

While manufacturing CAD systems are oriented towards describing the size and shape (and perhaps associated attributes such as materials or cost) of products, user interface CAD must not only describe the appearance and form of the user interface, but also the behavior of the interface. If, for a given interface, each interface element can have its own independent behavior, then a user interface often can be defined simply by combining and connecting pre-defined behavioral elements. But if there are interactions between the elements, if there is state to be maintained, or particular actions to be taken, then some other method for describing the behavior must be found. The usual approach is for the interface designer to write code in a traditional programming language, like C or Java, or text in a high-level interface description language.

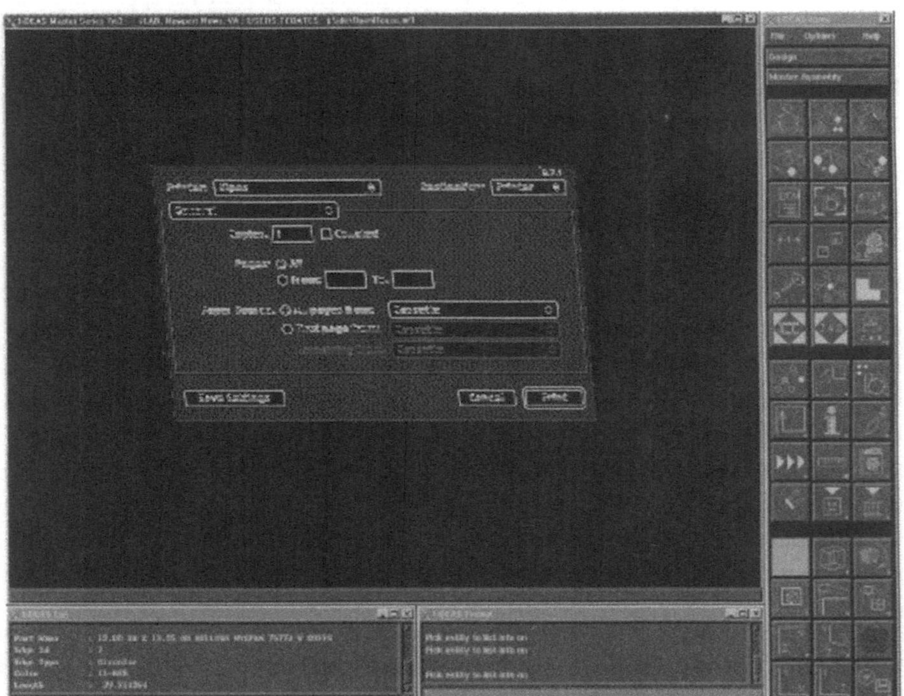

Figure 1. Can we design user interfaces the way we design CAD artifacts?

But writing and debugging in these languages is a difficult cognitive task for most people. To make the CAD analogy complete, it would be better if we could specify dynamic behavior by visualizing and editing virtual objects visually represented on the screen than by writing textual specifications, no matter how high level the language.

2. PROGRAMMING BY EXAMPLE

It is this goal which is the objective of *Programming by Example* (PBE, sometimes also called Programming by Demonstration). With Programming by Example, the user interface designer gets to "play user". He or she takes on the role of operating the user interface in the same manner as the intended end-user would, interacting with the on-screen interface components to demonstrate concrete examples of how to use the interface. The PBE system records the steps of the interaction, and synthesizes a program, in a similar manner to the way many interfaces contain so-called "macro" facilities that can record and playback interface steps. But in contrast to conventional macros, PBE systems have the ability to *generalize* programs, by using machine learning techniques to replace constants with variables, objects and actions with more general descriptions. The generalized program can then be used in situations analogous to, but not exactly the same as, those upon which it was taught. Programming by Example takes advantage of people's natural tendency to learn by example, and to teach by example.

Programming by Example systems have a long history, but PBE remains a minority viewpoint, relative to mainstream computer science. The PBE vision is quite radical, involving heuristics, machine learning, and agent approaches that conventional interface designers are not accustomed to. Over the years, a dedicated group of researchers has proved the feasibility of Programming by Example systems in an astonishingly wide variety of interesting domains as diverse as text editing, graphical editing, Web browsing and authoring, geographic information systems, animation, video games, educational applications, traditional CAD-CAM, and others.

There are two seminal collections of works in this field. The first, Allen Cypher's *Watch What I Do* [4], collects the initial works in this field dating back to David Canfield Smith's pioneering 1975 Pygmalion. It also includes a wealth of background material on this topic, such as a glossary, chronology, test suite and several survey articles. My recent book, *Your Wish is My Command* [12] brings together most of the important work in this field to date, detailing examples of over 17 different systems in the above-mentioned application areas, several of which are now commercially available. It incorporates a number of contributions from the international community of researchers in this topic.

3. PROGRAMMING BY EXAMPLE AND "INTERFACE BUILDERS"

Perhaps the closest conventional interface design tools to Programming by Example are the so-called "Interface Builders" – graphical editors that allow the interface designer to draw the position and size of so-called "widgets" – interactive interface elements such as menus, buttons, icons, text entry fields, etc. Interface builders trace their history to the early direct-manipulation interfaces, and were introduced in their modern form by Buxton [3]. More modern versions include the Microsoft Visual Basic editor, Apple's Hypercard and FaceSpan, or Macintosh Common Lisp's IFT Interface Tools. Animation editors used for interface "mock-ups" such as Macromind Director and Toolbook provide even more capabilities for including interactive elements and time-dependent behavior into interfaces. What's great about these systems is that they let you construct concrete examples of interfaces so that you can get immediate visual feedback as to the appearance to the end-user of the interface. They are the "poor man's" Programming by Example for interface design.

But all these tools break down at a certain level of complexity of the interface. It is usually not possible in such editors to allow the interface to take an arbitrary action in *response* to a user's selection of a button or menu item, except to invoke some already-defined function. The definition of such a function needs to be done in a conventional programming language, or, in many of the modern interface builder environments, in a so-called "scripting language". Visual Basic, Hypertalk, or Macromind's Lingo (which has a graphical representation) can also be considered scripting languages. Scripting languages are usually simplified programming languages that are deemed to be simpler for non-expert users to program, but they are typically quite limited in their ability to define new objects and new behavior, and most are quite poorly designed from the programming language standpoint. Worse, the interaction with the programming language is completely divorced from the interaction with the interface elements.

The approach of Programming by Example to interface design is to encourage the designer to switch roles, first casting the designer in the role of the end-user, where the designer simulates the actions that the end-user will eventually take in the interface. Then, in response, the interface designer simulates the role of how the interface will respond to the user's actions. The PBE system then records and generalizes the program. David Wolber refers to this as *stimulus-response PBE* [20]. An important aspect of stimulus-response PBE is that it generalizes on *time* as well as on example objects; the user demonstrates *when* to do something as well as *what* to do.

The first attempt to turn an interface builder into a true Programming by

Example system was Brad Myers' Peridot [15]. Peridot featured a "simulated mouse" that was used to demonstrate user actions so that it was not confused with the ordinary mouse used to interact with Peridot itself (Fig. 2). Peridot used inference to generalize geometric relations in the interface such as when objects line up, replaced constants with variables in situations such as looping through a displayed list of choices and generated some simple conditionals.

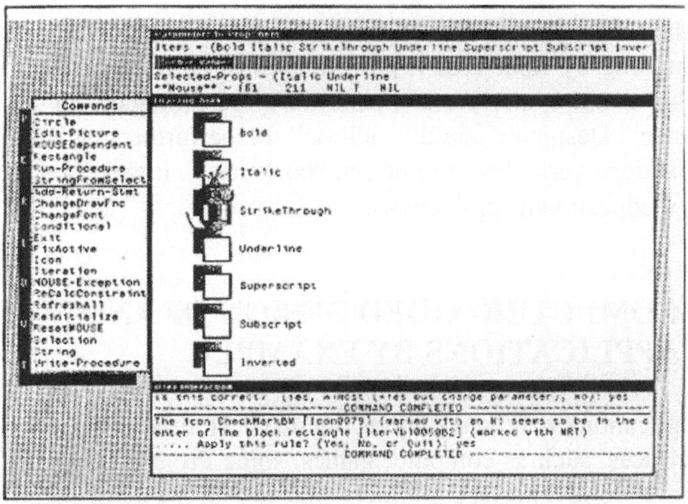

Figure 2. Peridot.

Myers and his group at Carnegie-Mellon University produced a long series of Programming by Example systems that operated in the Interface Builder domain. These are too numerous to describe in detail, but are surveyed in [14] and the papers referenced there. Notable among them were Lapidary; Jade, which created dialog boxes by example; Gilt, which permitted "callbacks" from interface elements; and, perhaps the most sophisticated, Marquise [16]. Several of these systems provided many ways for the user to edit properties of the generalizations constructed by the system. Elements of all these systems were incorporated in the general purpose User-Interface Management Systems produced by Myers and his group, first Garnet [15], then its successor Amulet.

Though not strictly an Interface Builder itself, my general purpose Programming by Example system, Tinker [9] used some Interface Builder-like techniques [interactive construction and placement of interface elements] and was used to construct interactive interfaces such as a spreadsheet-like interface [8] and a video game [9]. Tinker was perhaps the most procedurally general Programming by Example system, allowing functional abstraction, subroutines, and conditionals. Conditionals were defined from presenting multiple examples, one example for each branch of the conditional. Tinker did require the knowledge of the programming language, and it required more explicit programming steps than many of the other Programming by Example systems, but the interface designer got more procedural power as a result. The interface designer typed in snippets of code, which were immediately executed, and the resulting objects, either code objects or interface objects, were then available as examples to be used in subsequent steps of the demonstration. Generalizations were propagated through the tree of dependencies in the code.

Programming by Rehearsal [5] allowed constructing interfaces by using the metaphor that the interface elements were "performance" in the interface "performance". Designers could "audition" the performers to learn their capabilities. Hidden variables were placed "backstage". It was used by teachers and kids for educational applications.

4. COMPUTER-AIDED DESIGN OF ANIMATED APPLICATIONS BY EXAMPLE

For applications that make more intensive of time-dependent and animated interfaces, such as computer games, some Programming by Example systems go beyond Interface Builders that define standard menu-and-icon interfaces to provide extensive facilities for defining dynamic, autonomously acting objects and demonstrating transformations. Still mainly in the Interface Builder paradigm, David Wolber's Pavlov system [20] takes the scripting and timeline metaphor appearing in animation interface systems such as Macromind Director, and giving them a Programming by Example component to demonstrate the dynamic behavior of individual objects in the interface and their interaction. Wolber's article has a direct comparison of his system with the more conventional Director.

David Canfield Smith, and Allen Cypher's Stagecast Creator [18] and Alex Repenning and Corinna Perrone-Smith's AgentSheets [17] use a rule-based metaphor. Rules are defined by constructing before-and-after examples that specify the conditions under which a rule is to fire, and the action to take as a result, in terms of how it transforms the before state to the after state. The principal application is for children to build computer games. Both use a grid world and finite-state transitions to structure the domain to model the movable game characters and (relatively) fixed scenery.

A radically different approach is taken by Ken Kahn's Toontalk [6]. In Toontalk (Fig. 3), the programming environment itself is an animated video game. Programming language constructs are animated video characters. Robot characters represent user-defined programs whose thought-bubbles contain the code, animated actions demonstrated by example. A variety of physical-world metaphors, cities, houses and trucks, birds and nests, etc., are used to explain the behavior of the program constructs, which are based on an underlying model of concurrent logic programming.

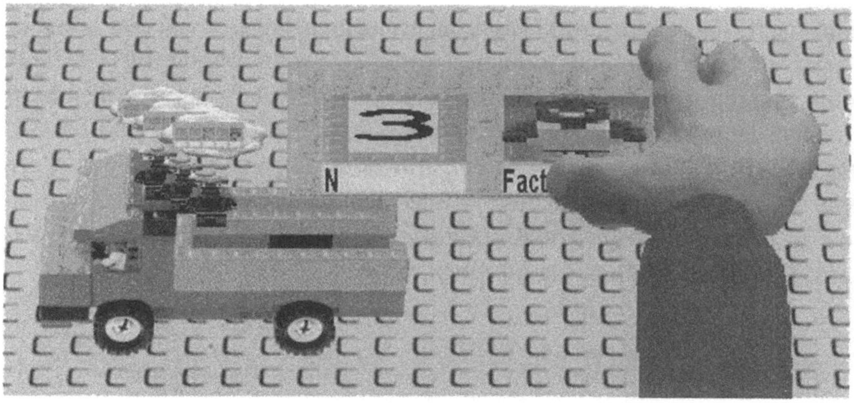

Figure 3. Toontalk.

5. COMPUTER-AIDED DESIGN OF WEB APPLICATIONS BY EXAMPLE

These days, many Web pages themselves can be considered user interfaces. Although a Web browser is often regarded as a specific application, Web pages that have embedded menus or forms, Javascript, Java applets and the like can be regarded as independent user interfaces, and Web page authoring amounts to interactive interface design. We are beginning to see Programming by Example applied in this domain as well. Web pages are constructed by operations of browsing, cutting and pasting from other Web pages, as well as giving advice to the system about how to interpret the format of Web pages.

Two examples are Atsushi Sugiura's Internet Scrapbook [19] and Matthias Bauer, Dietmar Dengler and Gabriele Paul's Trias [1]. Trias is especially interesting as a Programming by Example system because it embodies a mixed-initiative dialog – at any moment, either the user or the system may propose an action to be taken. The user and the system co-operate to define a "wrapper" – a description that describes how to extract example elements, like the price specification in an e-commerce Web page, from subsequent Web pages. This supplies the generalization for user actions.

6. COMPUTER-AIDED DESIGN OF CAD/CAM APPLICATIONS BY EXAMPLE

Perhaps the most direct analogy between Computer-Aided Design of products and interfaces is when those interfaces operated in the CAD/CAM domain itself. Patrick Girard [7] and his colleagues have developed some of the most sophisticated and industrial-strength Programming by Example systems as extensions to a traditional parametric CAD system for design of mechanical and electronic products. The systems, EBP (Fig. 4) and its successor GIPSE, notably incorporate constraints on the part descriptions. Constraints also play an important role in interface design. They paid careful attention to inference of control structures, and providing extensive example-oriented editing and debugging facilities.

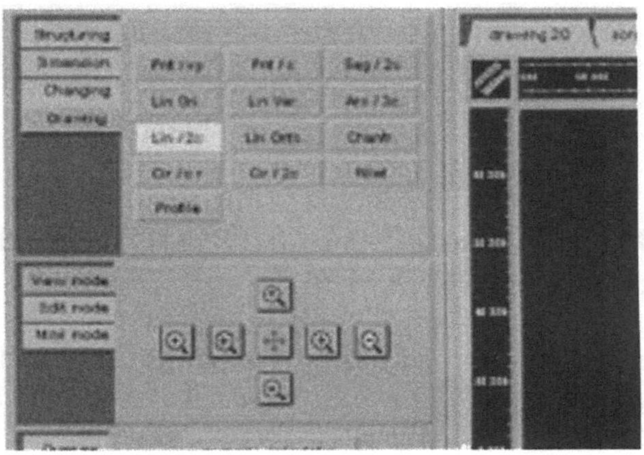

Figure 4. EBP: A CAD/CAM system with PBE.

7. COMPUTER-AIDED EXTENSION OF USER INTERFACES BY EXAMPLE

Strictly speaking, many Programming by Example systems, like EBP mentioned above, do not create arbitrary interfaces from scratch in the way that the Interface Builder-like PBE systems do. Instead, they already come with a user interface (the underlying CAD/CAM system in EBP's case), and they add the ability to *extend* rather than completely redefine, the interface with new capabilities demonstrated by example. The original interface remains accessible to the user. So they, too, can be considered as Computer-Aided Design systems for User Interface Design, but by extension rather than by construction *de novo*.

Almost all PBE systems extend the interface in some way. Some just record a single macro and allow playback of the last macro recorded. Some allow the recorded sequences to be named or otherwise referred to. But the best in this category try to deal with the issue of how to integrate the user-defined capabilities seamlessly into the existing underlying application's interface metaphor.

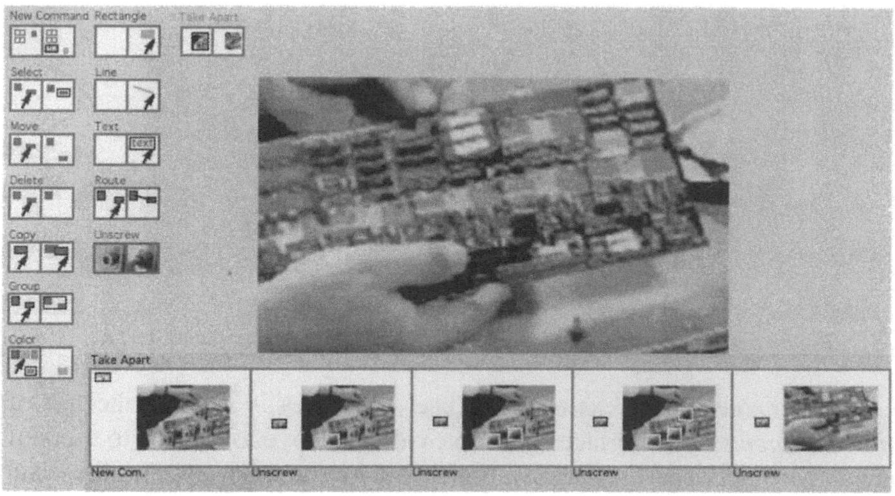

Figure 5. Mondrian.

My Mondrian system [10,11] represents the operations of the underlying graphical editor with "domino" icons that picture states of the screen before and after the operation. For example, the icon representing the "Draw Rectangle" operation consists of a left square showing a blank screen and a right square containing the rectangle (Fig. 5). When the user defines a new operation, the system constructs a new icon composed of the screen state before the demonstration on the left side, and the screen state after the demonstration (when it is completed) on the right side. Thus the user-defined operation is represented with the same visual language as used for the built-in operations, and user-defined operations may then take place as parts of further user-defined operations.

Mondrian is also unique in its ability to define *declarative* as well as procedural knowledge by example. Mondrian lets the user introduce new generalization descriptions by drawing *graphical annotations* on an object. In an example domain of learning operational and maintenance procedures from video input, Mondrian allows the user to select portions of the video frame to serve as the graphical representations of example objects. Objects can be grouped, and labelled with text labels to show their structure. Mondrian then learns part-whole hierarchies amongst the objects and the names of relations between the parts and wholes. When the user selects these objects in the future, Mondrian generalizes them according to their place in the part-whole hierarchy and their named relations (Fig. 6). This is a way of introducing new *concepts* by example as well as simply new procedures.

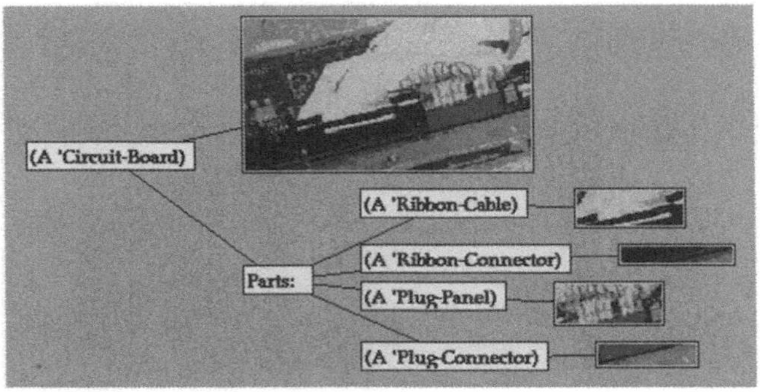

Figure 6. Graphical annotation in Mondrian, and inferred conceptual structure.

Another avenue for extension of user interfaces is through the use of *software agents* [2]. Interface agents provide proactive assistance to users of interactive interfaces by tracking user behavior, creating user profiles and user models, anticipating user needs, and accepting high-level goals and advice from the user. Agents effectively extend the capabilities of interfaces in dynamic ways not explicitly presented by the menu and icon operations, and in some cases, in ways not even anticipated by the interface designer.

Examples can play an important role in software agent interfaces because they can be the most effective means for a user to communicate their desires to the agent, obviating the need for more explicit instruction. We investigated an agent, Apple Data Detectors, that parses text occurring in naturally in e-mail, calendars and other applications, and applies semantically appropriate actions. We implemented a system, Grammex [13] for teaching the system new text patterns by presenting example text to be recognized and going through a dialog that interactively generalizes or specializes hypotheses about how to recognize substrings. This is the first interface that brings control of text recognition and parsing technology to non-expert users.

8. CONCLUSION

Like Computer-Aided Design systems for products and manufacturing applications, Computer-Aided Design systems for user interfaces can make the design process easier, more interactive and less-error prone. The success of CAD/CAM systems for product design is predicated on the fact that the system allows the user to interact with virtual examples of the artifact under construction. This takes advantage of people's natural tendency to teach and to learn by example. But user interfaces have dynamic and interactive behavior, and to define such behavior we need more mechanism then just specification of appearance of interfaces. By recording actions of a simulated end-user and generalizing them, Programming by Example provides the technology for bringing the success of the CAD/CAM applications to user interface design.

REFERENCES

[1] Bauer, M., Dengler, D., and Paul, G., *Programming by Demonstration for Information Agents*, in [12], pp. 7-20.

[2] Bradshaw, J. (ed.), *Software Agents*, MIT Press, Cambridge, 1996.

[3] Buxton, W., Lamb, M.R., Sherman, D., and Smith, K.C., *Towards a Comprehensive User Interface Management System*, in Proc. of ACM Conf. on Computer Graphics SIGGRAPH'83 (Detroit, 25-29 July 1983), Computer Graphics, Vol. 17, No. 3, ACM Press, New York, 1983, pp. 576-583.

[4] Cypher, A. (ed.), *Watch What I Do: Programming by Demonstration*, MIT Press, Cambridge, 1993.

[5] Finzer, W.F. and Gould, L., *Rehearsal World: Programming by Rehearsal*, in [4], pp. 79-102.

[6] Girard, P., *Bringing Programming by Demonstration to CAD Users*, in [12], pp. 135-162.

[7] Kahn, K., *Generalizing by Removing Detail: How any Program Can Be Created by Working with Examples*, in [12], pp. 21-44.

[8] Lieberman, H., *Constructing Graphical User Interfaces by Example*, in Proc. of Conf. Graphics Interface'82 (Toronto, May 1982), pp. 295-302.

[9] Lieberman, H., *Tinker: An Example Oriented Programming Environment for Beginning Programmers*, in R. Lawler and M. Yazdani (eds.), Artificial Intelligence and Education, Vol. 1, Ablex Publishing Company, 1987, pp. 49-66.

[10] Lieberman, H., *Mondrian: A Teachable Graphical Editor*, in [4], pp. 340-358.

[11] Lieberman, H., *A Demonstrational Interface for Recording Technical Procedures by Annotation of Videotaped Examples*, International Journal of Human-Computer Studies, Vol. 43, 1995, pp. 383-417.

[12] Lieberman, H. (ed.), *Your Wish is My Command: Programming by Example*, Morgan Kaufmann, San Francisco, 2001. Introduction accessible at http://lieber.www.media.mit.edu/people/lieber/PBE/Your-Wish/

[13] Lieberman, H., Nardi, B., and Wright, D., *Training Agents to Recognize Text by Example*, in [12], pp. 227-244.

[14] Myers, B. and McDaniel, R., *Demonstrational Interfaces: Sometimes You Need a Little Intelligence; Sometimes You Need a Lot*, in [12], pp. 45-60.

[15] Myers, B., *Garnet: Uses of Demonstrational Techniques*, in [4], pp. 219-238.

[16] Myers, B., McDaniel, R., and Kosbie, D., *Marquise: Creating Complete User Interfaces by Demonstration*, in Proc. of ACM Conf. on Human Aspects in Computing Systems INTERCHI'93 (Amsterdam, 24-29 April 1993), ACM Press, New York, 1993, pp. 293-300.

[17] Repenning, A. and Perrone-Smith, C., *Programming by Analogous Examples*, in [12],

pp. 351-370.
[18] Smith, D.C., Cypher, A., and Tesler, L., *Novice Programming Comes of Age*, in [12], pp. 7-19.
[19] Sugiura, A., *Web Browsing by Demonstration*, in [12], pp. 61-86.
[20] Wolber, D., *Pavlov: Where PBD Meets Macromedia's Director*, in [12], pp. 345-350.

Chapter 2

FOUNDATIONS FOR A THEORY OF CONTEXTORS

Joëlle Coutaz and Gaëtan Rey
CLIPS-IMAG, BP 53
F-38 041 Grenoble Cedex 9 (France)
E-mail: {Joelle.Coutaz, Gaetan.Rey}@imag.fr – URL: http://iihm.imag.fr/coutaz/
Tel.: +33-4-76 51 48 54/4-76 63 56 87 – Fax: +33-4 76 44 66 75

Abstract This article proposes an operational definition of the notion of context for the design and development of context-sensitive systems. Our definition draws upon the distinction between the notion of an instant snapshot of observables (a situation) and the composition of these observables over time (a context). Observables and their relationships, which are elicited at the design stage of the development process, can be mapped, at the implementation phase, as colonies of contextors. A contextor is a software abstraction that models relationships between observables. Contextors share a common I/O structure including control channels and meta-data to ensure and express QoS (e.g., precision, stability), as well as common properties such as reflexivity and remanence. They can be combined as oriented graphs or encapsulated into higher computational units.

Keywords: Context aware system, Ubiquitous computing.

1. INTRODUCTION

Since the mid-eighties, context has been considered as an important element in the design process of interactive systems. However, context was assimilated to the workplace and the workplace served as the foundation for contextual design [3]. With the advent of mobile devices and the availability of worldwide digital networks, the workplace is no longer limited to the confined space observed at design time.

Tasks that have been modeled for a particular environment may now be accomplished in multiple settings using different interaction devices. From

C. Kolski and J. Vanderdonckt (eds.), Computer-Aided Design of User Interfaces III, 13–33.
© 2002 *Kluwer Academic Publishers.*

context-confined, interactive systems are progressively becoming *context-sensitive* and/or *context-aware*.

Early experiences show that context-sensitivity is a tricky problem. For example, Cheverst et al. report that using context to simplify users' tasks is sometimes perceived by users as system preemption [7]. If the research community aims at developing context-sensitive systems that are effective for humans, we need to devise an operational model for the notion of context that can be used and refined at every step of the development process. The framework developed by Thevenin et al. is an example of how such a context model can be used in the development process of plastic user interfaces [5,6,21].

Although many papers in the literature make reference to context, there is no clear widely agreed definition [24]. In the next section, we present a brief analysis of the state of the art in context-aware computing that elicits the key concepts related to context. From these concepts, we then elaborate our own definition in Section 3. This conceptual abstract definition is then refined in Section 4 from an external user-centered perspective into an internal computational model called a contextor.

2. ANALYSIS OF THE STATE OF THE ART

In 1994, Schilit and Theimer define context as the location and the identity of "the collection of nearby people and objects, as well as changes to those objects over time" [18]. According to Schilit et al., context analysis boils down to answering the Quintilian questions such as "Where are you, Who you are with, Which resources are nearby? When this happens? Etc." [1,19]. Environmental entities including the season of the year, time of the day, and room temperature, are part of the context [4]. From these early studies, we observe that *state* and *time* are two key underlying concepts for context awareness [22].

Later, Pascoe introduces the notion of *relevance*: context is a subset of physical and conceptual states that may be "relevant to a particular entity" [15]. According to Dey, an entity is "a person, place, or object that is considered relevant to the interaction between a user and an application, including the user and the applications themselves" [8,9]. Surprisingly, it is only recently that relevancy is considered in relation to the user's task.

In summary, the state of the art related to context-aware computing brings in the following key concepts: *state*, *time*, *relevancy* to user's *task* and *entities* of which *location* and *physical environment* are first class components [10,12,22]. None of the definitions makes it explicit the composition of states over time and none of them explicitly considers the user as central.

We propose an operational definition for the notion of context that bundles the key concepts drawn from the literature, but where the *user* and the *task* are first class entities, and where relevant states are composed over time. Instead of referring loosely to context (without specifying its purpose), we consider more appropriate to use the term *context of interaction*. Thus, our definition of context is with respect to interaction.

3. THE NOTION OF CONTEXT

We elaborate our own definition of context in five points:

1. The definition per se in general terms.
2. The refinement of the definition in terms of gross and net contexts, of user and system contexts, and of observed and observable contexts.
3. The notion of peripheral state variables, one of the key items of a context.
4. The composition function used to express the effect of past on context.
5. A generalization of our definition of context in relation to ubiquitous computing, extending our user-centered perspective to an agent view whether agents are humans or artefacts.

3.1 Definition

Our definition of context draws upon the notion of situation. A situation at time t is a state vector, that is a set of observables at t. Context at t is a composition of multiple situations over a period of time. In addition, a situation as well as a context do not exist as autonomous things: they are always related to something. In the case of interest, they are related to users involved in a particular task. More precisely:

Given a set of users, U, a task, T, and two instants of observation, t_0 and t, where t_0 is the temporal reference for observations, the *Context* at t that relates to U for performing T, is the composition of the *Situations* observed between t_0 and t that relate to U for performing T.

$$\text{context}^{U,T}(t) = \text{COMPOSITION}(\text{situation}^{U,T}(t_0), \dots, \text{situation}^{U,T}(t))$$

where:

situation ^{U,T} (t) is the Situation at t that relates to U for performing T.

The *Situation*, situation ^{U,T} (t), is the set of the values observed (or observable) at t of the peripheral state variables that relate to U for performing T, as well as their relations.

Peripheral state variables denote the entities that are *not central* to U at t for performing T, but that may have an impact on T, *now* (i.e., at t) and/or in the *future* (i.e., at t+dt). The *impact of peripheral state variables* on a task may be one of the following:

- The task is aborted,
- The task is suspended, then resumed,
- The task is carried out but the nominal expected quality of the task is likely to be altered (for better or for worse). The quality of the task execution may be measured in terms of the quality of its product, the duration, the robustness (e.g., the number of user and/or system errors), etc.

The choice of U, the selection of the instants of observation t_0 and t, the granularity of the task and time, as well as the nature of the peripheral state variables are left opened. It is up to the designers to make the decision depending on the step in the design process as well as on the level of precision required.

For example,

- U may denote a single user, a class of users, multiple classes of users, the whole humanity. The choice depends on the degree of precision that the designers are seeking for.

- t_0, which is the temporal reference for elaborating a context, may denote the starting time of the session. It may correspond to the beginning of the execution of the task, to a new day or year, or to any event relevant to the case at hand.

- The *granularity of a task* can be measured by its depth within the task model that the computer system is supposed to support. (A computer system is composed of multiple software components that interoperate. It ranges from closed applications as we now them today, up to world-wide computing as envisioned by Weiser [23]).

  In classic HCI, a task model is a hierarchical decomposition of tasks where a task is defined by the couple "goal, procedure". The goal describes the system state that the user desires, and the procedure corresponds to the plan(s) available to reach the goal. The designer may decide that only specific subtasks of the task tree should be concerned with context-sensitivity. Conversely, the root of the tree will be considered if, from the analysis of the users' needs, context-sensitivity applies to the whole system.

- The *granularity of time intervals* ([t_0, t], dt) depends on the types of the state variables to be observed and/or the quality requirements defined early in the development process. For example, considering changes of light conditions, a time interval of 1 minute is reasonable for supporting the self-calibration of a computer vision algorithm, whereas 15 minutes is appropriate to automatically control the lights in the home.

- *Peripheral state variables* are discussed next.

3.2 Peripheral State Variables

The *peripheral state variables* that relate to a user U for performing a task T are those variables that are not central but that may have an impact on the task, now or in the future. The central state variables that relate to U for performing T denote the concepts that U necessarily manipulates (literally or mentally) for achieving T.

For example, consider the task of withdrawing money from a teller machine. The amount of money to be withdrawn and the state of the bank account are central to the task, whereas people waiting in line are peripheral. However, because the line is long, one may decide to skip the subtask that consists of checking the money left in the bank account. The peripheral state variable, length of the line, has an impact on the execution of the task. In our example, a subtask of T, checking the bank account, is not accomplished. The impact of the length of the line is the immediate abortion of T.

Note that state variables that are peripheral for T and U may be central for another task and/or for another set of users. Central and peripheral states variables are identified by the designers using sound design approaches such as Suchman's Situated Action approach [20], Activity Theory [2], Distributed Cognition [11], or Contextual Design [3,13]). Central variables are subsequently conveyed in task models (e.g., GOMS, ADEPT, DIANE), as task parameters or objects. Unfortunately, peripheral state variables are not explicitly expressed in current task models. As a result, they are lost during the development process. In ARTstudio, a software tool that supports the development process of plastic user interfaces, we have extended ConcurTaskTree [14] by ordering state variables so that when screen estate is insufficient, secondary variables are not observable but browsable [5].

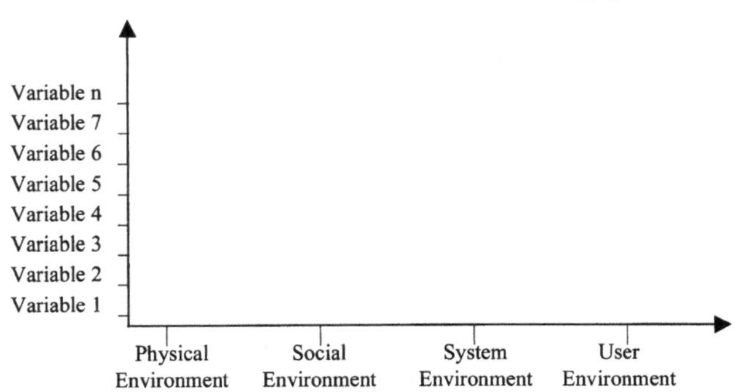

Figure 1. A simple classification space for eliciting and organizing peripheral state variables.

Because peripheral state variables potentially cover the entire universe, it is important that they be identified early in the design process. To assist the identification and classification process, we suggest using the design space shown in Fig. 1. A peripheral state variable V_i may belong to one or several of the following classes:

- The *physical environment* covers the peripheral state variables that characterize the physical spaces and places [12] where task T is likely to be performed by users U. Such characteristics include light conditions, temperature, and noise level. They cover architectural characteristics such as connectedness, as well as social values (a house is distinct from "home"). They also include real world objects such as chairs, pencils, and toys.
- The *social environment* denotes the people that are in the physical environment in relation to T and U: people waiting in line, colleagues that may come in, friends that we are likely to meet at the airport, family members, a companion robot, etc.
- The *system environment* covers the computational, communicational and interactional resources available or potentially available to U for accomplishing T (e.g., a PDA vs. a PC, a mobile phone, or any augmented object).
- The *user environment* corresponds to the characteristics of U with regard to the task T (e.g., expert in the domain covered by the task, special needs and preferences in relation to T, etc.).

3.3 Refinement: System and User Contexts, Gross and Net Contexts, Observed and Observable Contexts

In HCI, it is good practice to analyze a problem from at least two complementary perspectives: that of the user and that of the system. For example, one should check whether the dialogue controller of a running system is compliant to the task model defined during the design phase. For this reason, we need to consider the context and the situation both from the user and the system perspectives. As shown in Fig. 2, we introduce the notions of *user context* and of *system context* and relate them to the *gross* and *net* contexts. The same lines of reasoning hold for situations.

The *gross context* at t that relates to U for performing T, $context^{U,T}_{G}(t)$, is the composition of all of the gross situations that have been observed between t_0 and t and that relate to U for performing T.

The *gross situation* at t that relates to U for performing T, $situation^{U,T}_{G}(t)$, includes all of the universal facts (variables and their relations) observed (or observable) at t that relate to U for performing T.

The *system context* at t that relates to U for performing T at t, *context* $^{U,T}{}_{S}$ *(t)*, is the subset of the gross context, *context* $^{U,T}{}_{G}$ *(t)*, that the system is concerned with at t.

Similarly, the *user context* at t that relates to U for performing T, *context* $^{U,T}{}_{U}$ *(t)*, is the subset of the gross context, *context* $^{U,T}{}_{G}$ *(t)*, that the user U is concerned with at t.

The *net context* at t that relates to U for performing T, *context* $^{U,T}{}_{N}$ *(t)*, is the subset of the gross context, *context* $^{U,T}{}_{G}$ *(t)*, that the user and the system have in common at t. Thus, by definition:

- context $^{U,T}{}_{i}$ (0) = situation $^{U,T}{}_{i}$ (0) for $\forall$i $\in$[G,S,U,N]
- $\forall$t>0, context $^{U,T}{}_{i}$ (t) = situation $^{U,T}{}_{i}$ (t) $\otimes$ context $^{U,T}{}_{i}$ (t-1) where $\otimes$ denotes the composition operator and i $\in$[G,S,U,N]
- $\forall$t$\geq$0, situation $^{U,T}{}_{N}$ (t) = situation $^{U,T}{}_{U}$ (t) $\cap$ situation $^{U,T}{}_{S}$ (t) = situation $^{U,T}{}_{S}$ (t) $\cap$ situation $^{U,T}{}_{U}$ (t)

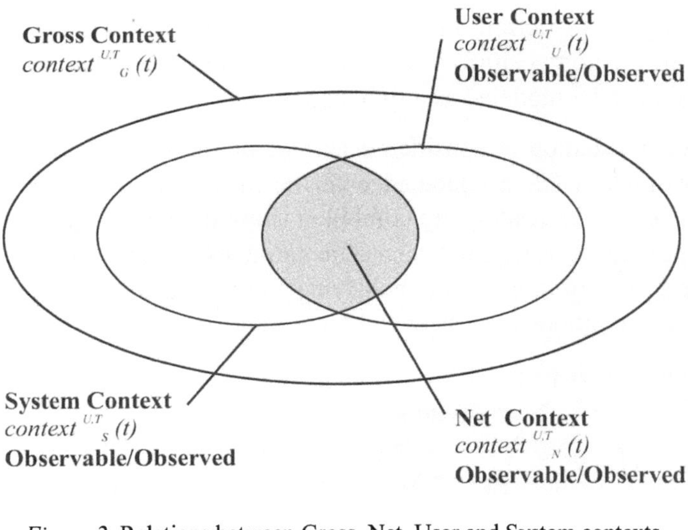

Figure 2. Relations between Gross, Net, User and System contexts.

As shown in Fig. 2, the adjectives "observable" and "observed" make explicit the distinction between the design phase and the run time phase of the development process. In the design phase, designers specify the peripheral state variables that should be observed at run time. We then refer to the *observable context* and to the *observable situation*. They are potentially observed. At run time, they are effective: peripheral state variables, either are observed effectively or not observed at all due, for example, to some system or user failure or to a loss of conformity between the design and the implementation phases.

The refinement of the notion of context (situation) as observed or observable, the distinction between Gross, Net, System and User contexts provide a means to define *quality metrics for context-aware computing*. For example, the cardinality of the Net Context is a way to measure the conformity of the system context sensitivity to users' expectation. A cardinality close to 0 would mean that the context sensitivity of the system is nearly of no use to the user. Similarly, the cardinality of the System Context compared to that of the Gross Context expresses the intrinsic sensitivity of the system. A cardinality of 0 denotes a context-unaware system.

The comparison between an observable context and its corresponding observed context may provide some useful insights into the design process and/or on the human and system behaviors. Having defined the foundations for our notion of context, we need to present one of its key components: the peripheral state variables.

3.4 Composing Situations

According to our definition, a context that relates to users U for a task T results from the composition of a set of situations. As shown in Fig. 3, the composition can be modeled as a two-step process:

- For every situation S considered as part of the context, the peripheral state variables of S are labeled with the time of S. Then the situations considered in the context are combined using the Union operator on sets. So far, the relationships between state variables are kept unchanged.
- The second step consists of modifying the relations between state variables: new relations are created whereas others may be deleted.

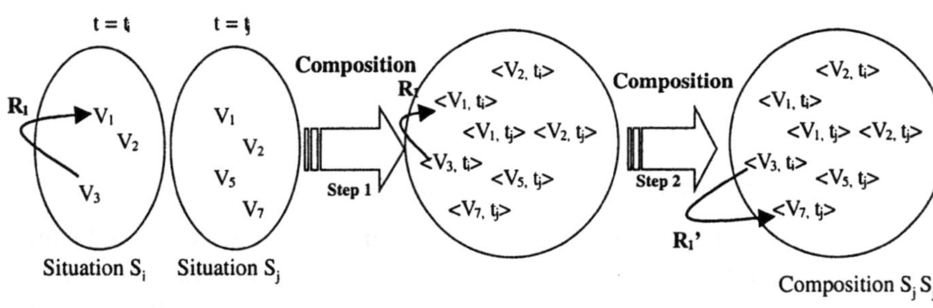

Figure 3. Capitalizing Situations to elaborate a Context.

For example, in Fig. 3, Variables V_1 and V_3 express the temperature of the room in Farenheit and Celsius respectively. In the situation S_i, relation R_1 indicates that at t_i, V_1 is derived from V_3 whose value is produced by a physical sensor (e.g., a thermometer). At t_j ($t_j > t_i$), because the Celsius thermometer is out of order, V_3 does not belong to S_j anymore. However, another device has been able to record the value of V_3 at time t_j. This value is represented by V_7 in S_j. In addition, at t_j, a Farenheit thermometer has replaced the faulty Celsius device, hence the presence of V_1 in S_j. The right-most picture of Fig. 3 shows the set that describes the context at t_j after the composition function has been applied to S_i and S_j: the faulty thermometer has been replaced by a new one, hence the presence of the couple "V_1, t_j". Because the value of V_1 at t_i may be useful in the future, it is kept in the context. Relation R_1 between V_3 and V_1 at t_i has been suppressed and replaced by a relation between V_3 and V_7.

Composition is a kind of history function that involves the emergence of new relations and peripheral state variables as well as the destruction of old ones. Although the concept of composition is easy to grasp, it requires well-thought design methods as well as sophisticated run time mechanisms. Run time mechanisms must be able to support the dynamic creation of relationships as well as the capacity to synthesize new peripheral state variables. Conversely, they must be able to eliminate ("garbage collect") useless state variables and relations. The risk is to erase information that may be useful in the future.

3.5 Generalization of the Notion of Context

We believe that context and situation can only be defined with respect to an entity for a given purpose. So far, we have developed the concept of context (and situation) in relation to a particular class of entities, the "user", for a particular class of purposes, the users' "task".

One way to generalize our definitions is to extend the scope of our first class entity to that of agents. An agent may be a human or a computational artefact such as an augmented physical object that interacts with the world, including humans. Thus:

Given a set of agents, A, a task, T, and two instants of observation, t_0 and t, where t_0 is the temporal reference for observations, the *Context* at t that relates to A for performing T, is the composition of the Situations observed between t_0 and t that relate to A for performing T:

$$\text{context}^{A,T}(t) = \text{COMPOSITION}(\text{situation}^{A,T}(t_0), \ldots, \text{situation}^{A,T}(t))$$

This generalization opens new issues including:

- Agents have different time scales. How can these be reconciled?
- What are the appropriate agents?
- What are the relationships between agent contexts?
- From an ethical perspective, how can we insure that the human agent has control over the computational world that is supposed to serve him?

In the following section, we describe the notion of contextor, a computational model we have derived from our definition of context.

4. CONTEXTOR: A COMPUTATIONAL MODEL FOR CONTEXT

Our notion of contextor is a conceptual extension of the context widget implemented in the Context Toolkit [17]. We first present the definition of a contextor followed in 4.2 by a taxonomy based on the functional aspect of contextors. Then, in 4.3, we show how contextors can be combined into richer computational units. Whether contextors are simple or composed, their properties, described in 4.3, have an impact on implementation mechanisms illustrated in 4.4.

4.1 Definition

A *contextor* is a software abstraction that models a relation between variables of an Observed System Context. As defined in Section 3.3, the Observed System Context is the composition of situations as observed by the system. From the values of a set of variables of an Observed System Context, a contextor returns the value of a variable (or of a set of variables) that belongs to that context.

As shown in Fig. 4, a contextor is comprised of a functional core and of *typed input and output communication channels*.

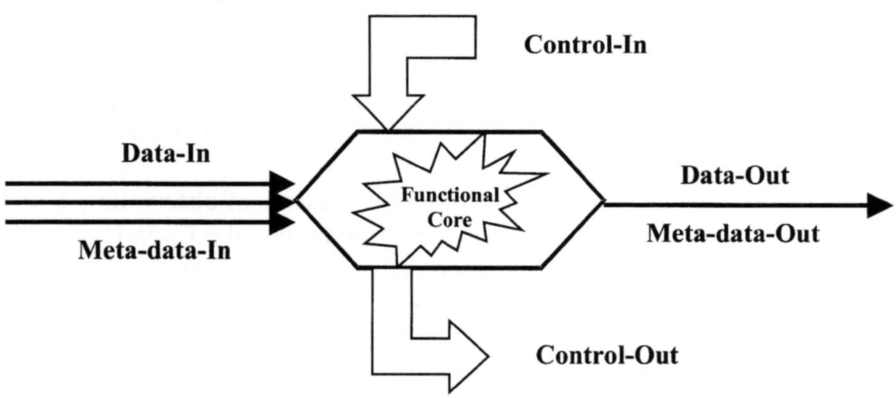

Figure 4. A graphical representation of a contextor.

The *functional core of a contextor* implements a relation between variables of the Observed System Context.

For example, in Fig. 3, relation R1 between variables V1 and V3 of situation Si can be computationally represented by a contextor whose functional core consists of translating Farenheit data into Celsius representation. The input channels of a contextor are of two types:

1. *Data-In* corresponds to the variables of the Observed System Context

that are used as inputs by the functional core of the contextor. Every input value is decorated with a *Meta-data-In* that expresses the quality of the input value.

2. *Control-In* corresponds to commands received from other contextors to set the internal parameters of the contextor. These parameters concern the functional behavior of the contextor as well as the non-functional behavior such as the QoS (Quality of Service) expected by other contextors. For example, a contextor may receive a "switch off" command on its Control-In because it has been recognized as faulty by another one. Or, it may receive a QoS request that expresses the level of precision of the values delivered on the Data-out channel.

Symmetrically, the output channels of a contextor are of two types:

1. *Data-Out* corresponds to the values of some variables of the Observed System Context returned by the contextor. As for input, output data are decorated with *Meta-data-Out* that describes the quality of the output produced by the contextor.
2. *Control-Out* is used by the contextor to send control commands to other contextors. For example, based on the meta-data associated with the data received from a contextor C, a contextor may decide to send a "switch off" command to C.

In addition:

- A Data-In channel receives data from a Data-out channel whose data type is compatible with that of the Data-In channel.
- A Control-In channel receives data from a Control-Out channel whose data type is compatible with that of the Control-In channel.
- The connections between input and output channels may be static (i.e., wired by the implementer) or semi-static (i.e., computed at run time when the system is launched), or transient (i.e., may be changed dynamically).

Given a contextor C, a *source contextor* is a contextor that provides C with Data-In values, and a *sink contextor* is a contextor that receives Data-Out values from C.

4.2 Taxonomy

By analogy with the software tools and concepts developed in Human-Computer Interaction, we propose a taxonomy for contextors based on the recurrence of the functional requirements of context aware systems. Table 1 shows an overview of the different types of contextors that we present in more detail in the following subsections.

Table 1. Contextor types based on their functional core. X, Y, Z denote distinct data types, but Z is at a higher level of abstraction that X and Y. {X} represents a set of values of type X.

Contextor type	Sensor connec-tivity	Number of input channels	Number of output channels	Input data types	Output data types
Elementary	Yes	0	1	-	X
History	No	1	1	X	{X}
Threshold	No	1	1	X	Boolean
Translator	No	1	1	X	Y
Fusionor	No	2 or more	1	X,X	X
Abstractor	No	1 or more	1	X,Y	Z

4.2.1 Elementary Contextor

An elementary contextor has no Data-In Channel. It offers a convenient way to encapsulate a physical sensor such as a thermometer, or any computational component that can be used as a source of physical data.

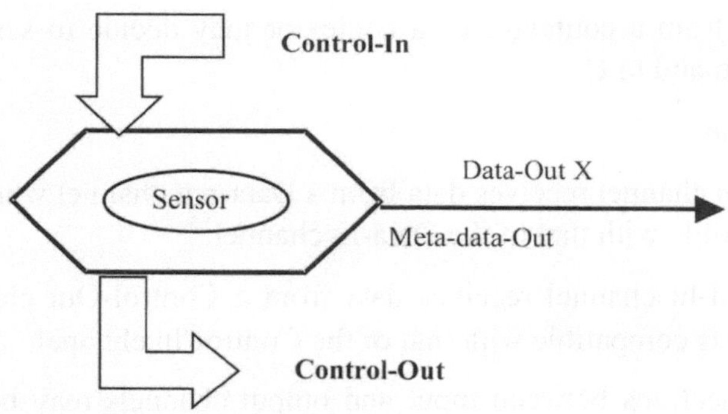

Figure 5. The elementary contextor.

For example, suppose we encapsulate a video camera within an elementary contextor. Then, Data-out corresponds to the video flow of images, Control-in allows other contextors to set the video rate, as well as the pan-tilt-zoom factors of the camera. Meta-data-Out can be used to express the resolution, the number of bits per pixel, and more generally, any factor that qualifies the images delivered by the contextor. Control-out is used by the contextor to acknowledge the execution of the commands received through the Control-in channel.

4.2.2 History Contextor

A history contextor saves the values and their meta-values that it has successively received through its Data-In channel. For example, the Data-In channel of a history contextor receives temperature values provided by a Thermometer elementary contextor. By definition, the history contextor saves the values it receives. Its Control-in channel allows other contextors to set the number of values to be maintained or the time interval before initiating garbage collection. Through its Control-Out, the history contextor is able to notify source contextors to slow down their emission flow rate because out of memory is nearly reached.

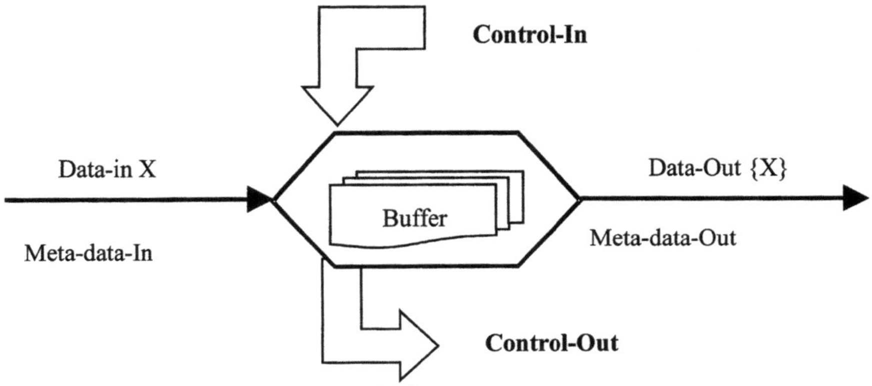

Figure 6. History contextor.

4.2.3 Threshold Contextor

A threshold contextor returns true if the Data-In value satisfies a threshold condition, false otherwise.

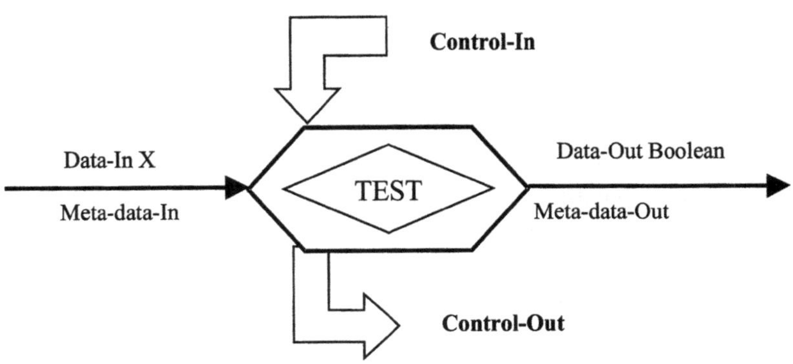

Figure 7. The Threshold contextor.

For example, suppose a threshold contextor receives temperature values from a thermometer elementary contextor. Data-Out expresses the answer to the question "Is it hot?". The Control-In channel allows the sink contextor to set the temperature threshold. Typically, in winter, the threshold would be set to 22°C whereas 35°C would be more adequate for summer. Through the

Control-Out channel, the threshold contextor can notify its source contextor to change the flow rate of its Data-Out channel.

4.2.4 Translation Contextor

A translation contextor performs type recasting but does not change the meaning, nor the level of abstraction of the values received on the Data-In channel. For example, a translation contextor is used to transform input temperatures from one representation system to another (for example Celsius, Farenheit, Kelvin). The Control-In channel allows the sink contextor to set up the desired data type for the Data-Out channel.

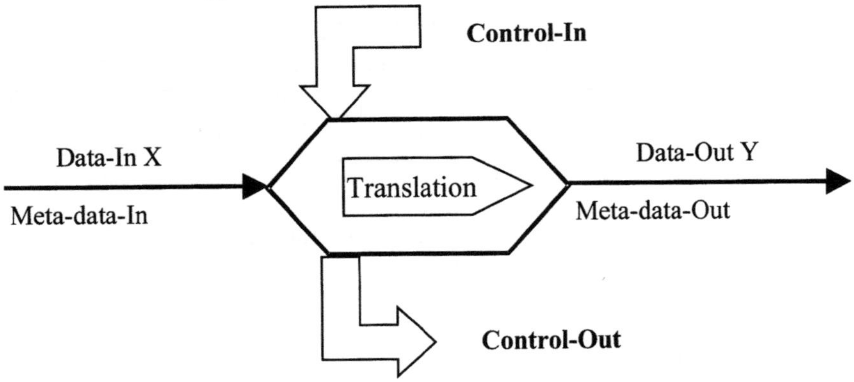

Figure 8. The Translation contextor.

4.2.5 Fusion Contextor

The Fusion contextor has multiple Data-In of the same type, each one with its own meta-data. The role of the fusion contextor is to produce a single Data-Out of the same type whose quality has been improved over that of the input data. Typically, a fusion contextor receives the number of persons in a room both from a video tracker and an audio tracker. It renders the number of people in the room but with a better confidence factor than that provided by the video and the audio trackers. Control-In is used to express the relative importance of the source contextors, whereas the Control-out sends commands to source contextors such as start/stop sending values.

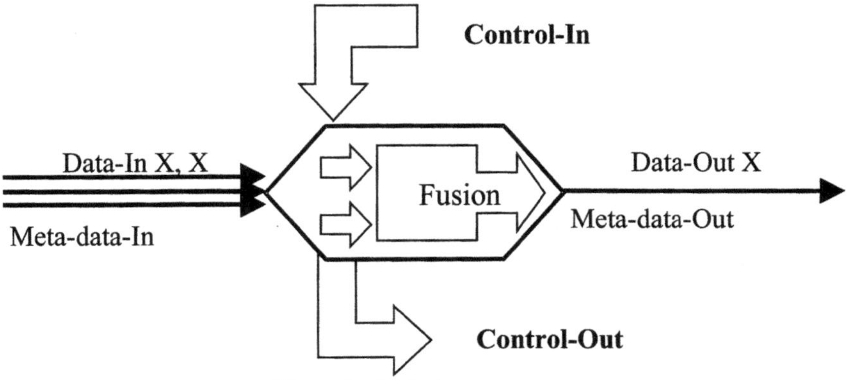

Figure 9. The fusion contextor.

4.2.6 Abstraction Contextor

The Fusion contextor has multiple Data-In. The role of the abstraction contextor is to produce a single Data-Out whose type is at a higher level of abstraction than that of the input data types.

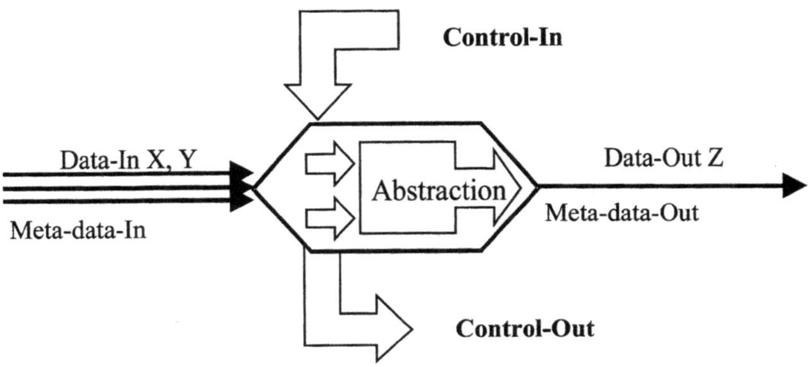

Figure 10. The abstraction contextor.

Example: A source contextor provides an abstraction contextor with the weight of moving things on the floor of a museum room. Another one provides the abstraction contextor with the ambient temperature of the room. From these two input streams, the abstraction contextor returns the level of occupancy of the room. So far, we have introduced the basic classes of interactors. In the following section, we consider their composition.

4.3 Composing Contextors

Contextors may be composed in two ways: through data channels connection and via encapsulation.

4.3.1 Data Channels Connection

Contextors are composed by connecting Data-In channels with compliant Data-Out channels to form an oriented graph. Two channels are compliant if they convey data of the same type. As shown in Fig. 11, the resulting oriented graph forms a colony of contextors. A colony of contextors is an oriented graph where Data-In channels are connected to compliant Data-out channels. Source interactors at the base of the graph are elementary contextors. Contextors at the top of the graph provide applications with contextual data at the appropriate level of abstraction.

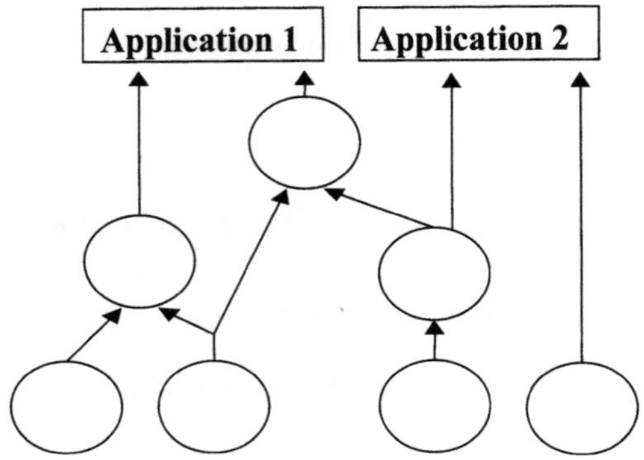

Figure 11. A colony of contextors.

We have not devised yet the connection rules between control channels. For now, we can say that the Control-in channel of a contextor is connected to the Control-out channel of its sink contextors. Consequently, the Control-out channel of a contextor is connected to the Control-in channel of its source contextors.

4.3.2 Encapsulation

Encapsulation is used to group a colony of contextors as a new class of contextor whose internal composition is hidden to other contextors. Fig. 12 shows an example of an abstraction contextor built from a colony of simpler contextors.

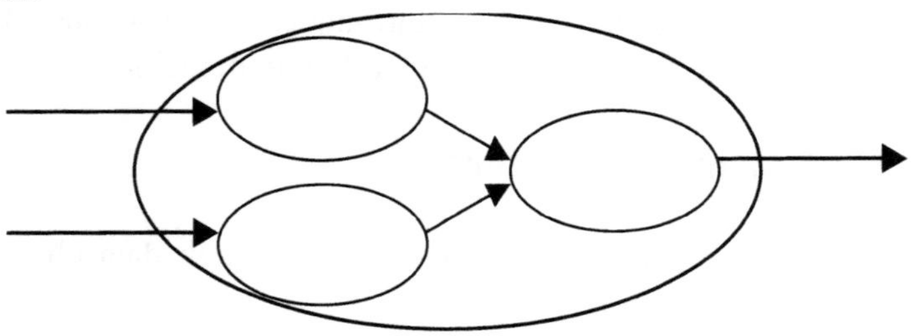

Figure 12. A colony of contextors encapsulated as a reusable class of contextors.

4.4 Quality of Service and Properties

In a world of uncertainty, the system must be able to auto-evaluate the quality of the services it provides in order to adapt its behavior. As a result, contextors are capable of measuring their own QoS. So far, we have identified metrics for elementary contextors. These include: resolution, latency, sample rate, stability, field of perception, field of action, autonomy, etc. (see [16] for more details). In addition, a contextor satisfies the following properties:

- **Reflexivity** – a contextor is auto-descriptive so that its class as well as its input and output channels are discovered by other software components (including other contextors). In addition, reflexivity provides the contextor with the capability to adapt its behavior based on the QoS requests received through its Control-In channel.
- **Remanence** – a contextor is able to disappear from its colony and, if necessary, to restore its state when resuming its execution within the colony (or within another colony).
- **Mobility** – a contextor may migrate within its colony by dynamically reconfiguring the connectivity of its input and output channels.

4.5 Illustration

To test our notion of contextor, we have implemented a server of contextors in Java. In this environment, a contextor is an autonomous software component with a life cycle that includes the following states: the contextor exists as a file but is unknown from the server; the contextor is identified by the server but is not running; the contextor is running; the contextor is suspended. The details of the contextors server can be found in [16].

Fig. 13 shows a simple contextor-based system that we have developed as an answer to a real life experience. In our lab, coffee cups are shared resources. As such, they are supposed to be kept in the cafeteria, at all time. However, we often end up sipping our coffee in the office and forget to bring the cups back at the appropriate location. As a result, flame messages are sent through email by the first person with no coffee cup available. Our system is aimed at automatically sending a warning email message when the number of cups available in the cafeteria is below a threshold.

Our contextor-based system includes 2 elementary contextors whose data-Out channel is connected to the data-In channels of an abstraction contextor: the first elementary contextor encapsulates a camera sensor whose function is to count the number of cups in the cafeteria.

The second elementary contextor computes the threshold whose value depends on the time of the day as well as on the date. The abstraction contextor synthesizes a new variable "cups will soon be missing" at the appropriate level of abstraction. The value of the variable is sent to the application which in turn can broadcast a warning message to the people of the lab.

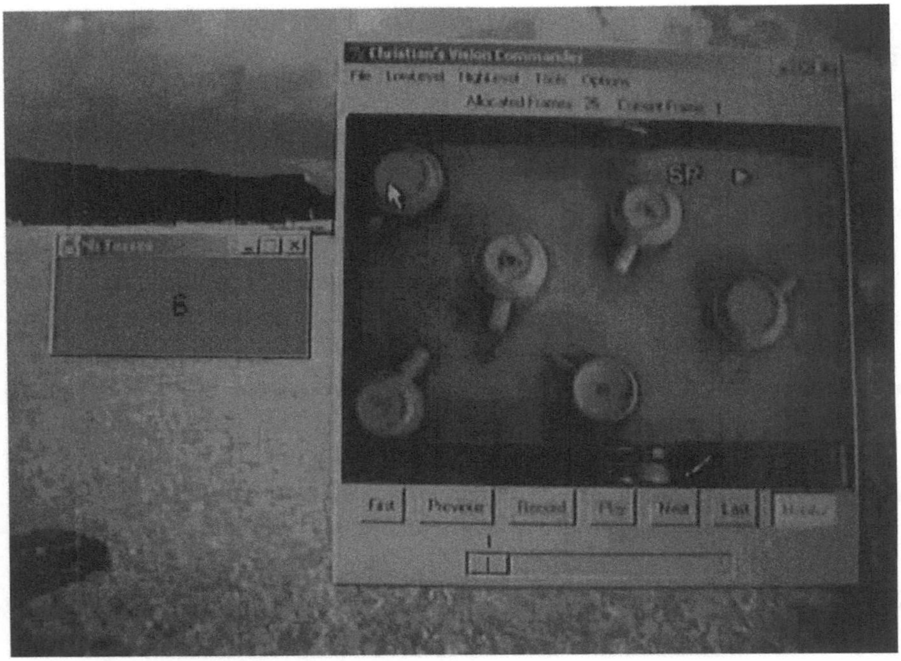

Figure 13. On the right, the scene as captured by the video contextor. On the left, the small red windows pops up to notify that cups should be brought back to the cafeteria.

5. CONCLUSION

In this article, we have presented a working definition for the notion of context for the design and development of context-sensitive systems. This definition draws upon the following key ideas:

- The distinction between the notion of an instant snapshot of "things" in the form of a state vector (a situation at t), and the composition of these state vectors over time (a context at t),
- The distinction between the user's view and the system's view of context (and situation), and their intersection to form the net context (situation). In turn, the cardinality of the net context can be used as a basis for evaluation,
- The distinction between the designer's view (the observables) and the run time view of context (the effectively observed variables) and their intersection usable as evaluation metrics,

- The transposition of the relations between the observables as software abstractions (the contextors),
- A common I/O structure for all contextors including control channels to ensure and express QoS (e.g., precision, stability), as well as common properties such as reflexivity and remanence,
- The definition of core contextors serving recurring functional requirements in ubiquitous computing (sensor encapsulators, translators, abstractors, etc.),
- The composition of contextors as oriented graphs or encapsulated into higher computational units.

There are very few tools available for the development of context aware systems. The Context Toolkit is a notable exception [17]. Although similar in spirit, the contextor model applies in a more systematic way at every level of abstraction.

One important aspect of the contextor is the notion of meta-data and control. Salber introduced similar ideas, but with subtle differences. In particular, in the contextor model, meta-data are not sent on a separate channel: they are decoration of the data in order to insure synchronicity. In addition, we generalize the role of the control channels as a way to dynamically express Quality of Service.

Although our model of context and contextors needs to be evaluated against large scale applications, it sets the foundations for a systematic approach to context-aware computing.

ACKNOWLEDGMENT

This work has been partly supported by the EEC project TMR TACIT (ERB-FMRX-CT-97-0133) and by the FET GLOSS project (IST-2000-26070). It has been conducted with the participation of G. Calvary, P. Reignier and J.L. Crowley.

REFERENCES

[1] Abowd, G., *Towards a Better Understanding of Context and Context-Awareness*, in G. Szwillus and T. Turner (eds), Workshop on The What, Who, Where, When, Why and How of Context-Awareness, Extended Abstract of the ACM Conference on Human Factors in Computing Systems CHI'2000 (The Hague, 1-6 April 2000), ACM Press, New York, 2000, pp. 371.

[2] Bardram, J.E., *Plans as Situated Action: An Activity Theory Approach to Workflow Systems*, in Proceedings of the Fifth European Conference on Computer Supported Cooperative Work ECSCW'97 Conference (Lancaster, 7-11 September 1997), Kluwer Aca-

demics Pub., Dordrecht, 1997.

[3] Beyer, H. and Holtzblatt, K., *Contextual Design: Defining Customer-Centered Systems*, Morgan Kaufman Publ., San Francisco, 1998.

[4] Brown, P.J., Bovey, J.D., and Chen, X., *Context-Aware applications: From the Laboratory to the Marketplace*, IEEE Personal Communications, Vol. 4, No. 5, 1997, pp. 58-64.

[5] Calvary, G., Coutaz, J., and Thevenin. D., *A Unifying Reference Framework for the Development of Plastic User Interfaces*, in M.R. Little and L. Nigay (eds.), Proc. of IFIP WG2.7 (13.2) Working Conference on Engineering the User Interfaces EHCI'01 (Toronto, May 2001), Springer-Verlag Berlin, LNCS, Vol. 2254, 2001, pp. 173-192.

[6] Calvary, G., Coutaz, J., and Thevenin, D., *Supporting Context Changes for Plastic User Interfaces: a Process and a Mechanism*, in A. Blandford, J. Vanderdonckt, and P. Gray (eds.), Proc. of HCI-IHM 2001, Springer-Verlag, London, 2001, pp. 349-363.

[7] Cheverst, K., Davies, N., Mitchell, K., Efstratiou, C., Using context as a Crystal Ball: Rewards and Pitfalls, Personal and Ubiquitous Computing, Vol. 5, No. 1, 2001, pp. 8-11.

[8] Dey, A., Kortuem, G., Morse, D., and Schmidt, A., *Situated Interaction and Context aware Computing*, Personal and Ubiquitous Computing, Vol. 5, No. 1, 2001, pp. 1-3.

[9] Dey, A., *Understanding and Using Context*, Personal and Ubiquitous Computing, Vol. 5, No. 1, 2001, pp. 4-7.

[10] Fitzmaurice, G.W., *Situated Information Spaces and Spatially Aware Palmtop Computers*, Communication of the ACM, Vol. 7, No. 36, July 93, pp. 39-49.

[11] Halverson, C.A., *Distributed Cognition as a theoretical framework for HCI: Don't throw the Baby out with the bathwater - the importance of the cursor in Air Traffic Control*, Tech Rep. No. 94-03, Dept. of Cognitive Science, Univ. of California, San Diego, 1994.

[12] Harrison, S. and Dourish, P., *Re-Place-ing Space: the roles of Place and Spaces in Colaborative Systems*, in Proc. of 6th Conference on Computer Supported Cooperative Work CSCW'96 (Boston, 16-20 November 1996), ACM Press, New York, 1996, pp. 67-76.

[13] Nardi, B., *Context and Conciousness. Activity Theory and Human Computer Interaction*, MIT Press, Cambridge, 1996.

[14] Paternò, F., *Model-based Design and Evaluation of Interactive Applications*, Springer-Verlag, Berlin, 1999.

[15] Pascoe, J., *Adding Generic Contextual Capabilities to Wearable Computers*, in Proc. of the 2nd *International Symposium on Wearable Computers*, 1998, pp. 92-99

[16] Rey, G., *Systèmes Interactifs Sensibles au Contexte. Ecole doctorale de Mathématiques et Informatique*, DEA d'Informatique, Systèmes et Communications, Université Joseph Fourier et Institut National Polytechnique de Grenoble, June 2001.

[17] Salber, D., Dey, A.K., and Abowd, G., *The Context Toolkit: Aiding the development of context-enabled Applications*, in Proc. of ACM Conf. on Human Aspects in Computing Systems CHI'99 (Pittsburgh, 15-20 May 1999), ACM Press, New York, 1999, pp. 434-441.

[18] Schilit, B.N., Adams, N.I. and Want, R., *Context-Aware Computing Applications*, in Proceedings of the 1st IEEE Workshop on Mobile Computing Systems and Applications WMCSA'94 (Santa Cruz, 8-9 December 1994), IEEE Computer Society Press, Los Alamitos, 1994, pp. 85-90.

[19] Schmidt, A., *Implicit Human Computer Interaction Through Context*, Personal Technologies,Vol. 4, No. 2&3, June 2000, pp.191-199.

[20] Suchman, L.A., *Plans and situated actions. The problem of human-machine communication*, Cambridge University Press, Cambridge, 1987.

[21] Thevenin, D., Coutaz, J., *Plasticity of User Interfaces: Framework and Research Agenda*, in A. Sasse and C. Johnson (eds.), Proc. of 7th IFIP International Conference on Human-Computer Interaction Interact'99 (Edinburgh, 30 August – 3 September 1999), IOS Press Publ., 1999, pp.110-117.

[22] Ward, A. Jones, A. Hopper, A New Location Technique for the Active Office. IEEE *Personnal Communications*, 1997, pp. 42-47.
[23] Weiser, M., *The Computer for the 21st century*, Scientific American, Vol. 265, No. 3 1991, pp. 94-104.
[24] *Dagstuhl Seminar on Ubiquitous Computing*, September 2001, accessible at http://www.inf.ethz.ch/vs/events/dag2001/.

Chapter 3

WSXL: A WEB SERVICES LANGUAGE FOR INTEGRATING END-USER EXPERIENCE

David Chamberlain, Angel Diaz, Dan Gisolfi, Ravi Konuru, John Lucassen, Julie Macnaught, Stephane Maes, Roland Merrick, David Mundel, TV Raman, Shankar Ramaswamy, Thomas Schaeck, Rich Thompson, and Charles Wiecha
IBM Corporation, T.J. Watson Research Center, P.O. Box 704,
Yorktown Heights, NY 10598 (USA)
E-mail: wiecha@us.ibm.com – Tel.: +1-914-784-7044 – Fax: +1-914-784-6324

Abstract WSXL (Web Services Experience Language) is a web services centric component model for interactive web applications. WSXL is designed to achieve two main goals: enable businesses to distribute web applications through multiple revenue channels, and enable new services or applications to be created by leveraging existing applications across the Web. To accomplish these goals, WSXL components can be built out of three basic web service types for data, presentation, and control, the last of which is used to "wire together" the others using declarative language based on XLink and XML Events. WSXL also introduces a new description language for adapting services to new distribution channels. WSXL is built on widely accepted established and emerging open standards, and is designed to be independent of execution platform, browser, and presentation markup.

Keywords: Components, Control, Data, Presentation, Web applications, WSXL, XML.

1. INTRODUCTION

In today's business environment, companies face an increasing array of unrelenting marketplace pressures. To be successful, they need to bring applications that support their business processes to market quickly and economically. They need to unbundle their business processes into core competencies so they can deliver a wide variety of increasingly sophisticated services and vary these services in response to changing market conditions. They need to exploit an increasing diversity of on-line distribution models – in-

C. Kolski and J. Vanderdonckt (eds.), Computer-Aided Design of User Interfaces III, 35–50.
© 2002 *Kluwer Academic Publishers.*

cluding both direct and multiple distribution channels – in order to reach a variety of customers.

As businesses attempt to insure that their Internet investments result in increased revenues, they often seek to optimize those investments across multiple distribution channels. For example, a company that sells Traveler Checks over the web could benefit from added exposure of their web applications (and therefore of their products) to a wider array of potential customers by using multiple business partner distribution channels. When doing so, the application provider may need to modify or give up brand relationship and navigation control to some, if not all, of its distributors. The technical challenge is to economically establish and maintain such re-distribution relationships in a way that can flexibly accommodate the demands of multiple business partners using different business models.

Take for example a vendor of financial visualization software. In order to support multiple new revenue opportunities, the vendor may need to support both direct access from a client (B2C), a re-distribution relationship from a value added reseller, and an OEM relationship with a business partner. Each of these approaches, when considered on its own, is clearly feasible today. However, time to market and cost of entry are critical factors that weigh heavily when a vendor is evaluating the expansion of distribution channels. A key business enabler would be a technology that allows the software to be expressed in a common format that minimizes the development and support requirements, for both software distributors and providers. Provided that it is flexible and easy to use, such a technology could improve both time to market and cost of entry, resulting in substantial new opportunities for Independent Software Vendors (ISVs) and substantial cost savings and time-to-market gains for their distributors and end customers.

1.1 The Demand for Dynamic Web Applications

Businesses need a new approach for developing and delivering applications to help reduce the cost of developing interactive web applications, delivering them to end users, and adjusting them over application lifetime to the changing requirements imposed by new business models. This new approach must enable enterprises to:

- Achieve an effective user experience that is appealing, efficient, and appropriately branded within each delivery channel.
- Maintain business flexibility – in particular, the flexibility to add new distribution partners and application content providers quickly, and to change and update applications both collaboratively (jointly with partners) and autonomously (i.e., without being dependent on the partners).
- Leverage existing skills and infrastructure.

Moreover, the new approach needs to support:

- Ease of change: to implement new and rapidly evolving business models, such as cross-selling, joint offerings, and outsourcing.
- Ease of adaptation: to deliver an application through new channels, such as a portals or third party web sites.
- Ease of aggregation: to group several applications into a single user experience, such as a portal.
- Ease of integration: to create a new presentation by tightly integrating elements of several web applications.

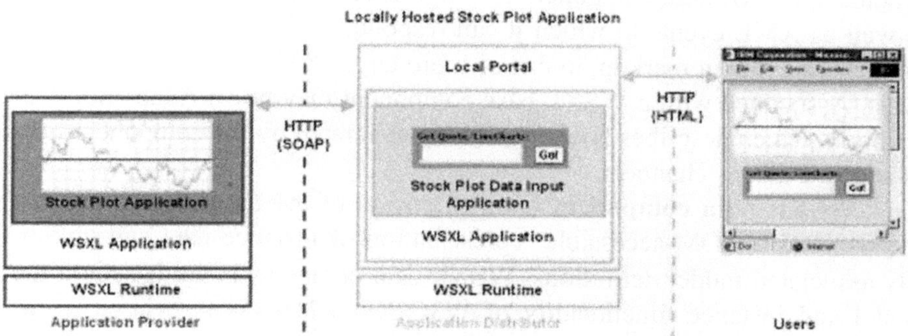

Figure 1. Distributed visualization services.

We seek to enable scenarios such as the one in Fig. 1 where a supplier of financial graphics utility services enables the flexible redistribution of these services. A portal company could in this case augment the utility service with a branded data input form. This approach would enable quick enhancements to the portfolio of portal services at a low cost of entry.

2. WEB SERVICES EXPERIENCE LANGUAGE

The approach taken in WSXL to meet the requirements listed above is to allow a web application to export one or more component interfaces that expose enough information to enable adaptation, aggregation and integration while still allowing the applications to evolve. WSXL enables applications to be built out of separate presentation, data, and control components; this helps developers to separate design issues that if left intermixed in more monolithic objects would make integration for re-use in multiple channels more difficult.

This section introduces the WSXL component framework for web applications (based on the well-known Model-View-Controller architecture) and relates it to existing standards such as XFORMS [5] and XLINK [6]. We also give a simple example of how data, presentation, and control components can be reused to produce new web applications by integration rather than programming them from scratch.

WSXL applications consist of one or more data and presentation components, together with a controller component which binds them together and specifies their interrelated behavior.

A WSXL base component has interfaces for life cycle management, event handling, and generation of output markup. The life cycle operations can be used to explicitly create and destroy instances of a WSXL base component. A WSXL base component may define XML events that it may raise, as well as XML events to which it can respond. A WSXL base component can generate output markup, in one or more target XML languages, upon request. Associated with a WSXL base component may be an Adaptation Description, which describes how the markup generated by the component may be adapted to new channels.

A WSXL data component is an extension of the base component that encapsulates a DOM-accessible representation of instance data and optionally associated model definitions. WSXL data components are based on the model and instance functionality of W3C XFORMS [5] (see http://www.w3c.org/tr/xforms). Data components may be bound to presentation components using WSXL control components. In addition, data components may be connected to data sources external to WSXL applications, but this is an implementation detail that is beyond the scope of WSXL.

A WSXL presentation component is an extension of the base component that encapsulates a DOM-accessible representation of the elements in a user interface (UI) "page". The namespaces for elements used in presentation components are not fixed by WSXL, though commonly useful "widget" sets may be available such as those defined in the XFORMS UI draft. WSXL presentation components may be bound to data components using the WSXL control component and must raise and respond to events defined by that component for updating and resetting interaction data values and updating the presentation.

A WSXL control component is an extension of the base component that manages the micro-control between instantiated data and presentation components in order to bind them together. It determines when to invoke event handlers to parse and reformat data values during updates in each direction. The WSXL control component reads declarations authored in an XLINK-based extensible control language specification to establish required arcs and implements the processing model for initiating, sequencing, and carrying out updates to synchronize the presentation with the state of the data. A second function of the control component is to manage the macro-control involving instantiation of entirely new data and presentation components as a user moves through the application. This aspect of control may be specified by state-machine notations or workflow languages using an extensible flow language interface.

WSXL interfaces can be described using the Web Services Description Language (WSDL). WSDL allows for a language-independent definition of the types, messages, and operations in a component's interface. WSDL separates these interface characteristics (the service's portType) from the binding of the portType to a particular transport mechanism. Many web services are accessed remotely over the network using SOAP messages. In other cases, components may be executed locally and use higher performance "transport" such as direct method invocation. We intend the WSDL definitions in this document to be interpreted independently of whether the WSXL components described are to be accessed remotely or locally.

WXSL Adaptation Descriptions can be expressed using the Adaptation Description Language described in this document. We separate the Adaptation Description Language from the Web Services Description Language to allow a component interface to be associated with a choice of Adaptation Descriptions.

2.1 Component Descriptions

In this section we describe the interfaces provided by the base WSXL component. Next, we show how three particular types of components – data, presentation, and control – are derived from the base component interfaces. In the following section, we discuss how applications can be built from groups of components.

2.1.1 Base Component

The base component in WSXL specifies the interfaces that are common for all WSXL components: life cycle management, event handling, and generation of output markup, along with the notion of Adaptation Descriptions, which describe how the markup generated by the component may be adapted to new channels. Other WSXL components, including data, presentation, and control, implement these base interfaces as well as the particular interfaces required for their functionality.

The specific categories of interfaces of a WSXL Base Component are shown in Fig. 2 and include:

- **Lifecycle:** the Lifecycle interface of a component provides operations that can be called by the container to implement its lifecycle. While in general there may be multiple lifecycles required – in order to support differing requirements of containers according to the types of compo-

nents they manage, the initial WSXL lifecycle operations will include operations such as those for creating and destroying instances of a component.
- **Events**: a WSXL component must implement the DOM Level 2 [3] EventTarget interface. XML event specifications will be used to describe event listeners.
- **OutputMarkup**: generates output markup, typically at the end of an update/refresh cycle. Returns an XML representation of the instance data document.

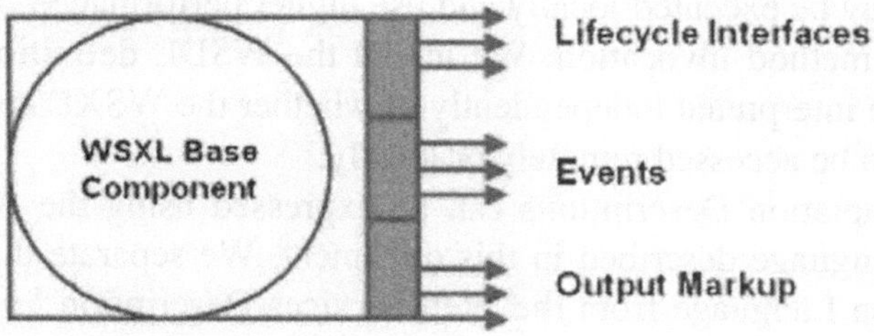

Figure 2. Base WSXL component and interfaces.

2.1.2 Data Component

In addition to the WSXL base component interfaces described above, the WSXL data component implements interfaces used to describe and maintain instances of DOM-accessible data in WSXL applications. The WSXL data component is based on the data functionality in XFORMS, and includes both XFORMS model and instance functions.

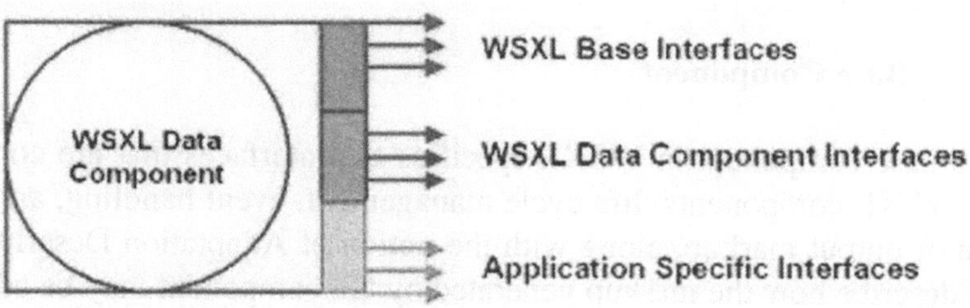

Figure 3. WSXL data component and interfaces.

The additional categories of interfaces of a WSXL data component are shown in Fig. 3 and include:
- **Access**: a WSXL data component describes the structure it wishes to expose using a subset of the DOM Level 2 interface [3]. The specific operations from DOM Level 2 required by WSXL have not yet been determined. At a minimum, a component must support reading and writing attributes on its DOM.

- **UpdateControl**: used to mark the start and end of group of updates. Use of this interface is optional, at the discretion of the container. Default behavior is to raise change notification events synchronously with each update.
- **Validation**: used to trigger evaluation of type constraints between the data instance and its model.
- **Recompute**: used to trigger evaluation of side effects from updates elsewhere in the data. Result is to call any handlers that are part of the internal implementation of the data component, i.e. those that will not be evaluated as a result of evaluating external control links (see control component below).
- **DataAvailability**: used to signal the availability of the component's instance data. While the way in which the component connects to external data is not itself standardized, states associated with that data connection could be, such as unconnected, data requested, data partial, data available.

2.1.3 Presentation Component

In addition to the WSXL base component interfaces described above, the WSXL presentation component implements interfaces used to describe and maintain DOM-accessible instances of presentation in WSXL applications. The WSXL presentation component is based on the UI specifications in XFORMS, and includes both XFORMS presentation instance and template functionality.

The WSXL presentation component does not specify any particular widget set. WSXL presentation components may consist of elements in arbitrary namespaces, and may generate output markup similarly in any target XML language. It is a goal for WSXL to be a foundational infrastructure for supporting particular XML widget sets for user interfaces as may emerge in the industry, including those in XFORMS [5], XUL [2], UIML [1], and so on.

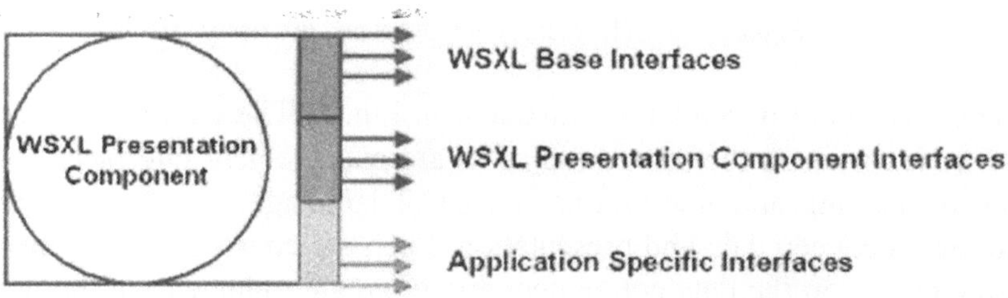

Figure 4. WSXL presentation component and interfaces.

Beyond the base component interfaces, the additional categories of interfaces of a WSXL presentation component are shown in Fig. 4 and include:

- **Access**: a WSXL presentation component describes the structure it wishes to expose using a subset of the DOM Level 2 interface. The specific operations from DOM Level 2 required by WSXL have not yet been determined. At a minimum, a component must support reading and writing attributes on its DOM.
- **Interaction**: used to indicate state of end-user interaction with elements in the presentation component, such as focus, selection, activation, execution, hide/expose. Draws on and extends the abstract UI events in DOM Level 2 event model. Physical events such as mouse probably of less import to server-side components. Keyboard events required.

2.1.4 Control Component

As shown in Fig. 5, the WSXL control component is an extension of the WSXL base component as are data and presentation components. In addition to the base WSXL component interfaces, the WSXL control component implements interfaces used to manage the arcs binding data components to presentation components, to parse and interpret the XLINK-based control language specification described below, and to implement a processing model that controls the propagation of event notifications in both directions between data and presentation.

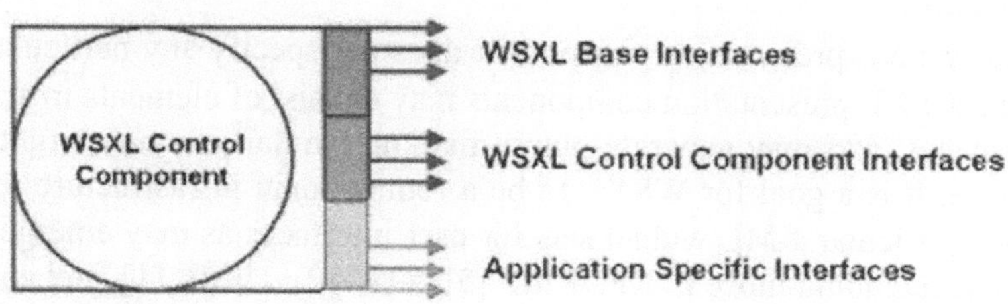

Figure 5. WSXL control component and interfaces.

The basic control model is illustrated in Fig. 6. The control component, either in response to the invocation of its arc management interface, or indirectly by parsing and interpreting a control language specification, establishes arcs between data and presentation. Each arc consists of a listener to a given element on the data component and to another element on the presentation component. Data and presentation components are not connected directly to each other. The control component establishes arcs and maintains itself at runtime to manage the order and timing of event notifications in each direction.

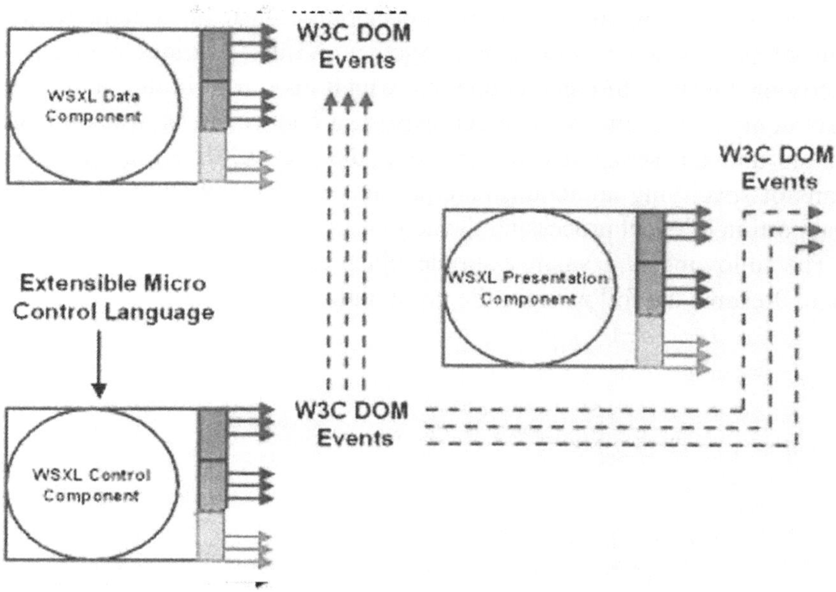

Figure 6. WSXL control component binding to WSXL data and presentation components.

Event handlers can be associated with arcs to provide control logic triggered in response to event notifications. This between-component, or "micro-level" control logic may (1) modify the values or structure of the data and/or presentation components, (2) make calls to external services, and (3) interact with across-component or "macro-level" control to trigger the possible instantiation of additional WSXL components for subsequent steps in the application.

Beyond the base component interfaces, the additional categories of interface of a WSXL control component are shown in Fig. 5 and include:

- **Arc definition and management**: used to create new arcs by providing source and destination service instances, XPATH locators within those instances, and event handlers to be associated with the arc. This interface supports operations for enumerate, change, delete, and create actions on arcs. This interface can be called directly, or via the control specification language described below.
- **Control specification parsing**: used to parse an XLINK-based control specification file and create arcs using the interface above. This interface supports a declarative way of defining the behavior of the control component without driving the underlying programmatic interface directly.
- **Update processing model**: used to maintain list of "dirty" links, order list of updates and update groups, apply updates according to policies set by binding language (synchronous or asynchronous), fire event handlers on arcs.

The control component supports a declarative means of binding components of type data or presentation together. XLink provides a means for specifying 'locators' to name endpoints, which may exist in the same or different components, and 'arcs' which express a connection between a pair of locators and the semantics of traversing the arc. XML Events provide a means of specifying an action, its type, the event, event source and during what portion of event processing the action should be triggered.

The following is a small example illustrating how these may be combined. Presume the following is the presentation markup:

```
<form id="Employee">
  <span>
      <div>First name</div>
      <input name="firstname"></input>
  </span>
  <span>
      <div>Last name</div>
      <input name="lastname"></input>
  </span>
  <span>
      <div>Employee #</div>
      <input name="employeeNum"></input>
  </span>
</form>
```

If the data contains:

```
<Employee>
  <Name><First/><Last/></Name>
  <SerialNumber/>
</Employee>
```

then an example Micro Control binding declaration could be:

```
<BinderLinks xmlns:ev="http://www.w3.org/2001/xml-events"
  xmlns:xlink="http://www.w3.org/1999/xlink"
  xlink:type="extended"
  xlink:title="Example binder link specification">

  <!-- First define the endpoint locators -->
  <loc xlink:type="locator"
   xlink:href="http://www.examples.com/presentation.html"
   xlink:label="Presentation Root"/>

<!-- 'parent' protocol indicates what follows is a label -->
  <loc xlink:type="locator" xlink:href="parent://
```

```
     Presentation Root#//form[@id='Employee']"
     xlink:label="Employee Form"/>

    <loc xlink:type="locator"
     xlink:href="http://www.examples.com/data.xml"
     xlink:label="Data Root"/>

    <loc xlink:type="locator"
     xlink:href="parent://Data Root#/Employee"
     xlink:label="Employee Data"/>

  <!-- Now define the arcs between the endpoints -->
  <bind xlink:type="arc"
        xlink:from="Employee Data#Name/First"
        xlink:to="Employee
         Form#.//input[@id='firstname']/@value"/>

  <bind xlink:type="arc"
        xlink:from="Employee Data#Name/Last"
        xlink:to="Employee
         Form#.//input[@id='lastname']/@value"/>

  <bind xlink:type="arc"
        xlink:from="Employee Data#SerialNumber"
        xlink:to="Employee
         Form#.//input[@id='employeeNum']/@value">

  <!-- validate the entered serial number -->
  <ev:listener ev:event="DOMCharacterDataModified"
               ev:observer="xlink:to"
               ev:handler=http://testit#VerifySerialNumber
               handlertype="WebService"/>
   </bind>
  </BinderLinks>
```

These declarations start with two locators that each reference a URL through their xlink:href attributes. The Micro Control Component will ask the container that instantiated it to resolve these URLs. If the container has not already instantiated these, it will fetch the referenced component and locally instantiate it (or a proxy to it). The handle to local instance will then be returned to the Micro Control component.

A couple of additional locators are declared relative to these two root level locators. The Micro Control Component will query the components referenced by the parent locators to resolve the supplied query string (in this case an XPath).

The processing of the arc declarations will establish listener relationships between the referenced components and the controller using the DOM Level 2 Event API. The default event type is DOMCharacterDataModified with a default action making the value of the endpoints of the arc equal. As can be seen from the last arc definition, both the event and handler can be declared using XML Event syntax. An extension is required to indicate which endpoint is the source of the handled event (the example specifies the input field with id='employeeNum' in presentation.html). These handlers may format the data during the traversal of the arc by returning a new value, abort the traversal by returning null, as well as any desired side effects (e.g. trigger a transition in the Macro Flow between components).

2.2 Adaptation Description Language

One of the issues in application syndication is that a component provider may want to control how the markup and operations provided by the component may be accessed, modified, or overridden. This need may be for brand preservation, to preserve a certain aesthetic design constraints, or for correctness reasons. Thus a "conforming" client/aggregator can use the information to reliably adapt the component output and to intercept user-input to the component within the constraints laid down by the provider.

To this end, WSXL includes an extensible Adaptation Description Language where explicit locations of adaptation points, the permissible operations on adaptation points (e.g. insert, delete, modify), and the constraints on the contents of adaptation (e.g. via an XML Schema) can be specified. The Adaptation Description Language can be used as a post-processing step where the output of a WSXL component can be adapted independently without invoking the component.

The core concept of this description language is the notion of an Adaptation point. Adaptation points define "observable characteristics" of a presentation stream. Adaptation points are used at design time, by both the application provider and the intermediary, to speed development and help ensure correctness. Further, these points are used at runtime, by supporting middleware, to safely perform the adaptations requested by an intermediary. Adaptation points allow a client to reliably: change background color or font variable used by the application, lookup a value in the output markup (e.g. an embedded product ID), overwrite/Add to a value in the output markup (e.g. a price), insert a value in a particular page (e.g. an extra text field, a new column in a table), or override/extend the action associated with an event (e.g. button press).

Adaptation Points are part of a WSXL component definition. An Adaptation Point specifies:

- An application-specific Adaptation Point name.
- The kind of operation (insert, replace, lookup).
- The names of pages that it applies to.
- A locator to the item[s] of interest. For instance, xpath, xquery are used for XML documents.
- An Adaptation Point category (XML, CSS, etc).
- Information specific to an adaptation of a given category.

The following categories of adaptations are initially introduced: CSS-Adaptation, and XMLAdaptation. Other categories can be introduced into the language as necessary.

2.2.1 XMLAdaptation

XMLAdaptation can appear as part of defininining an adaptation and used to provide information related to manipulating XML fragments. An example XMLAdaptation is shown below:

```
<adaptation name="ContactInfo" use="replace">
 <locator name="ContactLocator" type="xpath"
  xpath="//cntctInfo"/>
 <XMLAdaptation>
  <validTypes>ShortContactInfo LongContactInfo</validTypes>
  <schemaLocation>http://www.Sample.com/TypeInfo.xml
  </schemaLocation>
 </XMLAdaptation>
</adaptation>
```

In the above example, the provider is specifying an Adaptation Point to allow the replacement of the contact information in its output stream with the constraint that the replacing XML fragment should match one of the two specified types. The type description is available in the file at the URL specified in the schemaLocation element.

2.2.2 CSSAdaptation

CSSAdaptation elements have been introduced to accommodate the specification and manipulation of CSS attributes that do not conform to XML. An example instance of is shown below:

```
<adaptationGroup name="changeLookAndFeel">
   <adaptation name="backgroundColor" use="replace">
   <outputList>output1 output3 output10</outputList>
   <locator name="backgroundColorLocator"
            type="xpath" xpath="xhtml/body//table"/>
   <CSSAdaptation>
```

```
  <property>background-color</property>
  </CSSAdaptation>
  <comment>For help contact A.Jones.</comment>
  <toolingHint>Specify override for background color.
  </toolingHint>
  </adaptation>
</adaptationGroup>
```

In this description fragment, the adaptationGroup has only one Adaptation Point, which provides information to aggregator about how the background color of a XHTML table can be adapted. The "use" attribute on the adaptation specifies that a client can perform a replace operation on the item specified within the adaptation element. The outputList element consists of names that identify the subset of the different outputs to which the Adaptation Point applies. The locator element specifies where in the component's XML portion of the output the item of interest can be found while the CSSAdaptation specifies the CSS qualifying locator that identifies the specific attribute of interest. In this case the values in the property element must match one of the properties in the CSS specification.

2.2.3 AdaptationGenerator

AdaptationGenerators have been introduced to assist providers in creating markup for aggregators to use in adaptation, to retain control over markup fragments that are inserted, and to sidestep the limitations of the constraint language. The following example shows how an operation named "addColumnToXHTMLTable" can be included within an AdaptationGenerator.

```
<adaptation name="addColumnAtEndOfTableA"
            use="replace">
   <locator name="TableALocator"
             type="xpath" xpath="//..."/>
   <AdaptationGenerator>addColumntoXHTMLTable
   </AdaptationGenerator>
</adaptation>
```

The signature of an AdaptationGenerator is obtained from the WSXL specification of the service. Its' input message consists of two parts: a locator in the message, and the presentation content that the client wishes to be added to the provider's message. The output signature is a message containing any instance appropriate to the client's content.

3. WSXL EXAMPLE

Fig. 7 demonstrates how a portal provider could create a product that for access to financial graphics utilities. The distributor in the application supply chain is adding functionality beyond simply altering the look and feel of the provider's application. Additional Presentation and Data components are introduced at the distributor to create the data entry form required for the stock symbol to be charted. A Control component at the distributor links the data and presentation elements for the stock symbol, and carries an event handler on that arc for passing the entered data value to the provider's application control component to trigger the regeneration of a chart. From the standpoint of the end user there is a single application frame whose events are coordinated and delegated to the appropriate providers by the distributor.

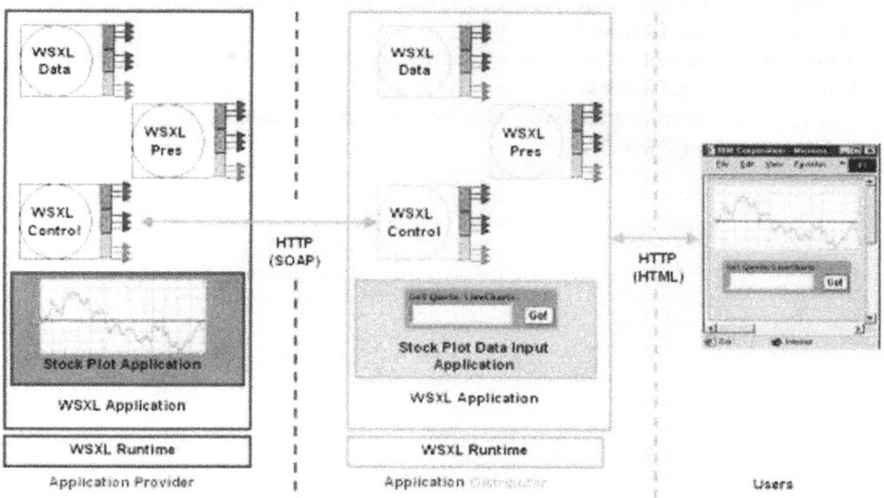

Figure 7. WSXL Implementation of Distributed Visualization Services.

4. SUMMARY

WSXL is the next piece of the web services stack. WSXL provides a web services standards based approach for web application development, deployment and maintenance. WSXL enables *Dynamic e-Business*, by moving from transactions driven by a single business entity to a world of electronic transactions involving multiple business entities who compose and aggregate re-usable web applications. As a result, these applications can leverage new and innovative revenue models.

REFERENCES

[1] Abrams, M., Phanouriou, C., Batongbacal, A.L., Williams, S.M., Shuster, J.E., *UIML: An Appliance-Independent XML User Interface Language*, in A. Mendelzon (ed.), Proceedings of 8th Int. World-Wide Web Conference WWW'8 (Toronto, May 11-14, 1999), Elsevier Science Publishers, Amsterdam, 1999. Accessible at http://www8.org/w8-papers/5b-hyper text-media/uiml/uiml.html

[2] Cheng, T., *XUL Coding Style Guidelines*, The Mozilla Organization, December 2001. Available at http://www.mozilla.org/projects/l10n/xul-styleguide.html

[3] DOM Level 2 Core, W3C (World Wide Web Consortium), Document Object Model Level 2 Core Specification, November 2000. Available at http://www.w3.org/TR/2000/REC-DOM-Level-2-Core-20001113

[4] DOM Level 3 Events, W3C (World Wide Web Consortium), Document Object Model Level 3 Events Specification, August 2001. Available at http://www.w3.org/TR/DOM-Level-3-Events

[5] Xforms, W3C (World Wide Web Consortium) XForms, August 2001. Available at http://www.w3.org/TR/xforms

[6] Xlink, W3C (World Wide Web Consortium) XLink, June 2001. Available at http://www.w3.org/TR/xlink/

[7] XSLT, W3C (World Wide Web Consortium) XSLT, January 2001. Available at http://www.w3.org/TR/xslt

Chapter 4

FROM FORMAL SPECIFICATIONS TO SECURE IMPLEMENTATIONS

Francis Jambon
LISI-ENSMA, Téléport 2 - 1 avenue Clément Ader, BP 40109
F-86961 Futuroscope Chasseneuil cedex (France)
E-mail: Francis.Jambon@ensma.fr – URL: http://www.lisi.ensma.fr/members/jambon/
Tel.: +33-5-49 49 80 70 – Fax.: +33-5 49 49 80 64

Abstract This paper proposes a new tool-supported technique for the complete development of safety-critical interactive systems from the specification to the implementation step. Safety as well as usability properties are continuously guaranteed during the development process. This technique relies on formal specifications of the requirements and so uses the model-oriented formal method B and a new ad-hoc software architecture model –CAV– which is an hybrid of MVC and PAC models. At the implementation step, this technique uses automatic code generation. Moreover, links from secure generated code to native non-secure libraries are clarified. This development process is illustrated by a fully implemented case study.

Keywords: B method, Development process, Formal specification, Safety-critical interactive system, Usability property.

1. INTRODUCTION

Graphical user interfaces relying mostly on software, are being more and more used for safety-critical interactive systems –for example aircraft glass cockpits– the failure of which can cause injury or death to human beings. Consequently, as well as hardware, the software of these interactive systems needs a high level of dependability. Besides, on the one hand, the design process must insure the reliability of the system features in order to prevent disastrous breakdowns. On the other hand, the usability of the interactive system must be carefully carried out to avoid user misunderstanding that can trigger similar disastrous effects. So, the software dependability of these

C. Kolski and J. Vanderdonckt (eds.), Computer-Aided Design of User Interfaces III, 51–62.
© 2002 *Kluwer Academic Publishers.*

safety-critical interactive systems rely as well on safety as on usability properties. Usually, safety-critical systems act in the real-word, i.e., they control the most of hardware –for example an aircraft engine. This represents the major cause of their safety-critical characteristic. As a consequence, most of the functional core of these systems are asynchronous, i.e., the system state – for example the engine rotation speed– can be altered independently of the user actions: a typical characteristic of process-control systems.

The verification of safety as well as of usability properties of software can be achieved by tests or proofs. For asynchronous systems, the former technique is rather difficult to set up: the needed number of test sequences to get a full cover may be not computable. That explains why the latter technique –proofs– is a relevant one for the verification of safety-critical interactive systems. In previous works, the adaptation of well-defined approaches, combined with interactive models, brought partial but positive results. For example, we can find the Interactors and related approaches [7,8], model-oriented approaches [7], algebraic notations [9], Petri nets [10] or Temporal Logic [4]. These techniques enable designers to prove some safety as well as usability requirements. However, these formal techniques are used in the development process in restricted conditions due to two constraints:

- They mostly rely on ad-hoc specification models –e.g. Interactors– and do not use well-known software architecture models such as MVC or PAC. The consequence is that these unusual models make the specification task to most interactive systems designers uneasy to achieve, and the refinement to implementation difficult to carry out.
- Few of them can preserve formal semantics of the requirements from the specification to the implementation steps. Most of them can prove usability properties at the specification level only. So, it cannot be proved that the final software is exactly what has been specified.

Our development process uses the B formal method [1]. On the one hand, compared to VDM and Z, the B method permits the definition of a constructive process to build whole applications, respecting of all the rules by the use of a semi-automatic tool [5]. Our first results [2] focus on low-level interaction mechanisms, such as mouse and windows control and use the Arch software architecture model [3]. Recent results detail the use of the new CAV software architecture model for the specification of process-control interactive systems [6]. We so demonstrated that the B method might be used with profit in interactive system specification. This paper shows that the B method and the CAV software architecture model can be used to specify and thoroughly to implement a safety-critical interactive system. Moreover, a tool –Atelier B– is used to prove automatically all the proof obligations and to generate C code. This work may be considered as a new step towards the definition of an actual tool-supported interactive development process based on formal approaches.

The paper is organized as follows: in section 2, our case study –the battery control panel– is presented. Section 3 focuses on the specifications and explains how the safety and usability requirements can be formally checked. The B method and the CAV architecture model are also briefly described. Then, in section 4, the implantation of the case study is detailed, and at last, there is a discussion about used programming philosophies.

2. CASE STUDY

The case study is a control panel for a set of three rechargeable batteries. The aim of this system is to produce continuous electric power supply. This system may be a part of a more complex safety-critical system as avionics. The operator is in charge of the selection of the switched battery.

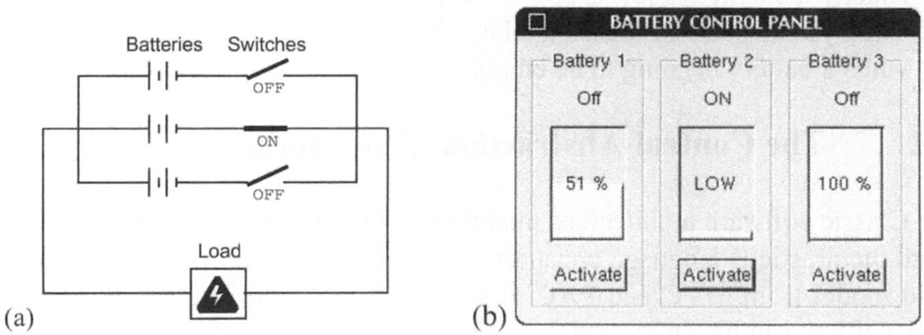

Figure 1. Electric diagram (a) and interface layout (b) of the electric power supply.

The functional core of the system is a set of three batteries and three switches. As shown on Fig. 1a, the load can be supplied by any battery. In order to prevent short-cuts between batteries, only one switch must be in position on at the same time. Moreover, to ensure power supply continuity, at least one switch must be in position on. For the same reason, an empty battery cannot be switched on. These three requirements of the functional core deals with the safety of the system.

The operator interprets the system state via the positions –on or off– of the switches and the levels of the batteries –in percentage of maximum. The operator can select the switched battery via three push-buttons. Fig. 1b shows the user interface layout. When a switched battery level is below 10% of its initial capacity, the percentage is replaced by a low warning message. The user interface must ensure conformity, i.e., the interface state must display exactly the functional core state. This last requirement deals with the usability of the system.

This case study is an elementary safety-critical process-control system: the operator can control side-effects on hardware –the switches– whereas the hardware state –the batteries levels– is altered asynchronously. Both safety and usability properties have to be ensured. We will reach such results thanks to the formal method B.

3. SPECIFICATIONS

This first required step of our design process consists in modeling the battery control panel requirements with the B language. Three kinds of requirements must be fulfilled:

1. The system must be safe, i.e., the system must avoid shortcuts and it must not be possible to switch on an empty battery.
2. The system must be conform, i.e., the user interface widgets must display exactly the batteries levels and switches positions.
3. The system must be insistent, i.e., the system must warn the operator when a battery is going to be empty.

3.1 The Control-Abstraction-View Model

Classic software architecture models as PAC or MVC are not compliant with the drastic B language constraints. That is why we proposed a new hybrid model from MVC and PAC to solve this problem. The design of this new software architecture model –CAV– cannot be detailed here. The reader should refers to [6] for a more detailed description of the model. Briefly explained, the model uses the external strategy of MVC: the outputs of the system are devoted to a specific module –the View– while inputs are concerned by another one –the Control– that also manages symmetrical inputs from the reactive system, that is directed by the third module –the Abstraction. Like PAC, the Control module synchronizes and activates both the View and the Abstraction modules in response to both user and functional core system events, assuming though its role of dialogue controller (center of Fig. 2).

3.2 Specifications Base

In the B method [1], abstract machines represent the specifications. The typical B abstract machine starts with the keyword MACHINE and ends with the keyword END. A set of clauses can be defined in between. In our case study, these clauses appear in the following order:

- INCLUDES is a programming in the large clause that allows to import instances of other machines. Every component of the imported machine becomes usable in the current machine. The included machine(s) can be renamed by a prefix. This clause allows modularity capabilities.
- VARIABLES is the clause where all the attributes of the described model are represented. Variables may be abstract or concrete, i.e. the latter can be directly implemented, the former not.
- INVARIANT clause describes the properties of the attributes defined in the variables clause. The logical expressions described in this clause remain true in the whole machine and they represent assertions that are always valid.
- OPERATIONS clause defines all the operations –functions and procedures– that constitute the abstract data type represented by the machine. Depending on the nature of the machine, the operations clause authorizes particular generalized substitutions to specify each operation. The substitutions used in our specifications and their semantics are described below.

Applying our CAV software architecture model to the case study is straightforward: each module corresponds to a B abstract machine that encapsulates few attributes in its VARIABLE clause. The *AbsrBatt* abstract machine models the Abstraction of the system –the batteries– and the variables of this abstract machine are the switches positions and the batteries levels. These variables are altered through two operations: one to switch on a battery and one to update the levels:

```
MACHINE
     AbstBatt
ABSTRACT_VARIABLES
     switch_batt1, level_batt1, ...
OPERATIONS
     changeBattery (batt) = ...
     updateLevels (level1, level2, level3) = ...
END
```

The *ViewBatt* abstract machine models the View –the interface layout– and the variables of this abstract machine represent the state of each widget: the batteries levels, the switches positions, the states –enabled or disabled– of the warning messages LOW and pushbuttons (Fig. 1b). Operations of the machine update the switches positions and the batteries levels:

```
MACHINE
     ViewBatt
ABSTRACT_VARIABLES
     display_level1, display_low1, display_on1, display_button1, ...
OPERATIONS
     showOn (batt) = ...
     showLevels (level1, level2, level3) = ...
END
```

The *CtrlBatt* abstract machine models the Control –the dialogue controller– of the user interface. This abstract machine includes instances of the

View and of the Abstraction. The variables of the controller refers to the validity of the events from the real word, i.e., if a button is disabled an event is not supposed to be generated by this button. Operations of the controller are events coming from the batteries or the user: the update of the batteries levels and the activation of one of the pushbuttons.

```
MACHINE
     CtrlBatt
INCLUDES
     abst.AbstBatt, view.ViewBatt
ABSTRACT_VARIABLES
     evt_valid1, ...
OPERATIONS
     evtLevels ( level1, level2, level3 ) = ...
     evtButton ( nb ) = ...
END
```

The above specifications are incomplete: the INVARIANT clauses and the operations bodies have not been specified yet. Now we are going to complete some of them while specifying the usability and safety properties of the system.

3.3 Usability Properties

Among the usability properties, the system is in charge of warning the user if a battery is going to be empty. This usability requirement has to be specified as: if the battery switch is in position ON and the level is below or equal 10%, a warning message must be shown. This must be specified in the INVARIANT clause of the View:

```
INVARIANT
     ((display_low1=TRUE) ⇔ (display_on1=TRUE ∧ display_level1≤10)) ∧
...
```

The operations of the View must be specified to fulfill this invariant. For the *showLevels* operation, the specification below means that for any new value of the variables, they must satisfy the invariant, whatever the way they are computed:

```
OPERATIONS
     showLevels (level1, level2, level3) =
     ...
     ANY low1, low2, low3 WHERE
               ((display_on1=TRUE ∧ level1≤10) ⇔ (low1=TRUE)) ∧ ...
     THEN
               display_low1 := low1 || ...
     END || ...
```

This Insistence property specification is restricted to the View abstract machine. So, it is fairly easy to handle. On the contrary, the Conformity property requires the Control mediation between Abstraction and View. Its specification is similar to the specification of safety below and has not been described in the paper for the explanation would be too long.

3.4 Safety Properties

Among the safety requirements, we detail now the prevention of user error: the operator must not be able to switch on an empty battery. At first, this safety requirement deals with the functional core of the system, i.e., it must be specified in the Abstraction.

Moreover, this requirement is not a static but a dynamic property: the battery can become empty while switched on, but an empty battery must not be switched on. This requirement is not static predicate, so, it cannot be specified in the invariant clause of the abstract machine. In the B language semantics this category of requirement must be specified in a precondition substitution of the operations.

In the Abstraction abstract machine this safety requirement is specified in the PRE...THEN... substitution of the *changeBattery* operation. This substitution means that the operation is defined only if the parameter is not an empty battery. At this point, the specification sets the safety requirements up. As a consequence, the B language semantics ensure that the operation will never be called with an empty battery as parameter.

```
OPERATIONS
      changeBattery (batt) =
      PRE
                batt ∈ 1..3 ∧
                ((batt=1) ⇒ (level_batt1≠0)) ∧ ...
      THEN
                ...
      END
```

In fact, we have delegated to the Control abstract machine –that includes the Abstraction– the safety requirements, i.e. the Control is in charge of the verification of the semantic validity of the parameters when it calls the operation of the Abstraction abstract machine. We call this technique the *delegation of safety*. This generates two consequences:

1. The operator cannot be aware of a battery could not be switched on.
2. An action on a pushbutton can be generated with a empty battery number as parameter, so some required proofs obligations cannot be proved.

The first consequence is easy to set up. We have to improve the interface layout and to update the state of the button: enabled or disabled. Of course, if a button is disabled, it is well known that this button cannot emit an event. This assertion may seem to be sufficient to solve the second consequence above. That is not exact: the B semantics cannot ensure that a disabled button cannot emit events because the graphic toolkit is not formally specified. So, the Control abstract machine must filter the input events with the button states specified in the View abstract machine. This is required by the formal specification. The benefit of this consequence is that our system is safe and so even if the user interface is defective.

```
MACHINE
    CtrlBatt
INVARIANT
    ((abst.level_batt1 = 0) ⇒ (view.display_button1 = FALSE)) ∧
    (¬(abst.level_batt1 = 0) ⇒ (view.display_button1 = TRUE)) ∧
    ((abst.level_batt1 = 0) ⇔ (evt_valid1 = FALSE)) ∧
    (¬(abst.level_batt1 = 0) ⇔ (evt_valid1 = TRUE)) ∧ ...
OPERATIONS
    evtButton ( nb ) =
    PRE
            nb ∈ 1..3
    THEN
            SELECT
                    ((nb=1) ∧ (evt_valid1=TRUE)) ∨ ...
            THEN
                    abst.changeBattery(nb) || view.showOn(nb)
            END
    END ; ...
END
```

The total specification of the abstract machines is too long to be reproduced in this paper, but the two latter requirements are characteristic examples of the specification problems we had to deal with. Now we focus on the second step of the development process: the implementation.

4. IMPLEMENTATION

This section details the second step of our development process, i.e., the implementation of the control panel from the formal specifications carried out in the previous section. The final objective of our study is to design a working program. So, on the one hand we must implement secure code from the formal specifications but on the other hand we need to link this code to existing software libraries because it is not realistic –if ever possible– to specify a complete system with formal methods.

4.1 Implementation of the CAV Model

The final program must be a set of software modules in which some of them are formally specified and implemented, and some other are developed with classic software engineering methods. In order to dissociate these two antagonists types of modules, interfaces have been inserted in between. So, at the implementation step, the CAV architecture supports some add-ons as shown on Fig. 2. We now focus on these three types of modules: secure code, interface and native modules.

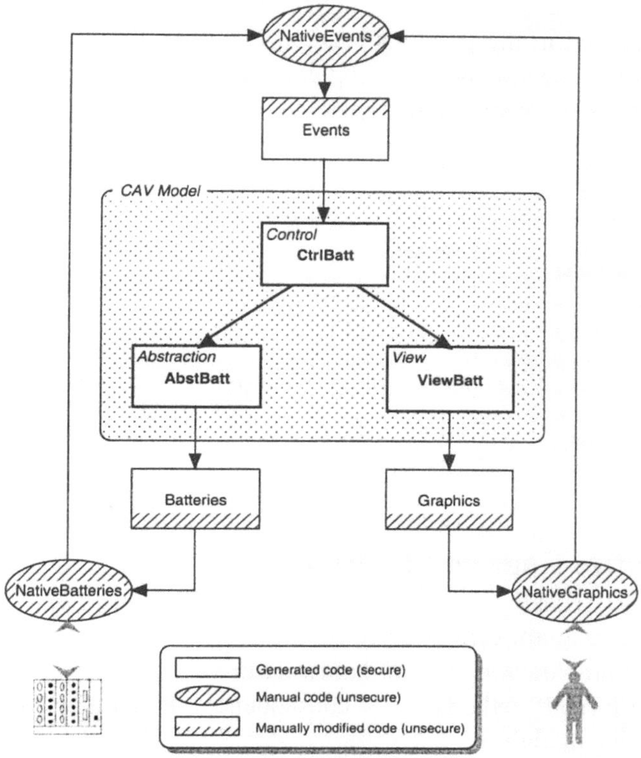

Figure 2. The CAV software architecture with interfaces and native modules.

4.2 Secure Code

The core of the interactive system has been specified in three B abstract machines. These machines specify the minimum requirements of the system but do not give any implantation solution. To do so, the B method uses implementation machines that refine abstract machines. The implementation machines are programmed in BØ pseudo-code that shares the same syntax with the B language and is close to a generic imperative programming language. In implementation machines, the substitutions are executed in sequence. BØ pseudo-code can be automatically translated into C code.

As implementation machines refine abstract machines, they must implement all the operations of the abstract machines. Moreover, the B method and semantics ensure that the side effects on variables of the implementation machines operations do respect the invariant as well as the abstract machines operations they refine. Providing the proof obligations are actually proved, the implementation machines respect the safety and usability requirements. So, the code is **secure** whether the specifications are adequate. As an illustration, we reproduce below the implementation of the Control operation *evtButton* specified in the previous section. Note that the SELECT...WHEN... non determinist specification is implemented by a determinist classic CASE...EITHER....OR... instruction.

```
IMPLEMENTATION
      CtrlBatt_i
REFINES
      CtrlBatt
IMPORTS
      abst.AbstBatt, view.ViewBatt
CONCRETE_VARIABLES
      evt_valid1, ...
OPERATIONS
      evtButton ( nb ) =
      BEGIN
                 CASE nb OF
                           EITHER 1 THEN IF (evt_valid1=TRUE) THEN
                                     abst.changeBattery(1) ; view.showOn(1) END
                           ...
                 END
      END ; ...
END
```

4.3 Native Code and Interfaces

A working program cannot be fully developed with formal methods because most of graphic widgets and hardware drivers libraries are not yet developed with formal methods. As a consequence, the battery control panel uses three native modules:

- The *NativeGraphics* software module controls the graphic layout of the user interface. It uses the GTk library.
- The *NativeBatteries* software module simulates the batteries with lightweight processes. It uses the POSIX thread library.
- The *NativeEvents* software module is in charge of merging the events coming from the user or the hardware and formats them to the data structure used by the BØ translator.

These three modules are not secure. However, the modules can be tested with a reduced set of test sequences because the procedures of these modules are only called by the secure code that do respect the formal specification. For example, the bar graph widget of *NativeGraphics* module is to be tested with values from 0 to 100 only because the secure modules are proved to use values from 0 to 100 only. Abnormal states do not have to be tested.

The interfaces modules roles are to make a syntactic filtering and translation between native modules and secure code:

- The *Events* software module receives integer data and translates them to 1..3 or 0..100 types. This module is secure because it as been specified and fully implemented in BØ but is called by non-secure modules.

- The *Graphics* and *Batteries* modules are specified in B and the skeleton of the modules is implemented in BØ and then manually modified to call the native modules *NativeBatteries* and *NativeGraphics* respectively.

4.4 Programming Philosophies

At last, the project outcome is a set of C source files. Some of these files are automatically generated from the BØ implementations, while others are partially generated or manually designed. The formal specification and implantation require about one thousand non obvious proof obligations to be actually proved. All these proof obligations can be proved thanks to the automatic prover in a few dozen of minutes with a standard workstation.

The core of the system is formally specified and developed. The programming philosophy used is called the *offensive* programming, i.e., the programmer do not have to question about the validity of the operations calls. The B method and semantics ensure that any operation is called with respect to the specifications. Most of the dialogue controller as well as the logic of the View and the Abstraction are designed with this philosophy. As a consequence, most of the dialog control of the system is secure.

On the opposite, the events coming from the real-word –user or hardware– have to be syntactically and semantically filtered. This programming philosophy is *defensive*. One the one hand the syntactic filtering is done by the Event module that casts the parameters types –from integer to interval. On the other hand, the semantic filtering is achieved by the Control module that can refuse events coming from disabled buttons. So, the system is resistant to graphic libraries bugs or transient errors with sensors. This filtering is required by the proof obligations that force upon the operations calls to be done with valid parameters.

There is no need to use the defensive programming philosophy in native modules. The procedures of these modules are called only by secure modules, so the parameters must be valid anytime. Neither verification nor filtering is necessary. The programming philosophy looks like the offensive philosophy except that the native modules are not formally specified but must be tested, so we name this philosophy *half-offensive*. As a consequence the development of high-quality native code can be performed with a reduced programming effort.

5. CONCLUSION

A previous work tends to show that the B method can specifies WIMP interactive systems [2] or process-control interactive systems [6]. This paper now shows that we successfully achieved the complete development of a safety-critical process-control interactive system from formal specifications. We proved that the system respects the requirements that deals with safety and usability. Moreover, this case study shows how the Control-Abstraction-View software architecture model can be successfully implemented. Some points may be enlightened:

- Safety and usability requirements may be specified by invariant or operation preconditions of B abstract machines.
- Incremental development from specifications to implementation of an interactive system can be achieved in a reasonable laps of time.
- Links between secure and insecure code are mandatory in the design of working programs and require interfaces.

This work is a new step toward an actual method for specifying, designing and implementing interactive systems with the formal method B and the use of an industrial tool. The next step is to overcome the lack of secure graphic libraries. That is the reason why we are currently developing a formal graphical widget library.

REFERENCES

[1] Abrial, J.-R., *The B Book: Assigning Programs to Meanings,* Cambridge University Press, Cambridge, 1996.

[2] Aït-Ameur, Y., Girard, P., and Jambon, F., *Using the B formal approach for incremental specification design of interactive systems*, in S. Chatty and P. Dewan (eds.), Engineering for Human-Computer Interaction, Vol. 22, Kluwer Academic Publishers, Dordrecht, 1998, pp. 91-108.

[3] Bass, L., Pellegrino, R., Reed, S., Sheppard, S., and Szczur, M., *A Metamodel for the Runtime Architecture of an Interactive System*, The UIMS Workshop Tool Developers, SIGCHI Bulletin, Vol. 24, No. 1, 1992, pp. 32-37.

[4] Brun, P., *XTL: a temporal logic for the formal development of interactive systems*, in P. Palanque and F. Paternò (eds.), Formal Methods for Human-Computer Interaction, Springer-Verlag, 1997, pp. 121-139.

[5] ClearSy. Atelier B - version 3.5, 1997.

[6] Jambon, F., Girard, P., and Aït-Ameur, Y., *Interactive System Safety and Usability enforced with the development process*, in Proc. Engineering for Human-Computer Interaction EHCI'01 (Toronto, May 11-13, 2001), PREceedings, 2001, pp. 61-76.

[7] Duke, D.J. and Harrison, M.D., *Abstract Interaction Objects,* Computer Graphics Forum, Vol. 12, No. 3, 1993, pp. 25-36.

[8] Paternò, F., *A Theory of User-Interaction Objects*, Journal of Visual Languages and Computing, Vol. 5, No. 3, 1994, pp. 227-249.

[9] Paternò, F. and Faconti, G.P., *On the LOTOS use to describe graphical interaction*, Proc. of HCI'92 Conf., Cambridge University Press, Cambridge, 1992, pp. 155-173.

[10] Palanque, P., *Modélisation par Objets Coopératifs Interactifs d'interfaces homme-machine dirigées par l'utilisateur,* Ph.D. thesis, Université de Toulouse I, Toulouse, 1992.

Chapter 5

JUST-UI: A USER INTERFACE SPECIFICATION MODEL

Pedro J. Molina*, Santiago Meliá*, and Oscar Pastor**
**CARE Technologies S.A., Pda. Madrigueres, 44, 03700 Denia,Alicante (Spain)*
E-mail: {pjmolina,smelia}@care-t.com – URL: http://www.care-t.com
Tel.: +34-96-643 55 55 – +34 96 643 55 54
*** Dept. of Information Systems and Computation, Valencia University of Technology,*
Camino de Vera s/n, Apdo. 22.012, E-46071 Valencia (Spain)
E-mail: opastor@dsic.upv.es – URL: http://dreyer.dsic.upv.es/~opastor/
Tel.: +34-6-387 93 59 – Fax: +34-6-387 73 59

Abstract A Model for the Specification of Abstract User Interfaces based on Conceptual Patterns is proposed to enhance the semantic captured by an object-oriented analysis method. The model gathers both Presentation and Navigation issues. A graphical notation is also provided to make easier the specification tasks. This simple graphical notation allows that a non analyst can understand and participate in the specification process.

Keywords: Conceptual modelling, Model-based user interface specification, User interface requirements.

1. INTRODUCTION

In this new millennium, the volume of data produced in the Information Society is increasing continuously on a daily basis. In this *data ocean*, tools for searching and navigating among data are really needed as never before to extract valuable information. On the other hand, better applications in less time are demanded. Nevertheless, developing good User Interfaces (UIs) for such Information Systems is a non trivial task which requires effort to build and maintain them in order to assure a good quality product.

Commercial business applications based on Information Systems have similar interfaces, mainly based on forms. JUST-UI tries to identify patterns in such UIs and abstract them to work in terms of the problem domain. The

C. Kolski and J. Vanderdonckt (eds.), Computer-Aided Design of User Interfaces III, 63–74.
© 2002 *Kluwer Academic Publishers.*

model is based on Conceptual Patterns to capture elemental UI requirements such as: *how to search?, how to order?, what to see?*, *and what to do?* Answering these questions in an abstract specification allows us to express the requirements without fixing any target environment. Design aspects, deliberately, are not collected in this phase in order to maintain the specification free of any design issues. The paper starts with the motivation and introduces the concepts used in the JUST-UI approach. Following, a graphical diagram based on these concepts is introduced. Then, a case study and generation issues are commented on. Finally, conclusions are given.

2. MOTIVATION

Traditional UML CASE tools such as Rational Rose [16], Together [22] or Argo [18] do not explicitly consider the specification of UIs. Therefore, specification with these tools is very complex and incomplete [14]. Collections of UI Patterns do exist. However, these collections are focused on design problems [21,23] and not on analysis problems. Indeed, surveys on Model-Based Interface Development Environments (MB-IDEs) [15,20] show that patterns at analysis levels are unexplored in classical MB-IDEs. The work here presented tries to bring UI Specification nearer to non-analysts (e.g., users, graphical designers, etc) with the ultimate intention of involving them in the process of specification.

3. THE JUST-UI APPROACH

Our contribution is focused on JUST-UI: a Model for the specification of UIs linked to Conceptual Modelling and code generation techniques to automatically implement the UI for business applications. Constantine *et al.* [6] proposes a technique to gather UI requirements prototyping with users using paper and Post-Its. In this technique, each Post-It represents an interaction unit (e.g. form or web page in the implementation). The user and analyst build together the navigation among interaction units drawing arrows. JUST-UI follows the same intuitive approach to describe UIs as it is used in [6] and Ruble [19].

The Conceptual Modelling stage is supported by an object-oriented method, the OO-Method [12], to obtain a conceptual schema of an Information System. OO-Method is a method that provides UML [5] compliant diagrams and is based on the formal language OASIS [11]. The model captures classes, properties for classes: attributes, services (methods), static, and dynamic constraints,..., following a classical object-oriented approach.

JUST-UI extends OO-Method to capture UI requirements to explore and navigate among data (information objects). The final goal is to collect interface requirements in an abstract way and to automatically generate the final UI to different target environments such as Web, Windows, X11, UMTS, or PDAs. The UI requirements captured by this approach are collected in the OO-Method Presentation Model. The following subsections describe the patterns used.

3.1 Simple Patterns

Simple patterns are single components that can be asked directly to user or customer by an analyst. These simple concepts constitute the primitive *bricks* to build the UI.

Filter. A filter is a criterion that is useful for searching for objects. Fixing a class, the user needs to search for objects satisfying a given condition. E.g. searching cars by fare or colour in a Car Rental Service. The analyst has identified the Vehicle class in the problem domain. Now she has to ask the user: *How do you need to search for Vehicles?* Each answer from the user constitutes a filter criterion. E.g. the formula for searching red cars with special fare is: `colour="red"` and `fare.code="special"`. Query By Example techniques [26] could be applied too, but previous experiences reveal us that, in general, users do not need a powerful search engine. Specific filters tailored for the current tasks increases the usability.

Order Criterion. After gathering search requirements, the analyst can inquire: *How must objects be ordered?, alphabetically?, by colour*? Again, each response given by our customer constitutes an Order Criterion Pattern. Order Criteria can be specified in terms of a list of attributes defined in the conceptual schema and an ordering direction for each attribute: ascendant or descendent. The semantic associated with this pattern is: sort the collection of objects using the criteria expressed in the list. E.g., to sort Vehicles by brand (ascending) and colour (descending), we have to express: `brand ASC, colour DES`.

Display Set. At this point, we have the objects filtered and ordered. But, what properties does the user need to see from a given object? The customer could answer for a Vehicle: *I need to see: brand, model, year, colour, state, location, and price per day.* A list of visible attributes from the given class is enough to capture the initial user requirement. E.g. the Vehicle Display Set example could be: `brand, model, year, colour, state, location, fare.price_per_day`. Up to now, the user has filtered, ordered and listed the objects. At this point, the user has enough power in the UI to search and select objects. In an object-action (noun-verb) paradigm the first step is to select the object to interact with. Once the object is selected, the second step can be proposed: What to do with such an object? Basically, two responses can be provided:

- To show information related to this object (*Navigation*).
- To execute methods to change the object's state (*Action*).

Note that *Navigation* is merely observation and it is innocuous by definition. Nevertheless, *Actions* may execute services or operations that could alter valuable data.

Navigation. Following with the analyst's questions to users, the next one to ask is: *When you have reached a Vehicle, do you need to see any other related information?* E.g.: *The user is exploring a Vehicle. The analyst has identified the need to navigate to additional information such as Contracts and Fare*. Beyond this kind of navigation, the analyst is refining aggregation or inheritance relationships between classes in the conceptual schema. The analyst must specify the subset of objects to be reached in the target. E.g. it can be expressed using roles of relationships, or filters.

Actions. The second kind of semantic associated to an object is the possibility of changing the state of the current object. In conventional object-oriented methodologies, this is performed executing methods (or services) defined in the class. Once again, in a given context, the analyst has to ask the user: *What actions the object can suffer*? The user can answer something like this: *In the fare scenario I need to work with fares for vehicles: I need to create, modify, and destroy fares. Additionally, If need to change the fare related to vehicles*.

With this information, the analyst has enough clues to complete the conceptual schema with new services in classes and to organize a subset of services to offer users in a given scenario. This list (ordered subset) of visible services is the representation of what we call *Offered Actions Pattern*.

3.2 Building Complex Patterns

An interaction unit is a particular scenario in the UI where users have to interact with them in order to carry out concrete tasks. The Presentation Units [2] abstract these contexts as a set of Abstract Interaction Objects (AIOs) [4] discarding design issues.

A reduced set of patterns focused on Presentation Units have been abstracted based on literature review [6,19], our experience exploring UIs of commercial applications and developing business applications. These patterns are going to be referred to as Presentation Patterns. The Presentation Patterns are used to abstract interaction units with common behaviour. This approach provides different advantages:

- Extensibility: new Presentation Patterns can be included in the model.

- Homogeneity: every interaction scenario is expressed with a Presentation Pattern.
- Design independence: no design details are collected in the model.

At this stage, we have identified four types of Presentation Patterns: *Service* (interaction with service execution), *Instance* (interaction with an object), *Population* (interaction with a set of objects), and *Master-Detail* (composed interactions).

Service Presentation Pattern. Service Presentation Pattern is in charge of modelling a dialogue to deal with a service. The user must provide the arguments and launch the service. In the problem domain, the analyst identifies a service associated with a certain class: e.g., to create a contract in the Car Rental Service and declares it in the object model. In terms of specification, the Service Presentation Pattern encapsulates the interaction unit to supply a service in the interface. In this context, the service specification can be completed asking the user: *What input data are needed for this service?, How must input data be grouped?, Are the input fields inter-related?, What kind of feedback do you need for each selected object*?, etc.

Many answers to this questions can be expressed using other auxiliary simple patterns: *introduction* (constrains the introduction of values), *defined selection* (defines by enumeration the valid values), *population selection* (expresses how to select objects), *dependency* (expresses dynamic interdependencies among objects), *supplementary information* (provides extra feedback for object identifiers), *Status Recovery* (recovers argument values from attributes), and *grouping* (logical grouping of arguments) [10,13].

Instance Presentation Pattern. Its mission is to model the data presentation of an instance and support interaction with it. It is oriented to object manipulation. In terms of the user, the Instance Presentation Pattern arises out of the necessity to observe single objects. In addition, the user may want to change the state of the object (by means of services) and to navigate to related objects. In the problem domain the analyst identifies a certain class, e.g. `Vehicle`. Once the class is defined, she could ask the user the following questions: *Which attributes of the object do you wish to view? What actions can be done on the object? Which additional info. (relationships) do you want to reach in the interface by navigation*? The specification of the Instance Pattern is defined using three of the simple patterns: A *Display Set* (what properties to show), *Actions* (what services could be executed for the instance) and *Navigation*: (the links to the inheritance and aggregation relationships which it is desirable to navigate to from this instance). In OVID [17], the concept of *view* plays a similar role to the Instance Presentation Pattern.

Population Presentation Pattern. This pattern models units of interaction focused on showing sets of instances of a class. This pattern deals with the necessity of working with object collections. It is composed of five smaller patterns: *Filters* (how to search), *Order Criterion* (how to order), *Display Sets* (what to show), *Navigation* (how to navigate from an object), and *Actions* (what can be executed on objects). In the problem domain, the analyst, as in the previous case, identifies a class with its attributes, services and relationships. Later, she can ask the user to identify these smaller components bricks.

Master-Detail Presentation Pattern. The last pattern models more complex units of interaction dealing with master/slave presentations. For this reason, the components are divided in two logical types; Master and Detail components. These components are related by means of an aggregation relationship crossed in a given direction: from master to detail. Therefore, when a Master Component changes, the Detail Components associated also do. In business applications, this pattern is very usual. For instance, an invoice and the possibility of introducing the lines of this invoice in the same scenario.

In order to specify them, the analyst has to detect and create the classes, the elemental components, and finally the Master Detail Unit. The Master component can be an Instance Pattern (it will display an object) or a Population Pattern (it will display a collection of objects). The patterns that act as Detail Component can be of several types: an Instance Pattern if the role path is univalued, a Class Population Pattern if the role path is multivalued or a Master/Detail Pattern as well, which makes it possible to have, recursively, more depth levels in the master/detail. The specification of the Master/Detail Presentation Pattern is expressed by means of the following concepts: Master class, Presentation Pattern acting as a Master, Role path (side of an aggregation relationship) visible of the Master class that acts as a detail and Presentation Patterns like Details.

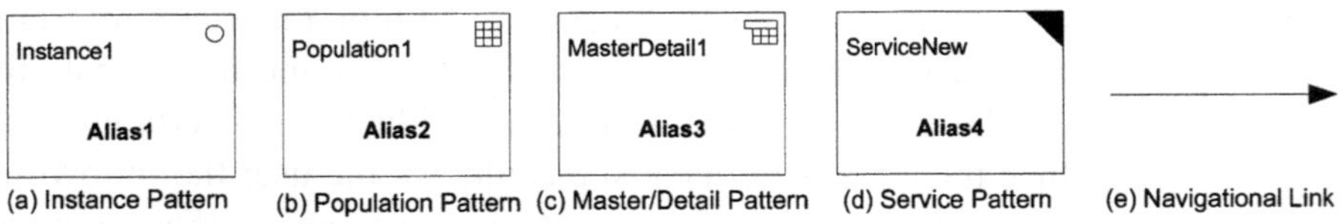

Figure 1. Navigational Diagram: Graphical primitives.

3.3 System Access

Finally, the user needs entry points to the interface in order to access the UI. To deal with this type of requirement, a tree structure is used to organize the access to interaction units: the Hierarchical Action Tree (HAT) [8]. This abstraction provides a tree for specifying how the user can access the system. Each intermediate node of the tree acts as a container with a label. Each leaf node contains a label and a link to an interaction unit.

This data is automatically mapped in the implementation phase to menus (in windows environments) or pages and links (in web environments). Using a tree structure is a good technique to support the *Gradual Approach Principle* [7]. For further references, see [8].

3.4 Navigational Diagram

Once the concepts have been introduced, a Navigational Diagram is going to be presented as a graphical representation of the stated concepts. Diagrams provide a more suitable workspace to deal with large projects and makes it easier to understand and edit the UI specification. The proposed diagram is a directional graph were nodes constitute Presentation Patterns (represented as boxes) and arcs represent navigational links between a pair of Presentation Patterns (represented as arrows). Fig. 1 shows the representation of each concept.

An example of the Navigational Diagram can be shown in Fig. 3. The diagram shows the scenarios specified to be present in the UI and the navigational relationship among them. The specification editing tasks could be very easy if a graphical editor for diagrams is available. A prototype of the editor (JUST-UI/VISIO) has been built programming in the VISIO [24] environment. In JUST-UI/VISIO, the left part of the window contains a component palette (called *Stencil* in VISIO terminology) and the right part of the window contains the drawing zone (work-area for diagrams). The user can select presentation pattern components on the palette and perform a *drag and drop* operation over the drawing zone.

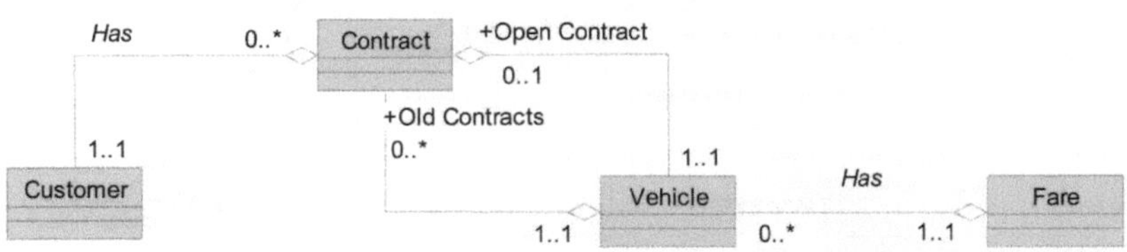

Figure 2. Class diagram for the Rent-a-car Schema.

4. A CASE STUDY: RENT-A-CAR

A brief case study based on a *Rent a Car* business system is going to be introduced. The example manages information about customers, vehicles, fares, and contracts. The classes of the Conceptual Schema of the quoted system are shown in Fig. 2.

The first step involves gathering the UI requirements from the customer explanations about the system. Once completed, the patterns identified in the process are shown. Initially, the user wants, as an entry point, a scenario capable of searching and showing the vehicles the company owns. Therefore, the user requires to search for vehicles with a contract associated to them. Next, the customer wants to select a vehicle and see the current contract associated in a scenario where vehicle and contract are displayed. In such a scenario, it will be possible to launch the operations *rent* and *return*. It will also be possible to select a vehicle to show the old closed contracts with theirs related customers and to launch operations on such customers as *change address*, or *delete*. Finally, the user wishes to see the related fares for each vehicle and the possibility of maintaining them (operations: *create*, *change* and *delete*).

With these requirements expressed in natural language, the analyst can identify some patterns in the interface (see Navigational Diagram shown in Fig. 3): The first scenario can be modelled as a Population Presentation Pattern for class Vehicle where a filter is defined to search for vehicles that have a current contract. In such a scenario, the user can browse a Master/Detail Pattern containing a Vehicle Instance Pattern as Master component and a Contract Instance Pattern as Detail component. The Master component also provides a set of Actions to reach *rent* and *return* operations. A navigation is identified from Vehicles to another Contract Population Pattern crossing over the aggregation relationship *old-contracts*. In this scenario, the user can jump again to a Customer Instance Pattern and select operations: *change address* or *delete*. Finally, the analyst can add a navigation from the Vehicle scenario to Fare Instance Pattern. In this pattern, three operations are allowed: *create*, *change*, and *delete* fares.

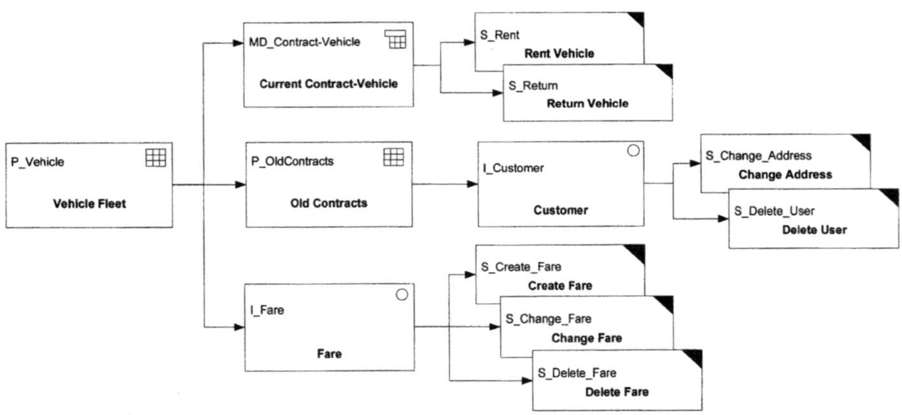

Figure 3. Navigational Diagram for the Rent-a-car Schema.

5. GENERATING THE USER INTERFACE

The specification collects the UI requirements expressed in terms of the problem domain. It constitutes a good documentation of the system itself. This specification can be also used to generate code in order to implement the UI for the Information System. Depending on the target platform, different translations must be done. In CARE Technologies S.A. we have developed translators to produce automatically such UIs. For the moment, we have developed translators for the following target languages (and platforms): Visual Basic (Windows), Java (Swing), JSP, ASP, and ColdFusion (Web pages). Depending on the target environment, a different style guide is used to obtain a homogeneous UI with respect to other applications. Each pattern in the Model can be expressed in terms of AIOs [4]. In the translation phase these AIOs are mapped to Concrete Interaction Objects (CIOs, controls or widgets) following a table of transformations based on ergonomic rules [3,9].

The implemented system is assumed to use an n-tier architecture. The UI layer acts as a client of a Business-Logic layer acting as a server in a client-server paradigm. Therefore, the UI contains the code to make calls to the Business-Logic layer: the responsible for executing the services and maintaining the consistency of the data. Code for error trapping is also produced to isolate the UI for any potential failure that could occur in communications or other layers.

6. CONCLUSIONS

A model for the specification of UIs based in Conceptual Interface Patterns and a graphical notation has been presented. JUST-UI provides a set of patterns that can be used as building blocks to create UI specifications for Information Systems. The whole concepts used are located in the problem domain, thus allowing an easy matching of requirements to the UI model. Analysts can create complete specification with very little effort. Besides, graphical designers can model without needing to be expert analysts. Users can also understand and review the navigational diagrams with analysts in order to validate the UI specification.

The specification obtained with JUST-UI is platform neutral. The specifications do not contain any design details. In this way, the specification is reused to provide similar UIs across several target platforms. At the same time, the concepts used have direct translation to the final implementation. Each presentation pattern is reified (mapped) to windows, forms, web pages or any other implementation of presentation unit that can be presented in the solution domain.

The need to obtain tailored UIs depending on the final platform (for example PDAs or UMTS devices) is beyond the scope of this paper, but this can be naturally achieved by providing design tools for specific environments capable of refining the initial JUST-UI specification to add and maintain such design topics.

Using Just-UI to specify the User Interface in conjunction with OO-Method to gather the functionality of the system, opens the door to automatically obtaining complete prototypes of Information Systems, copying with Data Persistence, Business-Logic, User Interface and User Help. If the specification is complete enough and non ambiguous, more and more code could be generated as final application code without additional manual changes. Therefore, the maintenance phases of software can be moved from code to specification as it was stated by Balzer in the Automatic Programming Paradigm [1].

REFERENCES

[1] Balzer, R., Cheatham, T.E., and Green, C., *Software Technology in the 1990s: Using a New Paradigm*, IEEE Computer, November 1983, pp. 39-45.

[2] Bodart, F., Hennebert, A.-M., Leheureux, J.-M., and Vanderdonckt, J., *A Model-Based Approach to Presentation: A Continuum from Task Analysis to Prototype*, in F. Paternò (ed.), Interactive Systems: Design, Specification, and Verification, Proc. of the 1st Eurographics Workshop on Design, Specification, and Verification of Interactive Systems, DSV-IS'94 (Carrara, 8-10 June 1994), Focus on Computer Graphics, Springer-Verlag, Berlin, 1994, pp.77-94, accessible at http://www.info.fundp.ac.be/cgi-publi/pub-spec-paper?RP-94-023

[3] Bodart, F. and Vanderdonckt, J., *On the Problem of Selecting Interaction Objects,* in G. Cockton, S.W. Draper, G.R.S. Weir (eds), People and Computers IX, Proceedings of the BCS Conf. on Human Computer Interaction HCI'94 (Glasgow, 23-26 August 1994), Cambridge University Press, Cambridge, 1994, pp. 163-178, accessible at http://www.info.fundp.ac.be/cgi-publi/pub-spec-paper?RP-94-018

[4] Bodart, F. and Vanderdonckt, J., *Widget Standardisation through Abstract Interaction Objects,* in A.F. Özok and G. Salvendy (eds.), in Proc. of 1st Int. Conf. on Applied Ergonomics ICAE'96 (Istanboul, 21-24 May 1996), USA Publishing, Istanboul-West Lafayette, 1996, pp. 300-305, accessible at http://www.info.fundp.ac.be/cgi-publi/pub-spec-paper?RP-96-019

[5] Booch, G., Rumbaugh, J., and Jacobson, I., *Unified Modeling Language (UML summary). Version 1.0*, Rational Software Corporation, January 1997.

[6] Constantine, L. and Lockwood, L., *Software for use. A practical Guide to the Models and Methods of Usage-Centered Design*, Addison-Wesley, New York, 1999.

[7] IBM, *Object Oriented Interface Design: IBM Common User Access Guidelines*. Que Corp., Carmel, 1992.

[8] Insfran, E., Molina, P.J., Martí, S., and Pelechano, V., *Ingeniería de Requisitos aplicada al modelado conceptual de interfaz de usuario (Requirements Engineering Applied to*

User Interface Conceptual Modeling), in Proc. of IDEAS'2001 (Santo Domingo, Costa Rica, April 2001), Ed. CIT, 2001, pp. 181-192.

[9] Molina, P.J., *Especificación de Interfaz de Usuario en OO-Method (User Interface Specification in OO-Method)*, Master Science Thesis, DISC, Technical University of Valencia, Valencia, 1998.

[10] Molina, P.J., Pastor, O., Martí, S., Fons, J., and Insfran, E., *Specifying Conceptual Interface Patterns in an Object-Oriented Method with Code Generation*, in E. Kapetanios and H. Hinterberger (eds.), Proc. of 2nd International Workshop on User Interfaces to Data-Intensive Systems UIDIS'2001 (Zurich, 31 May-1 June 2001), IEEE Computer Soc., Los Alamitos, 2001, pp. 72-79.

[11] Pastor, O., Hayes, F., and Bear, S., *OASIS: An OO Specification Language*, in P. Loucopoulos (ed.), Proc. of the 4th International Conference on Advanced Information Systems Engineering CAiSE-92 (Manchester, 12-15 May 1992), Lecture Notes in Computer Science, Vol. 593, Springer-Verlag, Berlin, 1992, pp. 348-363.

[12] Pastor, O., Insfran, E. Merseguer, J., Romero, J., and Pelechano, V., *OO-METHOD: An OO Software Production Environment Combining Conventional and Formal Methods*, in Proceedings of 9th International Conference on Advanced Information Systems Engineering CaiSE'97 (Barcelona, 16-17 June 1997), Lecture Notes in Computer Science, Vol. 1250, Springer-Verlag, Berlin, 1997, pp. 145-159.

[13] Pastor, O., Molina, P.J., and Aparicio, A., *Specifying Interface Properties in Object Oriented Conceptual Models*, in Proceedings of Working Conference on Advanced Visual Interfaces AVI'2000 (Palermo, May 2000), ACM Press, New York, 2000, pp. 302-304.

[14] Pinheiro da Silva, P. and Paton, N.W., *User Interface Modelling with UML*, in H. Kangassalo, H. Jaakkola, and E. Kawaguchi (eds.), Information Modelling and Knowledge Bases XII, Proc. of 10th European-Japanese Conference on Information Modelling and Knowledge Representation (Saariselka, May, 8-11 May 2000), IOS Press, Amsterdam, 2001, pp. 203-217, accessible at http://img.cs.man.ac.uk/umli/publications/imkb.ps.gz

[15] Pinheiro da Silva, P., *User Interface Declarative Models and Development Environments: A Survey*, in Ph. Palanque and F. Paternò (eds.), Interactive Systems: Design, Specification and Verification, Proc. of the 7th International Workshop on Design, Specification and Verification of Interactive Systems DSV-IS'2000 (Limerick, 5-6 June 2000), Lecture Notes on in Computer Science, Vol. 1946, Springer-Verlag, Berlin, 2000, pp. 207-226, accessible at http://img.cs.man.ac.uk/umli/publications/dsvis2000.ps.gz

[16] Quarani, T., *Visual Modeling with Rational Rose and UML*, Addison-Wesley, New York, 1998.

[17] Roberts, D., Berry, D., Isensee, S., and Mullaly, J., *Designing for the User with OVID: Bridging User Interface Design and Software Engineering*, MacMillan, 1998.

[18] Robbins, J., Hilbert, D., and Redmiles, D., *ARGO: A Design Environment for Evolving Software Architectures*, in Proceedings of International Conference on Software Engineering ICSE'97 (Boston, 17-23 May 1997), ACM Press, New York, pp. 600-601.

[19] Ruble, D.A., *Practical Analysis and Design for Client/Server and GUI Systems*, Yourdon Press Computing Series, 1997.

[20] Szekely, P., *Retrospective and Challenges for Model-Based Interface Development*, in J. Vanderdonckt (ed.), Computer-Aided Design of User Interfaces, Proceeedings of the 2nd International Workshop on Computer-Aided Design of User Interfaces CADUI'96 (Namur, 5-7 June 1996), Presses Universitaires de Namur, Namur, 1996, pp. xxi-xliv, accessible at http://www.isi.edu/isd/Mastermind/Internal/Files/DSVIS96/paper.ps.Z

[21] Tidwell, J., *Common Ground: A Pattern Language for Human-Computer Interface Design*, 1999, accessible at http://www.mit.edu/~jtidwell/common_ground.html

[22] TogetherSoft, accessible at http://www.togethersoft.com.

[23] van Welie, M., The Amsterdam Collection of Patterns in User Interface Design. 2000, accessible at http://www.cs.vu.nl/~martijn/patterns/index.html.

[24] Microsoft Corp, VISIO, accessible at http://www.microsoft.com/visio

[25] M. Zloof, *Query-By-Exaple: A Data Base Language,* IBM Systems Journal, Vol. 4, December 1977, pp. 324-343.

Chapter 6

DTS-EDIT: AN INTERACTIVE DEVELOPMENT ENVIRONMENT FOR STRUCTURED DIALOG APPLICATIONS

Fabrice Depaulis, Sabrina Maiano, and Guillaume Texier
LISI-ENSMA, Téléport 2 - 1 avenue Clément Ader, BP 40109
F-86961 Futuroscope Chasseneuil cedex (France)
E-mail: {depaulis, maiano, texier}@ensma.fr – URL: http://www.lisi.ensma.fr/members
Tel : +33-5-49 49 80 63 – Fax: +33-5-49 49 80 64

Abstract The structured dialog is an important concept as it is natural for a user to break down a main goal into several sub-goals. Meanwhile, no architecture model permits the systematic design of a system taking into account such a structured dialog. In previous works, we described a new architecture model allowing this and built a library that permits a designer to create a graphical interactive application dialog controller as easily as he would build the graphical user interface. After presenting these works and comparing our approach to existing solutions, this paper introduces a graphical tool which provides an interactive development environment for designing structured dialog applications.

Keywords: Model-Based Systems, Structured Dialog, User Interface.

1. INTRODUCTION

In the particular field of Computer-Aided Design (or CAD), the concept of structured dialog is very important. It consists of allowing a user to decompose a main goal into several sub-goals. In a CAD system, a standard interaction sequence to create an edge between two circle centers is: Pushing the "Create Edge" button - Pushing the "Get Circle Center" button - Selecting the first circle - Pushing the "Get Circle Center" button - Selecting the second circle. Thus, the system gets the two positions it needs to create the edge.

Despite the relevance of this concept, no user interface architecture

C. Kolski and J. Vanderdonckt (eds.), Computer-Aided Design of User Interfaces III, 75–82.
© 2002 *Kluwer Academic Publishers.*

model enables such a dialog. In order to fill this gap, a new architecture model – H^4 – was designed in our lab, several years ago [3]. It describes a dialog controller that takes the structured dialog into account. Then, we built a programming library: the Dialog Toolset (or DTS). This permits a user to create the dialog controller of an interactive application as he would design the graphical interface of an application with a standard toolkit [8]. The last step of our study was to provide a graphical tool which generates the H^4 dialog controller and verifies some useful dialog properties.

In this paper, we introduce the field that prompted us to create a new architecture model. Then, we present the existing architectural solutions and explain why they seem deficient for our study. In a third part, we outline our own model and the DTS. Finally, we show what our DTS Editor can do.

2. STRUCTURED DIALOG

Norman [7] argues that breaking down goals into sub-goals is the natural way for users to solve a complex problem. This decomposition is done recursively until the actions correspond to system functions. Such an analysis highlights the "structured tasks" paradigm that is a very important concern in the application field we address, i.e. the CAD.

During a structured dialog, each task can be executed in the context of another task. It is able to provide results that can be used by a higher abstraction level task. On the one hand, a hierarchical task organization results from this feature: **production** tasks (e.g. getting a circle center) are lower abstraction level tasks than **terminal** ones (e.g. edge creation). On the other hand, different tasks can be gathered in the same abstraction level. Thus, three different levels stand out : the "creation" level concerns terminal tasks; the "compute" level concerns tasks that extract object features; the "select" level concerns tasks used to select entities.

In the next part, we will study the different solutions used to create interfaces, and show why they are unable to integrate such a dialog.

3. EXISTING SOLUTIONS

In order to create interactive graphical interfaces, Bass and Coutaz [1] suggest two main ways: the bottom-up and the top-down methods.

The bottom-up method consists in creating the presentation layer, using a toolkit. A toolkit is composed of widgets. It permits a very simple control mechanism, using callback functions, that are activated as soon as any event occurs on a widget. This corresponds to the application behavior. To create an application with this method, the designer realizes the functional core. Then he creates the presentation layer and, finally, he links the presentation to the functional core with the callback functions. The main issue of this approach is that the dialog logic is spread through all the application widgets. Indeed, each one has a predefined behavior that represents a part of this dialog. In [5], E. Lecolinet presents a new way for designing interface with an original toolkit: UBIT (Ubiquitous Brick Interaction Toolkit). It manages to make the interaction control easier and to increase the designer freedom. Meanwhile the obtained behaviors cannot substitute for a genuine dialog controller.

The top-down method enables a designer to describe the application interface with a specific language. This description is used to generate the codes of the dialog controller and of the presentation. In this context, designing applications consists in: creating the functional core, describing the interface and, finally, linking the generated code to the functional core. In contrast to the generic bottom-up method, the top-down approach based systems (or model-based systems) are specialized in a peculiar application type. As an example, a generator of drawing applications is not able to build word processing software. Moreover, only experimental systems have been made with this method. The dialog of an interactive application can also be described in a formal way, e.g. with high level Petri nets. This approach permits, via a Petri nets editor, to specify the application dialog dynamically [6]. This method enables a task structuring: a Petri net that represents a given task is able to call another Petri net. But, as a Petri net high abstraction level task contains a lower abstraction one, the dialog logic must be planned.

As a conclusion, it seems that no solution permits to create a dialog controller that enables both structured dialogs and independent calls of tasks.

4. THE DIALOG TOOLSET

The architecture model H^4 has been created for CAD system designers. It is based on the Arch model [2] and details the role and the structure of any component. It involves a dialog controller, which manages structured dialogs, and consists of several elements described below.

4.1 Dialog Toolset Components

Tokens are information units that connect tasks together: the *"command tokens"* permit tasks activation, while *"parameter tokens"* hold typed values.

Questionnaires are the task abstractions within the dialog controller.

They are the function signatures that are called by the dialog controller to modify the state of the functional core. As entries, they own one parameterized token list. Their output is a single token that carries the result of the task execution. Moreover, each one has a link to a functional core method, called when the questionnaire has received all the needed tokens.

By analogy with the widgets (window + gadget), the name of the controller interactors is **diaget** (dialog + gadget) [8]. A single Diaget gathers several questionnaires of equal abstraction level. Each one contains an Augmented Transition Network (ATN) [9] that remembers and organizes the tokens it receives. Fig. 1 shows an ATN representing a Circle Creation Diaget: it accepts a command, a position (center) and a numeric value (radius).

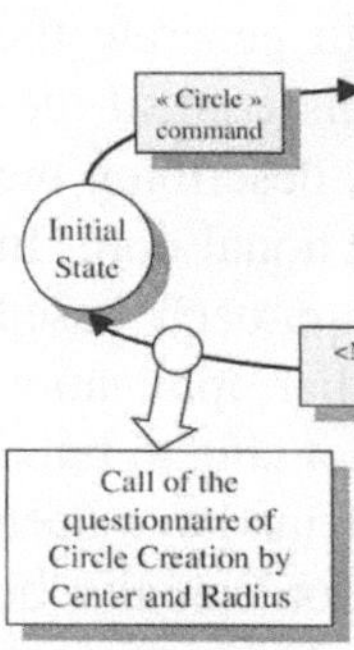

Figure 1. Dialog interactor functioning.

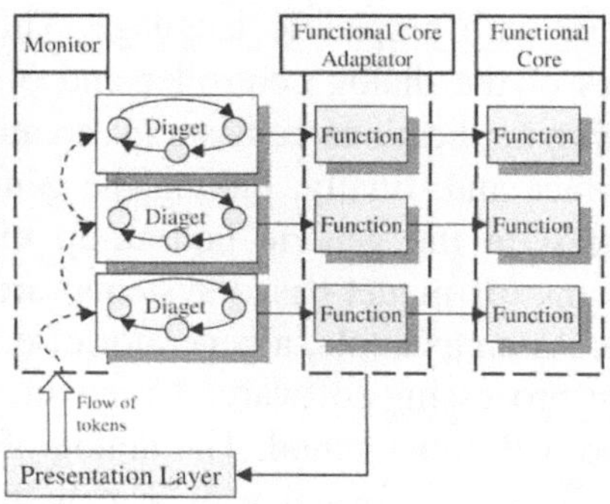

Figure 2. Dialog controller functioning.

The **monitor** organizes the diagets in a hierarchical way. They are sorted from bottom to top and the rank is given to the monitor. When getting a token from the presentation layer, the monitor transmits it to the first diaget in its hierarchy. If it is not consumed, the diaget gives it back to the monitor which proposes it to the next diaget and so on (Fig. 2). As a result, the tasks are independent, as they never know the source of the tokens they get and the destination of those they produce. Moreover, the monitor knows what tokens are expected by each diaget, and it is able to authorise only valid tokens to be produced, according to the current dialog state.

From this architectural model, we have created a library that permits to build an application dialog controller like an interface is made with a toolkit: the DTS (Dialog ToolSet).

4.2 Dialog Controller Coding Issues

Nevertheless, programming such a dialog is tedious and reluctant though, the dialog controller code is very redundant. Moreover, several dialog properties, that deal with task completeness, could be automatically checked:

- **Production / consumption consistency**. Is a diaget able to receive a given type of token? A least one lower diaget, in the monitor hierarchy, must be able to provide it. If there is not such a diaget, the corresponding system task will be available but will never be completed.
- **Questionnaires and command tokens**. Do two different questionnaires in two different diagets have the same signature? Such a situation will prevent the higher one, in the monitor hierarchy, and consequently the task, to be executed.
- **Overloading**. Do two questionnaires in the same diaget have the same beginning of entry token sequence? In this case, one of the corresponding task won't be able to be used.

In the next section, we present the Diaget Editor we have added to the DTS, that helps developers in coding their dialog and solves this problem.

5. A DIAGET EDITOR

The Diaget Editor main goals are to provide to an interactive graphical application a development environment for creating the dialog controller code and to verify some useful dialog properties.

5.1 Editing Diagets

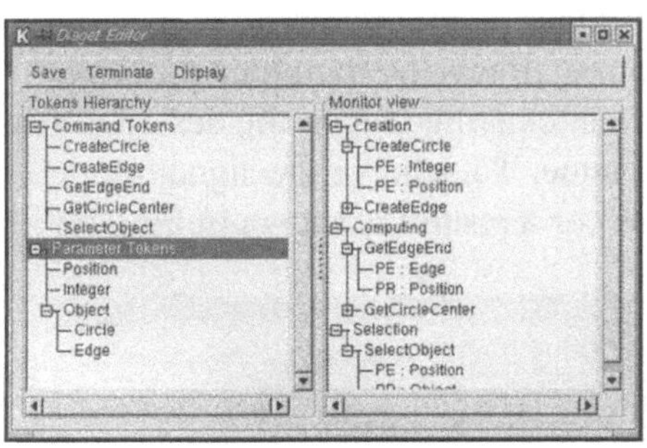

Figure 3. The Diaget Editor views.

The left part of the Diaget Editor (Fig. 3) displays information about tokens, while the right part deals with the diagets and questionnaire signatures. Direct manipulation has been largely used, and drag and drop from one side to another is possible. Saving and restoring DTS architecture is possible, either in Diaget Editor native format or in generated code format.

5.1.1 Tokens

The left part of the Fig. 3 presents the token hierarchy, which is split into two classifications. On the one hand, the command tokens carry the questionnaire name and are the only tokens able to make a questionnaire waiting for its sequence of parameter tokens. In most applications, they are provided by the user to the Dialog Controller via interface buttons or menus. On the other hand, parameter tokens carry functional core objects (circles, edges,...). They are organized hierarchically, as the functional core objects are. Hence, some of the questionnaires can be gathered together. For example, in a MacDraw like application, the user is allowed to create circles and edges, that inherit both from a "graphical object" class. Defining a single selection questionnaire for a "graphical object" is enough and combines both circle and edge selections.

In DTS-Edit, the two token classifications are displayed. The command tokens are ranked in a single depth tree. These commands are created automatically each time a new questionnaire is defined.

Parameter tokens are illustrated by a tree, which represents parent connections. Every sub-tree inherits from the tree it is part of. These tokens are not automatically created. Defining a new parameter requires the user to give its name and to declare its parent. It is then added to the hierarchy. It is important to notice that, to be able to add a parameter to a questionnaire signature, the parameter token has first to be described in the token hierarchy.

5.1.2 Monitor

The right side of the DTS-Edit interface displays the monitor view. On this panel, diagets and questionnaires can be created, and the monitor hierarchy can be described.

Creating some diaget implies clicking on the panel and giving a string for its name. All diagets are displayed according to the hierarchy. Changing a diaget position with drag and drop operation affects the monitor hierarchy.

In order to add some questionnaire to an existing diaget, the designer just clicks on the wanted diaget and gives a name. To achieve the signature definition, she can add either entry parameters or a result (as shown in Fig. 4).

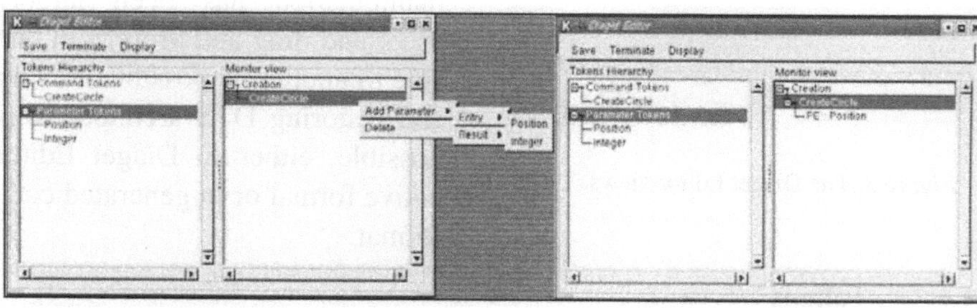

Figure 4. Adding a Parameter to a Questionnaire.

Once all diagets are described, including the questionnaires and the tokens they manage, the designer can achieve the process. She clicks on the

"Terminate" button and, then, the dialog controller code is generated. Moreover, the functional core adapting function headers are created thanks to the questionnaire signatures. Then, the user is given the possibility of programming the functional core adapting function bodies via an editing window. At this time, the system checks some properties of the dialog.

5.2 Checking Properties

Thanks to the architectural model, H^4, the tool is able to check several dialog properties.

- **Production / Consumption consistency**. In H^4, the diagets are sorted from top to bottom: the highest ones receive tokens from the lowest ones. According to the diaget ranking and to the tokens they produce and consume, the system knows and warns the user when a questionnaire of the highest diaget produce a not empty token and when it is impossible for a Questionnaire to receive a token that is necessary for its execution.
- **Questionnaires and Command tokens.** A questionnaire is able to receive its sequence of tokens once it has been provided with its command. This latter is usually provided by the presentation layer, via a button. If two questionnaires, set in two different diagets, have the same name, one of them will never be activated. The command token will always be caught by the lowest of the two diagets. The tool warns the user when such a situation occurs.
- **Overloading.** In the same diaget, two questionnaires can have the same name: they are activated with the same command token. Meanwhile, a problem happens if the entry list of the tokens from one questionnaire is a sub-set of the entry list of the tokens of the other one. It is impossible to guess what to do: if the diaget activates the first questionnaire, the second one will never be provided with a matched sequence of tokens. If it waits for other tokens, trying to complete the second questionnaire sequence of tokens, the first one is forgotten and will never be activated.

6. CONCLUSION – FUTURE WORKS

The existing interface architecture models do not easily enable the structured dialogs. For this reason, we have designed our own architecture model, H^4. We then wrote a library, the DTS, that permits any user to build the H^4 dialog controller like an application user interface with a toolkit.

Unfortunately, the DTS is very intricate to use, and the dialog controller code is very repetitive and error-prone. For this reason, we have created a tool that permits to interactively build the dialog logic of a graphical application. The redundant code is generated and the coding errors are reduced. Moreover, this tool checks some useful dialog properties. Automating these tasks, DTS-Edit makes our dialog library easier to use.

The described method to produce and verify the dialog controller will be soon improved with new features. Further challenges include:

- Adding some validation concepts. In [4], the authors show how it is possible, with H4, to check the interaction reachability and completeness. We will add this method to our tool.
- The H4 dialog controller uses tokens, which carry some functional core information. Instead of manually creating them, we want our tool to introspect the functional core classes and create the tokens on its own.
- Generating the interface description file, that links the dialog controller to the presentation layer, from the dialog description given by H4.

REFERENCES

[1] Bass, L. and Coutaz, J. *Developing Software for the User Interface*. Addison-Wesley, 1991.

[2] Bass, L., Pellegrino, R., Reed, S., Sheppard, S. and Szczur, M., *A Metamodel for the Runtime Architecture of an Interactive System*, The UIMS Workshop Tool Developers, SIGCHI Bulletin, Vol. 24, No. 1, 1992, pp. 32-37.

[3] Girard, P., Guittet, L., and Pierra, G., *H4: un modèle d'architecture d'applications graphiques interactives*, in Proceedings of AGI'96 (Tours, 6-7 June 1996), 1996, pp. 245-250.

[4] Jambon, F., Girard, P., and Boisdron, Y., *Dialogue Validation from Task Analysis,* in Proc. of Eurographics Workshop on Design, Specification, and Verification of Interactive Systems DSV-IS'99 (Braga, 2-4 June 1999), Springer-Verlag, Vienna, 1999, pp. 205-224.

[5] Lecolinet, E., *Réification et réplication dans les interfaces graphiques : le toolkit Ubit,* in Proc. of IHM'99 (Montepellier, 23-26 November 1999), Cépaduès-Editions, Toulouse, 1999, pp. 9-12.

[6] Navarre, D., Palanque, P., Bastide, R., and Sy, O., *Le Prototypage aussi peut être formel,* in Proceedings of ERGO-IHM'2000 (Biarritz, 3-6 Octobre 2000), 2000, pp. 153-160.

[7] Norman, D., *User Centered System Design*, Lawrence Erlbaum Associates, Mahwah, 1986.

[8] Texier, G. and Guittet, L., *Dialogue+Gadget=Diaget*, in Proceedings of IHM'99 (Montepellier, 22-26 Novembre 1999), Cépadues-Editions, Toulouse, 1999, pp. 70-77.

[9] Woods, W., *Transition Network Grammars for Natural Language Analysis*, Communications of the ACM, Vol. 13, No. 10, 1970, pp. 591-606.

Chapter 7

AUTOMATICALLY ELICITING TASK MODELS FROM WRITTEN TASK NARRATIVES

Michael Brasser[1]* and Keith Vander Linden**
Department of Linguistics, University of Southern California
Los Angeles, CA 90089-1693 (USA)
E-mail: michael@luomaike.com – URL: http://www.luomaike.com
Tel.: +1-213-740 29 86 – Fax: +1-213-740 93 06
*** Department of Computer Science, Calvin College*
Grand Rapids, MI 49546 (USA)
E-mail: kvlinden@calvin.edu – URL: http://www.calvin.edu/~kvlinden
Tel.: +1-616-957-7111 – Fax: +1-616-957-6501

Abstract Task models are a key element of model-based user interface design, but they are difficult to build. Written task narratives, on the other hand, are easier to write and helpful in design, but are not formal enough to be used rigorously. To bridge this gap, researchers have developed tools that aid in the extraction of formal task models from scenarios, but the process is still largely one of manually identifying key elements in the text. This paper proposes the use of shallow natural language parsing to automatically extract task information from narratives.

Keywords: Task models, Task scenarios.

1. INTRODUCTION

Task models are a key element of model-based interface design, but they are difficult to build. To address this problem, researchers have developed methods for the elicitation of task knowledge from domain experts. One promising approach is to collect written task narratives from domain experts and sift through them, identifying the key actions, actors and objects in the domain, and then constructing an appropriate task model. While in some

[1] This work was performed while Michael Brasser was a student at Calvin College.

C. Kolski and J. Vanderdonckt (eds.), Computer-Aided Design of User Interfaces III, 83–90.
© 2002 *Kluwer Academic Publishers.*

cases this sifting process is partially supported by an interactive tool, it remains a largely manual process of identifying key elements of the text and then constructing the task model in some sort of task model editor.

In this paper, we describe our initial efforts to use techniques from Information Extraction to automate the elicitation of task information from written task narratives. We have found that some of the more mundane tasks can be automated, but that the system is limited and the resulting model must be enhanced by an experienced interface designer. The paper begins by describing the background for this work, and then details a prototype system built in the context of the ISOLDE task modeling environment [11]. It closes with an assessment of the grammatical coverage of the system and with conclusions on the appropriateness and usefulness of the technology.

2. BACKGROUND

2.1 Task Modeling

A number of task modeling languages have been devised, many of which have task model editors to support them. These include CTT/CTTE [5,12], DIANE/ISOLDE [11,17], GOMS/QGOMS [2,4], and UML Use Cases and Statecharts/Rational Rose [3,14]. Though varied, both the languages and the editors tend to support the representation of: (1) basic tasks with some limited domain knowledge (i.e., who did what to whom), (2) basic procedural relationships between tasks, including hierarchical (i.e., purpose) relationships, (cfr. the *generation* relationship [7]), sequence, alternatives, enablement [7], and in some cases concurrency [5].

Because task models are hard to build, regardless of the power of the modeling tool, some systems include additional tools that support the automated or semi-automated construction of task models. For example, ISOLDE includes a GUI event recorder that records user actions on a system prototype in the form of a task model. One source of task model information is the task narratives written by domain experts, which can be manually analyzed by interface designers using system tools.

For example, U-TEL allows designers to mark the expressions of objects, actors, and actions in a narrative and to assemble them into an hierarchical task decomposition [16]. EL-TM is a similar tool, which is integrated with CTTE [13]. This paper presents an attempt to automate this process of identifying objects and actions, and assembling a task model. One note on written task narratives is relevant here. They are commonly used in the initial phases of analysis, but can take many forms, ranging from generic task descriptions, such as descriptions of UML use cases [3], through to highly specific descriptions of particular individual's work [10]. Furthermore, complete written narratives may not be produced at all for some systems. This paper, therefore, advocates the use of IE as one of a set of task modeling tools used by experienced interface designers. Discussions of other tools with complementary features can be found elsewhere (e.g., [11]).

2.2 Information Extraction

Information Extraction (IE) attempts to identify and return relevant information from a set of texts[2]. Most IE systems perform four basic steps towards this goal: lexical analysis, syntactic analysis (parsing), pattern matching, and information integration [8]. During the key step of pattern matching, the system attempts to fill pre-defined frames with information encountered. An example frame for a business merger might include information detailing the original company names, the merged company's name, and the date and price of the deal. These frame matches are usually triggered by domain specific keywords, such as "merger" or "take-over" for the preceding example.

Each of the above-mentioned steps can be performed by relatively simple and robust Natural Language Processing technologies. For example, during the syntactic analysis phase, a "partial" parser based on an Augmented Transition Network (ATN) is often used, rather than a full parser [9]. While a deep syntactic parse would provide more information, it is also computationally expensive and error-prone. Furthermore, much of the additional information is superfluous for extracting the basic "gist" of the text. However, use of simple techniques also means that IE systems perform best in a somewhat constrained environment – with the information being expressed in a straight-forward manner, using a relatively small number of forms, and with few long distance dependencies in the text [8].

The process of eliciting task models from written narratives can be seen as a form of IE that elicits basic tasks along with the various procedural relationships between them. There are two features of the task narrative domain, however, that distinguish it from typical IE applications: (1) Because critical task information can occur just about anywhere in the text, our system must examine every sentence, unlike typical IE systems which focus on certain portions of the text, and (2) Because task models come from a variety of domains, our system will not be able to trigger based on domain specific words or phrases but rather will have to search for closed-class words (e.g., "to", "and") and words from general classes (e.g., verbs and nouns). This will allow it to extract information in new domains without having to supply new keywords.

[2] Much of the research in IE has been spurred by the Message Understanding Conferences (MUCs) which began in the late 1980's [1].

3. THE SYSTEM

Our task elicitation tool works within the ISOLDE environment [11], although this type of tool could conceivably be designed for use in any task modeling environment. The core of the system is a natural language grammar built as a 25-state ATN. This grammar, shown at a high level in Fig. 1, deals with expressions of the key information we need to extract. To build a task model, we need to extract two kinds of information:

- **Basic Domain Information** – The key elements here are the *action* being performed, the *actor* performing the action, and the *object* being acted upon. Additional relevant information includes the source of an object, its destination, its location and the instrument being used. This domain information is useful for driving ISOLDE's text generation component [18].
- **Procedural Information** – We are also interested in assigning a procedural role to each task created by the system. These roles are used to determine the structure of the resulting task model. The default is to create a sequence of tasks based on a sequence of expressions, but we also distinguish *condition* and *purpose* expressions. The former are cued by the use of "when" or "if", e.g., "*When the user is finished*, they can exit the system.". The latter are cued by "to" or "by", e.g., "The user clicks the "Save" button *to save a file*." or "*The user opens a file* by clicking the "Open File" button on the toolbar.".

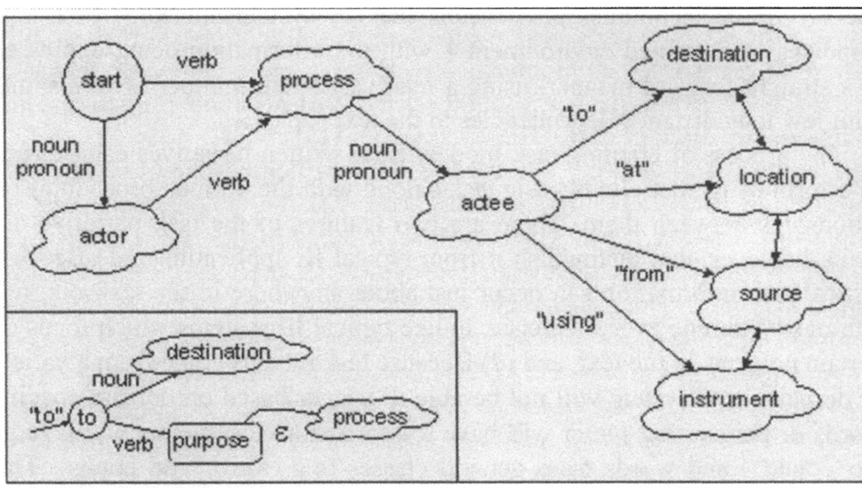

Figure 1. Overview of the ATN grammar.

The grammar decides when to break a text into separate tasks using both textual (e.g., periods, commas) and lexical (e.g., "and", "to") cues. The use of these cues is dependent upon context. For example, instances of "to" can indicate either a purpose expression (new task) or a destination (task subunit). The distinction is made in the portion of the grammar pictured in the inset of Fig. 1. There, a "to" followed by a noun leads to a destination, while a "to" followed by a verb leads to a purpose. The distinction between nouns and verbs is made based on classifications of WordNet [6]. While this is a simplistic way of dealing with grammatical ambiguity, it provides a workable starting point. Further work should go into the grammar at these points.

Fig. 2 shows the results of the system when run on the following portion of a task narrative from our testing corpus: *Click on "Add" button on the lower button panel, to schedule an event. This will bring up the "Event Info" screen (See Diagram 2). Fill in the blank information. Press DONE button, when finished.*

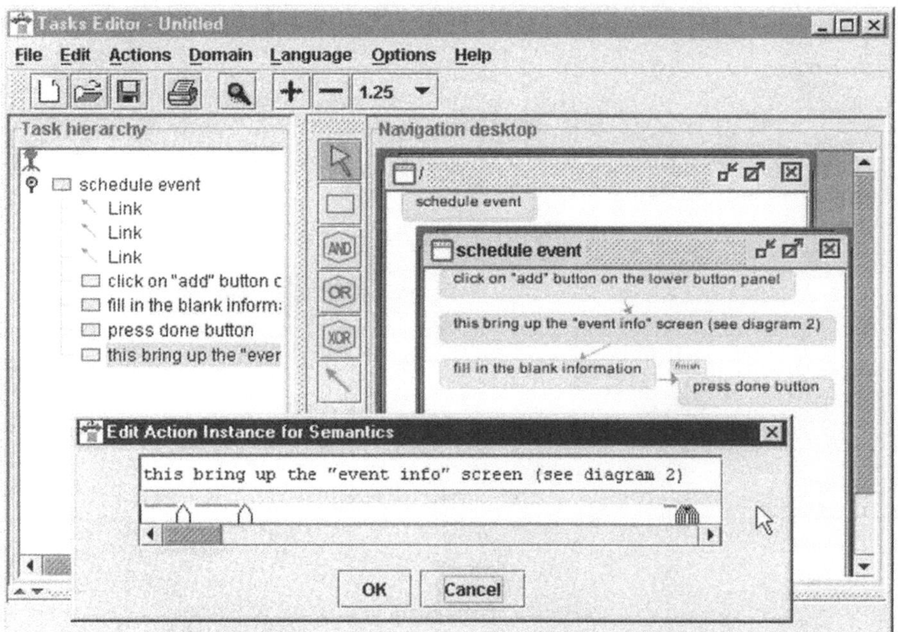

Figure 2. The System in Use.

In the figure, we see a tree-structured view of the procedure on the left and a graphical view of each level on the right. Note that the system has extracted the purpose of the procedure (i.e., "schedule event"), the sequence of actions (i.e., "click", "bring up", "fill in" and "press") and the condition on the last event (i.e., "finish"). There are, however, some problems. For example, the second task is one in which the system displays the "event info" screen; this should be recognized as an action by the system in DIANE+ and represented by a square box. The edit-action dialog box shows the parse of the sentence, with the constituent boundaries indicated by markers and the head words underlined. The grammar marks "this" as the actor, failing to recognize the reference to a system action. Neither does the grammar recognize the phrasal verb "bring up". However, the edit-action dialog allows the user to change the boundaries and head words assigned by the grammar. The results of such an edit are shown in Fig. 3. Note that the constituent boundaries and head words have changed. The user can also use the general task editing facilities of the Tasks Editor to make other changes, say if the parser misses a task entirely, or adds one inappropriately.

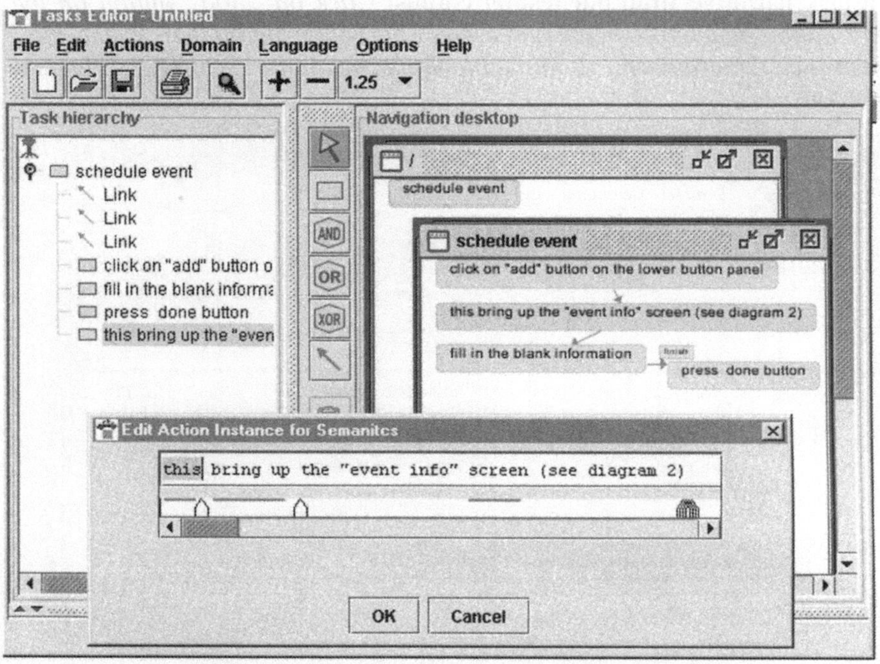

Figure 3. The System in Use.

4. ASSESSMENT

We built the ATN grammar used in the system by hand, based upon a set of 28 written narratives [15]. To help assess the coverage of this grammar, we collected an additional 9 narratives as well as the example text presented in Tam et al.'s paper [16]. These new task narratives were run through the system, and the resulting task models were judged against what we considered to be the correct task model from the text. We checked the correctness of the following three aspects of the resulting task models:

- *Did we split tasks at the right place?* The grammar attempts to divide the text into separate tasks. It did this correctly in 118 out of 186 cases (63%). In 55 cases, it made a split where it shouldn't and in 13 cases it failed to split when it should. The majority of the splitting errors involved "to", "and", or comma. A closer examination should be made of the heuristics for new task creation at these points.
- *Did we identify the correct procedural role?* The system handled only 5 of the 28 purpose expressions correctly (17.8%); the errors were due primarily to expressions such as "if you {want to/choose to} do *X*, then do *Y*, in which "want/choose" should be ignored and "do *X*" should be marked as a purpose. The system handled 3 of 8 preconditions correctly (37.5%), and did not recognize any postconditions (because this feature is not currently implemented).
- *Did we get the right domain information?* Of the 324 domain entities in the narratives, the system classified 155 (48%) correctly. An additional 67 could be handled (21%) if the system were extended to handle phrasal verbs and nouns. It would also be useful to add an anaphora resolution pass to the system. This would allow us to pair certain actors such at "it" or "he/she" with their appropriate referent. As with partial parsing, anaphora resolution is a robust NLP technology, with an accuracy in the mid-80% range [9].

The statistics presented here are informal, and as such are only intended to give a general picture of the capabilities of the system.

5. CONCLUSIONS

This paper has discussed an Information Extraction tool designed to elicit task models from written task narratives. The key features of the tool, as well as its limitations were noted, and the coverage of grammar was assessed. Based on the results, we believe that IE technology shows promise at extracting key task and domain information from narratives, particularly when the process is driven by experienced interface designers who have access to other task modeling tools whose features complement those of IE.

ACKNOWLEDGMENTS

The authors wish to thank the members of the ISOLDE team, including Nathalie Colineau, Thomas Lo, Shijian Lu, Robert Tot, and Stephan Wan, as well as Sandrine Balbo, Nadine Ozkan, and Jean-Claude Tarby. We also acknowledge the support of the Office of Naval Research (grant #N00014-99-0906), CSIRO and Calvin College.

REFERENCES

[1] Appelt, D.E. and Israel, D.J., *Introduction to Information Extraction Technology*, A Tutorial prepared for IJCAI-99, 1999.

[2] Beard, D.V., Smith, D.K., and Danelsbeck, K.M., *QGOMS: A Direct-Manipulation Tool for Simple GOMS Models*, in Proc. of ACM Conf. on Human Aspects in Computing Systems CHI'96 (Vancouver, 14-18 April 1996), ACM Press, New York, 1996, pp. 25-26.

[3] Booch, G., Rumbaugh, J., and Jacobson, I., *The Unified Modelling Language User Guide*, Addison-Wesley, Reading, 1999.

[4] Card, S.K., Moran, T.P., and Newell, A., *The Psychology of Human-Computer Interaction*, Lawrence Erlbaum Associates, Hillsdale, 1983.

[5] ConcurTaskTrees Environment (CTTE), accessible at http://giove.cnuce.it/ctte.html

[6] Fellbaum, C. (ed.), *WordNet: An Electronic Lexical Database*, The MIT Press, Boston, 1998.

[7] Goldman, A.I., *A Theory of Human Action*, Prentice Hall, Englewood Cliffs, 1970.

[8] Grishman, R., *Information Extraction: Techniques and challenges*, in M.T. Pazienza (ed.), Information Extraction - A Multidisciplinary Approach to an Emerging Information Technology, Lecture Notes in Artificial Intelligence, Springer-Verlag, Berlin, 1997, pp. 10-27.

[9] Jurafsky, D.S. and Martin, J.H., *Speech and Language Processing*, Prentice Hall, Upper Saddle River, 2000.

[10] Lewis, C. and Rieman, J., *Task-Centered User Interface Design*, On-line book, accessible at ftp://cs.colorado.edu/pubs/distrib/clewis/HCI-Design-Book.

[11] Paris, C., Tarby, J.-C., and Vander Linden, K., *A Flexible Methodology and Support Environment for Building Task Models,* in A. Blandford, J. Vanderdonckt, and Ph. Gray (eds.), People and Computers XV – Interaction withouth Frontiers, Joint Proc. of IHM-HCI'2001 (Lille, 10-15 September 2001), Springer-Verlag, London, 2001, pp. 313-329.

[12] Paternò, F., Mancini, C., and Meniconi, S., *ConcurTaskTrees: A Diagrammatic Notation for Specifying Task Models*, in S. Howard, J. Hammond, and G. Lindgaard (eds.), Proc. of 6th IFIP TC 13 Conf. on Human-Computer Interaction Interact'97 (Sydney, 14-18 July 1997), Kluwer Academics, Dordrecht, 1997, pp. 362-369.

[13] Paternò, F., Mancini, C., and Meniconi, S., *Developing Task Models from Informal Scenarios*, in M.W. Altom and M.G. Williams (eds.), Companion Proc. of ACM Conf. on Human Aspects in Computing Systems CHI'99 (Pittsburgh, 15-19 May 1999), ACM Press, New York, 1999, pp. 228-229.

[14] Rational Rose, 1999, see information at http://www.rational.com

[15] Scenario Corpus, taken from a variety of course projects: bmrc.berkeley.edu/~course ware/cs160, www.cs.unc.edu/stotts/comp204/s01, cs.calvin.edu/cs/247.

[16] Tam, R.C., Maulsby, D., and Puerta, A.R., *U-Tel: A Tool for Eliciting User Task Models from Domain Experts*, in Proc. of ACM Conf. on Intelligent User Interfaces IUI'98 (Redondo Beach, 5-8 January 1999), ACM Press, New York, 1998, pp. 77-80.

[17] Tarby, J.-C. and Barthet, M.-F., *The Diane+ Method*, in J. Vanderdonckt (ed.), Computer-Aided Design of User Intefaces, Proc. of 2nd Int. Workshop on Computer-Aided Design of User Interfaces (Namur, 5-7 June 1997), Presses Universitaires de Namur, 1996, Namur, pp. 95-119.

[18] Vander Linden, K., Paris, C., and Lu, S., *Where Do Instructions Come From: Knowledge Acquisition and Specification for Instructional Text*, in T. Becker and S. Busemann (eds.), IMPACTS in Natural Language Generation: NLG Between Technology and Applications, DFKI document D-00-01, Schloss Dagstuhl, 26-28 July 2000.

Chapter 8

FROM USAGE SCENARIOS TO USER INTERFACE ELEMENTS IN A FEW STEPS

Hermann Kaindl and Rudolf Jezek
Siemens AG Österreich, Geusaug. 17, A-1030 Vienna (Austria)
E-mail: hermann.kaindl@siemens.at
Tel.: +43-51707-43288 - Fax:+43-51707-53270
Siemens AG Österreich, Siemensstrasse 92, A-1210 Vienna (Austria)
E-mail: rudolf.j.Jezek@siemens.at
Tel.: +43 51707

Abstract In practice, designers often select user interface elements like widgets intuitively. So, important design decisions may never become conscious or explicit, and therefore also not traceable. In order to improve this situation, we propose a systematic process for selecting user interface elements (in the form of widgets) in a few explicitly defined steps, starting from usage scenarios. This process provides a seamless way of going from scenarios through (attached) subtask definitions and various task classifications and (de)compositions to widget classes. In this way, it makes an important part of user interface design more systematic and conscious. For an initial evaluation of the usefulness of this approach, we conducted a small experiment that compares the widgets of an industrial GUI that was developed as usual by experienced practitioners, with the outcome of an independent execution of the proposed process. Since the results of this experiment are encouraging, we suggest to investigate this approach further in real-world practice.

Keywords: Task analysis, Usage scenarios, User interface elements, Widgets.

1. INTRODUCTION

In current practice, user interface design is typically more an art rather than science or engineering and requires much experience. In particular, designers tend to select user interface elements in the form of widgets for productivity tools intuitively, based on their experience. So, we address the problem of selecting widgets for a GUI that will be built from those building

C. Kolski and J. Vanderdonckt (eds.), Computer-Aided Design of User Interfaces III, 91–102.
© 2002 *Kluwer Academic Publishers.*

blocks. Striving for a systematic process to be followed in a step-by-step fashion, we propose a task-based approach to widget selection.

Our approach is based upon *task analysis* and *scenario-based design*, assuming that envisaged usage scenarios of reasonable quality are already available. We propose to explicitly assign subtask descriptions to the interactions documented in such a scenario, to the steps of both users and the proposed system to be built. Through combining those subtasks that together make up an interaction, *interaction tasks* are identified. For these, the right granularity needs to be found, which may require task composition or decomposition. The resulting interaction tasks can be classified according to the kind of interaction they require, using a class hierarchy of interaction tasks that we developed for this purpose. From this classification, it is possible to map the interaction tasks to a class hierarchy of widgets that we developed as well. Up to this point, our process description is seamless, while the subsequent selection of concrete widgets is beyond the scope of this paper.

We wanted to get an idea of whether and how strongly the kinds of widgets selected with this approach might correspond with those in the development of an industrial GUI. So, we conducted a small experiment with such a GUI. The results are encouraging and make us believe that this approach is promising. This paper is organized in the following manner. First, we summarize related work in the literature. Then, we present our process for widget selection, with its focus on the identification of interaction tasks and their mapping to widget classes, and illustrate it with a running example. Finally, we describe the experiment and present its results.

2. RELATED WORK

In the literature, many approaches to *task analysis* and *task modeling* can be found (see, e.g., [1, 4, 10]). A task can be viewed as a piece of work that a person or other agent has to (or wishes to) perform. The granularity of tasks can vary from whole work tasks [4] to minute detail of how a user interacts with a computer at the command and input/output level [1]. Since we propose an approach to identifying user interface elements in this paper, our focus here is on the latter, more detailed level. Still, work tasks are the original starting point for the design of a user interface in our approach.

Concrete ways of performing work tasks can be described in scenarios such as those in our approach. Similar constructs to scenarios have occasionally been called *methods* or *plans* in the context of task analysis. The author of TKS (Task Knowledge Structures) [4] also dealt with scenarios, which in this context describe human activity [5]. Another role of scenarios in this approach is in depicting an account of a proposed course of action. Our approach fits in here as a proposal for systematically designing a *task model* based on such scenarios and developing an *abstract interface model* from it (these notions are taken from ADEPT [13]).

The approach most similar to ours for scenario-based GUI design is called *essential modeling* and can be found in [2]. While we stick with concrete scenarios, the basic idea behind essential modeling is *abstraction* from a concrete use case to an abstract use case and, to develop an abstract user interface with abstract interface elements from it and finally a concrete GUI with widgets. This approach is certainly useful and can possibly also be combined with ours, but there is no seamless process defined of how one should go from scenario descriptions to the user interface elements (widgets).

Even approaches to automatic generation of user interfaces can be found in the literature (see, e.g., [12]). They typically focus on input and output of data, based on data models (E/R models). In [12], there is a distinction between abstract and concrete interface objects and a focus on automatically mapping the former to the latter using selection rules. Other work has its focus on layout issues, proposing knowledge-based generation and evaluation [7] or creation and metric-based evaluation [11] of user interfaces. Rather than building on what is to be input and output, or elaborating on how the user interface should really look like, we focus on what is to be done with the resulting user interface once it will be available, and what its basic building blocks should be.

Our approach centers around (a taxonomy of) *interaction tasks*, a notion that can be found already in [9]. It is used there for abstracting from the details of window management, which is similar to our abstraction from concrete widgets. But we describe how to systematically determine such interaction tasks and to map them to widget classes.

3. A SYSTEMATIC PROCESS FOR WIDGET SELECTION

Our new process for widget selection is based on scenarios, more precisely envisaged interaction scenarios of the kind dealt with in [6], in the larger context of the method and tool named RETH (Requirements Engineering Through Hypertext). This approach combines scenarios both with functions and goals. Functions are required to make the desired behavior of some scenario happen in order to achieve one or more goals. Rather than giving elaborate theoretical explanations, we simply present the example scenario “Displaying a summary of changes” in Table 1 as an illustration, which was developed according to this approach. This scenario serves also as a running example for the explanations of the new process below. It is one of the 20 scenarios actually defined in the case study at hand.

In order to facilitate a better understanding of this scenario and the widgets resulting from it, let us briefly sketch the context. This scenario is part of a requirements specification for a versioning facility of the RETH tool, where it helped to acquire and to define the functional requirements. One might think that there would be a complication introduced through having RETH both as the target system and the tool. However, it is a common *bootstrapping* approach to use an existing tool for developing a subsequent release of the same but enhanced tool. In addition, our focus here is not on the use of the RETH tool, but rather on a specific part of the RETH method.

Table 1. A tabular representation of the scenario Displaying a summary of changes.

Scenario *Displaying a summary of changes*	
1. The user initiates the displaying of a summary of changes between any two versions. *Task:* To select Display Change Summary	
	2. RETH displays a list of all available versions and asks the user to select the first version. *Task:* To display version list
3. The user selects a version from the list. *Task:* To pick a version	
	4. RETH displays a list of all available versions and asks the user to select the second version. *Task:* To display version list
5. The user selects a version from the list. *Task:* To pick a version	
	6. RETH displays a summary of changes that have occurred between the two versions *Task:* To display change summary

Since such a scenario describes interactions between a user and the system to be built, it pre-determines to some extent the kind of interface that will support it. The extent depends on how concrete or abstract these interactions are specified. Abstract use cases [2] leave more room for later GUI design decisions. In fact, scenario descriptions may actually vary within a spectrum from concrete to abstract [6]. In this paper, we assume the availability of more concrete scenarios.

The creation of more concrete scenarios already involves more such design work. In some sense, designing more concrete scenarios also has to assume the availability of certain user-interface elements, in our case widget classes. As long as the usual functionality is covered, this should not constrain the design much. We deal with widgets from the MS Windows style guide [8] in the context of this paper. The process for widget selection as presented here selects appropriate widget classes from the ones available.

Since this process is seamless from concrete scenarios to widget classes through several steps of task manipulations, it facilitates traceability. Of course, some record linking the various tasks needs to be kept for this purpose. The difference to unguided GUI design in this respect is, however, that defined artifacts in the form of such task descriptions are available for such a record.

3.1 Interaction Scenarios with Attached Task Descriptions

As a unique feature of our scenario descriptions, the steps of the proposed system to be built have annotations that link to descriptions of functional requirements. Whenever this system performs such a step, it will need to accomplish these functions. In this sense, this relation between a step and a function is called *By-Function*. Since the scenarios are envisaged at the requirements stage, the functions are not yet available but they are still functional requirements.

Additionally, the steps of users of that system can have analogous attachments. Rather than talking about functions to be required from users, let us view them as attachments to task descriptions. In fact, we can also view the functional requirements as specifications of tasks that the proposed system to be built will have to perform. In the following, we assume that each and every step of an envisaged interaction scenario has an attachment of descriptions of one or more tasks that are associated with the step. In Table 1, only the names of these tasks are given. They are underlined in order to indicate that they link to the corresponding task descriptions (in the RETH tool itself or Web representations automatically generated from it, in the form of hypertext links). We assume that the actual task descriptions are not needed here for understanding this example.

In general, these are many-to-many relations between the steps of a scenario and such tasks. Therefore, a given set of scenarios is associated with a set of tasks which have to be performed for executing these scenarios. So, this set of tasks is related to the whole set of scenarios, rather than a single one.

3.2 From Task Descriptions to Widget Classes

The core of our new approach leads from the set of those task descriptions to widget classes in the following steps. It is systematic in that these steps can and should be performed in the given sequence.

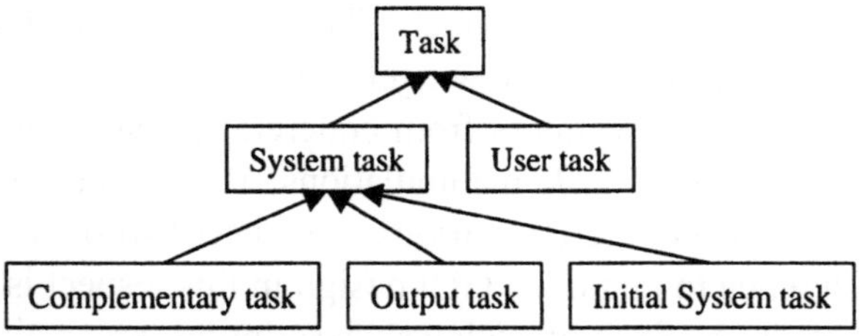

Figure 1. A hierarchy of task categories.

1. **Put tasks into predefined categories.** First, we propose to put each task into one of several categories that we define here with the intention to work out which of the tasks relate to the user interface and, in which way. As indicated above, we distinguish between tasks to be performed by the user (User Tasks) from tasks to be performed by the proposed system to be built (System Tasks). Fig. 1 illustrates this distinction in a UML class diagram, where the triangles denote a relationship between object classes that we can intuitively view as a specialization. That is, a User Task is a special case of a Task in general. In our running example, the following tasks are obviously put into the category User Task: "To select Display Change Summary" and "To pick a version". The latter occurs actually twice, which is a specialty of this scenario. A System Task is also a special case of a Task in general. In this diagram, we can even see a further specialization of System Tasks.
   - *Complementary Tasks* – These System Tasks are complementary to User Tasks in the sense that they together need the user interface for being performed. For each User Task, something needs to be prepared in the user interface so that it can be performed on it. That is what a Complementary Task of the system to be built does. In our running example, the task "To display version list" occurs twice, and we put it into the category Complementary Task, corresponding to the User Task "To pick a version" given above.
   - *Output Tasks* – These are tasks of the system to be built that output something without a User Task to complement with. That is, an Output Task does not prepare anything in the user interface that would be needed by a complementary task as defined above. In our running example, we understand the task "To display change summary" in such a way that the change summary output is not to be processed further in the user interface by a User Task. So, we put it into the category Output Task.
   - *Internal System Tasks* – These are System Tasks that do not have any effect on the user interface, since they are performed with computations inside the program only. Of course, Internal System Tasks are not directly involved in our process of widget selection, but we in-

clude them for the purpose of completeness. In our running example, there is no Internal System Task.

2. **Aggregate complementary tasks.** Then, the complementary tasks of users and the proposed system can be aggregated. For this purpose, we define an aggregate of such tasks and call it Interaction Task, since the complementary tasks together make up an interaction through the user interface. Fig. 2 illustrates this relationship in a UML class diagram, where the diamonds denote the aggregation relationship. A concrete Interaction Task (an object-oriented instance of this class) is the whole and, concrete User Tasks and Complementary Tasks are the parts in such an aggregation. In our scenario descriptions, not for every User Task a Complementary Task is explicitly given and vice versa. Since the point of this step is the identification of Interaction Tasks, this should not be much of a problem, as long as they can be identified from either a User Task or a Complementary Task. Output Tasks are special, since they ave no complementary User Tasks in our approach. Still, we think it is appropriate to view them as a specialization of Interaction Tasks (more precisely a specialization of I/O Tasks, see below). In our running example, we aggregate the tasks "To display version list" and "To pick a version" into the Interaction Task "To interact on selecting a version". For the User Task "To select Display Change Summary", no Complementary Task is explicitly given in this scenario. Its (implicit) precondition is that such a selection is possible before the scenario can be executed, i.e., a Complementary Task has been performed before. Still, it is possible to identify a corresponding Interaction Task "To interact on selecting Display Change Summary".

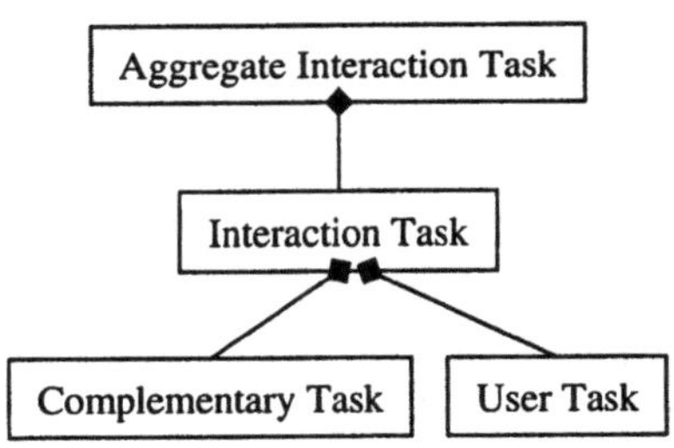

Figure 2. Task aggregations.

3. **Compose and decompose tasks**. This step is optional, since those Interaction Tasks may or may not yet have the right granularity. Either they might need to be composed with others to an Aggregate Interaction Task or they might need to be decomposed into "atomic" tasks, where the decomposed task is modeled as an Aggregate Interaction Task. This is again an aggregation relationship, which is illustrated in the top part of Fig. 2. In our running example, the Interaction Task "To interact on se-

lecting a version" occurs twice, once for the old and once for the new version to be compared. But according to the scenario description these selections are to be executed in sequence. So, no Aggregate Interaction Task is needed here and also none for the other Interaction Tasks in this scenario. Since all of them are "atomic", also no decomposition is needed here. In general, however, even recursive composition may occur, according to the quasi-recursion in UML between Interaction Task and Aggregate Interaction Task in Fig. 3. That is, an Aggregate Interaction Task aggregates Interaction Tasks. It is an Interaction Task itself and can, therefore, be aggregated by another Aggregate Interaction Task. This case actually occurred in the scenario "Displaying the List of Document Versions", where first the Interaction Tasks on selecting all versions and on major versions only are aggregated. The resulting Aggregate Interaction Task is itself aggregated with the Interaction Task on viewing a version list. It is clear that such task composition and decomposition is due to human judgement. Still, it occurs embedded in the systematic process and is done consciously.

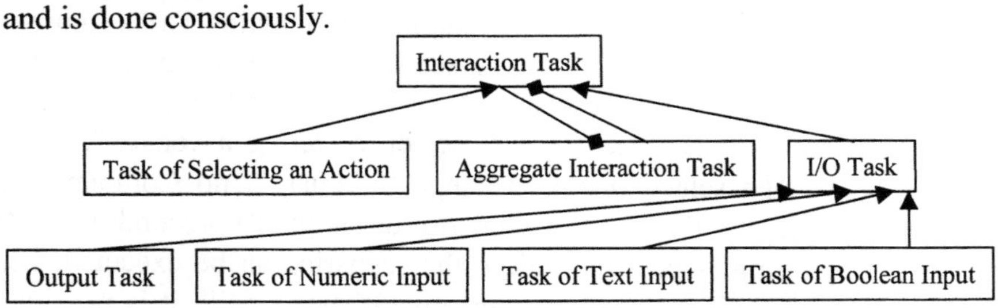

Figure 3. A classification hierarchy of Interaction Tasks.

4. **Classify tasks according to the kind of interaction required.** After that, we propose to classify the resulting Interaction Tasks according to the kind of interaction they require. Fig. 3 shows the classification hierarchy that we have defined for this step. (In fact, this is another possibility of specializing tasks than that illustrated above in Fig. 1.) Apart from the Aggregate Interaction Tasks, we distinguish here Tasks of Selecting an Action from I/O Tasks, which are further specialized according to what is input and output, e.g., text or Boolean values. In our running example, we obviously classify "To interact on selecting Display Change Summary" as a Task of Selecting an Action. Since "To interact on selecting a version" means I/O on the textual representation of the version name, we classify it as a Task of Text Input.

5. **Map to widget classes**. Finally, it is possible to map from the domain of classes of Interaction Tasks (see Fig. 3) to the domain of Widget classes (see Fig. 4) in such a way that a widget from the resulting class can support the corresponding Interaction Task in a GUI. More precisely, we

map I/O Task to Control, Task of Selecting an Action to Widget for Selecting an Action, and Aggregate Interaction Task to Container Widget. In addition, we map the specializations of I/O Task to their obvious counterpart in the specializations of Control in the widget classification hierarchy. Due to space restrictions, we show here only the top-most part of the hierarchy of widget classes, but the full and fine-grained hierarchy can be found in [3]. This object-oriented hierarchy reflects a breakdown according to the purpose of the widgets in the GUI, rather than a structural view of widgets. Structural composition, however, is modeled through aggregations of widgets. While we cannot show our full hierarchy of Interaction Tasks in this paper either, note that it is equally detailed as the hierarchy of widget classes. In fact, it is complete with regard to the functionality of the widgets of the MSWindows style guide [8]. In our running example, for the task "To interact on selecting Display Change Summary" a Widget for Selecting an Action should be appropriate and, for the task "To interact on selecting a version" a Widget for Text Input. We view text input not only in the sense of typing text here, but more generally, so that it includes selection of text from a list. For the Output Task "To display change summary", an Output Widget should be appropriate. So, this mapping looks rather straight-forward. In fact, this is partly due to the way we defined both hierarchies, so that there are more or less obvious one-to-one correspondences. However, it seems clear that for any reasonable and complete hierarchy of user interface elements, there will exist some mapping from our classification hierarchy of Interaction Tasks to it.

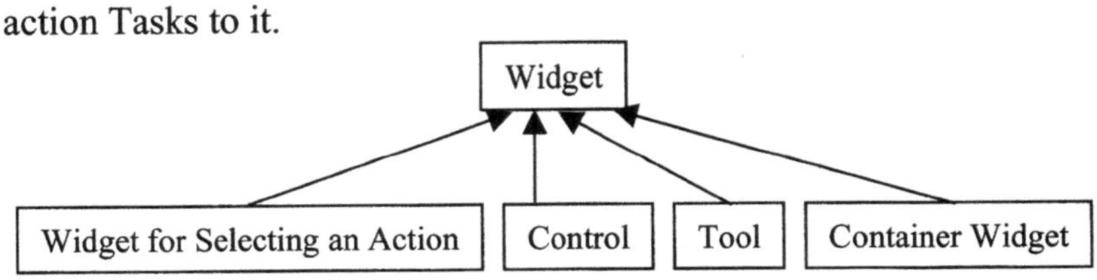

Figure 4. Our classification hierarchy of widgets (its top-most level).

4. AN EXPERIMENT WITH THIS APPROACH

Ideally, the usability of a user interface resulting from our process should be evaluated. However, it systematically covers the selection of widget classes only, while the selection of concrete widgets and their placement are out of its scope and require much human skill and experience. So, evaluating concrete widgets or even a complete user interface built by using our process would involve too much bias, because even more human judgement would be involved. Since a usability test requires a real user interface or at least a reasonable mockup, a selection of widget classes cannot be evaluated in this way. Even usability inspections cannot be applied to a set of widget classes.

Still, in order to get an idea about the validity of this new approach, we conducted a small experiment. The second author of this paper worked completely through the process described above for all 20 scenarios in the given requirements specification of the versioning facility of RETH (which was the only information available to him about this facility). This approach had the advantage that he knew our process already, of course, while we would have had to teach someone else first. Note, that he is less experienced in user-interface design than the key interface developer in the regular development.

For the various (re)classifications, he used the RETH tool itself. Primarily, he utilized the object-oriented features of the tool, which helped to avoid inconsistency. Of course, this was the RETH tool without the versioning facility, which the second author has never seen until this exercise was completely finished. In fact, the versioning facility was developed concurrently and independently. The real GUI of this facility was designed and implemented by experienced GUI developers. After both this exercise and the development of the real GUI was finished completely, we compared the results of executing our proposed process with the part of the RETH user interface for versioning of the tool itself.

Before this experiment was conducted, we formulated the following hypothesis: The kinds of widgets selected in both processes would correspond to a high degree.

A major issue was to define how to measure the proportion of the widget classes selected through execution of the new proposed process, from the widgets in the GUI developed as usual (which served as a kind of "oracle"). We defined the following way of measuring this degree of correspondence: How frequent is a widget of the real versioning GUI in the widget class that is the direct result of the mapping from the corresponding task in step 5 of our process as described above?

Table 2. Experimental results.

	No. of widgets	No. of corresp. Widget classes	Frequency of correspondence
Widget class mapped	75	64	85%
Widget class at level 1	75	65	87%

Table 2 shows the results. 85.3 percent of the widgets of the real versioning GUI were in the widget class that is the direct result of the mapping. Since the mapping is partly done on two levels of the hierarchies (1 and 2), we were also interested in how the results would differ between them. With 86.7 percent for the level 1 only, this result is more or less the same as that of the mapping overall. This means that the widgets of the real versioning GUI were also in the more specific classes most of the time when they were in the less specific class at level 1. This suggests that most of the different selections actually occurred close to the root of the widget class hierarchy. An analysis of these differences confirmed this and revealed that they came from different strategic design decisions made. The second author of this paper had rather straightforward enhancements, e.g., of the already existing menus in mind, while the designers of the real GUI decided to introduce an extra subpane for versioning, that provides a permanent display of versioning information whenever a versioned document is loaded. This implies that in the real GUI there is a permanent selection of versioning-related information, where an action can be immediately performed on. In essence, this amounts to a trade-off between less "real-estate" used on the screen and fewer interactions required. Based on this result, we tend to accept the hypothesis above. While the outcome is clearly not the same, the results are encouraging. The high frequency of the same widget classes on a higher level of classification after the mapping from the systematically determined Interaction Tasks suggests preliminary evidence that the proposed process delivers results that correspond to a high degree with what designers elaborate intuitively and based on their experience.

5. CONCLUSION

In this paper, we propose a new and systematic process for selecting user interface elements in the form of widgets. From given interaction scenarios, it leads in a few steps to classes of widgets, which specify the kinds of building blocks for a GUI that shall support the execution of these scenarios.

This process involves various manipulations of tasks, based upon task categories that we have defined for it. As a result of these task manipulations, *interaction tasks* are identified and categorized, which seems to be a new approach. These interaction tasks are finally mapped to widget classes. Preliminary evidence suggests that these are more or less the right kinds of building blocks.

For this mapping, we defined a hierarchy of widget classes according to a functional rather than the usual structural view of classifying widgets. This hierarchy covers the MSWindows style guide [8]. We also defined a hierarchy of interaction tasks that reflects this widget hierarchy. We conjecture, however, that it is more generally applicable in the sense that it could also be mapped to other classes of user-interface-elements (e.g., built in hardware). These classification hierarchies are new contributions of this paper, in addition to the process that builds upon them.

There should also be a certain completeness with respect to the given scenarios in the sense that no functionality in the GUI is missing for their execution based on the determined building blocks. These user interface elements should even be consistent with respect to the given scenarios, in the sense that the required functionality is provided by them. So, all of the given scenarios should be executable at least somehow with a user interface that contains widgets of the kind the derived interaction tasks are mapped to.

We hope that this systematic process contributes to a better understanding of the relationship between usage scenarios and user interface elements through the various tasks involved. More generally, it should help to better understand a certain part of user interface design.

REFERENCES

[1] Card, S.K., Moran, T.P., and Newell, A., *The Psychology of Human-Computer Interaction*. Lawrence Erlbaum, Hillsdale, 1983.

[2] Constantine, L. and Lockwood, L.A.D., *Software for Use*. ACM Press, New York, 1999.

[3] Jezek, R., *Methodischer Designprozeß von GUIs unter Verwendung von Scenarios.Diplomarbeit*, Universität Wien, Vienna, 2000.

[4] Johnson, P., *Human-Computer Interaction: Psychology, Task Analysis and Software Engineering*. McGraw-Hill, London, 1992.

[5] Johnson, P., Johnson, H., and Wilson, S., *Rapid prototyping of user interfaces driven by task models,* in Carroll, J.M. (ed.), Scenario-Based Design: Envisioning Work and Technology in System Development, John Wiley & Sons, New York, 1995, pp. 209-246.

[6] Kaindl, H., *A design process based on a model combining scenarios with goals and functions*, IEEE Transactions on Systems, Man, and Cybernetics (SMC) Part A, Vol. 30, No. 5, 2000, pp. 537-551.

[7] Kim, W.C. and Foley, J.D., *Providing High-Level Control and Expert Assistance in the User Interface Presentation Design*, in Proceedings of ACM Conference on Human Factors in computing systems InterCHI'93 (Amsterdam, 24-29 April 1993), ACM Press, New York, 1993, pp. 430-437.

[8] Microsoft, *The Windows Interface Guidelines for Software Design: An Application Design Guide*, Microsoft Press, Redmond, 1995.

[9] Myers, B.A., *A new Model for Handling Input*, ACM Transactions of Information Systems, Vol. 8, No. 3, 1990, pp. 289-320.

[10] Paternò, F., *Model-Based Design and Evaluation of Interactive Applications*, Springer Verlag, Berlin, 1999.

[11] Sears, A., *AIDE: A Step Toward Metric-Based Interface Development Tools*, in Proceedings of the 8th ACM Symposium on User Interface Software and Technology UIST'95 (Pittsburgh, 15-17 November 1995), ACM Press, New York, 1995, pp. 101-110.

[12] Vanderdonckt, J.M. and Bodart, F., *Encapsulating Knowledge for Intelligent Automatic Interaction Objects Selection*, in Proceedings of ACM Conference on Human Factors in computing systems InterCHI'93 (Amsterdam, 24-29 April 1993), ACM Press, New York, 1993, pp. 424-429.

[13] Wilson, S., Johnson, P., Kelly, C., Cunningham, J., and Markopoulos, P., *Beyond Hacking: A Model Based Approach to User Interface Design*, in Proc. of the BCS Conference on Human Computer Interaction HCI'93 People and Computers VIII (Loughborough , 7-10 September 1993), Cambridge University Press, Cambridge, 1993, pp. 217–231.

Chapter 9

EXPLORING DESIGN HEURISTICS FOR USER INTERFACE DERIVATION FROM TASK AND DOMAIN MODELS

Costin Pribeanu and Jean Vanderdonckt
National Institute for Research and Development in Informatics, Bd.Maresal Averescu Nr.8-10, R-71316 Bucharest (Romania)
E-mail: pribeanu@acm.org – URL: http://www.ici.ro/chi-romania/pribeanu/
Tel: +40-1-224 0736 / ext. 294, 163 – Fax: +40-1-2240539
BCHI - Université catholique de Louvain, Louvain-la-Neuve, Place des Doyens, 1, B-1348 Louvain-la-Neuve (Belgium)
E-mail: vanderdonckt@isys.ucl.ac.be – URL: http://www.isys.ucl.ac.be/bchi/members/jva
Tel: +32-10-47 85 25 – Fax: +32-10- 47 83 24

Abstract Task modelling and user interface design are iterative development processes. In this paper we will take a closer look to the relationship between three models: task, application domain and presentation. The objective is to explore heuristics aiming at progressively derive the presentation model from application-domain and task model.

Keywords: Basic tasks, Design heuristics, Task-based design, Task modelling, Unit tasks.

1. INTRODUCTION

Many limitations of existing model-based approaches are a consequence of putting too much emphasis on only one model. For example, although selection of interaction objects from the application domain model is currently a computer supported work, like in MECANO [4] or TRIDENT [7], existing tools failed to deal with more complex constructs like interaction objects groups and dialog units. This situation could be explained by the lack of integration between the models that are used in the computer-aided design of user interfaces.

The objective of this paper is to present an approach aiming to relate task

C. Kolski and J. Vanderdonckt (eds.), Computer-Aided Design of User Interfaces III, 103–110.
© 2002 *Kluwer Academic Publishers.*

modelling and user interface design. First we will take a closer look at task modelling in order to distinguish between two categories of goals: functional goals, related to what the user wants to do and operational goals related to how he is actually performing the task. The second layer makes possible to relate domain and task models to the presentation model. Then, in order to exploit both domain and task model a set of design heuristics is proposed.

The rest of this document is structured as follows. A conceptual framework for task modelling is presented in section 2. Heuristics used for grouping of interaction objects and further structuring of the presentation in dialog units are presented in section 3. The document ends up with conclusion in section 4.

2. TASK MODELLING

As pointed out by activity theory [2], tasks are goal driven, being performed consciously while actions are depending on operational conditions of the task and become automatic by practice.

This distinction is important since it reveals two levels in the task structure: a functional (planning) level that does not depend on a given interface and an operational level. In a more general sense, the planning level does not depend on the context of use (or the dependence is insignificant) while the operational level does. By variable context of use we understand variations in user knowledge, task specifics, user interface, hardware-software platform and work environment. The operational conditions is a concept which could be analysed from two points of view:

- variations in using an interface: there may be different actions required to manipulate the same interaction object;
- variations in the tools used to perform a task: the same goal could be achieved using different user interfaces.

The first situation clearly corresponds to actions that are performed upon interaction objects. In this case, the activity is not driven by goals but rather by requirements to adjust the work. The most frequent operational conditions are related to accommodate variations in data input, information display and user preferences. For example, reading the information displayed by an interaction object may need articulator actions like scrolling a list.

The second situation corresponds to tasks that are driven by operational goals. Depending on the technology used and the design decisions, there are several ways to operationalize a functional goal. Therefore we will consider goals at both levels of task decomposition, but with different relevance. Goal hierarchies are more relevant at functional level, since they are stable across different platforms and user interface designs. On contrary, task structures are more important at operational level since they are describing how the user can accomplish his goals with a given interface.

2.1 Goal Hierarchies

Analysing the relevance of the task from the user's point of view is important because it helps to identify the knowledge he needs. The first level in task decomposition shows how users are planning task performance by decomposing a task in sub-tasks and giving an ordering preference for each of them. In the *initial task model* goal hierarchy results from early task analysis and shows what the user really wants to do.

In order to show how application data could be used, an example will be chosen. The task is to record orders submitted by clients via phone call. First, the client is asked if he is an old client. If so, he provides his id number. If the search operation fails, he is asked to tell his name. If search also fails or if he is a new client, then he is asked to tell his full address: street, number, city name and zip code.

Second, the client is ordering the products only by specifying the product id (if he knows it) or the product name and the quantity ordered. The operator informs him on the total amount of the order after each product line. Finally, the client is asked to tell the delivery date and the payment mode (cheque, cash or bank transfer).

The leaves in the task tree are unit tasks, defined by Card, Moran and Newell [1] as the lower level tasks which the user really wants to perform. In this modelling context, unit tasks are defined as the lowest level tasks which is device independent. This definition focuses on well-defined and stable user goals. Under this level, the task structure is depending on the technology by which the goal is operationalized.

2.2 Operational Task Structures

Operational level is obtained by decomposing unit tasks. Fig. 1 illustrates the decomposition for the unit task "Identify by id". According to van Welie, van der Veer and Eliens [6] the relationship between unit tasks and basic tasks is important because it shows problems a user may have when he tries to accomplish his goals with a given interface.

Tauber defined the basic task as a task for which the system provides with one single command or unit of delegation [5]. In order to design the user interface he starts from the specification of the so-called User's Virtual Machine (UVM) which is the conceptual model of a "competent user", i.e. a user that knows how to delegate his task to the computer.

This definition relates basic tasks to user interface objects but it leaves outside the specification of user tasks that are not related to user interface objects. Basic tasks as defined by Tauber roughly correspond to interaction tasks in CTT [3]. However, the definition proposed by Paternò – tasks that are not further decomposed - is ambiguous and gives no indication on the stopping criterion.

The definition of Tauber is highlighting the underlying concept for basic tasks, which is task delegation. Basic tasks are closely related to the interaction process and they are resulting from a task design activity, which is concurrently performed with user interface design activity.

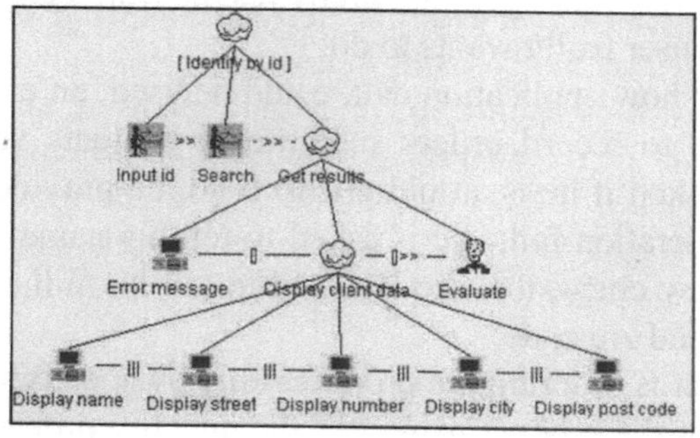

Figure 1. Task decomposition for "Identify client by id".

Therefore basic task is defined as the lowest level task that is using a single interaction object or a single external object or serves a communicational goal. In this respect, the stopping criteria for task decomposition are an interaction object (for interaction tasks, application tasks and cognitive user tasks), an external object (for manual user tasks), and a distinct step in communication (for communication user tasks).

2.3 Checking the Compatibility between Task Model and Application Domain Model

Interactive tasks are manipulating information. The user is interacting with a part of the data model that is made visible in the interface. In Fig. 2 is presented the ERA (entity-relationship-association) diagram for our example.

Following the relationships between domain objects several tasks could be developed: to record an order for a client (the example under consideration), to analyse orders of a particular client and to manage orders. For each case, cardinality of roles is important for the task structure. In the given example, recording orders and filling in the product line are iterative tasks.

➢ *Cardinality of roles played by domain objects reveals iterative tasks and helps in performing task decomposition*

All the attributes for the given example (except for stock quantity) are displayed in the interface by means of interaction objects. A first grouping of interaction objects is suggested by the semantics of data.

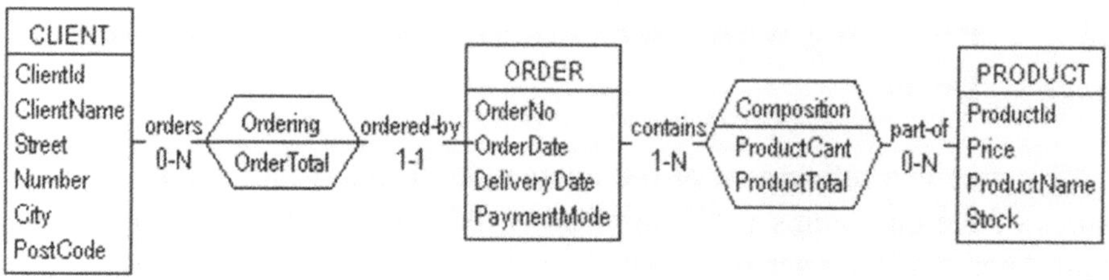

Figure 2. ERA diagram for application "Record order".

Usually, attributes of entities are grouped together. For entities that include internal groups, like address of the client, grouping is done according to task requirements. In our example, ClientId, ClientName, and ClientAddress all belong to the same entity but are processed in a different way.

➢ *Interaction objects that represent attributes of entities and relations are grouped according to semantic criteria and task requirements*

3. DERIVING THE PRESENTATION

3.1 Specification of Interaction Objects

Abstract interaction objects (AIO) are supporting a generic interaction task like selecting an item from a list, choosing an option from a menu or pressing a button that triggers a transaction. Interaction objects are dynamic if they accept input from or display information to the user and static if they are only used to present or to organise the information on the screen. However both categories could be termed as interaction objects since the user is actually interacting with them either perceptually or physically.

The first step is to select appropriate interaction objects that support the required interaction techniques and to apply data properties (extracted from the application-domain model) to them. Although information control IOs could be automatically generated by exploiting the domain model based on ergonomic criteria, function control IOs (like command buttons or menus) could only be added to these groups according to task requirements.

- ➢ *First level of interaction object groups are mirroring the unit task structure. In this respect, information control IOs are grouped around a function control IO.*

A static interaction object having as label the name of the data item could also be generated. Function control interaction objects will use as initial label the name of the basic task (for example, "Search" in Fig. 1).

3.2 Providing with User Guidance at Interaction Object Level

This step is a refinement of the interaction object specification. Usually, names of the data items in the application domain are rarely satisfying the requirements of the user guidance. Therefore, static interaction objects that were automatically generated should be changed.

Additional static interaction objects could be added in order to increase the usability of the interface. If interaction object groups are generated from the task model then static interaction objects denoting the unit task goal are also examined and additional static objects could be created to emphasise the grouping.

- ➢ *Assign a static interaction object to each goal at unit task level.*

At this stage, consistency of interaction object placing is checked and the results of applying generation rules are evaluated. It is recommended that first level interaction object groups should be finalised in order to get a bigger building block for working with in subsequent design stages.

Ideally, an additional specification of interaction object groups should be elaborated. This specification should record the unit task goal and the area occupied by each group. Then only the goal hierarchy at planning level and temporal relations are needed, thus reducing the cognitive workload for the designer. Even for computer aided generation, this approach reduces the solution space for dialog unit allocation. Further grouping of interaction object groups (unit tasks) is done by exploiting the task model. The same algorithm used for the generation of first level groups could be used.

- ➢ *Higher grouping of interaction objects should mirror the goal hierarchy.*

3.3 Structuring the Presentation

The initial user interface model is structured only up to the level of unit tasks. As we saw in the previous section, this is a bottom-up process that aims at a computer aided generation of the operational level of the user interface. Further structuring of the presentation requires a top-down approach.

First, dialog units are identified starting from the task model. The task model is examined layer by layer in order to identify the possible allocations. Second, interaction groups are grouped to form higher level groups within a dialog unit.

There are several criteria and/or constraints to apply for the structuring of presentation in dialog units: strategy of allocation (platform oriented, task oriented, content oriented), built-in capabilities, available screen space. Regarding the strategies of allocation it is important that they are applied in a uniform manner to ensure the consistency of the user interface. No matter which strategy is applied, the user will perceive the underlying structure of the presentation and any inconsistency will impact negatively on his attempt to build a correct metal model of the interface.

Temporal relations provide with important information making possible to derive constraints for the allocation of dialog units [3]. In order to effectively exploit temporal relations for the identification of dialog units we need to examine the task model in a top-down direction. This way, it is possible to reduce the solution space by eliminating the solutions that are not acceptable. An example of task-based allocation is given in Fig. 3.

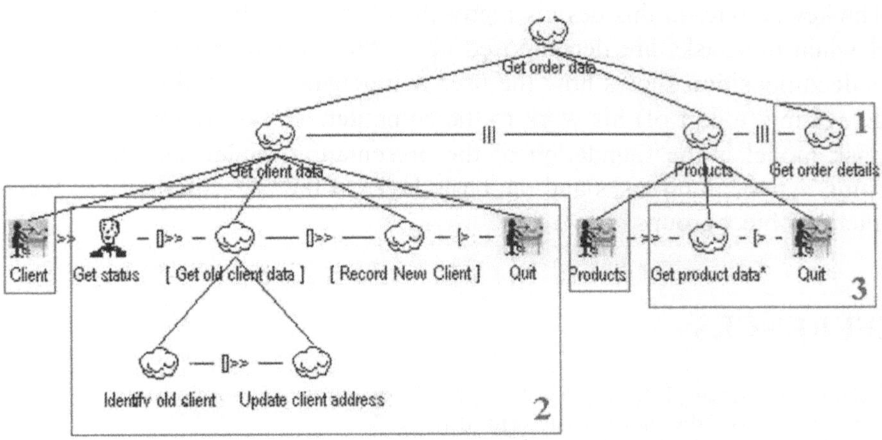

Figure 3. A task-based allocation.

We consider that an allocation solution is not acceptable when tasks that are part of different branches (sub-tasks of the same task) are brought together while tasks belonging to a branch are left outside, except for the case navigational enabling task (usually, the first sub-task). A problem is to apply this method when a strategy of allocation is considered. There are several possible situations, depending on the strategy. Platform dependent strategies lead to minimal vs. maximal allocations when the variation is mainly in the available screen space. This case fits the general one.

Task oriented strategies require to reconsider the task model. In this case, the virtual space is first transformed into a structured space in order to satisfy the allocation strategy. Then temporal relations could be analysed in order to fit the available screen space. Normally, this type of allocation is based on a clear separation between (sub-)tasks and leads to derive independent task trees. Regarding the content oriented strategy, the most typical case is the web site which is divided in web pages. In this case, the structure of the interface takes precedence over the task model. The problem is not to identify the dialog units from the task model bur rather to build a task model in a constraint presentation.

4. CONCLUSION

In this paper we presented design heuristics aiming to progressively derive the presentation from task model and application domain model. The task-based approach undertaken in this work is intended to provide with a better understanding of the relation between task modelling and user interface design.

The key activity in this design approach is task modelling at operational level when unit tasks are decomposed up to the level of basic tasks. Unit tasks decomposition shows how the user will actually accomplish his goals by delegating (a part of) his work to the computer. The operational level in the task model is the foundation of the presentation model and enables a mapping between unit tasks and the basic layer of the user interface i.e. the interaction object groups.

REFERENCES

[1] Card, S.K., Moran, T.P., and Newell, A., *The Psychology of Human-Computer Interaction*, Lawrence Erlbaum Associates, Hillsdale, 1983.

[2] Leontiev, A.N., *Activity, consciousness and personality*, Englewood Cliffs, Prentice Hall, 1978.

[3] Paternò, F., *Model based evaluation of interactive applications*. Springer Verlag, 1999.

[4] Puerta, A., *The MECANO project: Comprehensive and Integrated Support for Model-based Interface Development*, in J. Vanderdonckt (ed.), Computer-Aided Design of User Interfaces, Presses Universitaires de Namur. Namur, 1996, pp. 19-36.

[5] Tauber, M.J., *ETAG: Extended Task Action Grammar - a language for the description of the user's task language*, in D. Diaper et al. (eds.), Proc. of Interact'90, Elsevier, Amsterdam, 1990.

[6] van Welie, M., van der Veer, G.C., and Eliens A., *An Ontology for Task World Models*, in Proc. of DSV-IS'98 (Abingdon, 3-5 June 1998), Springer-Verlag, Vienna, 1998.

[7] Vanderdonckt, J. and Bodart, F., *Encapsulating Knowledge for Intelligent Automatic Interaction Objects Selections*, in Proc. of InterCHI'93, ACM Press, 1993, pp. 424-429.

Chapter 10

A USER MODELING DESIGN TOOL BASED ON A COGNITIVE ARCHITECTURE FOR COMPARING INTERFACES

Frank E. Ritter, Dirk Van Rooy, and Robert St. Amant*
School of Information Sciences and Technology, The Pennsylvania State University
004 Thomas Building, University Park, PA 16802 (USA)
E-mail: {ritter, dvanrooy}@ist.psu.edu – URL: http://www.frankritter.com/
Tel.: +1- 814-865-4453 – Fax: +1-814- 865-5604
**Department of Computer Science, North Carolina State University*
E-mail: stamant@cs.ncsu.edu – URL: http://www.csc.ncsu.edu/eos/users/s/stamant/www/
Tel.: +1-919-515-7938 – Fax: +1- 919-515-7925

Abstract Usability evaluation has long been recognized as an indispensable part of the development of interactive software. Evaluation can still be a difficult and labor intensive task with conventional tools and user studies, however. Results can vary with the knowledge and experience of the evaluator and with the subjects. We describe an approach to evaluation, based on cognitive modeling, that will alleviate some of these problems. We are building a general-purpose, cross platform architecture in which user performance in an interactive environment is simulated by a cognitive model. The results of the model can be analyzed and fed back into the development lifecycle. This project is still preliminary, but progress is accelerating..

Keywords: Cognitive modeling, Usability analysis.

1. INTRODUCTION

Research in automated user interface generation has traditionally concentrated on the specification, design, and implementation stages in the software development lifecycle (e.g. [13].) Over the past several years, however, attention has increasingly focused on the evaluation stage, with tools growing more sophisticated to assist with a greater part of the analysis process. Tools for user interface evaluation vary along several dimensions of ef-

C. Kolski and J. Vanderdonckt (eds.), Computer-Aided Design of User Interfaces III, 111–118.
© 2002 *Kluwer Academic Publishers.*

fectiveness: at which development stage the technique can be applied; how much knowledge, time, and effort are required in its application; the formal underpinnings of the technique; the reliability and replicability of its results; and the role of the user in the evaluation. An approach to evaluation that provides novel solutions in several of these areas is outlined in a recent issue of the *International Journal of Human-Computer Studies*, which describes cognitive models that test user interfaces [11]. The approach treats the design of human-computer interfaces as a form of engineering design. Cognitive models provide a means of applying what is known about psychology to predict time, errors, and other measures of user interaction.

If cognitive models are to be used for evaluation, their development and application must be fast and routine. A recent trend is for models to be built within the fixed framework of a cognitive architecture that supports these needs [9]. Increasingly, cognitive architectures are being extended by simulated eyes and hands, enabling the construction of embodied models. Being embodied allows models to interact directly with interfaces. The resulting models can be used to evaluate the interfaces they use and serve as explanations of users' behavior.

There are several advantages to this approach. While we like users (and the authors are themselves users), running usability studies is time consuming and expensive. Performance varies across time and across users, and results are often not reusable. This variability complicates the task of evaluation. Using a cognitive model based on advanced theories of human cognition—that have been validated by user studies—will support a more uniform evaluation, with detailed information collected at a lower cost than with actual users.

Our research has produced simulated eyes and hands for cognitive models that interact with user interfaces [10, 12]. We are now working on ways of making their application more routine. In this paper we present an approach to comparing interface designs through the application of user models based on a cognitive architecture. This approach will generate what we call Cognitive Model Interface Evaluation (CMIE) tools, systems that support the display of the user interface, experimental control over the cognitive model and its simulation runs, feedback on model execution, model execution diagnostics, and simple display facilities for model traces. No such CMIE tools currently exist (though APEX is a step in this direction [4]); however, significant functionality can already be found in each of these areas.

2. A PROTOTYPE

As a step towards creating and using a CMIE tool, we have recently started a project targeted at the evaluation of human-robot interfaces. Human-robot interfaces are a challenge that will provide all the types of interface interaction and mental models that we could want.

Fig. 1 shows a prototype implementation of the interface to the CMIE tool. This interface has been realized in Visual Basic, and will be translated as we note below. Creating a mockup design provides several useful lessons, a way to summarize our progress and the open tasks.

A cognitive modeling architecture. Our first need is to choose a language or theory in which to create our user models. The ACT-R cognitive architecture [1], as seen in the general-purpose Lisp interaction window at the top of the figure, is a suitable candidate. It provides accurate timing predictions, which are important for predicting and producing user strategies. It is used by a wide community of psychologists and user modelers. In time, this will provide us with components to add to our system, including user models, model optimization techniques, and improved versions of the software.

A model of perceptual/motor behavior. A cognitive model needs a way to interact with a user interface. One effective approach is to extend a user interface management system (UIMS) to support cognitive models as users, creating a cognitive model interface management system (CMIMS). A CMIMS manages the interactions of a cognitive model with the interface in the same way that a UIMS manages a real user's interaction with the interface, by managing input and output between the user interface and the model. CMIMSs have been built for several domains, including air traffic control, telephone dialing, and puzzle solving [10], and are now routinely used to tie cognitive models of users to interfaces [2, 8, 10]. ACT-R/PM [1] is an example of a CMIMS. It is suitable because it is integrated with ACT-R, and provides a strong psychology theory on how interaction occurs.

Recently, a potentially more general and robust approach has been developed. It is possible to provide cognitive models access to interfaces based on reading the screen bitmap, parsing it, and passing the results to the model [12]. We will use this approach to provide ACT-R/PM more direct access to the interface, removing the need to create a CMIMS based on a specific UIMS. This will provide a platform- and application-independent architecture for the evaluation of user interfaces based on cognitive user models.

A tasking language. A given cognitive model may be designed to carry out any number of distinct tasks. The tasks window, upper right, allows the modeler to select and refine a specific task, such as dialing a specific number from memory.

The decomposition of this task into subtasks and primitive operations can also be under the modeler's control. The figure shows a checklist of tasks for the model to perform, rather than a set of ACT-R production rules. In general, we will provide users with a convenient graphical interface for defining tasks, or a high-level programming language, as was presented by John Anderson at an ACT-R workshop in July, 2001 (http://act.psy.cmu.edu/ACT-R 5.0). Anderson's interpreter takes instructions in a Prolog-type language and creates an ACT-R model that performs the task. This type of interface will be necessary for this approach to be successful.

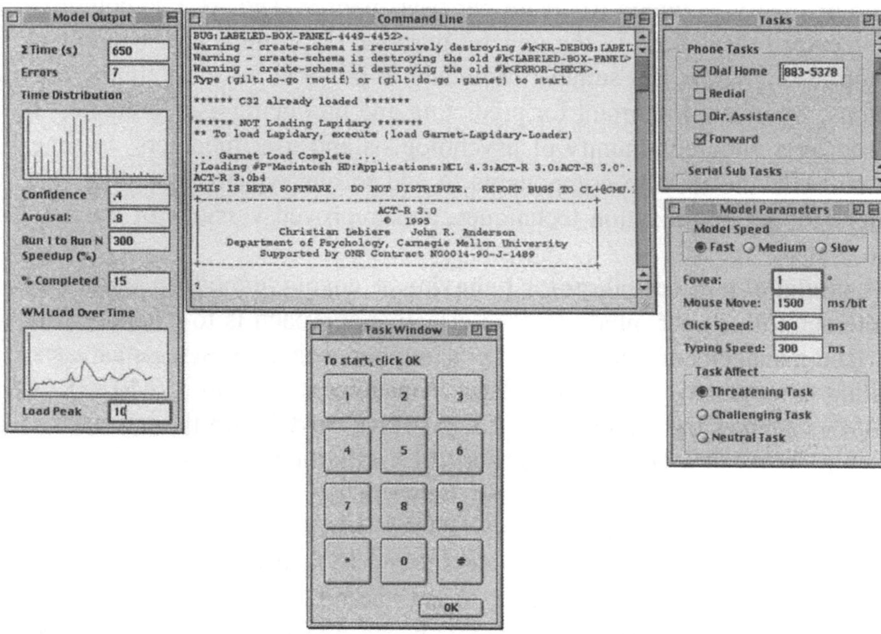

Figure 1. A draft design for a cognitive model-based interface evaluation (CMIE) tool.

A theory of individual differences. With different parameter settings, cognitive models can be tailored to reproduce the performance of different classes of users, as shown in the window in the lower right. These settings deal with reaction times (e.g. slow, medium, or fast [3]), properties of the visual system (e.g. the size of the fovea in degrees), and motor performance. We will also take advantage of recent working modeling user's different working memory capacities, which will be an important moderator of behavior and an important measure as well. One class of inputs, task affect, is related to a novel aspect of our cognitive modeling work. In realistic settings, external time constraints and other environmental pressures as well as internal uncertainty can drastically influence performance for even routine tasks. Experimenting with task affect can provide insight into variations in user performance.

Multiple models of user behaviors. We will initially be able to create simple models of menu use and we have in hand models of telephone dialing. This is where we benefit from using the ACT-R cognitive architecture. Many others have created models in ACT-R that are appropriate and useful in a CMIE tool.

Recent models include mathematics, graph reading (a list is available at http://act.psy.cmu.edu/papers) These models may not be directly usable, but this project will be a natural consumer of such models, promoting reuse.

Tasks to evaluate. The task window at the bottom of Fig. 1 shows the user interface, to be operated by the model. In most cases this will be identical to the interfaces seen by real users. A telephone interface is shown; the user selects a sequence of buttons and then presses OK to finish [6].

Output displays. Cognitive modelers may be well prepared to interpret a model's run, but other users (e.g., software developers) may not. We thus provide more than the model trace. The output window, on the far left, gives a running summary of the model's performance over some number of trials. The window shows general information, such as the number of trials to be carried out and the distribution of trial duration, as well as model-specific information: the running average and peak load on working memory. All of these measures are directly available from ACT-R, and we are displaying such variables in other projects using strip chart displays.

A graphics toolkit. One final component we will need is a language with which to build interfaces for the CMIE tool. We have found that it is most efficient to use the language that the cognitive architecture resides in. The Garnet toolkit [7], while no longer supported, is still quite usable. We are using it in several related, ongoing modeling projects working with ACT-R [5]. Importantly, it is free, and we are able to run it on multiple platforms with multiple version of Lisp (Mac, Unix, and most recently Windows). This multi platform support is crucial to our claim for the generality of the CMIE approach.

3. RECENT PROGRESS

We have taken significant steps towards the realization of the prototype sketched above. For our human-robot interface project, a task has been selected, namely the Mars rover game developed by National Media Technologies (http://www.natlmedia.com/html/fun mars.html). The type of inter face (plan view, controls) and the behavior required from the user (one is on patrol in Mars and the job is to collect alien specimens) are typical of human-robot interfaces.

Furthermore, because it is free, it can be modified and run at multiple sites. In later stages, this will be replaced by a more elaborate interface, which may include, for instance, a first person view.

The team at the North Carolina State University, under supervision of St. Amant, has succeeded in letting a simulated eyes and hands module called SEGMAN, interact with the Mars rover game (http://www.csc.ncsu.edu/faculty/stamant/cognitive-modeling.html). At the moment, the module can extract enough information from the scene to allow effective interaction, processing features such as color, position and size. Furthermore, they are establishing software-level integration between Java-based image processing algorithms and Lisp-based modeling software.

Concurrently, Ritter and his collaborators at the Applied Cognitive Science Laboratory are establishing a stable interaction between ACT-R 5.0 (http://act.psy.cmu.edu/ACT-R 5.0) and SEGMAN. Compared to previous implementations, this version of the ACT-R cognitive architecture has qualities that make it even more suitable for projects like ours (more tightly integrated with a perceptual and motor module, event-centered processing allowing interruption).

At the moment, the system (ACT-R 5.0 and SEGMAN) runs routinely on Windows machines. A GOMS-like [3] user knowledge structure of the Mars rover game has been generated that can be easily implemented into the production system ofACT-R5.0, which will allow the model to observe and manipulate objects in the interface. Furthermore, an overlay exists for the ACT-R model that allows modeling the influence of behavioral moderators, such as task appraisal and cafeine (http://ritter.ist.psu.edu/html/acs-lab#emotions). This overlay will enable the system to simulate individual differences between users, the influence of task affect, and also the influence of substances like nicotine and cafeine on the performance of users. As a result of these joint efforts, a demo of an ACT-R 5.0 model interacting with the Mars rover game is, at this point, clearly within reach.

4. SUMMARY

This approach to applying cognitive models to design offers a way to summarize and apply what is known in psychology to interface design. It further promises to make interface evaluation more routine and more accurate, helping to make interface design more like engineering design.

As with all evaluation techniques, the CMIE approach has disadvantages and restrictions. A CMIE evaluation with a cognitive model can be applied only late in the development process, with complete interfaces. The models require empirical validation before they can be applied effectively, and while a CMIE tool decreases the reliance on user studies, considerable knowledge is required to develop appropriate cognitive models.

The novelty of our approach to applying cognitive modeling to evaluate interface designs is that the tool itself is designed for ease of use. It provides generality across platforms and development environments. It makes cognitive modeling tools more readily available, complementing less formal techniques.

This approach is not a panacea, and it is not complete. But it is becoming much more within reach, and we, and others, are striving to achieve it.

ACKNOWLEDGMENTS

This project is sponsored by the National Science Foundation, award IIS-0083281, and by the Space and Naval Warfare Systems Center, San Diego. The views in this paper do not necessarily reflect the position or the policies of the U.S. Government, and no official endorsement should be inferred.

REFERENCES

[1] Anderson, J. and Lebiere, Ch., *The Atomic Components of Thought*, Lawrence Erlbaum, Mahwah, 1998.

[2] Byrne, M.D. and Anderson, J.R., *ACT-R/PM and menu selection: Applying a cognitive architecture to HCI*, International Journal of Human-Computer Studies, Vol. 55, No. 1, 2001, pp. 41-84.

[3] Card, S.K., Moran, T.P., and Newell, A., *The Psychology of Human-Computer Interaction*, Lawrence Erlbaum Associates, Hillsdale, 1983.

[4] Freed, M.A., Shafto, M.G., and Remington, R.W., *Using simulation to evaluate designs: The apex approach*, in Proceedings of Engineering for Human-Computer Interaction EHCI'98 (Crete, Greece, 1998), Kluwer Academics Publishers, Dordrecht, 1998.

[5] Jones, G., Ritter, F.E., and Wood, D.J., *Using a cognitive architecture to examine what develops*, Psychological Science, Vol. 11, No. 2, 2000, pp. 93-100.

[6] Lonsdale PR. and Ritter, F.E., *Soar/Tcl-PM: Extending the Soar architecture to include a widely applicable virtual eye and hand,* in N. Taatgen and J. Aasman (eds.), Proceedings of the 3rd International Conference on Cognitive Modelling (Veenendaal, 2000), Universal Press, pp. 202-209.

[7] Myers, B.A., Giuse, D., Dannenberg, R.B., Vander Zanden, B., Kosbie, D., Pervin, E., Mickish, A. and Marchal, Ph., *Garnet: Comprehensive support for graphical, highly-interactive user interfaces*, IEEE Computer, Vol. 23, No. 11, November 1990, pp. 71-85.

[8] Norling, E. and Ritter, F.E., *Embodying The Jack Agent Architecture*. Under review.

[9] Ritter, F.E., Jones, R.M., and Baxter, G.D., *Reusable Models and Graphical Interfaces: Realising the Potential of a Unified Theory of Cognition*, in U. Schmid, J. Krems, and F.Wysotzki (eds.), Mind modeling—A cognitive science approach to reasoning, learning and discovery, Pabst Scientific Publishing, Lengerich, 1998, pp. 83-109.

[10] Ritter, F.E., Baxter, G.D., Jones, G., and Young, R.M., *Supporting cognitive models as users*, ACM Transactions on Computer-Human Interaction, Vol. 7, No. 2, June 2000, pp. 141-173.

[11] Ritter, F.E. and Young, R.M., *Embodied models as simulated users: Introduction to this special issue on using cognitive models to improve interface design*, International Journal of Human-Computer Studies, Vol. 55, 2001, pp. 1-14.

[12] St. Amant, R. and Riedl, M.O., *A perception/action substrate for cognitive modeling in HCI*, International Journal of Human-Computer Studies, Vol. 55, No. 1, 2001.

[13] Sullivan, J.W. and Tyler, S.W. (eds.), *Intelligent User Interfaces*. ACM Press, New York, 1991.

Chapter 11

A MODEL-GUIDED AND TASK-BASED APPROACH TO USER INTERFACE DESIGN CENTERED IN A UNIFIED INTERACTION AND ARCHITECTURAL MODEL

Claudia Veronica Serey Guerrero[1] and Bernardo Lula Jr.
Coordenação de Pós-Graduação em Informática, Universidade Federal da Paraíba
58109-970 - Campina Grande – Paraíba (Brazil)
E-mail: cvserey@dsc.ufpb.br, lula@dsc.ufpb.br – URL: http://www.gia.dsc.ufpb.br/cvserey
Tel.: +55-83-310 1120 – Fax: +55-83-310 1124

Abstract This paper presents a model-based and task-based methodology to User Interface Design (MEDITE) which main characteristic is the use of explicit conceptual models in all stages of the design process. An interaction model unified with the interface architecture model (EDITOR) is proposed as a solution to the problems faced by user interface designers in applying similar methodologies. The proposed approach emphasises the use of models as opposed to the use of tools.

Keywords: Conceptual Model, Ergonomical Rules, Human-Machine Interface, Model-Based and Task-Based Approach, UI Design.

1. INTRODUCTION

1.1 Model-Based and Task-Based Approaches to UI Design

User interface designers find in model-based and task-based approaches an expressive support for the design of ergonomical user interface. Model-based methodologies start with the description of the task, the user's profile

[1] This work was partly supported by a grant from the Brazilian Minister of Education (CAPES).

C. Kolski and J. Vanderdonckt (eds.), Computer-Aided Design of User Interfaces III, 119–129.
© 2002 *Kluwer Academic Publishers.*

and ergonomical principles in order to build an interface that takes into account the user goals. Amongst the different methodologies found in this context, we considered ADEPT [9, 11, 21], ERGO-START (AIDE) [7] and MCI [19]. The main stages of the design process as defined by these methodologies are illustrated in Fig. 1: task analysis and user characteristics; an abstract representation of the interaction; a specification for the implementation; and an evaluation of an interface prototype. These methodologies define models (task model, operator model, interaction model, architectural model, etc.) and offer computational tools to support the specifications for each phase of the process.

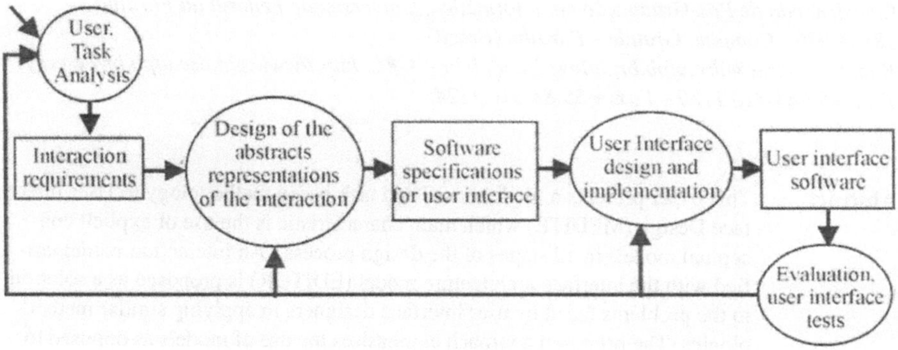

Figure 1. Model-based and task-model approach [7].

Although, these methodologies represent a valuable support to the interface design process, their use still introduce some difficulties, such as:

- Difficulties in choosing and using ergonomical rules adequate to the stage in the process. In general, the taxonomy of rules have no univocal relation with the stages in the process.
- Difficulties in transforming the task model into an interaction conceptual model.
- Strong dependency of computational support to produce the desired specifications.
- The interface code does not reflect the proposed interaction conceptual model.

1.2 Model-Guided Approach

This work is based on the hypothesis that the causes for the problems mentioned above are:

1. The interaction model used does not have a very clear relation with the task model causing difficulties in the process of transformation, as well as in the identification of rules that relate the two models. For example,

the ICS interaction model used in the AIDE methodology defines an interaction as a graph of states while the task model uses MAD* [5,7], which represents a task as a tree of sub-tasks.
2. The conceptual model used by these methodologies doesn't have an appropriate graphic description that allows a visualization of the structure of the presentation of the interface hindering the generation of a prototype and consequently demanding the use of specific computational tools. For example, the interaction conceptual models of ADEPT and MCI relate task actions with interaction objects, but do not offer an effective guide to the designer nor a general vision of the artefact being produced.
3. They lack an explicit interface architecture model. In general, none of these methodologies present a well defined architectural model. They are based mainly on computational tools whose product (interface code) does not reflect implicitly or explicitly the interaction model used. This lack of an interface model has direct consequences in the evaluation process of the prototype because one modification in this stage implies changes in the interaction model (previous stage) and not directly in the interface prototype.

Our proposal overcomes these problems with a model-based and task-based methodology context, defining: (i) a simple and explicit interaction conceptual model clearly related to the task model and (ii) an architectural model which structures the interface code to reflect with fidelity the interaction model used. Summarising, our proposal is a model-guided and task-based methodology to UI design based on an unified interaction and architectural model.

In this paper, we will present the proposal of a unified interaction and architectural model (EDITOR model) [10] within a model-based and task-based UI design approach (MEDITE), and the rule-based process to transform the task model (MAD*) into the interaction model (EDITOR).

2. THE EDITOR MODEL

The EDITOR model as an architectural interface model is inspired in the PAC model [1] and as a conceptual interaction model adopts the concept of *edition* as the central paradigm for interaction [18]. The EDITOR is an architectural model which associates aspects of the Seeheim model [14] with the advantages of a multi-agent model [1]. The PAC multi-agent aspect allows modelling not only non-sequential but also parallel activities of users. PAC structures the interactive system architecture as a hierarchy of PAC agents: an interactive system is a compound PAC agent decomposed into intermediate agents up to its elementary PAC agents. Every PAC agent has three facets: *Presentation*, *Abstraction* and *Control*. The Presentation facet defines the way an agent can be perceived (associates one graphical object of a graphical toolkit). The Abstraction facet defines the concept and the function of the application associated with the agent (associated to one object or function of the application). The Control facet defines the dialog between the other two facets and maintains the coherence between them. In PAC, the three functional facets (P, A, C) are distributed throughout all levels of abstraction: the control is distributed and recursive. Thus, it is possible, in PAC, to model multithread dialogues and enabling many communication lines with the system. As a result, PAC is more rigorous than Seeheim and provides a modular and distributed architecture. However, the PAC model, just as the Seeheim model, is more a "construction" model than a "design" model, because it does not provide any means or support to the design of its components: it does not includes an interaction model nor makes explicit the stages and/or the rules which allow the designer to identify its components from the analysis of the domain and/or task.

The EDITOR model associates the architectural advantages of the PAC model to the advantages of using a conceptual interaction model, allowing for the identification of its elements from task description through clear and objective rules. EDITOR finds in the object oriented approach an adequate computational model for representation and accomplishment. EDITOR adopts the concept of *edition* as the central paradigm for interaction: an *edition* process is considered as being any sequence of interactions between a user and a system, where the user perceives (sees, listens, etc.) and controls (modifies, manipulates, etc.) the application state. An editor is a software component supporting this process by presenting to the user a particular view of the application state and mechanisms (interactors) for controlling and modifying these states.

EDITOR defines an interface (editor) as a composition of three PAC-style agents, respectively: the *Editor*, the *View*, and the *Interactor*. An *Editor* agents defines an array of vision of the application (*View* agents) presented and organized in a frame (or window) on the screen. A *View* agent defines a vision of the application state as a set of entities (*Interactor* agents) visualized on a window (or sub-window). An *Interactor* agent defines a way of visualizing and manipulating an application object by using an interactor object taken from the virtual graphical toolkit. Both the *Editor* and *View* agents are complex PAC agents. *Interactors* can be simple or complex agents. Fig. 2 illustrates the complete description of the multi-agent organization of an interface as defined by the model. This hierarchical, multi-agent organization of an interface reflects the visual composition of its image and the nature of its elements.

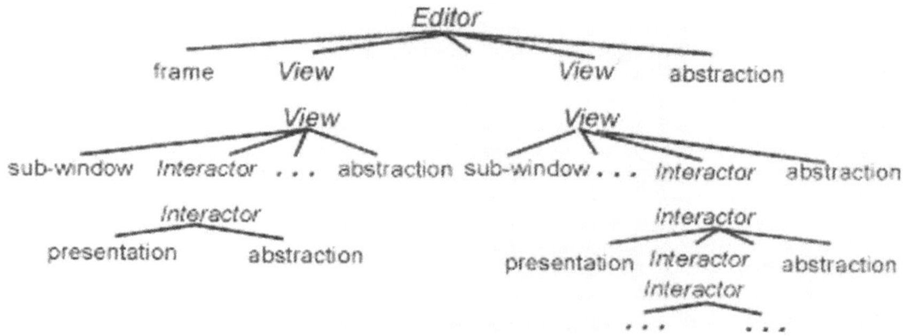

Figure 2. Multi-agent organization of an editor.

The EDITOR model as a conceptual interaction model is in accordance with the Norman's Theory of Action [12] in which the process of accomplishing a task through a computational system includes two fundamental stages which come about during the interaction: evaluation and execution. As an architectural interface model, it reflects precisely the concepts and structure of the interaction model and has in the object oriented programming paradigm a natural accomplishment framework .

We present in the next section the MEDITE approach, with emphasis on the mechanism used to proceed from the task model (MAD*) to the interaction model (EDITOR).

3. THE MEDITE METHODOLOGY

In this paper, we propose a model-guided and task-based methodology to aid the UI designer in the design process of ergonomical interfaces, namely the MEDITE methodology (MAD* + EDITOR + ERGONOMIC). MEDITE differs from other methodologies in the following aspects: (i) the existence of a simple, explicit and intuitive conceptual interaction model, whose structure reflects the task structure; (ii) the existence of an interface architectural model that reflects with fidelity the interaction model; and (iii) the objectiveness of the rules, which allows the designer a rapid and easy understanding of the method. MEDITE is an iterative and incremental approach which allows both descendant (from the task description we can obtain an initial partial and abstract representation of the interaction) and ascendant (a representation is incrementally completed with the definition of the attributes) design. Fig. 3 illustrates the processes, the products, the stages, and the models involved in the MEDITE methodology.

The MEDITE stages will be presented and exemplified by a very simple example (a tutorial design for Web [6]) which was developed manually.

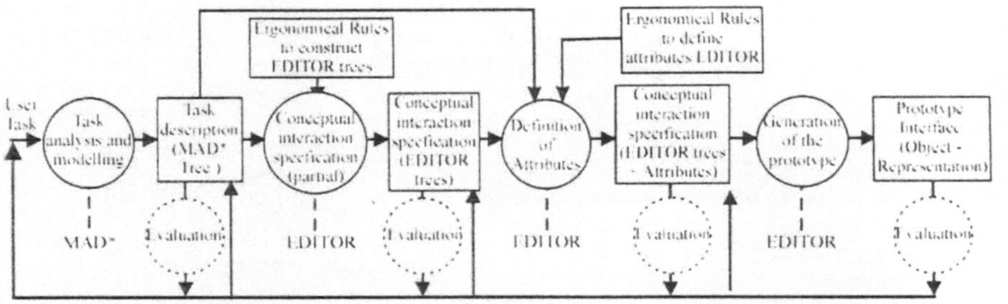

Figure 3. MEDITE approach.

The first stage of our approach consists in the analysis and modelling of a MAD* task generation, as illustrated in Fig. 4.

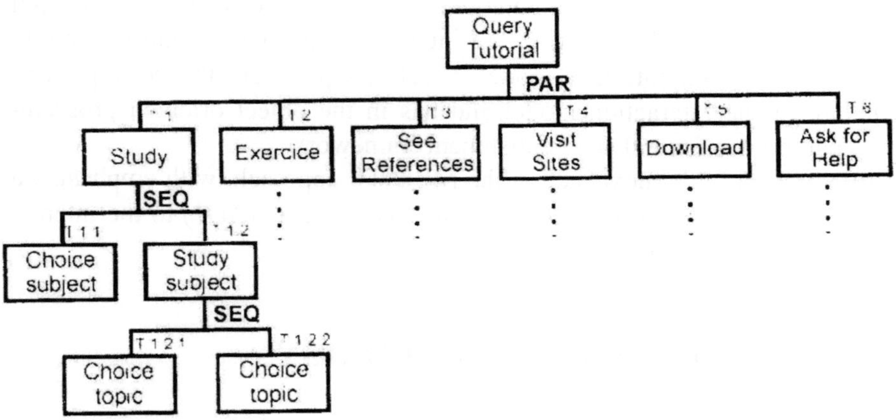

Figure 4. Part of the task tree: "Query Tutorial".

The second stage consists in the production of an initial partial and conceptual specification of the interaction. It consists of the construction of the EDITOR trees, defining each agent of the model: *Editor*, *View*, and *Interactor* agents from the MAD* task decomposition tree. This stage determines the structure and styles of the interaction aspects, that is, a general and initial (draft) vision of screens or interface windows to be built. This transformation can be conceptualized and accomplished easily through rules, since an *Editor* agent has a very close relation (isomorphism) with the structure (tree) of a MAD* description.

As in other methodologies [4,5,7], each rule used by the MEDITE approach is originated by one or more ergonomical recommendations extracted from various sources [2,8,13,16,17,20]. A Rule Base was defined as containing 2 types of rules used in two different stages of the specification process: (i) rules to build the tree EDITOR; (ii) and rules to define the attributes of each agent.

The ergonomical rules (the first type) considered for building the EDITOR trees are, amongst others:

- Rule 1 (R1): IF the task is of high-level (MAD*) THEN define an *Editor* (Editor Model) whose Presentation must be of type *Window* [16].
- Rule 2 (R2): IF the task is of intermediate-level (MAD*) THEN define an *Editor* (EDITOR model) whose Presentation must be of type *Sub-Window* or *Window* [16].

These two rules were extracted from the following recommendation: "The choice of one or more windows is determined by the task decomposition in sub-tasks" [16].

- Rule 3 (R3): IF the tasks are connected by the PAR (MAD*) constructor THEN define for this set of tasks a *View* (or Vision) (EDITOR model) whose Presentation must be of type *Menu Bar* and each task must be an *Interactor* (EDITOR model) of type *Menu-item* of this *View* [17].
- Rule 4 (R4): IF the tasks are connected by SEQ (MAD*) THEN define a *View* (EDITOR model) only for the first sequence task. The remaining will occupy the place of another view or a view of its own (depends on the dialogue) [8].
- Rule 5 (R5): Define for each *Editor* (EDITOR Model) a specific *View* (EDITOR model), whose Presentation will be of type *Region*. The *Interactor* of this *View* must have a Presentation of type *Text Field*. (This object must include guidance text, explaining in which state the user is, and which procedures must be done in this state) [16].

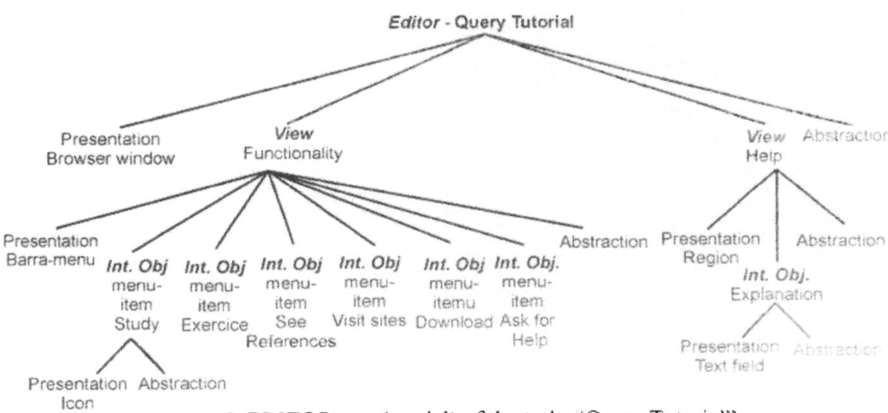

Figure 5. EDITOR tree (partial) of the task: "Query Tutorial".

Based on the task model and aided by the ergonomical rules above, a partial Editor tree is generated for the example. The EDITOR tree is illustrated in Fig. 5. The third stage consists in defining the attributes of the EDITOR trees. This complements the tree generated in the previous stage with the definition of the attributes of the Presentation facet for each agent (localization, format, font size, etc.), the Abstraction facet (in relation to the application domain), and the Control facet, which defines the linking of the dialogue (inter and intra *Editors*). In this stage, ergonomical rules of the second type are used to define these attributes. We present below examples of these rules:

- Rule 6 (R6): IF the task is of high-level (MAD*) THEN the size, format and localisation of the *Window* will be predefined by the type of platform being used. Ex. Browser Area (considering systems for the Web).
- Rule 7 (R7): IF the task is of intermediate-level (MAD*) THEN the size, format and localisation of the *Sub-windows* will be defined inside a *Region* of the window in a standard format [8].
- Rule 8 (R8): IF the centrality of the task is important and its frequency high (MAD*) THEN choose an iconical interaction (menu type) [16].
- Rule 9 (R9): IF the centrality of the task is important and its frequency high (MAD*) THEN choose a dialogue of type hierarchical menu types (menu type) [16].
- Rule 10 (R10): If the task frequency is elevated (MAD*) THEN spread the menu structure in an area which allows immediate access to the user (localization) [17].

This stage generates a complete Editor tree for the example considered. The tree is illustrated in Fig. 6.

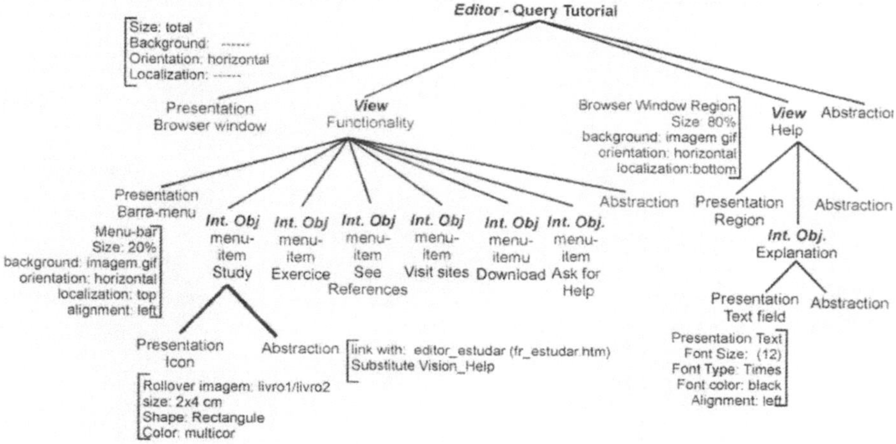

Figure 6. EDITOR tree (complete) of the task: "Query Tutorial".

The fourth stage consists in generating the interface prototype from the EDITOR trees produced by the previous stage. The implementation of this prototype can be done automatically because the architectural model reflects exactly the interaction model. That is, the PAC agents are adequately represented by an object oriented structure, as shown in [10].

The fifth stage is distributed in all previous stages of the process and consists of the evaluation of each artefact produced in each stage.

4. CONCLUSION

This paper focused on a model-guided and task-based approach (MEDITE) to UI design. The emphasis is on the model-based aspect as opposed to the strong emphasis on the tool-based aspect of other methodologies mentioned earlier in this paper (ADEPT [9,11,21], ERGO-START (AIDE) [7] and MCI [19]).

Each stage in MEDITE is directed by a well defined model which guides the construction of an adequate and consistent description of each artefact or product generated (task description, conceptual specification of the interaction, software specification of the interface).

The EDITOR model is the main differential of the MEDITE approach in relation to other methodologies due to the following reasons:

- The EDITOR interaction conceptual model saves, with the MAD* task model, two additional relations: (i) structural, that is, an EDITOR tree has the same structure as a MAD* tree; (ii) procedural, that is, the construction process of an EDITOR tree is similar to the construction process of a MAD* tree (ascendant and descendant). This makes the identification process of the rules to obtain the EDITOR trees from MAD* description simple and easy to be accomplished.
- Most methodologies considered in this work do not permit the handling by the designer of the artefacts created in some stages, only allowing it through the use of specific tools inherent to each one. On the other hand, MEDITE proposes that all created artefacts in all stages have a well-defined and accessible representation, independent of the existence of supporting tools.
- Most methodologies considered in this work do not use an explicit model of the interface architecture. The structure of the code generated for the interface prototype does not bare any relation with the interaction conceptual model, making difficult or even impractical, to modify the prototype without modifying the interaction conceptual model.

- The use of a well-defined task model (MAD*) and a well-defined and formal unified model for both interaction and architectural description (EDITOR), in all stages of MEDITE allows the automatization of great part of the UI design process.

Other methodologies that use task-based and model-guided approach to UI design, as MEDITE, have emerged, among them are MACIA [4] and the one used by ALACIE [5].

The advantage in using MEDITE is centered in the use of conceptual models to understand the processes and to guide the production of the artefacts of each stage. This assertion is supported by many studies of cognitive psychology which have shown the fundamental role of the use of conceptual models in order to learn, to design and to operate complex interactive devices [3, 14, 15].

In the current stage, MEDITE is being experimented in the development of an interface for a computer network simulator at the Federal University of Paraiba (UFPB), in Brazil.

REFERENCES

[1] Coutaz, J., *Interfaces Homme-Ordinateur – Conception et Réalisation,* Bordas, Paris, 1990.

[2] Cybis, W.A., *A Identificação de Objetos de Interfaces Homem-Computador e de seus Atributos Ergonômicos,* Ph.D. thesis, UFSC, Florianópolis, Brazil, 1994.

[3] Falzon, P., *Ergonomie Cognitive du Dialogue,* Presses Universitaires de Grenoble, France, 1989.

[4] Furtado, E., *Integrando Fatores Humanos no Processo de Desenvolvimento de Interfaces Homem-Computador Adaptativas,* II Workshop sobre Fatores Humanos em Sistemas Computacionais, Campinas, SP, Brazil, 1999.

[5] Gamboa, F.R., *Spécification et Implémentation d'ALACIE: Atelier Logiciel d'Aide à la Conception d'Interfaces Ergonomiques*, Ph.D. thesis, Université de Paris XI, October 1998.

[6] Guerrero, C.V.S. and Lula, B. Jr., *Um Tutorial na Web: obtenção do modelo da interação a partir do modelo da tarefa com o auxílio de regras ergonômicas*, Relatório Técnico RT- DSC-002/2001, UFPB/DSC/CCT Campina Grande, PB, October 2001.

[7] Hammouche, H., *De la modélisation des tâches utilisateurs au prototype de l'interface homme-machine*, Ph.D. thesis, Université de Paris VI, France, Décembre 1995.

[8] ISO 9241, *Ergonomic requirements for office work with visual display terminals*, Draft International Standard ISO 9241 (Parts 10, 12, 14), 1993.

[9] Johnson, P., Wilson, S., Markopoulos, P., and Pycock, J., *ADEPT – Advanced Design Environment for Prototyping with Task Models*, in Proc. of ACM Conf. on Human Aspects in Computing Systems InterCHI'93 (Amsterdam, 24-29 April 1993), Vol. II, ACM Press, New York, 1993, p. 56.

[10] Lula, B. Jr., *Contribution à la Conception Orientée Objet: Elaboration d'un Environnement de Génération Interactive d'Interfaces à Manipulation Directe pour le Language OBJLOG*, Ph.D. thesis, Université de Droit d'Economie et des Sciences d'Aix-Marseille III, Faculté des Sciences et Techniques de Saint–Jérôme, France, 1992.

[11] Markopoulos, P., Pycock, J., Wilson, S., *ADEPT - A task based design environment*, Queen Mary and Westfield College, UK, 1992.

[12] Norman, D.A., *Cognitive Engineering*, in D.A. Norman & S.W. Draper (eds.), User Centered Systems Design, Lawrence Erlbaum Associates Ltd., Hillsdale, 1986.

[13] Parizotto, R., *Guia de Estilos para Serviços de Informação em Ciência e Tecnologia*, Florianópolis, SC, Brazil, November 1997.

[14] Pfaff, G.R., *User Interface Management Systems*, Eurographics Seminars, Springer-Verlag, 1985.

[15] Rasmussen, J., *The Human as a Systems Component*, in H.T. Smith and T.R.G. Green (eds.), Human Interaction with Computers, Academic Press, 1980, pp. 67-96.

[16] Scapin, D.L., *Guide Ergonomique de Conception des Interfaces Homme-Machine*, Rapports Techniques, Unité de Recherche INRIA - Rocqencourt, France, 1986.

[17] Smith, S.L. and Mosier, J.N., *Guidelines For Designing User Interface Software*, The MITRE Corporation, Bedford, 1986.

[18] Smith R.G., Barth, P.S., and Young, R.L., *A substrate for Object-Oriented Interface Design*, in Shriver and Wegner (eds.), Research Direction in Object-Oriented Programming, Computer Systems Series, MIT Press, Boston, 1987.

[19] Turnell, M.F.Q.V., *Projeto de Interface para Web*, Notas de aula, Laboratório de Interfaces Homem-Máquina – LIHM/DEE/CCT/Universidade Federal da Paraíba, Brazil, March 2000.

[20] Valiati, E.R.A., *Guia de Recomendações para o desenvolvimento de interfaces com usabilidade em Softwares Educacionais do tipo hipertexto/hipermídia Informativo*, Instituto de Informática da Universidade Federal do Rio Grande do Sul (UFRGS), Porto Alegre, Brazil, 2000.

[21] Wilson, S., Johnson, P., Kelly, C., Cunningham, J., and Markopoulos, P., *Beyond Hacking: A Model Based Approach to User Interface Design*, in Proc. of the BCS Conference on Human Computer Interaction HCI'93 People and Computers VIII (Loughborough, 7-10 September 1993), Cambridge University Press, Cambridge, 1993, pp. 217–231.

Chapter 12

USING USER INTERFACE MODELS IN DESIGN

Hallvard Trætteberg[1]
Dept. of Computer and Information Sciences (IDI), Norwegian University of Science and Technology (NTNU), Sem Sælands v. 7-9, N-7491 Trondheim (Norway)
E-mail: hal@idi.ntnu.no – URL: http://www.idi.ntnu.no/~hal/
Tel.: +47-7359-3443 – Fax: + 47-7359-4466

Abstract We introduce a framework for classifying user interface design representations, and argue that multiple representations are must be used in the design process, and that modelling languages must support the transition between them. We present languages for modelling domain, task and dialog and show how they provide increased support for design, through flexibility and integration. Design patterns based on model fragments from these languages are suggested as a design and engineering tool.

Keywords: Dialog model, Design pattern, Task model, User interface model.

1. INTRODUCTION

With the standardization of UML and its emergence as a de-facto industrial standard, modelling of systems and software artefacts seems to be accepted in the engineering community. User interface modelling and model-based user interface design has however, not reached the mainstream software developer [12]. RedWhale's MOBILE [16] cover several models but lack integration with software engineering tools, while database-oriented tools like Genera's Genova (www.genera.no) have a more narrow focus on concrete interaction object selection and layout. It seems that lack of tool support for going from comprehensive visual model diagrams to executable code may be a reason for this difference. But very few UML diagramming tools provide full code- generation support, yet developers are using these tools to draw UML diagrams, e.g. for *communication* purposes. The lack of

[1] This work is part of a Dr.ing study funded by The Research Council of Norway.

C. Kolski and J. Vanderdonckt (eds.), Computer-Aided Design of User Interfaces III, 131–142.
© 2002 *Kluwer Academic Publishers.*

penetration of model-based user interface design methods may instead be due to pragmatic aspects of UI modelling languages, e.g. they are difficult to understand, inflexible and impractical to use and lack the appropriate integration with each other. Although formality in itself is important, it may be that the focus should be language *usability* rather than theory, if the goal is reaching the mainstream. A *uniform user interface modeling language* must *integrate* sub-languages for domain, task and dialog modelling, be *unconstraining* and *flexible*, i.e. provide support for expressing design ideas, suggestions and decisions throughout the design process.

In this paper we will first introduce a framework for classifying design representation. The framework provides a means for understanding how they are utilized in the design process, which in turn has implications for language design and usage. We then briefly present modelling languages for tasks and dialogs and discuss how our understanding affected their design. We then turn to how design knowledge can be represented in the same languages in the form of model-based user interface design patterns. Finally, we suggest how these modelling languages may be integrated with UML, to provide better integration with contemporary methods.

2. DESIGN PROCESS AND REPRESENTATIONS

To better understand how design representations are used and the role they play, we use a model of *organizational knowledge creation* as a starting point [13]. According to this theory, there must during product development, be a constant conversion of knowledge between *tacit* and *explicit* forms using the four *transfer modes* shown in Fig. 1. Hence, to better support product development, the process and *design representations* used, must support these transfer modes. By "design representation" we mean any design relevant knowledge that is externalized in a *human-readable* medium, whether textual, graphic or multimedia.

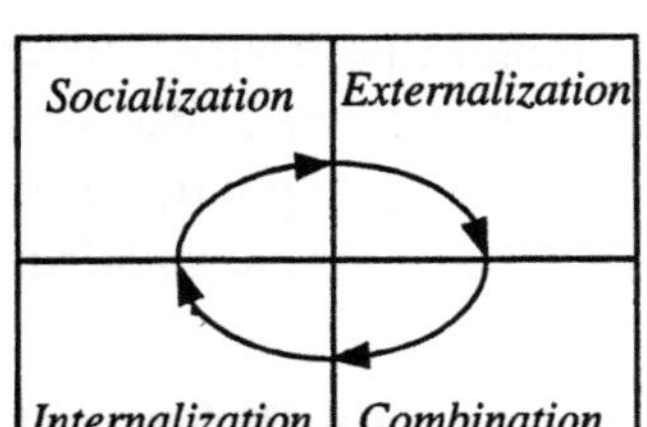

Figure 1. Nonaka's four modes of knowledge transfer.

To support *socialization*, the representation must support social interaction, for which flexible and informal representations are best suited. In the process of *externalization* and further *formalization*, the representation needs to shift from informal to formal, and the medium or language used will need to change. Throughout the development process there will be a drift towards increased formality, as the design is committed to and the need for transfer to "outsiders" increases [7]. Systems like SILK [8] and the Cocktail Napkin [5] target this transfer mode. During *combination* new knowledge is created by linking existing explicit knowledge, so the representations must supports analysis and reasoning. It is this transfer mode that model-based methods typically focus on. Finally, activities like usability testing and end-user validation requires a process of *internalization*.

The need for using and transferring between different design representations, implies that there exist different classes of representations. We have found it useful to classify representations along three dimensions, as shown right in Fig. 2: 1) the perspective, ranging from problem- to solution-oriented, 2) the granularity of the objects covered and 3) the level of formality. A language or method will usually cover a large part of this space, while a particular diagram covers a smaller part. E.g. contemporary task modelling languages are typically problem-oriented and formal, and suited for mid- to low-level actions. Workflow languages on the other hand, support a higher level view of actions. All the nine user interface models listed in [24] can be placed in the 2 dimensional space spanned by the perspective and granularity axes.

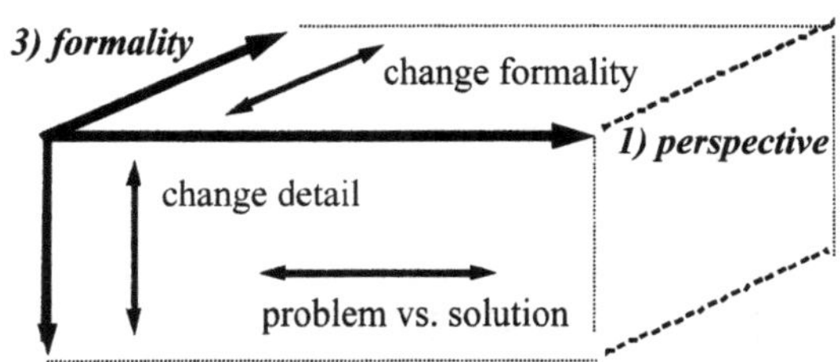

Figure 2. Dimensions of the representation space and movements within it.

Nonaka's transfer modes correspond to movements along the formality dimension, i.e. the top double-arrowed line in Fig. 2. There will be similar movements along the other two dimensions, according to the needs of the development process and the participants, and the intended role of the representation. Different roles are summarized in Table 1:

1. *Perspectives* – Movements from *solution to problem* is the "textbook" flow of a problem solving: first specify the problem, then solve it according to the constraints expressed in the specification. The representation should support looking "forward" towards constructing one or several solutions. Moving from *solution to problem* is used when analyzing a solution for the purpose of comparing it against a previously formulated specification.

2. *Granularity* – Moving *downwards*, details are constructed from a high-level description. This is similar to the problem-solution movement, in that it requires satisfying the constraints given by a more abstract specification. In the *upwards* movement, the aggregated characteristics are constructed from an analysis of one level, and relies on the *compositionality* of the language used.
3. *Formality* – When *formalizing* a design vague ideas are made less ambiguous and more precise. The common tacit understanding of design ideas must be made explicit through communication. Making a formal representation *less formal* may seem unnatural, but makes sense in a context where participants are unfamiliar with formal notations.

Table 1. Roles the design representation plays.

Role	**Objective**
Semantic	Capture domain knowledge.
Communicative	Communicate domain as represented among participants
Constructive	Guide and constrain further design
Analytic	Interpret and evaluate current representations

The model-based design approaches usually focus on the movements from left to right, and top to bottom within the formal "plane". Movements are just as relevant, e.g. when using more exploratory and informal approaches. To develop a more industry- friendly model-based approach, we should design modelling languages with better support for all movements in the representation space.

3. INTEGRATED USER INTERFACE MODELLING

We have developed three languages for domain, task and dialog modelling, with the goal of making model-based user interface design more developer-friendly. The domain modelling language, mainly developed by Arne Sølvberg [17], is used in the context of both task and dialog modelling. The task modelling language is based on ([19]) the APM workflow language [3], and is a hybrid of hierarchical task and workflow modelling languages.

The dialog modelling language combines interconnected interactors for expressing information flow and the Statechart language for control and activation. The three languages will be briefly presented below. Although they all have a formal basis, the focus will be on expressiveness and flexibility, to illustrate how we believe they provide better support for the different movements discussed above.

3.1 Domain Modelling with RML

Our domain modelling language, the Referent Modelling Language [17], provides constructs for naming concepts and their extensions (sets), partitioning them, relating them to each other and defining their attributes, all based on set theory. Fig. 3 illustrates our notation in an RML model of task modelling concepts, similar to the ontology suggested in [21].

The rectangle labeled 'Task' defines the TASK concept, which is related to a set of RESOURCES, through the REQUIREMENT and ACHIEVEMENT relations (lines). Each TASK requires at least one RESOURCE, expressed by the small black circle. There are three kinds of resources that a task may require: ACTORS, CONCEPTS/SETS (domain data) and TOOLS. The encircled '+' sign indicates that these *specializations/ subsets* are disjoint. Each task is related to an ACTOR through the PERFORMANCE relation, and this relation is a *specialization/subset* of the REQUIREMENT relation. Tasks are related through an aggregation relation, indicated by the encircled 'x'. Each task's participation in the aggregation is the basis for classifying it as either SUPERTASK or ACTION and either TOPLEVEL or SUBTASK.

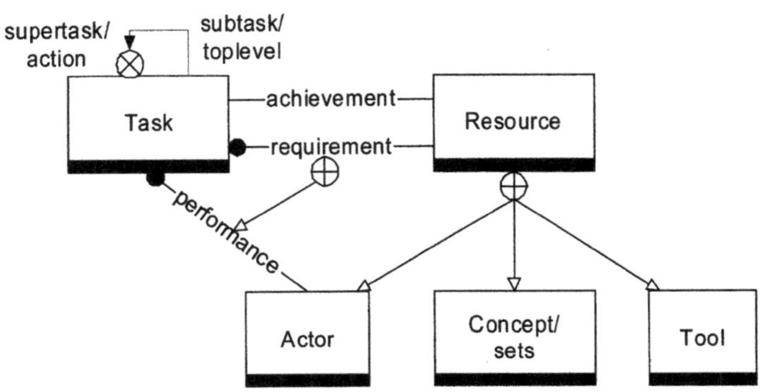

Figure 3. Generic model of tasks and their performance.

In RML, instances may be (re)classified many times in their lifetime as their characteristics change. This differs from most object-oriented modelling languages like UML, where the instance-class relation is static. Compared to UML's class diagrams RML provides a richer and more flexible visual notation, e.g. attributes may be grouped in separate boxes and cardinality is visually indicated. RML provides better support for modelling differing world-views in a single diagram, e.g. by allowing several orthogonal specializations for the same concept.

Although its philosophical roots are distinct from UML's, most RML constructs have UML correspondences, so RML most models may be translated to UML for software engineering purposes.

3.2 Task Modelling with TaskMODL and RML

Our task modelling language TaskMODL, utilizes and builds on RML in three ways. First, it is used for modelling the domain, as shown in Fig. 4, upper right, where the model of MESSAGES and MAILBOXES provides a context for the READ EMAIL task. The second usage is for expressing contextual information, dataflow and pre- and post-conditions. In Fig. 4, the IN mailbox instance is required for performing GET NEW EMAIL, a set of messages is required for MANAGE EMAIL and each MESSAGE in MESSAGES provides a context for a MANAGE MESSAGE task. The *cardinality* of the MANAGE EMAIL-MANAGE MESSAGE aggregation corresponds to the size of the set of messages. This exemplifies the tight coupling between the static domain and dynamic task model; the static structure constrains what is meaningful action, and is the reason these should be integrated both theoretically/formally and practically/visually.

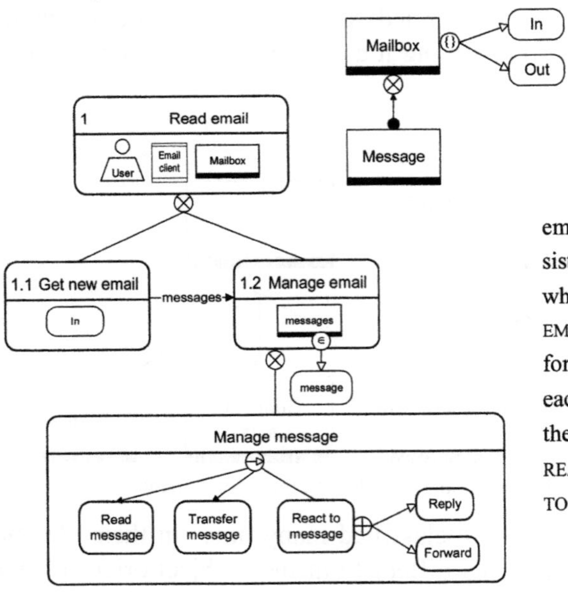

Figure 4. Model of Read email task: READ EMAIL consists of GET NEW EMAIL which triggers the MANAGE EMAIL TASK. The latter performs MANAGE MESSAGE for each new message, through the three sequential steps READ, TRANSFER and REACT TO MESSAGE.

TaskMODL's third usage of RML is for its own definition and notation. In the RML model in Fig. 3, it is expressed that SUPERTASKS contain SUBTASKS. This is a generic constraint, and in specific task models we express more specific constraints, e.g. that a GET NEW MESSAGES task will be performed as part of a READ EMAIL task. In a standard use of meta-models, the READ EMAIL task would be an *instance* of the TASK concept, but we have chosen to define it as a *specialization* of TASK, i.e. at the *same meta-level* as the generic task model in Fig. 3. This means that TaskMODL models are really RML models in disguise, and therefore the integration is straightforward. In fact, most of RML's notation is carried over, including cardinality and specialization.

RML lacks features for modelling how a domain evolves over time, so a set of standard sequence constraints have been added. Repetition is expressed through the cardinality of the SUPERTASK-SUBTASK aggregation. Abstraction of human action is important [9], and this is supported by the dual use of the choice operator (+) inherited from RML. In the example model, the REPLY TO MESSAGE and FORWARD MESSAGE are *specializations* of REACT TO MESSAGE. The meaning of specialization is inherited from RML: the static constraints of the general task must be met by the specialized tasks. Several specializations of a task may defined for different conditions, e.g. classes of input data, user stereotypes and use of different interface designs.

Compared to ConcurTaskTrees [15], TaskMODL provides several advantages:

1. TaskMODL is semantically and visually integrated with a domain modelling language. A corresponding integration should be possible with UML, providing a smoother integration than that suggested between CTT and UML in [14].
2. Specialisation is given a natural interpretation, providing means for managing task knowledge.
3. The notation is more flexible: The hybrid tree and containment-based hierarchical notation, provides better support for a combination of traditional hierarchical and dataflow-oriented style. Anonymous tasks can be used when a supertask is needed for grouping, but no name is needed for readability, as shown left in Fig. 5, where a complex constraint is expressed using two anonymous tasks.
4. The sequence constraints are more flexible than CTT's binary operators. They can be decoupling from supertasks, which in the left fragment in Fig. 5 can be used to removed the anonymous tasks altogether. TaskMODL also supports non- strict constraint trees, as illustrated in the right fragment, which makes expressing complex sequence constraints even more practical.

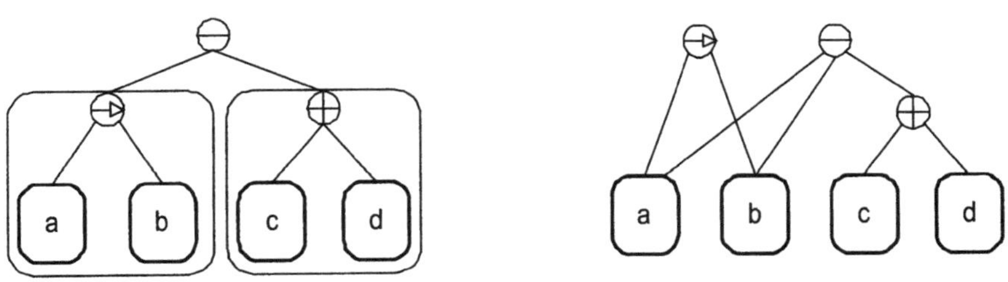

Figure 5. Left:order(sequence(a,b),choice(c,d))-Right:sequence(a,b)&order(a,b, choice(c, d)).

3.3 Dialog Modelling with DiaMODL and RML

Our dialog modelling language DiaMODL is based on the interactor abstraction from [4] and [11] for expressing information flow. We avoid basing control and activation on LOTOS and use Statecharts [6] instead, a trade-off between utilizing previous theoretical results and making the language more practical. The choice is due to Statecharts' simplicity and the fact that it is already part of UML.

As previously mentioned, we are interested in supporting movements within the design representation space introduced in Section 2. The compositionality of interactors directly supports movements along the granularity dimension. Moving between abstract and concrete interaction is supported by providing an interactor definition for every standard widgets, as exemplified in Fig. 6. The left RML fragment identifies the information that the interactor at the right can input and output. The interior represents a suitable widget supporting this interactor signature. If a folder view appears in a design sketch, we can suggest this interactor as its abstraction. Alternatively, if an abstract dialog model is consistent with this fragment, we can use the folder view in our concrete design, or for explaining our abstract model. We have modelled most standard widgets as interactors, and are working on ways to mix abstract interactors and concrete widgets in a GUI builder, to support the abstract-concrete movement in both directions. Traditionally, interactors have been applied to structured dialogs and forms, but our inclusion of Statecharts provides support for direct manipulation, in the way suggested in [18].

In [10], it is suggested that the structure of interconnected interactors can be represented by UML's objects diagram. With our use of Statecharts, the control part could be represented as well. Our way of mixing interactors/objects with Statecharts is not directly representable, though, since UML's State diagrams are local to an object and the composition of Statecharts in objects aggregations is unclear.

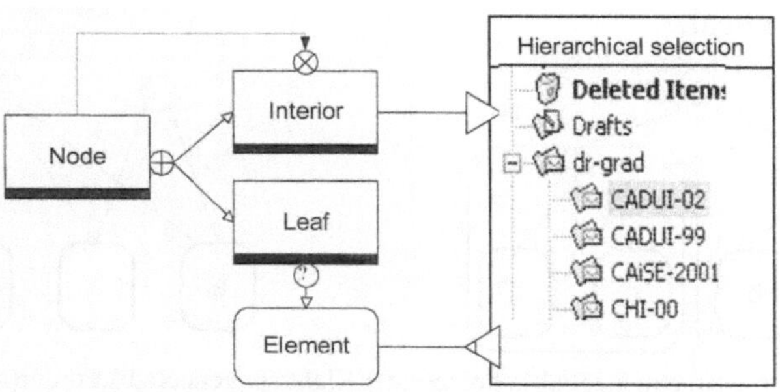

Figure 6. Interactor for selecting a leaf element from a hierarchy, and corresponding folder view.

4. MODEL-BASED DESIGN PATTERNS

Design is about making *choices* concerning *which* sequences of action the user should be able to perform, *which* design elements are used and *how* they are composed to support this behavior. The movements presented in Section 2, correspond to such design choices, e.g. how tasks are mapped to dialog structure, how formal specifications are derived from design sketches and how dialog structures are decomposed. Making these choices or movements requires knowledge, and accordingly, our framework can be used for classifying design knowledge. E.g, rules for mapping from abstract dialog elements to concrete widgets would be placed as shown in Fig. 7.

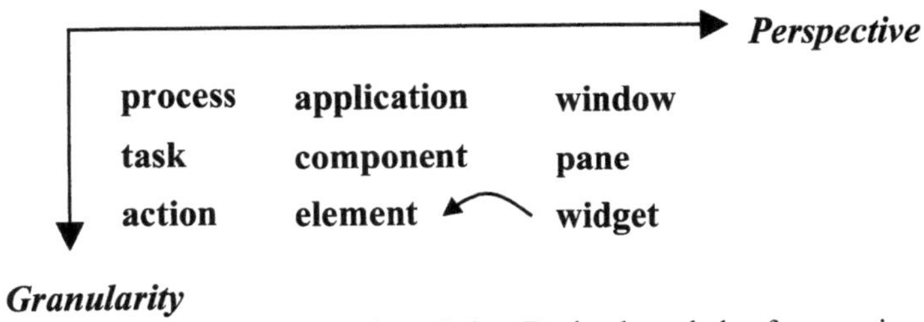

Figure 7. Classifying design knowledge: Design knowledge for mapping dialog elements to widgets.

The UID community has a long tradition of formulating design knowledge in principles, rules and guidelines, and there exists some attempt to formalize it, e.g. [23]. A problem is that such knowledge is either very high-level and general or very specific [22]. For capturing "middle-level" design knowledge, the use of *UID patterns* is gaining interest and momentum. The pattern concept originated in architecture ([2]), and simply stated, represents a generic, proven and accepted solution to a reoccurring design problem, in a way that facilitates (re)use in a new design context.

We believe patterns can become a useful design and engineering tool, if we are pragmatic about philosophical and often almost religious issues concerning pattern discovery and formulation/formats. In our context, design patterns can simply be interpreted as recipes for how to perform sound movements within our representation space.

As such, they can be used bottom-up as building blocks, top-down for design refinement and to move between perspectives. In a model-based approach to design, it is natural to use model fragments, and in our own experience, the abstraction and precision they provide is very helpful when formulating a pattern [20]. It is crucial that the modelling languages support combination of several perspectives, and this is part of the motivation for integrating them. We are currently experimenting with using model fragments utilizing our three modelling languages in pattern formulations.

Problem: The user needs to browse the elements of a hierarchy and select one.
Principle: Provide separate connected panes for specialised viewers.
Context: Many application contains aggregated data, which the user must browse through. and the user often wants to invoke a function taking one of the parts as input parameter.
Forces: 1) Freedom for the application to visualise the set of containers, parts and individual items in specific ways. 2) Freedom for the user to resize each viewer.
Solution: Split a window into three panes, one for the viewing a set of containers, one for viewing a set of parts, and one for viewing individual parts.The former two must provide item selection. The selection of a container should determine the content of the parts pane, and the selected part should determine the content of the part pane.

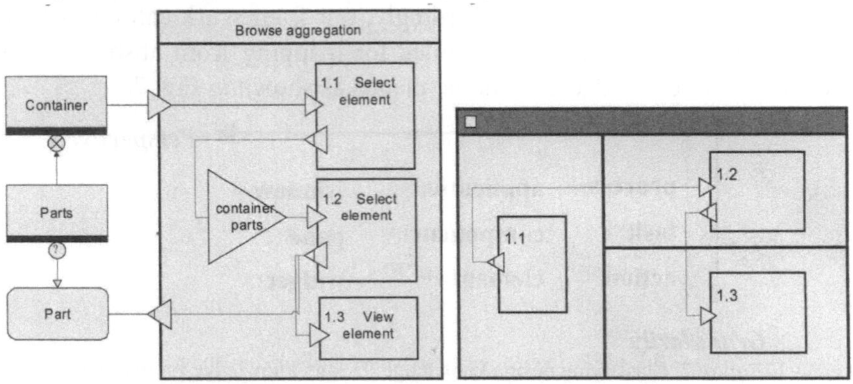

Figure 8. The *Browsing a container* design pattern for browsing aggregations.

Fig. 8 shows a pattern for browsing aggregation hierarchies and selecting an element. The interactor signature can be seen as a specification, and its composition a suggested solution to a design problem. A layout is suggested for configuring them in window panes. This particular pattern concerns two movements, decomposition of dialog and mapping from abstract to concrete design. We have formulated patterns for selecting concrete dialog elements from abstract interactors, based on mappings like the one shown in Fig. 6, and for mapping from tasks to dialogs, e.g. the Managing Favorites pattern found at [1]. The latter kind is in our experience the most difficult to "find".

Use of formal model (fragments) in design patterns is controversial, partly because of the non-engineering pattern tradition, and partly because formal user interface models are rarely used. The theory of knowledge creation presented in Section 2 suggests that a patterns format should use both formal and informal representations, the former for precision and the latter for supporting recognition and application. In our experience, the most immediate effect of using formal model fragments in patterns is mental, e.g. enhancing the understanding of design and increasing the consciousness of (abstract) design knowledge. What tools and techniques are needed for more practical results, remains to be seen.

5. CONCLUSION AND FURTHER WORK

The use of formal methods and languages in user interface design, has always been a source of debate, mirroring the discussion on systems development approaches. UML is criticized for both being too informal and too formal, depending on the context. Most however, agree that an integrated language is important and UML's pragmatic line of compromise wrt. different modelling traditions may be fruitful also in the community's work towards a *uniform user interface modeling language*.

We have argued that there is a use for both formal models and informal design representation methods in user interface development. The role of informal representations is to support creativity, involvement and dialog, among both developers and end- users. Formal representations allows detaching the representation from the meaning- giving context, and supports reflection, analysis and transition to executable representations. More effort should be put into understanding:

- How (design representation) language is used throughout the design process.
- The need for integration of modelling languages across perspectives.
- How design knowledge can be integrated into a model-based approach to user interface design.

REFERENCES

[1] Accessible at http://bscw.gmd.de/pub/english.cgi/0/17771476.

[2] Alexander, C., Ishikawa, S., Silverstein, M., Jacobson, M., Fiksdahl-King, I., and Angel, S., *A Pattern Language,* Oxford University Press, 1977.

[3] Carlsen, S., *Action Port Model: A Mixed Paradigm Conceptual Workflow Modeling Language,* in Proceedings of 3rd IFCIS International Conference on Cooperative Information Systems CoopIS'98 (New York, 20-22 August 1998), IEEE Computer Society Press, Los Alamitos, 1998, pp. 300-309.

[4] Duke, D., Faconti, G., Harrison, M., and Paternó, F., *Unifying views of interactors,* in Proceedings of the Int. Workshop on Advanced Visual Interfaces AVI'94, ACM Press, 1994, pp. 143-152.

[5] Gross, M.D. and Yi-Luen Do, E., *Ambiguous Intentions: A Paper-Like Interface for Creative Design,* in Proceedings of 9th Annual Symposium on User Interface Software and Technology UIST'96 Seattle, 6-8 November 1996), ACM Press, New York, 196, pp. 183-192.

[6] Harel, D., *Statecharts: A Visual Formalism for Complex Systems*, Science of Computer Programming, Vol. 8, 1987, pp. 231-274.

[7] Jones, S. and Sapsford, J., *The role of informal representations in early design,* in P. Markopoulos and P. Johnson (eds.), Proceedings of DSV-IS'98, Springer-Verlag, Vienna, 1998, pp. 117-133.

[8] Landay, J.A. and Myers, B.A., Interactive Sketching for the Early Stages of User Interface Design, in Proceedings of ACM Conf. on Human Aspects in Computing

Systems CHI'95 ()Denver, 7-11 May 1995), ACM Press, New York, 1995, pp. 43-50.
[9] Malone, T.W., et. al., *Tools for inventing organizations: Toward a handbook of organizational processes,* Management Science, Vol. 45, No. 3, March 1999, pp. 425-443.
[10] Markopoulos, P. and Marijnissen, P., *UML as a representation for Interaction Design*, in C. Paris., N. Ozkan, S. Howard, and S. Lu (eds.), Proceedings of Annual Conference for the Computer-Human Interaction Special Interest Group (CHISIG) of the Ergonomics Society of Australia OZCHI'2000 (Sydney, 4-8 December 2000), 2000, pp. 240-249, accessible at http://www.ipo.tue.nl/homepages/pmarkopo/papers/P.Markopoulos OZCHI2000.pdf
[11] Markopoulos, P., *A compositional model for the formal specification of user interface software*, Ph.D. thesis, Department of Computer Science, Queen Mary and Westfield College, University of London. 1997.
[12] Myers, B., Hudson, S.E., and Pausch, R., *Past, Present and Future of User Interface Software Tools,* ACM Trans. on Computer-Human Interaction, Vol. 7, 2000, pp. 3-28.
[13] Nonaka, I. and Takeushi, H., *A theory of the firm's knowledge-creation dynamics,* in A.D. Chandler jr, P. Hagstrøm, and Ø. Søvell (eds.), The dynamic firm. The role of technology, strategy, organization and regions, Oxford University Press, Oxford, 1998.
[14] Nunes, N.J., *Object Modeling for User-Centered Development and User Interface Design: The Wisdom Approach*, Ph.D. thesis, Universidade da Madeira, April 2001.
[15] Paternò, F., Mancini, C., and Meniconi, S., *ConcurTaskTrees: A Diagrammatic Notation for Specifying Task Models*, in S. Howard, J. Hammond, and G. Lindgaard (eds.), Proc. of 6th IFIP TC 13 Conf. on Human-Computer Interaction Interact'97 (Sydney, 14-18 July 1997), Kluwer Academics, Dordrecht, 1997, pp. 362-369.
[16] Puerta, A.R., Cheng, E., Ou, T., and Min, J., *Mobile: User-Centered Interface Building,* in Proceedings of the ACM Conference on Human Factors in Computing Systems CHI'99 (Pittsburgh, 15-20 May 1999), ACM Press, New York, 1999, pp. 426-433.
[17] Sølvberg, A., *Data and what they refer to,* in P.P.Chen *et al.* (eds.), Conceptual Modeling, Lecture Notes in Computer Science, Springer Verlag, 1999, pp. 211-226.
[18] Trætteberg, H., *Modelling Direct Manipulation with Referent and Statecharts*, in P. Markopoulos and P. Johnson (eds.), Proc. of DSV-IS'98, Springer-Verlag, Vienna, 1998, pp. 278-292.
[19] Trætteberg, H., *Modelling work: Workflow and Task Modelling,* in Proc. of 3rd Int. Conf. on Computer-Aided Design of User Interfaces CADUI'99 (Louvain-la-Neuve, 21-23 October 1999), Kluwer Academic Publishers, Dordrecht, 1999, pp. 275-280.
[20] van Welie, M. and Trætteberg, H., *Interaction patterns in user interfaces*, in Proc. of 7th. Pattern Languages of Programs Conference PLoP'2000 (Monticello, 13-16 August 2000), Washington University Technical Report number wucs-00-29, accessible at http://jerry.cs.uiuc.edu/~plop/plop2k/proceedings/Welie/Welie.pdf
[21] van Welie, M., van der Veer, G.C., and Eliëns, A., *An Ontology for Task World Models*, in P. Markopoulos and P. Johnson (eds.), Proceedings of DSV-IS'98 Abingdon, 3-5 June 1998), Springer-Verlag Vienna, 1998, pp. 57-70.
[22] van Welie, M., van der Veer, G.C., and Eliëns, A., *Patterns as Tools for UI Design,* in J. Vanderdonckt and Ch. Farenc (eds.), Proc. of Int. Workshop on Tools for Working with Guidelines (Biarritz, 7-8 October 2000), Springer-Verlag, London, 2000, pp. 313-324.
[23] Vanderdonckt, J.M. and Bodart, F., *Encapsulating Knowledge for Intelligent Automatic Interaction Objects Selection*, in Proceedings of InterCHI'93, ACM Press, New York, 1993, pp. 424-429.
[24] Vanderdonckt, J.M. and Puerta, A.R., *Introduction to Computer-Aided Design of User Interfaces*, Preface of J. Vanderdonckt and A.R. Puerta (eds.), Proc. of 3rd Int. Conf. on Computer-Aided Design of User Interfaces CADUI'99 (Louvain-la-Neuve, 21-23 October 1999), Kluwer Academic Publishers, Dordrecht, 1999, pp. 1-5.

Chapter 13

ONE MODEL, MANY INTERFACES

Fabio Paternò, Carmen Santoro
ISTI, CNR Institute, Via G. Moruzzi 1
I-56010 Ghezzano, Pisa (Italy)
E-mail: {f.paterno, c.santoro}@cnuce.cnr.it – URL: http://giove.cnuce.cnr.it/~fabio/
Tel: +39-050-315 30 66 – Fax: +39-050-313 80 91

Abstract The wide variety of devices currently available, which is bound to increase in the coming years, poses a number of issues for the design cycle of interactive software applications. Model-based approaches can provide useful support in addressing this new challenge. In this paper we present and discuss a model-based method for the design of nomadic applications showing how the use of models can support their design. The aim is to enable each interaction device to support the appropriate tasks users expect to perform and designers to develop the various device-specific application modules in a consistent manner.

Keywords: Context, Model-based design, Multi-platform user interfaces.

1. INTRODUCTION

Recent years have seen the introduction of many types of computers and devices (e.g. cellular phones, PDA's, WebTV, etc.) and the availability of such a wide range of devices has become a fundamental challenge for designers of interactive software systems [8]. Users wish to be able to seamlessly access information and services regardless of the device they are using, even when the system or the environment changes dynamically. To this end, computer-based applications need to run on a wide spectrum of devices.

Designing applications that exploit new technology is often a difficult problem. For software developers this introduces the problem of constructing multiple versions of single applications and endowing these versions with the ability to dynamically respond to changes in context. Creating different versions of applications for different devices engenders extra development and expensive maintenance cost of cross-platform consistency, com-

C. Kolski and J. Vanderdonckt (eds.), Computer-Aided Design of User Interfaces III, 143–154.
© 2002 *Kluwer Academic Publishers.*

plicates the problems of configuration management and dilutes the resources available for usability engineering. Additionally, current development tools provide little support for creating applications that change dynamically in response to changes in their environment, or that have to share data amongst heterogeneous device types. Although many dimensions must be considered when designing context-dependent applications (actors, platforms, environments, system resources, etc.), in this paper we focus on how to support a design addressing change of platforms.

Nowadays companies need to better consider the thorny issues involved in designing applications supporting multiple platforms. Currently, they often address different contexts of use by building different applications, even if supporting similar tasks accessing similar data. Different versions of applications should differ in their presentation, rather than trying to address different input/output platforms by just resizing the elements of the user interface. Versions may also differ in the tasks they can realistically support – for example, the PDA permits reading reviews, the phone permits ordering books, and the desktop PC supports both. In addition the set of functionality supported can change dynamically.

Technological advances solve some of the problems of engineering applications for multiple devices: XML (eXtensible Markup Language) documents supported by XSL (eXtensible Stylesheet Language) stylesheets allow creating customised presentations for different devices or users. Wireless Markup Language (WML) permits to produce device-independent presentations for a range of small display devices. Wireless Internet gateways automatically translate HTML documents into WML documents (although they may produce unusable results if they rely on large displays). XSL (and related technologies) help with user interface presentation, but are limited by the fact that a different interaction design may be necessary when moving between radically different device types. While these solutions help with parts of the problem, they do not provide high-level guidance for guaranteeing quality across multiple versions of applications.

The goal of this paper is to present and discuss a method to support design and development of highly usable context-sensitive interactive software systems. To this end we discuss the state of art in addressing issues related to multi-platform applications. Next, we identify the main phases of the proposed method and also illustrate how the information provided by task models can be useful for the design of user interfaces. Then, we analyse more in depth the method and show its application to an example taken from the design of a museum application. Lastly, some concluding remarks are provided.

2. RELATED WORK

In a recent paper, discussing the future of user interface tools, Myers, Hudson, and Pausch [7] indicate that the wide platform variability *encourages a return to the study of some techniques for device-independent user interface specification, so that developers can describe the input and output needs of their applications, so that vendors can describe the input and output capabilities of their devices, and so that users can specify their preferences. Then, the system might choose appropriate interaction techniques taking all of these into account*. The basic idea is that instead of having separate applications for each device that exchange only basic data, there is some abstract description and then an environment that is able to suggest a design for a specific device that adapts to its features and possible contexts of use. This is also called user interface plasticity [14]. Methods for modelling work context [2] can provide useful information for this type of approach.

This problem is a novel challenge for model-based design and development of interactive applications. The potentialities of these approaches have been addressed in a limited manner. In the GUITARE Esprit project a user interface generator has been developed: it takes ConcurTaskTrees (CTT) task models [9] and produces user interfaces for ERP applications according to company guidelines. However, automatic generation is not a general solution because of many, varying factors that have to be taken into account within the design process. Semi-automatic support is more general and flexible: Mobi-D [11] is an example of a semi-automatic approach but it only supports design of traditional graphical desktop applications.

UIML [1] is an appliance-independent XML user interface language. While this language is ostensibly independent of the specific device and medium used for the presentation, it does not take into account the research work carried out in the last decade on model-based approaches for user interfaces: for example, the language provides no notion of task, it mainly aims to define an abstract structure. The W3C consortium has recently delivered the first version of a new standard (XForms) that presents a description of the architecture, concepts, processing model, and terminology underlying the next generation of Web forms, based on the separation between the purpose and the presentation of a form. If it shows the importance of separating conceptual design from concrete presentation, it also highlights the need for meaningful models to support such approaches.

More generally, the issue of applying model-based techniques to the development of UIs for mobile computers has been addressed at a conceptual and research level [3, 4], but there are still many issues that should be solved to identify systematic, general solutions that can be supported by automatic tools. Our approach aims to support design and development of nomadic applications providing general solutions that can be tailored to specific cases, whereas current practise is still to develop *ad hoc* solutions with few concepts that can be reused in different contexts.

3. THE PROPOSED METHOD

The design of multi-platform applications can follow different approaches. It is possible to support the same type of tasks with different devices by changing the set of interaction and presentation techniques taking into account the resources available in the device considered. Another, more promising option is to consider different devices also with regard to the choice of the tasks to support (e.g. phones more suitable for quick access to limited information, desktop systems more suitable for browsing through large amounts of information). To complicate matters, even within the same class of devices there are different presentation models that need to be handled: for example, in WAP-enabled phones a number of micro-browsers tend to accept slightly different versions of WML, must interact with slightly different phones (for examples, phones with a different number of softkeys) and interpret the softkey interactions differently.

Our method tries to address such problems, and is composed of a number of steps that allows designers to start with an overall envisioned task model of a nomadic application and then derive concrete and effective user interfaces for multiple devices:

- *High-level task modelling of a multi-context application.* In this phase designers need to think about the logical activities that have to be supported and relationships among them. They develop a single model that addresses the various possible contexts of use and the various roles involved and also a domain model aiming to identify all the objects that have to be manipulated to perform tasks and the relationships among such objects.
- *Developing the system task model for the different platforms considered.* Here designers have to filter the task model according to the target platform. This involves creating task models in which the tasks that cannot be supported in a given platform are removed and the navigational tasks deemed necessary to interact with the considered platform are added. Thus, we obtain the system task model for the platform considered. Such models are specified using the ConcurTaskTrees notation. The CTTE (CTT Environment) tool (publicly available at http://giove.cnuce.cnr.it/ctte.html) supports editing and analysis of task models specified using this notation.

- *From system task model to abstract user interface.* Here the goal is to obtain an abstract description of the user interface composed of a set of abstract presentations that are identified with the support of the enabled task sets and structured by means of various operators. Then, still with the help of the task model, we identify the possible transitions among the user interface presentations considering the temporal relationships that the task model indicates.
- *User interface generation.* In this phase we have the generation of the user interface. This phase is completely platform-dependent and has to consider the specific properties of the target device. For example, if the considered device is a cellular phone, such information is not sufficient as we also need to know the type of micro-browser supported and the number and the types of soft-keys available.

In the following sections we better explain such steps while showing their application to a specific example.

We have defined XML versions of the language for task modelling (ConcurTaskTrees), enabled task sets and the language for modelling abstract interfaces and started development of the transformations among these representations.

4. MODEL-BASED DESIGN

Various models have been proposed to highlight important aspects in the design of user interfaces [5, 9, 12, 13, 15]. In our method we focus on models that can support development of user interfaces while preserving usability, in particular task models specifying the different activities that are supposed to be performed in an interactive system. Task models should be developed involving users so as to represent how they prefer to perform activities. By analysing the temporal relationships of a task model, it is possible to identify the sets of tasks that are enabled over the same period of time according to the constraints indicated in the model (*enabled task sets*). Thus, the interaction techniques supporting the tasks belonging to the same enable task set are logically candidate to be part of the same presentation though this criteria should not be interpreted too rigidly in order to avoid too modal user interfaces.

In addition, several criteria can be considered to derive concrete user interfaces from task models. Examples of such criteria are:

- The logical decomposition of tasks can be reflected in the presentation by explicitly grouping interaction techniques associated with tasks that share the same parent task.

- Sequential tasks can be supported in various modalities: for example with separate presentations for each task rendered at different time, or with all the interaction techniques corresponding to the sequential tasks rendered in the same presentation.
- The type of task, the type of objects manipulated and their cardinality are other useful elements. For example, for single choice among low cardinality values we can select a radio-button.
- Tasks that interrupt (or activate) other activities should be represented in the same manner (e.g.: buttons with specific graphical attributes) and located in the same part of the layout (e.g.: the right bottom part of the screen) for consistency.

5. THE EXAMPLE AND ITS TASK MODEL

The example considered is about the design of a nomadic application for accessing museum information. A possible scenario is a user who comes across the museum while surfing the web at home. S/he accesses the web site and starts to look at the information contained and afterwards s/he proposes to some friends a visit to the Marble Museum. As they seem to be a bit reluctant, s/he accesses the WAP server trying to convince them by showing some more concrete element of what the museum offers. Finally, they decide to have a visit, so they access again the WAP server to check its location and schedule. When they arrive at the museum, they receive a guide implemented in PDA that provides audio-visual support for their visit.

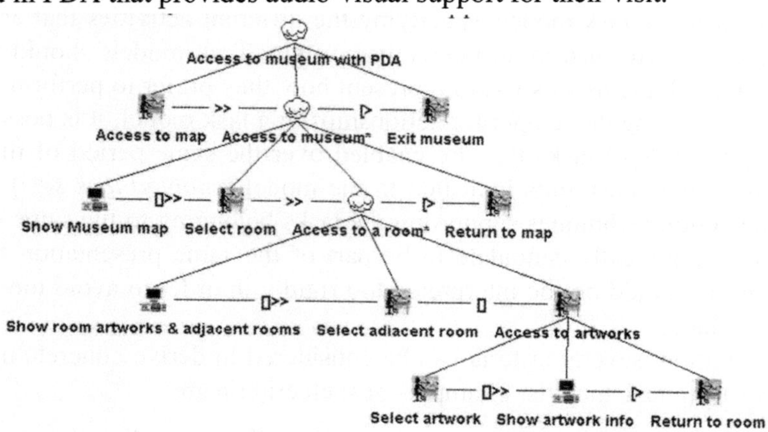

Figure 1. Part of the system task model for the PDA access.

For space reasons we provide only part of the system task model for the PDA (Fig. 1). Users can access the museum map (*Access to map*), and then (see the enabling CTT operator ">>"), after such map is displayed (*Show museum map*), they can select a room (*Select room*). When they select a room, the presentation shows the different types of artwork in the room, so as to allow visitors to locate them. After the visitor selects a specific artwork (*Select artwork*), depending on the selection (see the enabling with information passing operator "[]>>") the PDA delivers information about the artwork (*Show artwork info*), with the possibility of returning to the previous room. Further actions will be made available to the user: either return to the global map (*Return to map*) or exit the museum (*Exit museum*), both appearing at the right of a disabling operator ("[>").

6. FROM THE TASK MODEL TO THE ABSTRACT USER INTERFACE

Starting with the task model of the system, we aim to identify the specification of the abstract user interface in terms of its static structure (the "*presentation*" part) and dynamic behaviour (the "*dialogue*" part): such abstract specification will be used to drive the implementation.

6.1 The Presentation Part

The first step is to calculate the Enabled Task Sets (ETSs) according to the system task model. The CTTE tool automatically performs the identification of these sets. For the considered example, the ETSs are:
ETS1: {Access to map}
ETS2: {Show Museum map, Exit museum}
ETS3: {Select room, Exit museum}
ETS4: {Show room artworks&adjacent rooms,Return to map, Exit museum}
ETS5: {Select adjacent room, Select artwork, Return to map, Exit museum}
ETS6: {Show artwork info, Return to room, Return to map, Exit museum}

6.1.1 Heuristics for Obtaining a Lower Number of Task Sets

Once ETSs have been defined, we need to specify some rules to reduce their number by merging two or more ETSs into new sets, called *Task Set* or TS (as the union of several ETSs is no longer an ETS). The reasons (and the aims) to do such step are various: first of all, reducing the initial number of ETSs which —as we previously noted— in some cases can be very high; secondly, keeping and highlighting in the same presentation significant information (as a data exchange is) even when the involved tasks belong to different ETSs; lastly, avoiding repeatedly considering groups of tasks which all share a similar structure. Up to now, the heuristics that have been identified are the following:

- *H1*: If two (or more) ETSs differ for only one element, and those elements are at the same level connected with an enabling operator, they could be joined together with the Ordering operator.
- *H2*: If an ETS is composed of just one element, it should be joined with another ETS that shares some semantic feature.
- *H3*: If some ETSs share most elements, they could be unified. For example if the common elements all appear at the right of the disabling operator, they could be joined in only one TS.
- *H4*: If there is an exchange of information between two tasks, they can be put in the same TS in order to highlight such data transfer.

For example, ETS2 and ETS3 differ by only one element: applying H1 they could be unified into *TS1={Show museum map, Select room, Exit Museum}*. Also, ETS4 and ETS5 share most elements: H3 can be applied to obtain *TS2={Select adjacent room, Select artwork, Show Room Artworks & Adjacent Rooms, Return to map, Exit museum}*.

6.1.2 From TSs to Abstract Presentations

The set of TSs obtained is the initial input for building the abstract user interface specification which will be composed of interactors [10] (abstract interaction objects) associated with the basic tasks. Such interactors are high-level interaction objects that strongly depend on the particular corresponding task type. For simplicity now we focus only on a subset of the operators that have been identified taking into account criteria typically considered by user interface designers [6], namely:

- ***Grouping (G)**:* the idea is to group together two or more elements, so this operator should be applied when the involved tasks share some characteristics. A typical situation is when the tasks have the same parent (they are activities needed to perform a high level task).
- ***Ordering (O)*** operator: it is applied when some kind of order exists amongst elements. The more intuitive one is the temporal order.
- The ***Relation (R)*** operator should be applied when a relation exists between n elements y_i, i=1,…, n and one element *x*. Referring to the task model, a typical situation is when we have a leaf task *t* at the right side of a disabling operator: all the tasks that could be disabled by t (at whatever task tree level) are in relation with *t*.

Now we have to map each task of the task set into a suitable interactor and build a presentation structure that reflects the different relationships between such interactors by using the operators, whose applicability depends on the different temporal relationships specified in the task model. In order to derive the presentation structure associated to the specific task set and deduce the operators that should be applied to them, we have to consider the part of the task model regarding the tasks belonging to a specific task set. In this process we have to consider that temporal relationships existing between tasks are inherited also by their subtasks. For example, the presentation structure obtained for TS2 is:

O (*Show Room Artworks & Adiacent Rooms*, **G** (*Select adjacent room, Select artwork*)) **R** *Return to map* **R** *Exit museum*

This is because the Ordering operator highlights the information transfer (specified by the []>> operator) between the *Show Room Artworks & Adiacent Rooms* and both *Select adjacent room* and *Select artwork* tasks (which are grouped together because of the choice "[]" operator). Each task is in turn in relation with *Return to map* and *Exit museum* because they both appear at the right of a disabling operator ([>). In the same way we can identify the abstract presentation associated to TS1 which is: **O**(*Show museum map, Select room*) **R** *Exit Museum*

In addition, we have to map each task into a suitable interactor, by considering relevant dimensions specified in the task model. For example with regard to a *selection* task (as *Select adjacent room* task) we identify the *type of selection* (single/multiple), the *type* of manipulated objects (boolean/quantitative/text, etc) and the *cardinality* (low/medium/high) of the dataset from which the selection should be performed, as relevant dimensions. Once such attributes have been identified, we define some rules to indicate in which case a widget is more appropriate than another one depending on the different values that each attribute assumes and on the specific platform and/or device considered. For example, as the *Select adjacent room* task is single selection task managing spatial information and the set of manipulated objects has a low cardinality, the interaction technique to be provided must allow a choice of elements by providing an interactive map.

6.1.3 The Dialogue Part

Once the *static* arrangement of the abstract user interface is identified, we have to specify its *dynamic* behaviour. To this aim, an important role is played by the so-called *transition tasks*. For each task set T, we define *transition tasks(T)* the tasks whose execution makes the abstract user interface pass from the current task set T into another task set T'. For each task set T, a set of rules (*transition_task, next_TS*) should be provided whose meaning is: when *transition_task* is executed, the abstract user interface passes from T to *next_TS*. For example, TS1 has two transition tasks: *Select Room* and the task *Exit Museum*. To express that via the transition task *Select room* the abstract interface passes from TS1 to TS2 we can use the following rule:

<task_set **TS1** */task_set><behaviour><rule>*
<transition_task **Select room** */transition_task>* *<next_TS* **TS2** */next_TS>*
</rule></behavior>

6.2 From the Abstract User Interface to its Implementation

Once the elements of the abstract user interface have been identified, every interactor has to be mapped into interaction techniques supported by the particular device configuration considered (operating system, toolkit, etc.), and also the abstract operators have to be appropriately implemented by highlighting their logical meaning: a typical example is the set of techniques for conveying grouping relationships in visual interfaces by using presentation patterns like proximity, similarity and continuity [6]. A possible implementation for the presentation corresponding to TS2 is shown in Fig. 2, supposed that the current room is about Roman Archaeology.

Figure 2. One presentation of the PDA user interface.

With the suggested scenario it is possible to show how the same task can be supported differently depending on the platform used. Consider accessing the artworks list grouped by the material used: in the desktop application this task could be supported by buttons whose colour is similar to the material used and a long textual introduction to the section is presented too (right part of Fig. 3). However, this solution cannot be implemented in the WAP interface (left part of Fig. 3) as it does not support colours and there is no room for buttons and long texts, so a list of links is used in this platform.

Fig. 4 shows another example of different presentation of some visual information between a desktop system and a WAP phone: as you can see from the bottom part of the picture, while in the desktop system it is possible to have details of the work (title, type, description, author, material, and date of creation), in the WAP interface we can have only low resolution images allowing to have just a rough idea of what the work of art is, together with the indication of the title and the related museum section.

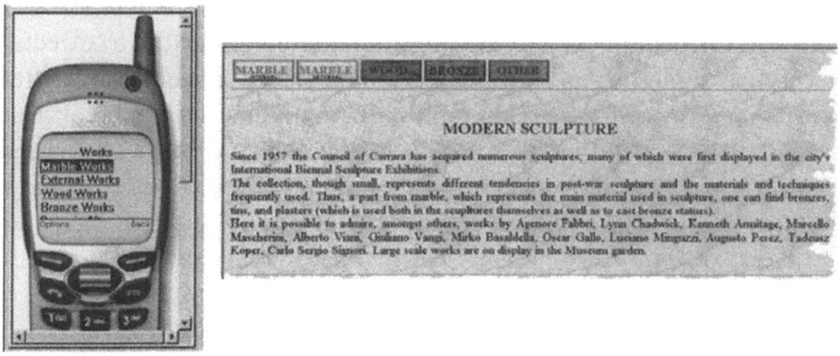

Figure 3. An example of different support for the selection task.

The top part of Fig. 4 shows how in the CTTE tool it is possible to specify for each task that each platform (PDA, desktop system, cellphone or other platforms) can support different sets of objects manipulated during the task performance. For example, for the "*Show artwork info*" task considered in the picture, the designer has specified that the title is available on all the platforms considered (all the checkboxes labelled "*PDA*", "*Desktop*", and "*Cellphone*" have been selected), whereas the description is available only for the desktop system.

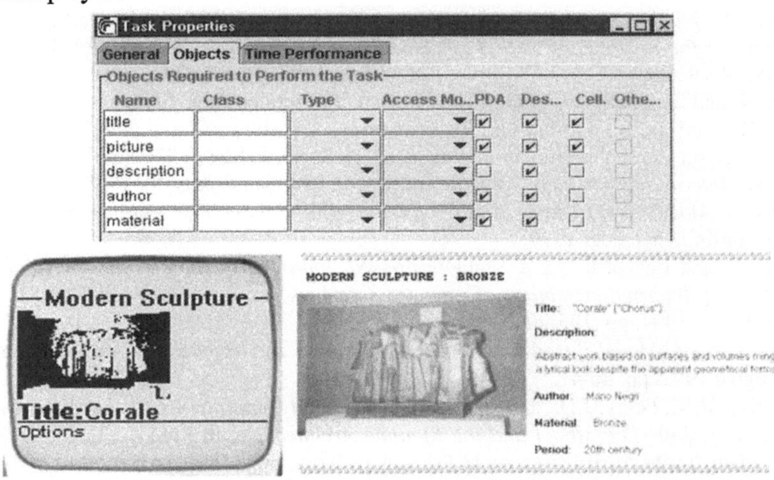

Figure 4. Example of different presentations of a work of art.
Figure 4. Example of different presentations of a work of art.

This information has been used to generate different user interfaces for the cellular phone and the desktop system: Fig. 4 shows that the title is available on both the platforms whereas the description is available only for the desktop system.

7. CONCLUSIONS

In this paper we have described a method for designing multi-device, nomadic applications starting from their task model and using a number of abstractions in the design cycle to obtain final applications able to effectively support the users' activities through various devices accessed in different contexts. The application of the method helps maintain a high-level of consistency across the multiple user interfaces developed. As the tool support in the user interface generation phase is still limited, future work is planned to extend it and create a complete semi-automatic environment implementing the presented method.

REFERENCES

[1] Abrams, M., Phanouriou, C., Batongbacal, A., Williams, S., and Shuster, J., *UIML: An Appliance-Independent XML User Interface Language*, in Proc. of WWW'8 (Toronto, May 1999).

[2] Beyer, H. and Holtzblatt, K., *Contextual Design: Defining Customer Centred Systems*, Morgan Kaufman, San Francisco, 1998.

[3] Einsenstein, J., Vanderdonckt, J., and Puerta, A., *Applying Model-Based Techniques to the Development of UIs for Mobile Computers*, in Proceedings of ACM Conference on Intelligent User Interfaces IUI'2001, ACM Press, New York, 2001, pp. 69-76.

[4] Calvary, G., Coutaz, J., and Thevenin, D., *A Unifying Reference Framework for the Development of Plastic User Interfaces*, Proc. of EHCI'2001, Springer-Verlag, 2001.

[5] Johnson, P., Wilson, S., Markopoulos, P., and Pycok, J., *ADEPT - Advanced Design Environment for Prototyping with Task Models*, in Proceedings of InterCHI'93 (Amsterdam, 24-29 April 1993), ACM Press, New York, 1993, pp. 56-57.

[6] Mullet, K. and Sano, D., *Designing Visual Interfaces*, Prentice Hall, 1995.

[7] Myers, B., Hudson, S., and Pausch, R., *Past, Present, Future of User Interface Tools*, ACM Trans. on Computer-Human Interaction, Vol. 7, No. 1, March 2000, pp. 3-28.

[8] Olsen, D., *Interacting in Chaos*, Keynote address, IUI'98, San Francisco, 1998.

[9] Paternò, F., *Model-based Design and Evaluation of Interactive Applications*, Springer-Verlag, Berlin, November 1999.

[10] Paternò, F. and Leonardi, A., *A Semantics-based Approach to the Design and Implementation of Interaction Objects*, Computer Graphics Forum, Blackwell Publisher, Vol.13, No. 3, 1994, pp. 195-204.

[11] Puerta, A.R., *A Model-Based Interface Development Environment*, IEEE Software, July/August 1997, pp. 40-47.

[12] Sukaviriya, P.N., Foley, J.D., and Griffith, T., *A Second Generation User Interface Design Environment: The Model and the Runtime Architecture*, in Proc. of InterCHI'93 (Amsterdam, 24-29 April 1993), ACM Press, New York, pp. 375-382.

[13] Szekely, P., Luo, P., and Neches, R., *Beyond interface builders: Model-based interface tools*, in Proceedings of InterCHI'93, ACM Press, New York, 1993, pp. 383-390.

[14] Thevenin, D. and Coutaz, J., *Plasticity of User Interfaces: Framework and Research Agenda*, in A. Sasse and C. Johnson (eds.), Proc. of Interact'99 (Edinburgh, August 1999), IOS Press Publ., 1999, pp. 110-117.

[15] Vanderdonckt, J. and Bodart, F., *Encapsulating Knowledge For Intelligent Automatic Interaction Objects Selection*, in Proc. of InterCHI'93 (Amsterdam, 24-29 April 1993), ACM Press, New York, 1993, pp. 424-429.

Chapter 14

COMBINING HANDCRAFTING AND AUTOMATIC GENERATION OF USER-INTERFACES FOR PERVASIVE DEVICES

Lawrence Bergman, Guruduth Banavar, Danny Soroker, and Jeremy Sussman
IBM T.J. Watson Research Center, 30 Saw Mill River Rd
Hawthorne, NY 10532 (USA)
E-mail: {bergmanl, banavar, soroker, jsussman}@us.ibm.com
URL: http://www.research.ibm.com/PIMA/
Tel.: +1-914-784-7946 – Fax: +1-914-784-7455

Abstract Application development for multiple pervasive devices requires a methodology that requires less development and management effort than simply rewriting the application for each device. We describe an approach that combines the advantages of automated generation from a single model-based UI description, with handcrafting of interfaces for specific devices. We discuss the infrastructure required to support a hybrid automated generation and handcrafting system, with particular attention to the issues that arise during application evolution.

Keywords: Application adaptation, Model-based UI, Pervasive application development.

1. THE PROBLEM

Today's world of rapidly proliferating computing devices, particularly mobile devices such as cellular phones and hand-helds, poses new challenges for the application developer. No longer can a developer custom-build an application for a single desktop device- carefully tuning layout for that device. In developing pervasive applications intended to run across a range of devices, the designer must be concerned with wide variation in a number of factors including screen size, interface objects such as hard-buttons, and computing resources, including connectivity.

C. Kolski and J. Vanderdonckt (eds.), Computer-Aided Design of User Interfaces III, 155–166.
© 2002 *Kluwer Academic Publishers.*

Multiple specification – developing one specification per platform – is today's commonly employed approach to pervasive application development. The application interface may simply be rewritten for each device, for example, using Java Server Pages [4]. Another approach is to transform a declarative representation of either data or interaction into concrete presentations, for example, using HTML with XSLT [20]. Both approaches require large development investments and management of a significant number of artifacts. An alternative is model-based UI design – a single specification that can be used to automatically generate interfaces for any device. Although automatically generated interfaces may produce good results for selected devices, they typically do not have the visual appeal and usability of handcrafted interfaces.

Multiple specification and model-based UI's with automatic generation represent end-points on a continuum – from complete customization for each device type to single specification. In this paper we explore an intermediate strategy – automated generation of application interfaces from a high-level semantic description, combined with an override facility that allows for tailoring the interface to specific devices. This strategy is a compromise between the desire to reduce and manage complexity by dealing with a single specification – what we call "write once, right anywhere" – and the commonly recognized fact that automated systems rarely produce perfect interfaces. We seek a hybrid approach that minimizes development time, while giving the developer as much control over the appearance of the final application as desired.

In this paper we present a very brief overview of the model-based approach to user-interface specification we employ, and how it is used to automatically generate presentations for a variety of platforms. We then focus on support for handcrafting these interfaces for individual platforms, a process we call *tweaking*. In addition to describing tooling and infrastructure to support tweaking, we discuss issues associated with maintaining a set of associated presentations, both automatically generated and manually tweaked, as an application evolves through iterative development.

2. A SEMI-AUTOMATED APPROACH

Our architecture, called PIMA (Platform Independent Model for Applications) focuses on the user-interface design, including accompanying interface logic. We assume that application logic is encapsulated as a set of *services* (EJB's or CORBA objects, for example) that are invoked from a PIMA application. The services may reside on the presentation device or may be accessed via a network; issues of service access and location are beyond the scope of this paper.

Fig. 1 gives a high-level overview of our application design process. The designer of a PIMA application creates a device-independent *generic application model.* This model consists of interactors, which are abstract interface widgets; dialogs, used to group interactors, transitions between dialogs (navigation), and event-handlers.

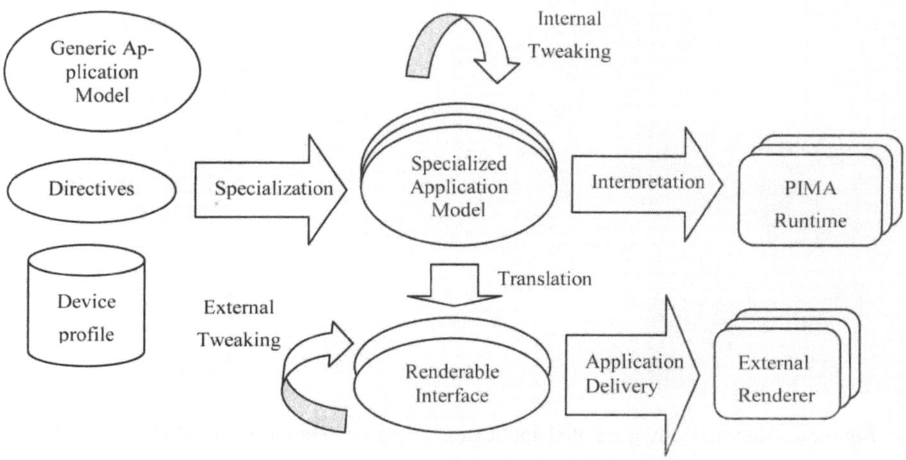

Figure 1. PIMA application development architecture.

Specialization is the automated process of converting the generic application model into multiple device-specific representations (called *specialized application models*), each consisting of concrete pages, page transitions, and additional information (such as layout) about the interactors in the generic application model. Our specialization algorithm performs page splitting – assigning interactors to pages; automated navigation generation – creating interface widgets to permit navigation between the generated pages; and page layout. One of the inputs to the specialization process is a set of directives to guide the process. These directives provide page splitting hints, navigation pattern hints, and device-independent layout hints for graphical devices including alignment, sizing constraints and page-splitting hints. A specialized application model can either be translated into a renderable interface such as Java Server Pages producing a presentation markup, e.g., HTML or WML, or it can be interpreted directly by a PIMA runtime such as a servlet.

Fig. 2 shows a portion of an automatically generated online ordering application rendered on three different platforms. Each of these interfaces was produced via specialization from a single generic application model, specified using the PIMA workbench. On the left is a Java version, rendered using the PIMA fat-client runtime. In the middle is an HTML rendering. On the right are shown three separate screens that represent the same portion of the application rendered on a WAP phone (WML).

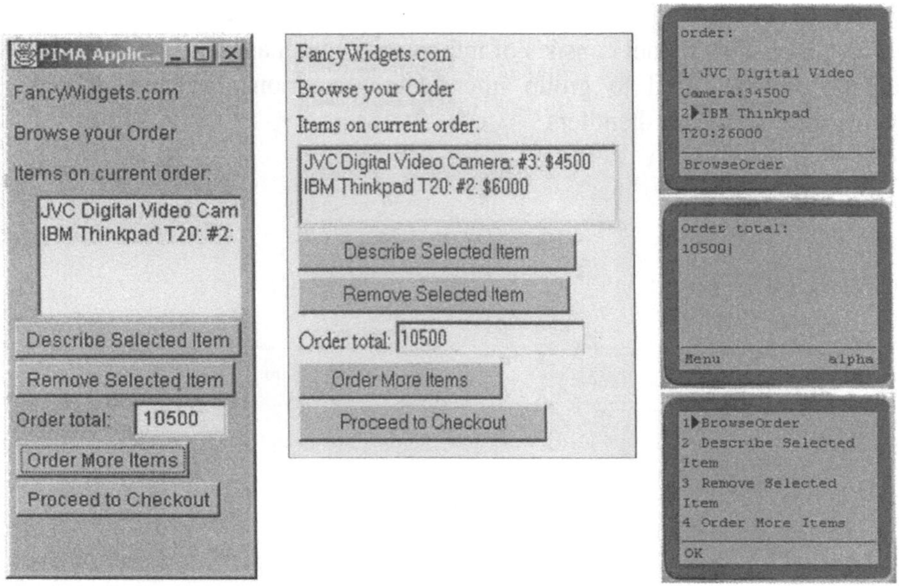

Figure 2. Automatically generated application pages rendered in Java, HTML, and WML.

The device-specific specialized application model created by the specialization algorithm is typically quite usable, but may not be completely visually satisfying in some cases. The specialized model can be hand-tailored through tweaking. This can involve adding additional material such as logos, images, or text; altering the appearance of interface elements; rearranging elements; or removing elements. Tweaking can be performed internally on the specialized application model (within the PIMA development environment) or externally on the renderable interface, using a device/language-specific editor. The infrastructure and implications for application evolution are different for the two approaches; both are discussed in a later section.

Fig. 3 shows an example of tweaking. On the left we have the automatically generated HTML interface. On the right we have a version of the same interface, after the page has been externally tweaked using an HTML editor. Note that the background has been changed, an image added, font styles changed, and widget sizes and positions (e.g., centering) specified.

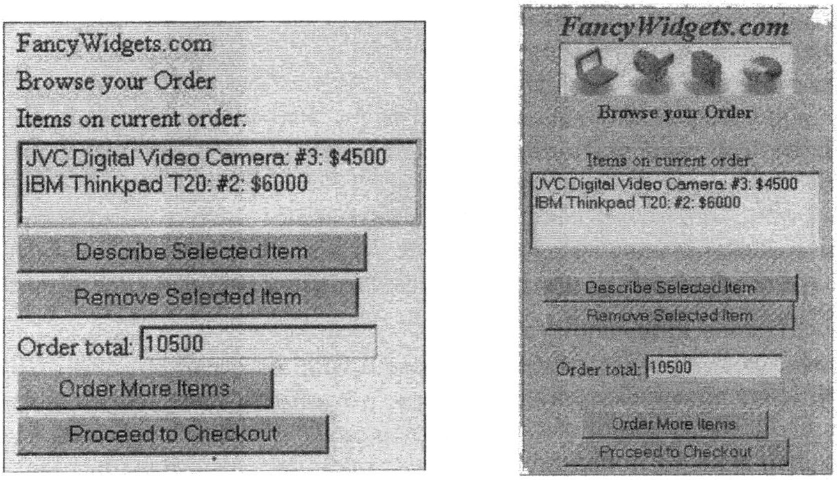

Figure 3. Automatically generated and tweaked versions of an HTML page.

3. THE HANDCRAFTING PROCESS

We provide two different mechanisms for tweaking an interface – either internally within the PIMA developer's workbench, or externally using a native editor. We will discuss each of these in turn, describing the interface provided to the designer, and the internal mechanisms for managing information about the tweaks.

Internal tweaking (Fig. 1) is performed directly within the workbench. The developer is presented with views of the application on specific devices, as well as a set of controls for altering the representation. We generate views either by invoking emulators, or by *greeking* the interface. A greeked view [2] is a simplified, stylized representation of the interface. This allows the developer to tweak the application for devices for which no emulator is available, an important facility in light of the rapid development of new devices and the difficulty of managing multiple third-party emulators.

The developer tweaks the application by changing the properties of individual interactors, or the relationships between interactors. There are several possible types of tweaks:

1. Overriding the default value of an interactor property. Properties include sizing, positioning information, and appearance such as font or color.
2. Removing an interactor from the application. This allows the designer to reduce the functionality, or streamline the appearance of an application for particular devices

3. Adding an interactor to the application. Note that only appearance elements (e.g., text and images) can be added to an application, since any other type would result in a change to the application semantics.
4. Reordering interactors. The order of interactors within a dialog is used by the specialization engine to layout pages. Part of the tweaking process can involve moving interactors, resulting in changes in this ordering.
5. Changing page-splitting assignments. The specialization algorithm determines the assignment of widgets (instantiated interactors) to pages for each output device. The designer may wish to manually adjust these assignments, moving widgets between existing pages, or creating new pages.

The various types of tweaks are stored within the particular specialized application model that is affected. Property overrides (item 1) are stored with the interactor to which they apply. Each interactor within the specialized application model has a vector of property overrides. Any properties that are not contained in that vector retain the value specified in the generic application model.

The other types of tweaks are easily retained by simply adding, moving, or removing elements within the specialized application model. The specialized application model stores a set of pages, each containing a set of interactors to be rendered on the device. Pages can be simply added and removed as needed, as can any interactors that have been added, moved, or removed.

External tweaking (Fig. 1) is accomplished by creating pages in the markup language required by the external editor (i.e., the language used for rendering the final application). These could be, for example, HTML pages. External tweaks are retained by storing the renderable interface (e.g., the HTML pages). At runtime, the PIMA engine checks to see if any given page has been translated from the internal representation into a renderable interface. If not, translation occurs on the fly. If it has, the stored page, which may have been tweaked, is delivered.

External tweaking has several advantages. First, the user is able to employ any editor with which he/she is comfortable. Second, it provides easy extensibility; there is no need to integrate new emulators into the PIMA development environment. Third, the developer can add additional content or appearance elements to individual pages. Background images, logos, descriptive text, and informational links can all be used to enhance the application without changes to the underlying generic model. Note that since there is an intermediate renderable interface between the specialized application model and the device, information that is not even representable within the PIMA generic application model can be added to a page.

4. TWEAKING AND EVOLUTION – ONGOING WORK

Although managing tweaks, as described above, is relatively straightforward, the picture becomes more complicated when changes are made to the underlying generic application model. Tweaks may no longer be applicable once the model that created them has changed. This is known as the software evolution or round trip problem.

The underlying problem is that any tweaking causes a divergence between the expected device specific representation corresponding to the generic application model and the tweaked representation. If the generic application model is changed subsequent to tweaking, conflicts may ensue between these two representations. Our goal is to merge generic application model changes and tweaked changes, but the conflicts make this difficult.

We attack this problem by dividing tweaking information into two types – those that affect only one interactor, which we call *local changes*; and those that affect sets of interactors, which we call *global changes*.

Local changes are changes to individual interactors that do not affect page layout. Only those property changes that do not affect an interactor's size or position can be considered local changes. For local changes, we adopt the policy that any tweaked properties are to be retained. This is implemented by keeping track of interactor properties that have been tweaked. The record-keeping and property updating is managed through the specialized application model in the case of internal tweaking – easily accomplished, since interactors in the specialized application model contain pointers to the interactors in the generic application model from which they are derived. For externally tweaked pages, we store Xpath expressions [19] that point from the interactors in the generic application model to DOM elements on the generated page. This allows us to determine which properties have been tweaked by comparing the previous generated page's and the tweaked page's property values. When the model changes, we re-specialize the application and then apply these tweaks to the relevant widgets.

Global tweaks include all other types of changes: adding, moving, or deleting interactors, property changes that affect interactor size or position, and changes to page splitting. Each of these tweaks potentially affects more than the single interactor touched by affecting the layout of the page. The problem in this case is due to a lack of information about the semantics of the change – there is no basis on which to determine how updates are to be applied. Consider, for example, adding a text interactor with the contents, "Welcome to our site. We hope you find everything you need!" between the text "FancyWidgets.com" and "Browse your Order" for the application page shown in Fig. 3. For the untweaked page, shown on the left, this is no problem – the text is simply inserted. For the tweaked page on the right of Fig. 3, the outcome is less certain – text may be inserted above the image, or below it. The problem here is that the system has no way of knowing that the image inserted during tweaking should be associated with the text "FancyWidgets.com," and nothing should be inserted between them.

Resolving such ambiguities in the case of global changes requires additional feedback from the developer. We are currently developing update policies and a user-in-the-loop interface that will permit the designer to identify portions of an updated interface that have been handled incorrectly, and specify additional semantics to resolve ambiguities. This will be an iterative process. First, the user is presented with a specialized application automatically generated by the system – a "best guess" at how the tweaks and model changes should be merged. The developer evaluates the output from the specialization algorithm for that platform, and either provides additional semantic information for another cycle, or tweaks the resulting page to get what he/she wants.

The semantic information includes information about how tweaks are to be retained and updates incorporated. One possibility is for the designer to explicitly specify semantic information – in our example, that "FancyWidgets.com" and the image are to be grouped. Another possibility is to use inference to derive a semantic rule. When the designer indicates that the text, "Welcome to our site! ..." is out of place (perhaps by manually moving the text), the system might infer that the image added through tweaking and the "FancyWidgets.com" text are to be grouped. If more than one likely hypothesis can be inferred, the system could present the user with a set of choices.

Based on this additional input, the system can then generate a new specialization that performs the automated layout subject to constraints from previous tweaking and the newly provided semantic information. The newly generated pages can be the start of another round of iteration.

Note that the designer has complete control over how much information is specified: there is no required additional information. If no semantic information is provided, the designer may need to completely re-tweak pages each time the model is changed. As more semantic information is provided, the system is more and more likely to "get it right," reducing the need for additional handcrafting.

It is important to recall the goal here: minimizing development time and effort. Since handcrafting is supported, the automation within a hybrid system does not need to get the layout perfect. A system that simply throws away all tweaks whenever there is a change to the generic model will be unacceptable, since the tweaks may represent a large time investment. On the other hand, a system which can integrate model changes with previous tweaks to present an "almost right" interface requiring only a bit of additional tweaking may represent a big win over existing approaches.

5. RELATED WORK

The general concept of loosening the coupling between logic and presentation is well established, thanks to work on user interface management systems (UIMS) [7,8,11, and others]. Using this approach naively, however, still requires that the developer design separate user-interfaces for each platform type, something we have argued is impractical.

The main alternative today for multi-device authoring is that provided by XML & XSLT [20]. In this approach, the XML abstractly represents the data to be presented, and separate sets of XSLT rules represent the transformations needed to present that data on different devices. In our approach, we represent not only the data, but also the *user interaction* abstractly. We seek to automatically transform this abstract description into usable device-specific presentations. Furthermore, if the output is not satisfactory, we allow developers to specify the *end-result* directly, instead of specifying the *transformation rules* for getting there.

Model-based user interface systems [12, 13], allow interfaces to be specified by constructing a declarative model of how the interface should look and behave. The work described here is a model-based UI system whose design was driven specifically by the requirements of multi-device application development. In general, model-based systems pose a usability challenge, since they make it difficult for developers to maintain a mental model that connects an abstract interface specification with multiple concrete realizations of it. Previous work, such as Puerta and Eisenstein [10], has proposed techniques to help developers inspect and set the mapping of abstract interface elements to concrete elements. The MIMIC language [3] enables separate modeling of platform, presentation and task structure for multi-device authoring. In this methodology, the model is significantly abstracted away from the resultant device-specific application. Our work aims to give the developer more control over the automatically generated interface by allowing him to tweak the generated output to improve its presentation. In particular, our goal is to provide a model that is flexible enough to be suited for multi-platform authoring, but to be concrete enough so as to have a straightforward correspondence to resultant device-specific application. This has the dual advantage of providing a more familiar model to the application developer, and enabling better integration of tweaks in the abstract model.

There are several companies and consortia active in designing and standardizing an abstract representation for device-independent applications, such as XForms [18], Mobile Web Forms [6], MobileXML [9], and UIML [1]. The goal of the work presented here is not to propose yet another device-independent language. We focus on developing methodologies and tools for helping developers start from one of these languages and arriving at usable presentations on several device platforms.

Several approaches are known for dealing with the "round trip" problem of code evolution (e.g., [5]). The simple-minded approach of discarding tweaked information upon re-generation is typically unacceptable. One common approach for code builders (such as VisualCafe [15]) is to generate stylized comments (place holders) in the generated code. As long as the developer makes "structured" changes (i.e., within the "allowed places"), the tweaked code is unchanged upon re-generation. However, if an "unstructured" change is made, then it will likely be lost upon re-generation. A more integrated approach (such as that supported by Together ControlCenter [14]) is to keep the model and generated code continually synchronized. In other words, changes in the model are reflected in the generated code and vice versa. This approach is most effective when the developer make the changes and tweaks within the IDE. An additional approach [16], which applies to languages that support inheritance, is to have an object for each element of the model, and a corresponding subclassed object for each element of the presentation. Thus, changes to the model are made to the model objects, and tweaks are made to the corresponding presentation objects. This approach has been formalized in the "Generation Gap" pattern [17]. The approach we take is based on having the abstract level correspond fairly directly with the concrete (device-specific) level, and to involve the developer when the system needs assistance in reconciling changes in the different levels.

6. SUMMARY AND CONCLUSION

This paper describes an approach for writing an application once that can be run on many different device types. This approach includes an abstract programming model for device-independent applications, a specialization mechanism that automatically adapts the application to a variety of target devices, and a means for the application developer to override portions of the automatically generated interface for particular platforms. We also describe a system that we have implemented which follows this approach.

The main contribution of this work is a methodology for combining automatically generated interfaces with handcrafting for particular devices. The developer is not forced to rebuild the application for each deployment platform, nor are they forced to accept automatically generated interfaces that may work well for some platforms and poorly for others. Our approach gives the developer an automatically generated interface as a "reasonable" starting point and then, using tools within our development environment or external page editors, they can manually change properties of appearance elements on a platform-by-platform basis.

We contend that the benefit of this approach is timesavings in developing and maintaining applications, both through reducing the number of artifacts that are produced, and by providing a uniform development methodology for a wide diversity of device types. Validation of this claim will require user experience and user studies. We are currently in the process of designing studies that will help to determine whether the automated generation plus tweaking approach (a) produces interfaces that are comparable in quality to totally hand-built interfaces, (b) results in a faster and/or less painful development cycle. We are also developing methodologies for maintaining these hybrid interfaces as an application evolves.

REFERENCES

[1] Abrams, M., Phanouriou, C., Batongbacal, A., Williams, S., and Shuster, J., UIML: *An Appliance-Independent XML User Interface Language*, in Proceedings of the Eighth International World Wide Web Conference, May, 1999.

[2] Bergman, L.D., Kichkaylo, T., Banavar, G., and Sussman, J., *Pervasive Application Development and the WYSIWYG Pitfall*, in Proceedings of IFIP Conf. on Engineering the User Interface EHCI'2001 (Toronto, May 2001), Springer-Verlag, Berlin, pp. 203-217.

[3] Eisenstein, J., Vanderdonckt, J., and Puerta, A.R., *Adapting to Mobile Contexts with User-Interface Modeling*, in Proceedings of the 3rd IEEE Workshop on Mobile Computing Systems and Applications WMCSA'2000 (Monterey, December 7-8, 2000), IEEE Press, Los Alamitos, 2000, pp. 83-92.

[4] Accessible at http://java.sun.com/products/jsp/

[5] Medvivovic, N., Egyed, A., Rosenblum, D.S., *Round-Trip Software Engineering Using UML: From Architecture to Design and Back*, in Proceedings of the 2nd Workshop on Object-Oriented Reengineering WOOR'99 (Toulouse, 6 September 1999), pp. 1-8.

[6] Accessible at http://msdn.microsoft.com/vstudio/nextgen/technology/mobilewebforms.asp

[7] Myers, B., *Separating Application Code from Toolkits: Eliminating the Spaghetti of Call-Backs*, in Proceedings of the Fourth Annual ACM SIGGRAPH Symposium on User Interface Software and Technology UIST'91 (Hilton Head, 11-13 November 1991), ACM Press, New York, 1991, pp. 211-220.

[8] Olsen, D., *The Menu Interaction Kontrol Environment*, ACM Transactions on Graphics, Vol. 5, No. 1, 1986, pp. 318-344.

[9] Accessible at http://www.oracle.com/mobile/

[10] Puerta, A.R. and Eisenstein, J., *Towards a General Computational Framework for Model-Based Interface Development Systems Model-Based Interfaces*, in Proceedings of

the ACM Conference on Intelligent User Interfaces IUI'99 (Los Angeles, 5-8 January 1999), ACM Press, New York, 1999, pp. 171-178.

[11] Singh, G., Kok, C., and Ngan, T., *Druid: A System for Demonstrational Rapid User Interface Development*, in Proceedings of the Third Annual ACM Symposium on User Interface Software and Technology UIST'90 (Snowbird, 3-5 October 1990), ACM Press, New York, 1990, pp. 167-177.

[12] Sukaviriya, P.N., Foley, J.D., and Griffith, T., *A Second Generation User Interface Design Environment: The Model and the Runtime Architecture*, in Proceedings of ACM Conference on Human Factors in Computing Systems InterCHI'93 (Amsterdam, 24-29 April 1993), ACM Press, New York, 1993, 1993, pp. 375-382.

[13] Szekely, P., Luo, P., and Neches, R., *Beyond Interface Builders: Model-Based Interface Tools*, in Proceedings of ACM Conference on Human Factors in Computing Systems InterCHI'93 (Amsterdam, 24-29 April 1993), ACM Press, New York, 1993, pp. 383-390.

[14] Accessible at http://www.togethersoft.com/us/products/index.html

[15] Accessible at http://www.webgain.com/products/visual_cafe

[16] Vlissides, J.M. and Tang, S., *A Unidraw-based User Interface Builder*, in Proceedings of the Fourth Annual ACM Symposium on User Interface Software and Technology UIST'91 (Hilton Head, 11-13 November 1991), ACM Press, New York, 1991, pp. 201-210.

[17] Vlissides, J.M., *Pattern Hatching: Design Patterns Applied*, Addison Wesley, New York, 1998.

[18] Accessible at http://www.w3c.org/MarkUp/Forms/

[19] Accessible at http://www.w3.org/TR/xpath

[20] Accessible at http://www.w3.org/Style/XSL/

Chapter 15

CONCEPTS FOR GENERATING MULTI-USER INTERFACES INCLUDING GRAPHICAL EDITORS

Alfons Brandl

Institut für Informatik, Technische Universität München, Arcisstr. 21
D-80290 München (Germany)
E-mail: brandla@informatik.tu-muenchen.de - URL: http://www2.in.tum.de/persons/brandla
Tel: +49-89-289-28136 – Fax: +49-89-289-28180

Abstract In this paper concepts for generating multi-user interfaces including graphical editors will be discussed. These concepts are applied in the runtime architecture of multi-user interfaces generated automatically by the generator EMUGEN. The main contribution of this paper is the integrative application of the concepts which are mostly already established in computer science.

Keywords: Compiler construction, Model-based development, User interfaces, Workflow.

1. INTRODUCTION

With today's user interface development tools, the development of multi-user interfaces (MUI) still remains expensive. Therefore, we explore generative tools [7] for the model-based development [8] of MUIs. Our current prototype is called *EMUGEN*. *EMU* stands for *e*xpandable models of *m*ulti-*u*ser interfaces, *GEN* simply for *gen*erator.

A generative approach always needs an adequate abstraction. Our abstract view of a running MUI application consists of a set of users working with their user-adapted single user interfaces on one – generally very complex – data structure (the functional core). Such a scenario is formally specified by the data model, the task model, and the user model of EMUGEN (Fig. 1). Given these input models, EMUGEN generates automatically a

C. Kolski and J. Vanderdonckt (eds.), Computer-Aided Design of User Interfaces III, 167–178.

© 2002 *Kluwer Academic Publishers.*

MUI application. The generated user interfaces include forms and graphical editors provided with a default presentation.

Furthermore, EMUGEN provides an API (*Application Programming Interface*) for implementing additional aspects of MUI applications. These optional aspects include the interaction between the generated MUI and an associated DBMS or WFMS (database/workflow management system) and the adaptation of the default presentation of the data in the user interfaces according to specific requirements. The API is sketched as *Presentation* and *ExternalSys* in Fig. 1.

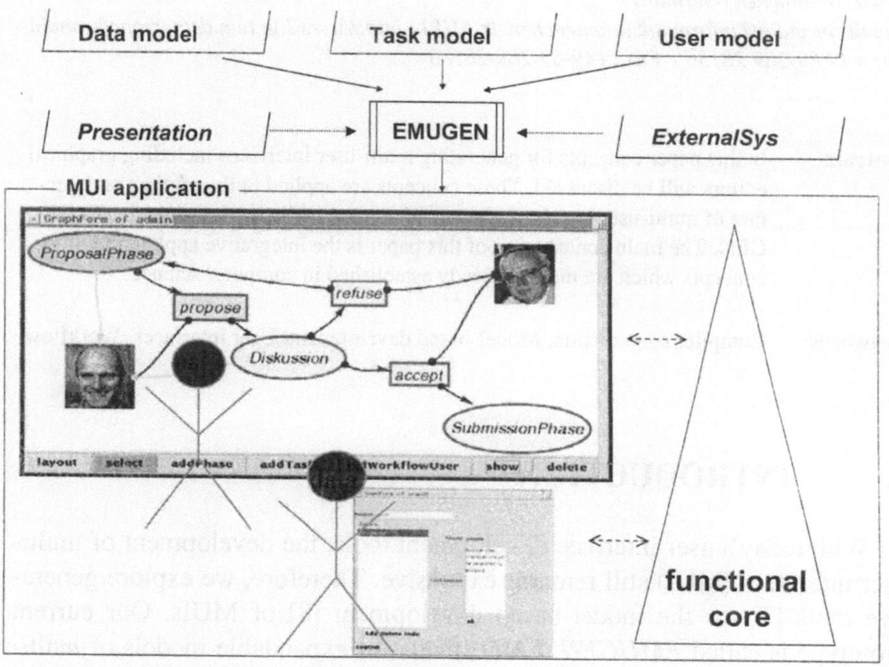

Figure 1. The overall architecture of EMUGEN.

Running examples of MUI applications generated with EMUGEN have already been given. The example *Ad-hoc Workflows* [1] shows the application of graphical editors for visually defining workflows at runtime (using the upper UI in Fig. 1). Here, the execution of the different tasks can be fulfilled by the assigned users via automatically generated forms (lower UI in Fig. 1). The example *Practical Course* [2] describes a MUI application managing the execution of a practical course with the collaboration of an arbitrary number of students and one supervisor.

The input specification (i.e. all input models together) of EMUGEN is rather compact. For instance, the input specification for the examples *Ad-hoc*

Workflows and *Practical Course* consists of no more than 200 and 70 lines, respectively.

In this paper, we try to give an impression of the underlying concepts applied in the runtime architecture of MUIs generated by EMUGEN. Some of the concepts are advanced compiler construction techniques and were already applied in the MB-UIDE BOSS [7].

Section 2 describes the general (i.e. not application-specific) requirements on MUI applications and their assignment to the different input models of EMUGEN. Subsequently, in section 3, the various concepts are discussed separately. The topic of section 4 is the integration of the different concepts in EMUGEN. Finally, we give some concluding remarks.

2. REQUIREMENTS

When using a MUI application, various users access common and private data. Using EMUGEN, the data is formally described by productions in the *data model*, and, at runtime, managed by the functional core (Fig. 1).

Additionally, the users may collaborate in performing complex tasks and execute atomic actions independently from each other. Using EMUGEN, these aspects are specified in the *task model*.

According to different rights, interests, or skills, the users may have different access to the data and actions managed by the functional core. The access is defined in the *user model* of EMUGEN. At runtime, the characteristics of the users are modelled by parts of the functional core and can be shown and edited via the user interfaces by the users (depending on their rights). Hence, CSCW-related aspects like the awareness of other users can also be specified. For instance, in the *Practical Course* example a participant sees all the other participants (more precisely, the data modelling them) in her form.

As already mentioned, the adaptation of the automatically generated presentation (e.g., selecting alternative interaction objects for editing the data) and the interaction with external systems can be fulfilled using an API.

The transformation of informally given requirements into the various input models of EMUGEN is described in [1,2]. There, a more detailed description of the modelling elements of the various models is given as well.

3. CONCEPTS

3.1 Model-View-Controller

The scenario in Fig. 1 shows two users working on the functional core of a MUI application using a graphical editor and a form, respectively. Such an architecture is obviously an application of the classical *Model-View-Controller*-paradigm (*MVC*) [6]. Both, the graphical editor and the form take the part of the *view/controller*-pair, and the functional core represents the *model*. When changing the functional core via the graphical editor the content visualized by the form is changed and vice versa.

A more detailed consideration of the example *Ad-hoc Workflows* (Fig. 1) shows that the user working on the graphical editor takes the role of the workflow administrator responsible for defining and monitoring the workflow execution. The user working on the form does not see the entire workflow execution, but only the tasks (more precisely, the interaction objects necessary to fulfil the tasks) assigned to him.

To facilitate such different kinds of access in multi-user systems, DBMSs support the description of access rights based on a role concept.

In order to allow the same possibilities when specifying a MUI application using EMUGEN, the properties of the users are formally described in the task model similarly to the usage of the role concept of a DBMS. For instance, in the *Practical Course* example there is a role *Participant* describing all users who are participants of the course.

For managing the access of the particular users during runtime, again the MVC-paradigm is applied, but now on a more abstract level. Here, the *view* and *controller* part of a single user interface consists of exactly those parts of the functional core which are readable (*view*) and writeable (*controller*), respectively, for the particular user at the current state. The functional core itself can be regarded as the *model* part of the MVC-paradigm.

3.2 HIT-instances

HIT-instances (HIT stands for *hierarchical interaction templates*) are the runtime models of user interfaces generated by BOSS [7]. Formally, a HIT-instance is a dynamic attributed tree which can also used as attributed syntax tree during a compilation process. Roughly spoken, the syntax tree together with some of the attributes correspond to the *model* of the MVC-paradigm, whereas a special synthesized layout attribute (more exactly, the value of its occurrence at the root of the tree) forms a (usually rather complex) interaction object and can be regarded as the *view/controller*-pair of MVC.

We want to emphasise two of the most important characteristics of HIT-instances. Firstly, a HIT-instance can dynamically change its structure upon user interaction, and as a consequence, the value of the layout attribute is recalculated according to the new structure. Secondly, this usually rather complex calculation need not be implemented by the developer by hand. It can be generated automatically from a formal description of a layout model using advanced techniques of compiler construction [7].

In the following, we regard the example *Ad-hoc Workflows* where the tasks are defined at runtime by the workflow administrator. Here, the functional core changes its structure (e.g. when the workflow administrator inserts or deletes tasks), and at least some of the various single user interfaces of the particular users have to change their visualized contents. For instance, when a new task is defined and assigned to user A, the user interface of A has to visualize the interaction objects necessary for performing the task.

In order to generate interactive systems fulfilling such requirements, an extended form of HIT-instances can be used for recalculating the user interfaces of the different users when the functional core is changed. Here, the access rights of the various users defined in the task model must be taken into account when performing the recalculation of the user interfaces.

In Fig. 2 the example *Ad-hoc Workflows* (more precisely, one state during an execution) is shown in more detail (but not complete). The circles represent the nodes of the extended HIT-instance (i.e. the nodes of the functional core), and the rectangles sketch the layout attributes. The concrete user interfaces (more precisely, their contents) are calculated as synthesized attributes [7]. The forms of the "team members" show the tasks assigned to them. The graphical editor of the workflow administrator (attribute at the root) visualizes the workflow execution.

The extension of the HIT-instances sketched in Fig. 2 includes the usage of one form layout attribute for each user and the usage of a graph as the possible value of a layout attribute. In fact, the set of users in EMUGEN may change at runtime, and therefore there is an arbitrary number of layout attributes necessary for managing a MUI application.

3.3 Adapter Pattern

For integrating the different requirements on MUI applications in a runtime architecture, further design patterns [4] (besides MVC) are applied. One of the most important patterns for the runtime architecture of MUI applications generated by EMUGEN is the *adapter pattern* [4].

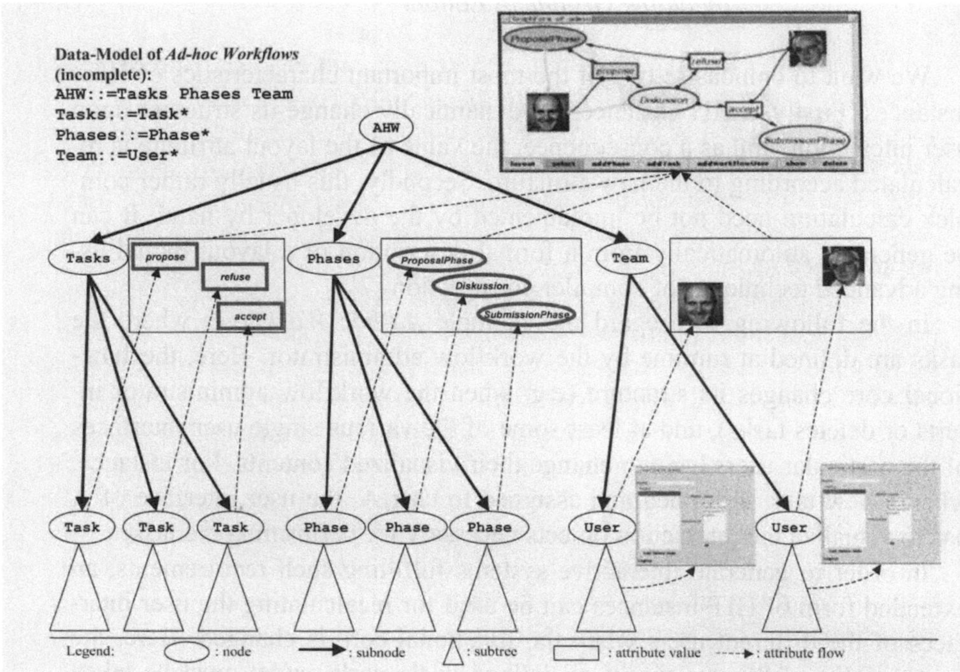

Figure 2. One state during the execution of the MUI application *Ad-hoc Workflows.*

The adapter pattern facilitates the communication of components (we use the term *component* instead of *object* because we use the pattern on a more abstract level) which cannot communicate via a common interface.

Theoretically it would be possible to generate components which communicate via a common interface. But for implementing a relatively complex generator like EMUGEN it is useful to apply different sub-generators e.g. FORMGEN [3] for **gen**erating **form**s and GRACE [5] for **g**enerating **gra**phical **e**ditors. Both generate single user interfaces which again follow the MVC-paradigm but do not use a common interface. Further, looking at the technical details, the graph model of graphical editors generated by GRACE includes attributes (e.g. the set of input edges assigned to a node) which are not necessary for the form model of a form generated by FORMGEN.

Hence, adapters are used as graph and form models enriching the visualized parts of the functional core with the attributes necessary for the models of the specific user interface. These adapters are called *graph adapter* and *form adapter*. For instance, a graph adapter manages the set of input edges assigned to each node visualized by the graph editor. In order to fully understand this approach a knowledge about the usage of the adapter pattern [4] is necessary.

The user interface of a user of a MUI application only show (according to user's current access rights) parts of the functional core. Since the user's access rights may change during runtime a flexible mechanism has to be used for managing the access. For that task again the adapter pattern is applied by using so called *access adapters*. There is one access adapter for each user. Each access adapter consists of all nodes of the functional core which are accessible by the user in the current state.

3.4 Bootstrapping

One of the most powerful techniques originating from the field of compiler construction is *bootstrapping*. Once there is a compiler for compiling a program written in language A in executable code, it is possible to write an executable compiler in language A which can be compiled by the first compiler and be used itself afterwards. Then the compiler can be extended using the features of language A.

EMUGEN is powerful enough to apply the bootstrapping principle for extending its front-end. We consider the following requirements.

> *Until now, the input language of EMUGEN is textual. In the future a graphical way is desired for describing the user's access on the data objects of a MUI application depending on the user's properties and the phases of a workflow. The graphical syntax should be related to activity and use-case diagrams of UML [9].*

In [2] an example for a text-oriented specification of the user access is given. Developing a single user interface with EMUGEN fulfilling the requirements above, means using EMUGEN for extending its own input language as sketched in Fig. 3. Here, four steps are drawn in. In the first step (top left side) the construction of the graphical editor allowing the graphical specification of the **t**ask and **u**ser **m**odel (therefore we call it *TUM*) is shown.

In the second step a developer graphically models the task and the user model. The developer is the only user working on the *TUM* application. Currently, she models the *TUM* of the *Practical Course* example (Fig. 4). When finished, the developer triggers the construction of the textual specification by executing an appropriate action. In the third step, again EMUGEN is used. Now, the *Practical Course* application is generated.

In step 4, the *Practical Course* application is executed by several users collaborating on the functional core for performing a practical course (an execution of the example is discussed in [2]).

In the following, we describe the first step more detailed.

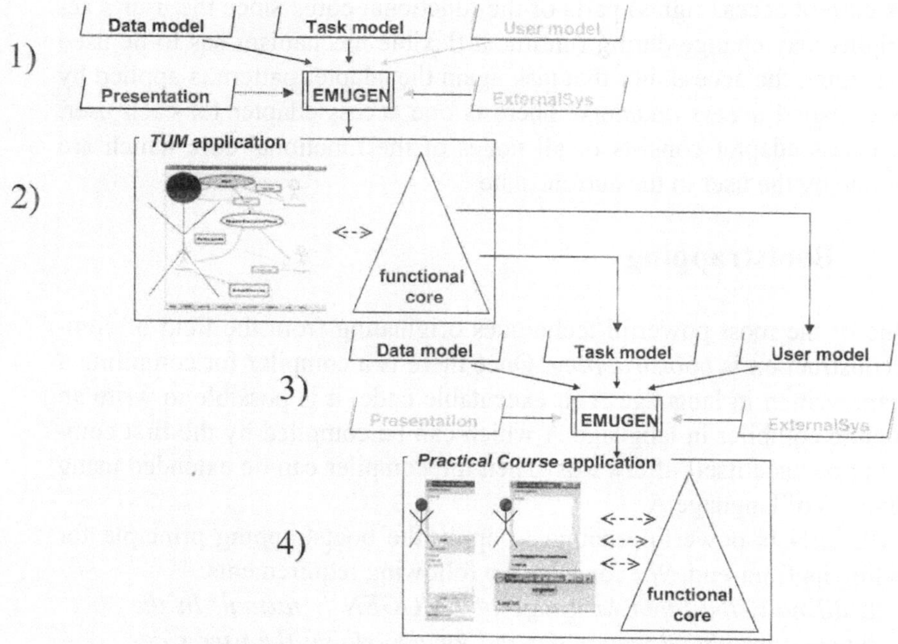

Figure 3. Bootstrapping the front-end of EMUGEN.

3.4.1 Generating the User Interface for TUM

Since *TUM* is a standalone application with a single user interface neither a user model nor an interface to external systems has to be given.

3.4.1.1 Data Model

In addition to well known data type productions of functional programming languages like tuples, variants, and lists, the data model of EMUGEN consists of an interactive reference concept which allows the end user to manipulate reference objects directly. Here are some of the productions forming the data model of *TUM*.

```
TUM::=Phase*:Phases Actor*:Actors
      DataObject*:DataObjects
      Transaction*:Transactions
Phase::=String:Name NextTransaction*
NextTransaction::=Name->Transaction
Actor::=String:Name Formula PhaseRef ReadAccess*
        WriteAccess* ExecAccess*
ReadAccess::=Name->DataObject
PhaseRef::=Name->Phase
..
```

The tuple TUM consists of lists for Phases, Actors, DataObjects and Transactions. Each Phase has a name and a list with element type NextTransaction. NextTransaction is a reference on Transactions using the Name of the Transaction as a handle for manipulating the reference value on the screen by the end user. Now, we consider the tuple Actor (this term is adopted from use-case diagrams [9]). Its Formula component allows the definition of users and their properties modelled by the actor. The PhaseRef component may associate Actor with a phase. If an actor is associated with a phase, the actor is only active if the phase is active as well. Further, each actor may have an arbitrary set of read, write and exec accesses to data objects and transactions, respectively.

3.4.1.2 Task Model

The task model of *TUM* consists just of one action for triggering the construction of the textual specification out of the current state of the functional core e.g. for constructing the MUI application on the lower right side as sketched in Fig. 3 out of the *TUM* shown in Fig. 4. For producing the textual specification we use the functional core of the *TUM* application as an abstract syntax tree as in the field of compiler construction.

3.4.1.3 Presentation

At runtime, the graphical editor shows the tuple objects of the functional core using graphical nodes and the reference values by graphical edges. It is possible to overwrite the default layout of the graphical nodes to generate a graphical editor allowing the definition of the graph shown in Fig. 4.

3.4.2 Working with the Graphical Editor for TUM

Fig. 4 shows the graphical editor for a *TUM* visualizing the MUI application *Practical Course*. During the start phase (as initial phase marked grey) the supervisor can start (black edge) the RegularExecutionPhase and read (grey edge) the list of the current participants. Students who are not already participants (NoParticipant) can register for the course. When the supervisor executes the start action, the RegularExecutionPhase is active. Now, participants can submit their solution and read the exercise given by the supervisor. Further, the list of all participants is readable for a participant.

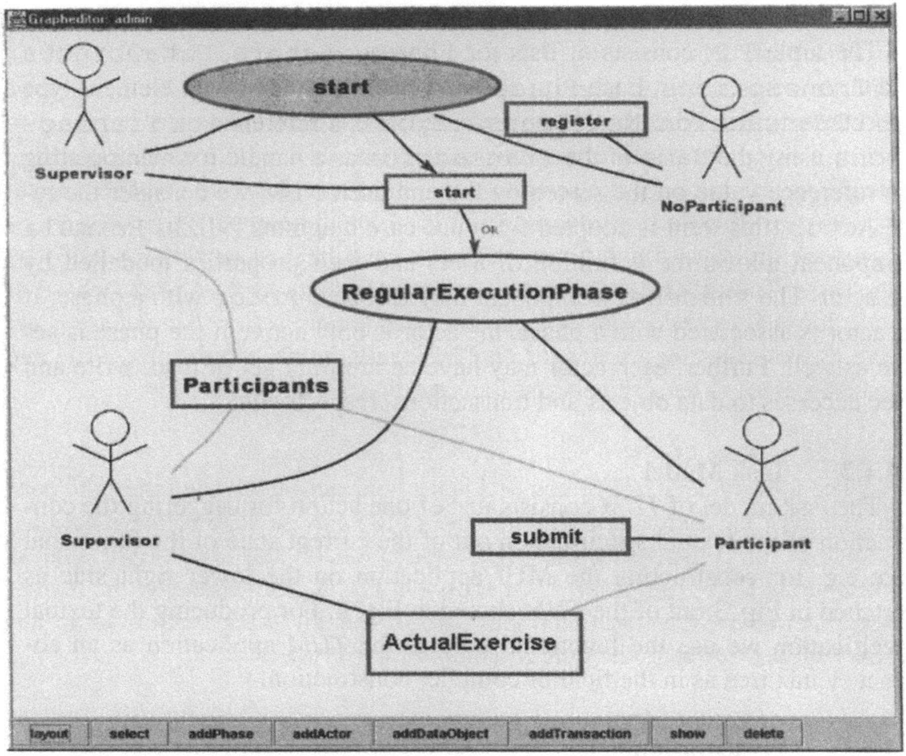

Figure 4. A *TUM* for *Practical Course.*

4. INTEGRATION

Fig. 5 sketches the integration of the concepts in EMUGEN using the tools GRACE and FORMGEN which can also be used standalone. The components PREGRACE and PREFORM can be regarded as pre-processors feeding GRACE and FORMGEN. The components USEGEN and MAKGEN generate the access adapters and the functional core, respectively.

The bottom part of Fig. 5 shows the runtime architecture of MUI applications generated by EMUGEN. The models (cf. section 3.1) of the graph editors and forms are composed of graph and form adapters (cf. section 3.3), respectively. The different user access are managed by access adapters again using the MVC-paradigm and the adapter pattern.

The functional core can be regarded as extended HIT-instance as discussed in section 3.2. The bootstrapping principle is not included in Fig. 5 because it pertains to the extension and not to the internal functionality of EMUGEN or MUI applications generated by it.

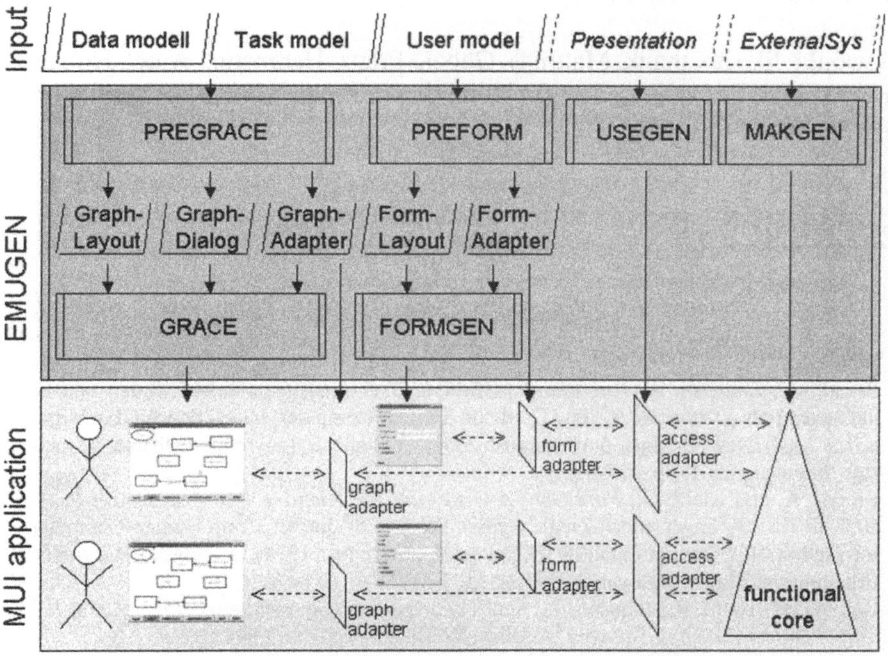

Figure 5. Integrating the concepts.

5. CONCLUSIONS

The concepts discussed in this paper give an impression of the functionality of the MUI applications generated by EMUGEN. We have seen that relatively complex prototypes can be generated (i.e. produced automatically) out of short problem descriptions. The examples show the potentials and the universality of our approach. The example *TUM* discussed in Section 3.4 introduces a new way for graphically modelling the tasks and the access rights of users depending on execution states.

At the chair of Prof. Eickel at the TU München there are regularly courses in compiler construction where teams of three graduate students develop simplified variants of EMUGEN during one semester successfully. I.e. the students apply the concepts described in this paper for implementing user interface generators (not just examples) using different technical platforms. So, there is evidence that the concepts are adequate for describing a generative approach for developing user interfaces on an abstract level.

ACKNOWLEDGMENTS

I would like to thank Matthias Göbel, Franz Haßmann, Aurel Huber, Marion Sperle, and the anonymous reviewers for their critical comments on draft versions of this paper.

REFERENCES

[1] Brandl, A., *Generating User Interfaces for Ad-hoc Workflows*, Poster demo at ACM Int. Conf. on Intelligent User Interfaces IUI'2001 (Santa Fe, January 2001), ACM Press, New York, 1991.

[2] Brandl, A., *EmuGen: A Generator for Multiple-User Interfaces*, in M.J. Smith and G. Salvendy (eds.), Proc. of 9th Int. Conf. on Human-Computer Interaction HCI International'2001 (New Orleans, 5-10 August 2001), Volume 2, Lawrence Erlbaum Associates, Mahwah, 2001, pp. 657-661.

[3] Brandl, A. and Klein, G., *FormGen: A Generator for Adaptive Forms Based on Easy-GUI*, in H.J. Bullinger and J. Ziegler (eds.), Proc. of 8th Int. Conf. on Human-Computer Interaction HCI International'99 (Munich, 22-26 August 1999), Volume 1, Lawrence Erlbaum Associates, Mahwah, 1999, pp. 1172-1176.

[4] Gamma, E., Helm, R., Johnson, R., and Vlissides, J., *Design Patterns: Elements of Reusable Object-Oriented Software*. Addison-Wesley, New York, 1994.

[5] Klein, G., *Generating Graphical Editors for Graph-like Datastructures*, Diploma thesis, Technische Universität München, 1999, accessible at http://www.gerwin-klein.de/grace.

[6] Krasner, G.E. and Pope, S.T., *A cookbook for using the model-view-controller user interface paradigm in Smalltalk-80*, Journal of Object-Oriented Programming, Vol. 1, No. 3, 1988, pp. 26-49.

[7] Schreiber, S., *Specification and Generation of User Interfaces with the BOSS-System*, in B. Blumenthal et al. (eds.), Proceedings of 4th East-West International Conference on Human-Computer Interaction EWHCI'94 (St. Petersburg, 2-6 August 1994), Lecture Notes in Computer Science, Vol. 876, Springer-Verlag, Berlin, 1994, pp. 107-120.

[8] Vanderdonckt, J. and Puerta, A.R., *Introduction to Computer-Aided Design of User Interfaces*, in J. Vanderdonckt and A.R. Puetra (eds.), Proc. of 3rd International Conference of Computer-Aided Design of User Interfaces CADUI'99 (Louvain-la-Neuve, 21-23 October 1999), Kluwer Academics Publisher, Dordrecht, 1999, pp. 1-5.

[9] Object Management Group, *OMG Unified Modeling Language Specification*, Version 1.4, ftp://ftp.omg.org/pub/docs/formal/01-09-67.pdf, 2001.

Chapter 16

DIGBE: ONLINE MODEL-BASED DESIGN AUTOMATION

Robin R. Penner and Erik S. Steinmetz
Iterativity, Inc.
Minneapolis, MN, 55404 (USA)
E-mail: {robin, erik}@iterativity.com – URL: www.iterativity.com/resumes/PennerCV.html
http://www.iterativity.com/resumes/SteinmetzCV.html
Tel.: +1-612-722-4493 / +1-612-789-6940

Abstract We describe the results of a research and development program which led to the implementation of a model-based system which automatically generates user interfaces to digital control systems. This system, called DIGBE, is based on constraint-based collaboration between three models. DIGBE produces interfaces on demand; each detail of the interface is tailored to the user, the task, and the available data. The models in DIGBE include: a domain model, which builds a representation of the objects in the control system; an interaction model, which builds an abstract representation of the human-computer interaction; and a presentation model, which presents the interaction to the user on a particular hardware device such as a personal computer or a PDA.

Keywords: Automated Interface Generation, Model-Based Design, User-Interface Design.

1. INTRODUCTION

In the domain of digital process control, individual user interfaces are currently developed for each installation, process, and user. In addition to being expensive, such systems pose a number of other problems for good user interface design. First, each digital control system is unique in its components, organization, tasks, users, computing systems, control programs, and interaction devices. Second, these individual features change over time, sometimes very quickly. Third, the users and tasks in this environment are diverse, and multiple separate software applications are required in order to support them. Finally, even with proper usability engineering applied to each

C. Kolski and J. Vanderdonckt (eds.), Computer-Aided Design of User Interfaces III, 179–192.
© 2002 *Kluwer Academic Publishers.*

application, user interfaces to various systems and functions will differ, and each site that needs a particular application will require manual user interface specialization.

We undertook a long-term research and development program (described in [4,5]) to reduce the cost and improve the usability of a subset of digital control interfaces: those in the domain of building management. We began with standard usability engineering practices, performing extensive task and domain analyses, functional requirements allocations, user interface design, interaction prototyping, and iterative usability evaluations. The result was a framework specification for that specific domain, including the tasks, users, and components involved. In addition, a user interface style guide (in paper and hypertext formats) was developed to guide the design and implementation of individual applications and individual sites requiring those applications, and a general windowing framework for applications was specified and included in the style guide.

Although better usability, more consistency, and better domain integration were the results, it was still time consuming and expensive to manually craft each interaction for each task and user at each installation. To explore other approaches, we undertook an additional research program to explore and develop automated solutions to providing user interfaces to complex digital control systems. This program had several explicit goals, including reducing the need for human-supplied user interface software development efforts, maximizing the appropriate application of user interface knowledge, and minimizing end user and design engineer configuration requirements. Functional requirements included the need to provide for multiple types of functionality, data, and users, support reuse of user interface designs, support multiple types of hardware devices, and support evolution in control systems, user functions, user interface design knowledge, user interface devices, and human-computer interaction paradigms.

The result of this research was the design and implementation of an online model-based system that creates, displays, and modifies all user interfaces required by each user of a building management system. All aspects of the user interface are created dynamically on demand, specialized for the situation: that particular installation, and those specific users and the interface devices they choose to use. The system, called DIGBE (Dynamic Interface Generation for Building Environments [6]), allocates domain knowledge, interaction design, and presentation heuristics into separate, collaborating models. Each model contains knowledge about a particular aspect of interface design, and uses this knowledge to dynamically create each user interface that is needed.

The model-based approach we took to DIGBE incorporates the findings of numerous other researchers in this area. For example, SAGE [9] generated

2D static presentations of relational data, and emphasized the importance of multi-dimensional representations of data and the effect of user goals on effective design. BOZ [1] took a task analytic approach to interface automation, included some rules of composition that responded to situational parameters, and separated interaction content from user interface format. IBIS [10] had a separate presentation component, and included representation knowledge of users, tasks, and contexts. Later work on IBIS included an emphasis on data characterization [14] and hierarchical decomposition of visual lexicons [15].

Investigations in the area of User Interface Design Environments (UIDE) also informed the DIGBE program, including modeling of user interface design knowledge [2], separation of design environments into multiple layers for the domain, the interactions, and the presentations [13], the use of declarative user interface design models [11], and the use of domain models to provide the underlying semantics for user interface design [8].

This paper presents a short overview of the DIGBE system and each of its models, illustrating the major design decisions for each model, followed by a discussion of the implications of such an approach and the next steps for this research program.

2. DIGBE OVERVIEW

Fig. 1 shows a screen shot of a DIGBE-generated user interface for a manager a large building environmental control system. The basic tasks for this user are presented as panes of an application window, and include system navigation (left pane), system monitoring (top right) and detail data interactions (lower right). With these displays, the user is automatically presented with the display of (or access to) all necessary tasks and system components, through a consistent and "usability engineered" user interface, specialized to the particular building and combination of control systems. To create that display, DIGBE starts with an existing flat database (like those used in current building management systems) that describes the objects in a control system for a building management system. Using a simple schema that describes the format of the application's database, DIGBE translates the inventory of systems and equipment into an object model representing the control situation. It also creates a Java executable to provide access to a user interface to interact with that control system.

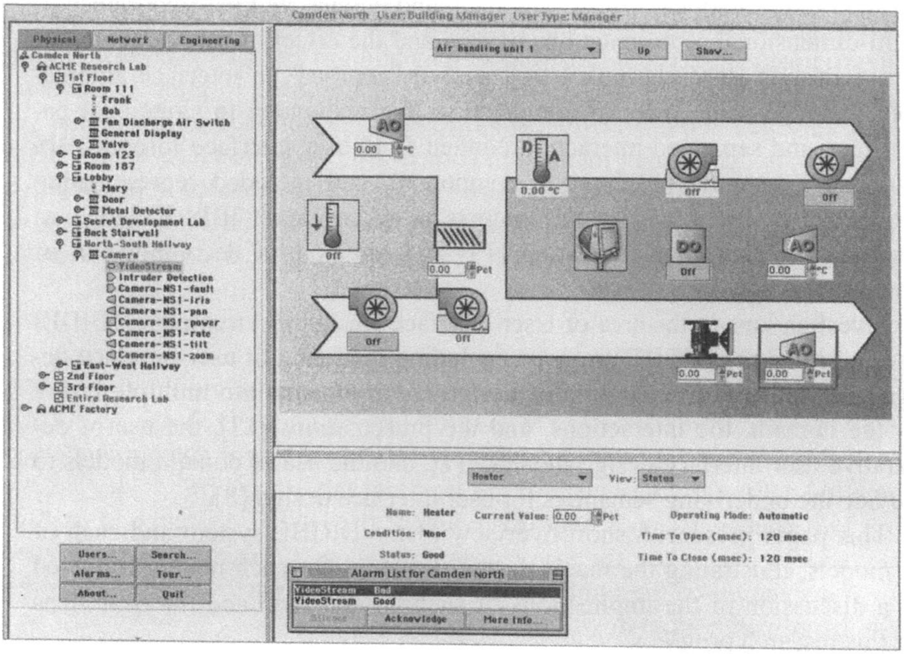

Figure 1. DIGBE-Generated User Interface for a Building Manager.

When a building management system user (a building manager or technician, for example) "double-clicks" the executable, and logs on, the various parts of the user interface are immediately created, assembled, and presented to the user as a well-designed operational user interface to the building's functions. This interface facilitates only the tasks that this particular user requires, and includes only the objects and actions that user requires and/or has access to. As the user operates within the interface or as the situation changes in the control system, DIGBE continuously refines and updates the contents, format, and presentation of the user interface.

DIGBE is able to provide a well-designed, specialized user interface for each situation because it uses internal models of good design (as we currently understand them) to create and tune each interface. Responsibility for the various aspects of an interface design is distributed into different models that collaborate to produce the user interface. DIGBE's knowledge is stored in three object-oriented models.

The **Domain Model** provides the semantic basis for interaction design, allowing control system independence and an object-oriented representation of control system components. It instantiates an object-oriented **Domain Representation** containing a representation of the site-specific digital control system. A Domain Representation exists for each installation, and is shared by all users at that installation.

The hierarchical, task-based **Interaction Model** provides the design knowledge required to design appropriate tasks and interactions, allowing dynamic application of the principles of usability engineering. It instantiates an **Interaction Design** (for each user, each time they log on) to support the specific user's interaction with the control system.

The **Presentation Model** converts Interaction Designs into user interfaces, allowing hardware and operating system independence. It formats and presents the Interaction Design as a **User Interface**. Interaction Designs have access to multiple presentation models, one for each of the types of devices that can be used to access DIGBE.

2.1 Domain Model

The domain of building management is fairly well understood, and numerous domain models with information about data types and information roles have been constructed (e.g., [12]). The domain model required to support automatic user interface design in DIGBE, like other representations of buildings and their control systems, contains information about control objects, their location within the building structure, and their hierarchical organization within control systems. To represent this, we developed a simple model of building objects and systems, based on a general object called Artifact. We used generic templates, like "Building", "Analog Input", "Chiller", and "On/Off Switch", to represent the hierarchically organized elements present in buildings.

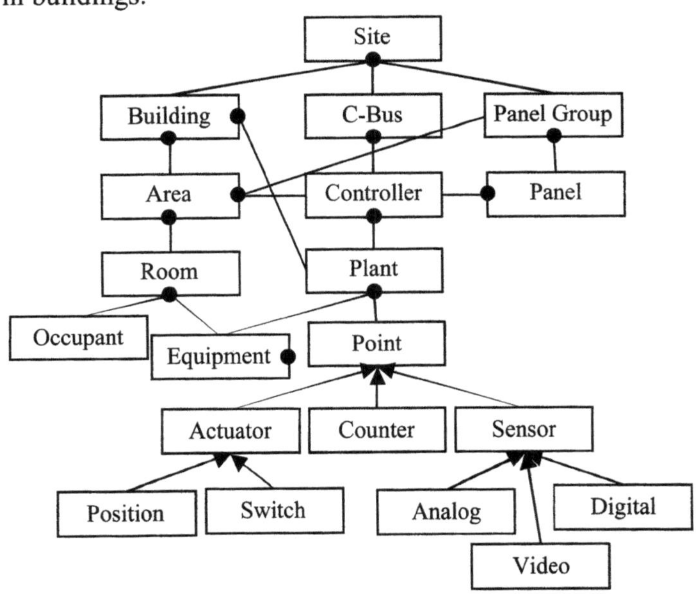

Figure 2. Portion of DIGBE's Domain Model.

Fig. 2 shows a portion of the DIGBE Domain Model. In this and other depictions of model components, an arrow from one component to another indicates inheritance; the arrow points at the superclass from the subclass. A line from one component to another with a filled circle at one end indicates a compositional relationship, where the component at the circle end "has" the other component as a part.

When a DIGBE system is installed at a particular installation, the Domain Model is used to create the site's Domain Representation. This is a dynamic representation of the control system, including control components, data, and users. A Domain Representation that might be created for a very small portion of an actual control system is shown in Fig. 3.

2.1.1 Domain Data

A Domain Model consisting only of physical artifacts provides important semantic information about objects and their relationships. However, it doesn't capture the semantics of their data and control parameters. There are a number of different types of data present in different aspects of the control system, and different types of interactions that are required with different types of equipment. While sensors cannot be controlled, only read, actuators need to be both readable and controllable, but only by authorized users. Different types of actuators have different control and display requirements; for example, a temperature control has a continuous range with high and low limits, while a heat mode switch is a three-state control.

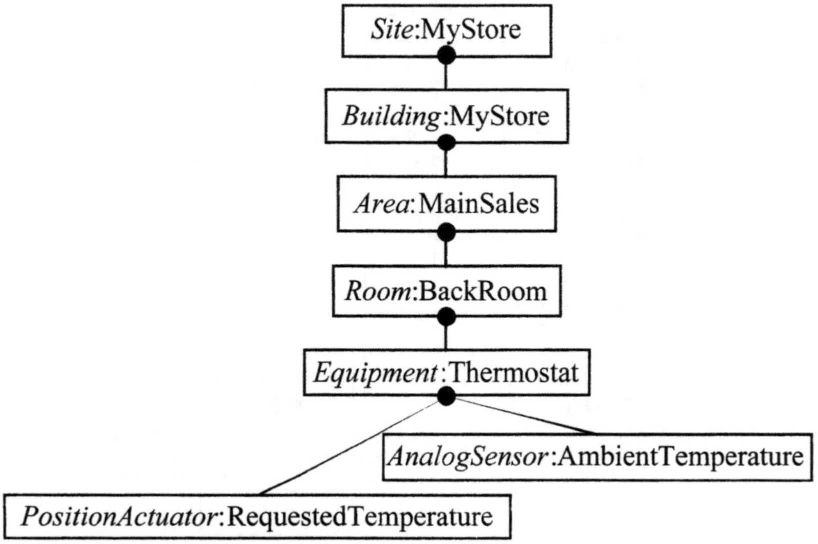

Figure 3. Small Portion of a Domain Representation for a Particular Site.

To represent these constraints, we modeled classes to represent the data values associated with objects. Each artifact in the domain model has a set of Domain Data Objects, representing its properties (such as the current value, permissible settings, or operational limits). When an artifact is created, its data properties are also instantiated as one or another type of Domain Data Object. We have identified eight basic data types required to represent the properties and data of objects in use in digital control systems: accumulator (simple counter), continuous (range), discrete (setting choices), file (data file), state (Boolean), text, time, and video.

For example, the data objects associated with an analog sensor (e.g., a temperature or humidity sensor) include status (a State Data), access level (a Discrete Data), various Continuous data values representing the sensor's current value and alarm limits, and File data objects representing pointers to history files.

2.1.2 Domain Roles

In order to be maximally applicable, we wanted the DIGBE system to be as domain independent as possible. To separate the knowledge of the domain and interaction models, we developed a set of Java singleton classes called Roles. These roles are associated with domain objects, and used by the interaction design system to guide the interaction design. This provides a useful separation between the knowledge in the interaction model and the knowledge in the domain model; as long as a domain model codes its objects and data according to the roles of those objects and data, the Interaction Model can be used with any domain model.

There are four types of Roles provided in DIGBE's Domain Model:

Agent roles are associated with a user when that user is created or redefined, and currently include engineer, guard, maintainer, manager, and operator. These roles are used by the Interaction Model to select the task set for the initial user interface design. For example, suppose that the agent role of "operator" is associated with a particular security guard. Then, only certain tasks (operations tasks, but not maintenance, management, or technical tasks), will be presented to this user.

Process roles represent the different kinds of processes and systems that can use DIGBE to mediate the human end of mixed initiative control. Process roles are assigned to both plants and users when each is created, and are used to constrain information for particular users. For example, a particular security guard has the process role "security". When the Interaction Model composes the interaction design to support this user, not only will the agent role constrain the tasks that are presented, the process role will also constrain the plant components that are available to this user. The security operator will not be shown or have access to environmental control system components. Process roles are assigned to objects in the Domain Representation when they are created, based on the systems they are associated with in the configured building.

Referential roles are used to provide information about the kind of thing referenced by each object in the domain model. They are statically preassigned to each object in the Domain Model, and their instantiations retain the referential role assigned to them. All artifacts are assigned an Object Referent role, to indicate that they refer to objects in the world. Data Objects are assigned individual referential roles that are used by the interaction design objects to provide a basis to choose between different user interface components. State Data objects have a Boolean referential role, for example, to generically represent that any data object that is a specialization of a state data object refers to Boolean data. Continuous Data objects, in contrast, are associated with a Number referential role, to represent that they operate on numerical, continuous data.

Data roles provide semantic information about the purpose of the information represented by each data object, in the context of the artifact it is associated with. For example, the objects representing the current value of a temperature sensor, a fan switch, and thermostat are represented by, respectively, data objects of the type Continuous, State, and Continuous. Each of these current values is assigned a data role that indicates the type of information they represent for the object they are associated with. The temperature sensor provides a measured value, and is given the data role of Value. The fan switch, in contrast, is a setting that determines how the system will operate; the current value for the fan switch is assigned an Operational Parameter data role. The thermostat is not a measured value, but a desired setting, and so is given the data role of Setting. These data roles are used to constrain the subtasks to contain only the information that is needed in the current situation. Data roles are created when the initial Domain Representation is built from the raw configuration files.

2.2 Interaction Model

DIGBE's automated design capabilities stem from the knowledge that the Interaction Model possesses about interaction design, and its ability to use the semantic information in the Domain Representation to drive the compositional design process. This knowledge is contained in the Interaction Model, organized as a (hierarchical) cellular automaton driven by local behavior rules [7]. Its purpose is to model the process of designing the interactions between the user and the information contained in the current situation. The Interaction Model is made up of five levels:

- *Applications* (e.g., Building Management), composed of tasks;
- *Tasks* (e.g., Monitoring), composed of subtasks;
- *Sub-Tasks* (e.g., Selection), composed of elements;
- *Elements* (e.g., Value Over Time), composed of primitives; and
- *Primitives* (e.g., Labeler), the basic units of an interaction.

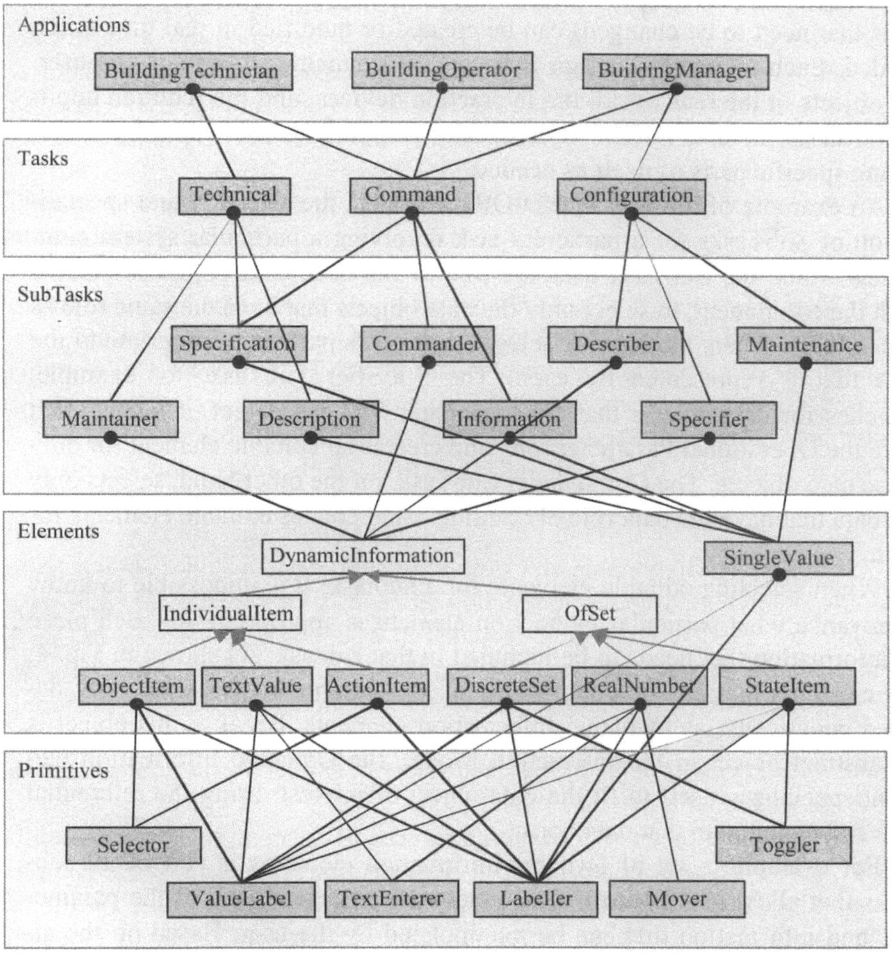

Figure 4. Portion of the DIGBE Interaction Model.

Fig. 4 illustrates a portion of the DIGBE Interaction Model. To simplify the diagram, we have only included the Technical, Command, and Configuration Tasks, and have removed the parts of the hierarchies at each level that are not directly involved in these three tasks.

The Interaction Model is a task-based *self-composing productive system.* When an instance of any interaction object is created for a particular user and a particular set of domain objects, that instance is responsible for adapting to the current situation, using internal rules and constraints based on current practice in task analysis, requirements management, and interaction design. Interaction objects also select their sub-components for the specific context, based on appropriateness to the situation and the user. Each subcomponent then tunes itself by selecting and tuning its own subcomponents.

Using this process of self-composition, an entire interaction (or only the parts that need to be changed) can be created or modified in real time when needed. Each interaction design is specialized dynamically to suit the user, the objects in the real world, the interaction devices, and the required application tasks. In use, DIGBE dynamically responds to user input by redesigning specific parts of itself as needed.

An example of the way that DIGBE works is the selection and specialization of SubTasks for a particular task involving a particular system component. First, the SubTask uses the role of the each data object associated with the component, to select only the data objects that have the same role as that subtask. Then, the subtask selects each of its parts as appropriate to the data that is represented by each. The Specifier SubTask, for example, searches for data objects that are associated with the object of interest that have the Operational Parameter role, and creates an editable element for only those data objects. The Commander SubTask, on the other hand, selects only the data that have the data role of "Setting", and creates editable elements for each.

When selecting editable elements for a subtask, it is impossible to know in advance what particular interaction element is appropriate for each piece of information that needs to be included in that subtask. As shown in Fig. 4, the elements that are subcomponents of the editable subtasks are only defined generically, as Dynamic Information elements. Because this object is an abstract object in the Interaction Model, the Dynamic Information element specializes itself to fit the data object of interest, using the referential role associated with that data object.

For example, a set of DynamicInformation elements is part of all subtasks that allow user control. These elements represent each of the parameters and information that can be manipulated by the user. Based on the attributes of the data being represented, the DynamicInformation elements themselves use rules of element selection and composition to specialize into the most appropriate element (an On/Off picker, for example, for a Fan On/Off command). Each concrete specialization of DynamicInformation (e.g., a StateItem or a TextValue) then picks its subparts (Primitives) according to the data represented in the domain.

Fig. 5 shows a representation of an Interaction Design for a configuration task representing a freeze thermostat (stat) for a building manager. Only the Specifier subtask is shown; this subtask is used to set the operating role data for the freeze stat. Because the Specifier subtask is associated with the Operational Parameter data role, only the parameters of the freeze stat that have an operational role are selected to fill the subtask. There are therefore four elements in this subtask: the operating mode, the alarm delay, the active state, and the log hours.

In this example, only the primitives for the operating mode element are shown, composed of the interaction primitives representing the label for the operating mode, its current value (false or Automatic), the labels for the two states, and the on/off picker that would allow a user to select a different state.

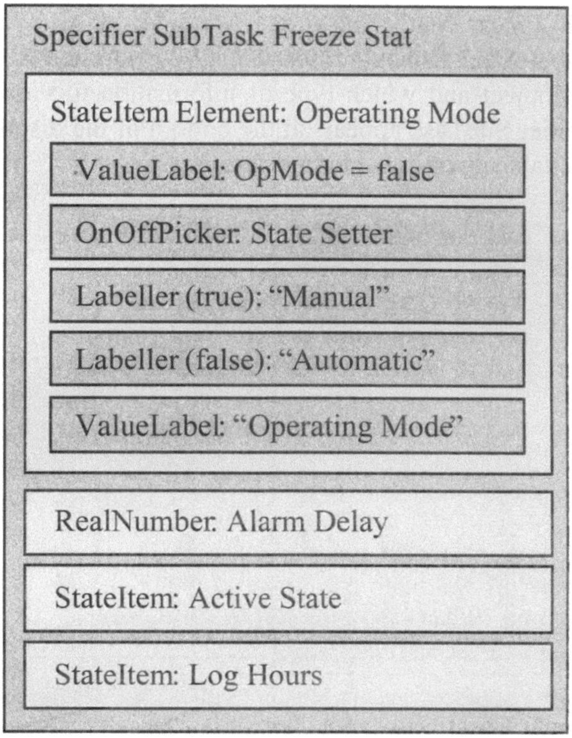

Figure 5. Portion of an Interaction Design for a SubTask.

2.3 Presentation Model

The presentation model in DIGBE is separate from the interaction model and the interaction design, in order to make DIGBE adaptable to multiple types of user interface devices. Each type of device has a Presentation Model; the appropriate model is selected based on the device currently in use. The DIGBE Presentation Model converts the interaction design into a presentation by selecting user interface components like windows (for applications), frames (for subtasks), and widgets (for elements), and specializing them according to the parameters of the objects in the Interaction Design.

In addition to the device-specific knowledge about translation from interaction objects to presentation objects, each presentation model also contains a number of heuristics that specify how to select and specialize presentation objects, and how to code and present the interaction object information (for example, how to line up widgets, add appropriate status coding, and represent objects graphically).

Fig. 6 presents a portion of a user interface presentation for the interaction defined in Fig. 5, showing only three subtasks. The ObjectSelection Subtask (labeled "Freeze Stat") and the ActionSelection SubTask ("View: Details"), at the top of the display, present the interactions that allow the user to specify which object and which type of information to view about that object. The Specifier SubTask appears at the bottom of the display, and provides access to settable operational parameters.

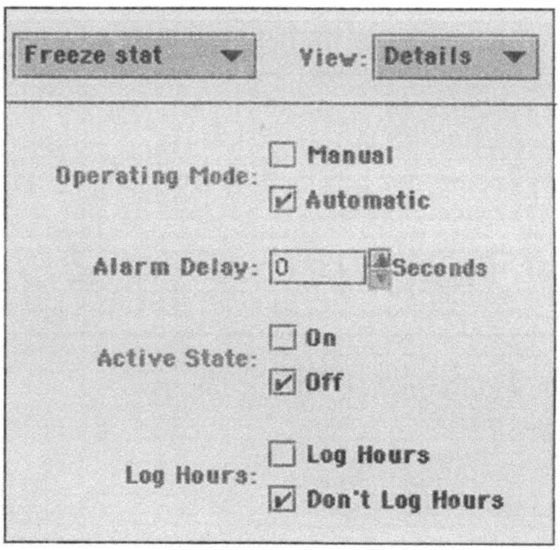

Figure 6. Presentation of a Specifier SubTask for a Freeze Stat.

3. DISCUSSION

An important principle that was applied during the development of DIGBE is the object-oriented principle of decoupling, where each part of a system needs only limited access to the other parts. Implementation of the DIGBE system in a real world domain revealed a number of domain model requirements, particularly in the representation of data and in the semantic information about users, processes, references, and data functions. While there may be multiple ways of embodying this information and applying it to help guide interaction design, the use of roles in Java provides a useful mechanism for exploring domain independence.

In the DIGBE system, the upper levels of the Interaction Model define users and tasks. While the specific tasks associated with each building control application were developed with these applications in mind, it is expected that the task set is of sufficient generality to extend to other domains. We are currently continuing the approach we took with the DIGBE system, beginning with research into its applicability to a military command and control domain. Further work will include extension of the current architecture to allow the incorporation of independently developed models of tasks, users, interaction design processes, and domains; integration of a modularized, compositional DIGBE approach with efforts whose primary emphasis are the development of robust models; and improvements to the modeling of actions available to the user (both in the domain and the interface).

REFERENCES

[1] Casner, S., *A task-analytic approach to the automated design of graphic presentations*, ACM Transactions on Graphics, Vol. 10, No. 2, 1991, pp. 111-151.

[2] Foley, J., Gibbs, C., Kim, W., and Kovacevic, S., *Knowledge-based user interface management system*, in Proceedings of the ACM Conference on Human Factors in Computing Systems CHI '88, ACM Press, New York, 1988, pp. 67-72.

[3] Penner, R., *Developing the process control interface*, in Engineering for Human Computer Interaction, Elsevier Scientific Press, Amsterdam, 1993, pp. 317-334.

[4] Penner, R., *Multimedia interfaces for process control*, in Proceedings of the Energy-Sources Technology Conference, ASME petroleum Division, 1994, pp. 375-383.

[5] Penner, R. and Soken, N., *Consistent Honeywell Interface: Tools for developers*, Scientific Honeyweller, 1993, pp. 106-109.

[6] Penner, R. and Steinmetz, E., *DIGBE: Adaptive user interface automation*, in Proc. of *AAAI Spring Symposium* (Stanford, 2000), pp. 98-101.

[7] Penner, R. and Steinmetz, E., Model-based automation of the design of user interfaces to digital control systems, IEEE Transactions on Systems, Man and Cybernetics, in press.

[8] Puerta, A., Eriksson, H., Gennari, J., and Musen, M., *Model-based automated generation of user interfaces*, in Proceedings of the National Conference on Artificial Intelligence, 1994, pp. 471-477.

[9] Roth, S. and Mattis, J., *Data characterization for intelligent graphics presentation*, in Proceedings of the Conference on Human Factors in Computing Systems (CHI'90), ACM Press, New York, 1990, pp. 193-200.

[10] Seligman, D. and Feiner, S., *Automated generation of intent-based 3D illustrations*, Computer Graphics, Vol. 25, No. 4, 1991, pp. 123-132.

[11] Szekely, P., Luo, P., and Neches, R., *Beyond interface builders: Model-based interface tools*, in Proceedings of InterCHI'93, ACM Press, New York, 1993, pp. 383-390.

[12] Torcellini, P., *Supervisory Control for Intelligent Building Systems*, Ph.D. thesis, Purdue University, 1992.

[13] Wiecha, C., Bennett, W., Boies, S., Gould, J., and Greene, S., *ITS: A tool for rapidly developing interactive applications*, ACM Transactions on Information Systems, Vol. 8, No. 3, 1989, pp. 204-236.

[14] Zhou, M., and Feiner, S., *Data characterization for automatically visualizing hetrogeneous information*, in Proceedings of IEEE Information Visualization'96, 1996, pp. 13-20.
[15] Zhou, M., and Feiner, S., *Top-down hierarchical planning of coherent visual discourse*, in Proceedings of the ACM Conference on Intelligent User Interfaces IUI'97, ACM Press, New York, 1997, pp. 129-136.

Chapter 17

MEETING ACTIVITY THEORY THROUGH TASK-BASED AND USER-ORIENTED DEVELOPMENT OF USER INTERFACES

Chris Stary
Communications Engineering Group, Department of Business Information Systems
University of Linz, Freistädterstraße 315, A-4040 Linz (Austria)
E-mail: stary@ce.uni-linz.ac.at – URL: http://instserv0.ce.uni-linz.ac.at/institut/about/staff.asp?mitarbeiter_id=0 – Tel.: +43-732-2468-7102 – Fax: +43-732-2468-7111

Abstract Activity theory describes (socio-technical) systems with respect to the interacting partners, objects and results of work, as well as the tools and conditions for work processes. As soon as interactive software systems become part of work systems those entities become essential parts of the designer's workspace. This paper tries to bridge the gap between the activity theory and a task-based design approach that spans from analysis to prototyping. Task-based and user-oriented interface design approaches utilize and reflect knowledge about user tasks, roles, and preferences. Thus, they are promising candidates to implement activity theory and embed knowledge about users and their work into the development of technological artefacts. In order to achieve that goal in the proposed approach a unifying notation for task analysis and design specification, comprising problem domain data, work processes, users and interaction features, is used. For prototyping, a corresponding support tool provides an interpreter. It executes the design specification and enables early feedback on task-based artefacts by users.

Keywords: Activity theory, Intelligent user interface management, Object-oriented systems, Prototyping, Task analysis, Task-based design, User-centred design,

1. INTRODUCTION

Activity theory has already gained the attention of HCI researchers, e.g. by Bedny et al. [3]. Activity theory is expected to help facilitate the development of task- and user-centred software systems [15]. Although a variety

C. Kolski and J. Vanderdonckt (eds.), Computer-Aided Design of User Interfaces III, 193–204.
© 2002 *Kluwer Academic Publishers.*

of techniques exists for the analysis of user needs and work tasks, e.g., [6], as well as for designing user interfaces and prototyping, e.g., [20], few techniques are capable to structure and maintain knowledge about the context of use, i.e. work actors, tasks etc. In case workers are not able to navigate their task space and manipulate problem domain data accordingly, i.e. with respect to the process of task accomplishment, computer support might decrease quality of work rather than improving it, e.g., [10,16]. Hence, designers need to be supported with a frame of reference and design elements reflecting the context of user interface development.

Activity theory attempts to model human activities in their organizational and societal context. It provides a variety of elements that has already been considered to be relevant for context-sensitive interactive-system development, and might well be embedded into existing task-based and user-oriented approaches to interactive-system design. In this paper activity theory is revisited with respect to capturing context elements of human-computer interaction. The candidates for design elements are derived from the theory in section 2. Section 3 briefly revisits TADEUS (Task Analysis / Design / End User Systems), a task-based and user-oriented development technique. Section 4 shows how the various context elements can be implemented through TADEUS. Activity theory consequently, combined with proper instruments for task acquisition, provides conceptual support and further inputs for a structured development procedure, starting with task analysis, proceeding with task-based and user-oriented interaction design and prototyping.

2. ACTIVITY THEORY AND ITS ELEMENTS FOR DESIGNING INTERACTIVE SYSTEMS

Activity theory reflects systems design and thinking in a way that, for practical use, systems have to take into account the diversity of individual views, the variety of motives (stemming from the actors involved) and the organizational setting activities are embedded [1,2,4,5]. This approach has several consequences, namely both, at the process and the content level: If we consider development processes leading to technological artefacts to be part of development systems, designers should have access to the context of development, and reflect each development activity in the light of the acquired context. For user interface development, this means to maintain a representation of the work tasks, the ingredients for design as well as intermediate results along the several phases of development (analysis, design, coding, functional testing, usability evaluation).

Secondly, activities related to human-oriented system design, either targeting towards technological artefacts or other systems (e.g., organizations), have to take into account the context of those activities that are going to be tackled or addressed by the design of systems. For user interface design, all relevant factors addressing the involved tasks and individuals should be represented throughout the design process. Finally, design knowledge has also to be kept in a context-sensitive way, since system-development processes are team processes. The latter require to communicate requirements, results, issues to be clarified etc. Target-system-specific information, such as class descriptions in case of exclusive technical system development, is not very likely to serve as basis for successful communication. Hence, context representation is required to guide the members of the development team to handle the core questions, such as classes required for a particular style of interaction at the user interface, in a successful way.

According to activity theory [8,11,17,18,21] activities might occur at the level of individuals as well as of collections of individuals. Each activity of an individual is implemented through a set of actions according to the individual's motivation. The motives for setting an action might be part of the structure of the activity, as individuals might not be aware of their motives when performing actions. As each activity is related to a motive, following the set of descriptions in each level of the hierarchy, each action is linked to a goal. In contrast to motives, goals are consciously defined, in order to achieve a certain state of an object of concern.

Actions can be decomposed into operations like activities can be decomposed into actions. The execution of actions depends on the actual conditions under which activities can be performed. Operations are not reflected directly (as actions are through checking achievements against goals), but the result of manipulations are, namely, according to the goal of the superior action. This layered approach of activity theory is neither meant to be a stringent sequence of decomposition steps nor is it neglecting systems dynamics. According to situations and individual experiences actions might become operations (e.g., for experienced individuals). In addition, the principle of development reflects the continuous and permanent change of activities, allowing even for contradictions. The reason for human behaviour being highly dynamic might lie in the fact that thoughts, as soon as they are externalised, lead to questioning of existing goals and motives. This questioning might lead to immediate adjustments of goals and thus, changes of actions [11,12].

With respect to collective activities (and systems where these activities occur) a comprehensive description of systems has to comprise (i) the situatedness of activities, (ii) the understanding of individuals being part of the group, (iii) the semiotic means for cooperation, and (iv) the dynamics of coordination and cooperation. The production of work results as well as the generation of knowledge occurs as a process in so-called communities of practice. The latter are permanently changing. In order to reflect these changes the context of system developments has to be made transparent and kept for further development. Kuutti [14] considers the activity to be the minimal meaningful context for an action. This understanding is in conformance to activity theory, since it assigns the individual to the action level. According to Engeström [8] activities cannot occur at the level of individuals, they rather occur at the group level. As he understands human labour to be of cooperative nature, activities, located at the top level of the hierarchy, have to be assigned to a set of individuals.

The elements of activity theory and their mutual relationships reflect the observation that each human activity is influenced through the social setting of operation and the operative means by which activities are performed. An ICT-infrastructure might support even distributed activity systems [8,18]. In case of collective work systems influences are given for actors and objects, in terms of the *social setting*: informal rules and the formal organization of work, and in terms of *operative means*: means of productions, means of orientation.

In case of software-supported work processes an actor A is supported through software features (i.e. means of production) that help an actor B to orient him/herself. The products resulting from this process can be seen as symbolic externalization of a certain way accomplishing a certain task. It is a way expressing individual experiences (actor A for actor B), without ensuring the usability of this knowledge along the work and the knowledge transfer process (since it is an abstraction of the content of work). Nevertheless, it demonstrates the dual character of human activities and actions. By setting the action or activity, not only objects are manipulated to produce certain results, but also individuals demonstrate their (cap)ability to accomplish a certain task in a certain way. Experiences uttered this way can become input for another actor or group of actors to develop novel skills.

This understanding of systems dynamics allows to develop another perspective on software-system development with respect to the accumulated knowledge along the development process. Wehner et al. [22] have addressed systems' dynamics in the context of accumulating knowledge. This process might lead to questioning existing solutions, discussions about them, and the collaborative exploration of new knowledge (sources): "[…] *in co-construction an attempt is made to generate organizational solutions that transcend single cases. Co-construction, as a specific form of expansive co-operation, differs in its underlying structure from coordination and cooperation because the focus of attention now lies in the common redefinition of roles, work objectives, and patterns of interaction*" [22, p. 990]. Hence, the cooperation of analysts, designers, programmers and usability engineers can be beneficial for the product as well as further development projects.

3. TADEUS

TADEUS (Task Analysis / Design / End User Systems) [19] targets towards task-conform user interfaces that support navigation and data manipulation in a way users are able to perform their tasks in an effective and efficient way. The user interface has to reflect the world of tasks as perceived by users, and has to take into account individual skills and preferences, as far as they are required and relevant for task accomplishment and for interaction. Task-conform user interfaces are based on the design representation of both, end user tasks and user skills, experiences and preferences. They are the result of a task-based and user-oriented design process. TADEUS provides an object-oriented representation of the users' workflow that is decomposed to data, role, and interaction specifications within the context of the workflow specification. It also enables the generation of user interface prototypes directly from the design specification.

In the course of designing tool support for meeting the objectives mentioned above, (i) a unifying notation for representation, and (ii) high-level semantic constructs for analysis and design have been developed. The unifying notation provides elements for representation throughout analysis, design, and prototyping. Concepts from object-oriented specification have been used, as they are already in use not only for design, but also for systems analysis (enabling semantically expressive specifications, see e.g., [7]). A task can be expressed in terms of a class description. The underlying data for that task, such as person for a human resource management task as well as the elements used for presenting tasks and data to the users, such as windows, are also being represented through class descriptions and proper relationships.

As the notation has to support the human-oriented expression of tasks and user characteristics, semantically rich language constructs, however with a tight (syntactic) definition, have to be provided. They enable to break the specification barrier that could be caused through the use of traditional (formal) specification languages for analysis and design. When breaking this barrier development can start with high-level declarative statements that are continuously refined to executable user interface procedures in a consistent way. For instance, a temporal relationship between tasks might be declared in the structural description of the task domain, and consequently be refined to a sequence of operations performed on dialog elements, such as check boxes.

The TADEUS technique is based on the following steps: After setting up a project, several steps have to be performed to bridge the gap between task-support requirements and user-interface prototyping: (1) Work analysis, resulting in a business representation - the business intelligence model; (2) Task-based design, resulting in an application model; (3) Workflow-based prototyping, resulting in a running user interface.

The analysis of work (step 1) is performed using TATAR (TADEUS Task Analysis and Representation technique) which leads to the TADEUS business intelligence representation, i.e. a representation of user requirements in terms of an organizational structure (name of the company, hierarchical layers of operation, tasks), and work flows. This model serves as the basis for the subsequent design activities (step 2):

- *Task modelling* capturing the parts of the task hierarchy relevant for user interface design, according to the organisation of work and the users' perception of the organisation.
- *User modelling* by defining specific views on tasks and data (according to the functional roles of users), as well as individual user characteristics or particular features for user-adapted interaction, such as left-hand assignments to interaction media (e.g., mouse buttons).
- *Data modelling* in terms of a semantic data model derived from the tasks and the users' organisation of work in the problem domain.
- *Interaction Modelling*, in order to establish a generic user interface architecture. It takes into account those features, i.e. devices, media, modalities and their combinations that are considered to be relevant for the presentation of tasks, the content (problem domain data) and navigation.
- *Application Modelling* which integrates the various perspectives on the design specification, namely the task, user, data, and interaction model, mutually in a static and dynamic way, thus defining the structure and behaviour of the entire interactive-software system.

The activities described in step 2 do not have to be performed in a linear way, except starting with the business intelligence representation to identify a more or less complete task model for further refinement during design. As a matter of fact, the application model (that is finally required for implementation) is constructed through jumping between the different models, i.e. views of the specification of the application. For instance, as soon as the designer might recognize that some users need a mouse for interaction, he/she might select those interaction elements from the platform the mouse is part of. Then he/she might switch (back) to the user model and proceed with detailing roles.

Finally, in step 3 a prototype can be generated directly from the specification, namely from the application model. The output of the design activities is a set of representations of the application that serves as input for a run time system for workflow-driven prototyping. The benefits of workflow-driven executions are (i) the correct sequencing of activities, and (ii) the completeness of inputs from specification to be provided for the execution of activities. Hence, deadlocks and decreasing performance can be avoided when the causal and temporal constraints for task accomplishment have been specified. The current version of the TADEUS-environment supports the interpretation of methods according to the constraints and activities (sub tasks) of the workflow specified in the task model. Hence, all behaviour diagrams are executed according to the specified state transitions and constraints. The designer may directly execute the workflow either step-by-step or continuously using a prototypical version of the system generated from the design specifications.

Table 1 shows the types of links representing conceptual relationships of the TADEUS representation scheme for business intelligence. They do not only support the structural perspective on a business, but also the dynamic one at a declarative level of description. In particular, the flow of work, i.e. how things are actually getting done, is modelled. TADEUS is open to the definition of further relationships, in case the provided ones do not suffice in accuracy or in semantics. In the table the link types are categorized according to their type of activity in the course of analysing user and work, and designing user interfaces. The categorization of analysis and design tasks stems from a cross-check of several TADEUS case studies.

Table 1. Typical activities and use of semantic relationships in the course of analysis and design.

Set up	Refine & Abstract	Relate
Employs Has	Is a Has part	Handles, Creates, Concerns, Informs, Controls, Requires, Before, Is based on, Corresponds to

The *set up* of a business specification requires basic relationships, such as 'employs' or 'has'. The first relationship enables to assign functional roles to the identified organization, whereas the second one enables the specification of properties (attributes) to any node, such as 'social security number' to 'employee'. *Refinement* and *abstraction* are performed using the common generalization / specialization and aggregation relationships, namely 'is a' and 'has part', respectively. *Relating*, the third type of development activity when using TADEUS, means setting those relationships that make up organizational intelligence. It is that part where TADEUS differs from most specification techniques, since these relationship are checked for correct use through particular algorithms according to their semantics. This way, the semantics of the entire development knowledge can be preserved along the different phases of development. For a detailed discussion of TADEUS the reader is referred to [19].

4. ACTIVITY THEORY AND ITS IMPLEMENTATION THROUGH TADEUS

As explained above, TADEUS follows the traditional lines of model-based interactive-software development, but extends them for the sake of context-sensitive, i.e. task-based and user-oriented, specification: it

- follows the approach of structured top-down development, but leaves space to switch consistently between views on and layers of design representations;
- is integrative, since, although it models problem domain data separated from tasks and user characteristics, it allows to keep their mutual dependencies throughout the different phases of development;
- is based on a single notation rather than a set of different languages for specifying tasks, user roles, problem domain data, and interaction features in the different phases of development.

As such, TADEUS meets the demand for taking account the diversity of individual views, the variety of goals (stemming from the users, analysts, designers and programmers involved) and the organizational setting the development activities are embedded. Hence, at the **process level**, designers have access to the context of development, and are able to reflect each development activity in the light of the acquired content in its context. The specification of work tasks, user characteristics and the initial interaction model are accessible at any time of development. This utility of design representation is enabled through the (additional) semantic relationships between design elements, the maintenance of consistency, and the use of the unifying object-oriented notation. The latter also supports the **communication** among the members of the development team, since it captures both, the structure and behaviour of the work system and the artefact to be developed.

Fig. 1 shows a snapshot of how the instantiation of activity theory at the process level looks like. It addresses the phases analysis and design. Located at the intermediate level of the activity hierarchy (activity-action-operation) the behaviour of the actors' involved has to be goal-oriented (namely, according to their role in a development project). The analyst creates a business model (B. Model) that is subsequently refined to a TADEUS task model by the designer. The analyst is guided through guidelines and is constrained in his/her work according to project constraints. The analysis is performed through using an analysis technique. Its results are represented in terms of a representation of the business intelligence. The designer (team) takes this specification as an input and produces relationship, behaviour, and interaction diagrams with the help of the TADEUS' model-based design technique. The resulting specification will be implemented through prototyping or programming.

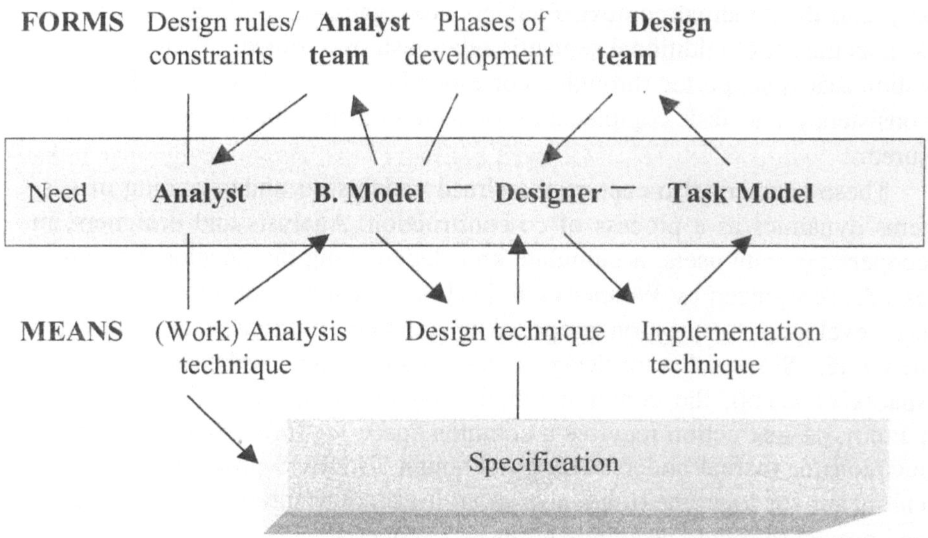

Figure 1. Activity theory's instantiation through TADEUS at the process level at the interface between analysis and design.

As shown, development knowledge is kept in a context-sensitive way as well as in a way to be communicated among different developers, in the example in Fig. 1 among analysts and designer. Hence, the context representation helps members of the different development teams to better understand the other's actions. The layered approach of activity theory supports the idea of model-based and context-sensitive processes throughout software development. Although there exists a formal division of development labour, namely analysis has to be performed before design and by respective specialists, it does not work as a linear procedure. This nature of work is captured through the non-stringent sequences and dynamics of the activity theory, as well as by TADEUS. In correspondence to the theory, TADEUS allows actions to become operations when particular specifications are reused or existing specifications are reused for the case at hand. The same holds for changing requirements and shift of focus in design. TADEUS also cares about the theory's principle of development. It allows to shift the focus either in terms of switching between perspectives (tasks, data, user, interaction, synchronization (i.e. application)) or in changing interaction or task requirements in the course of development.

Software development is a team process. Based on the adequate means for communication, according to activity theory, the level of individuals as well as of collective actions have to be represented. This demand is met in

TADEUS in line to activity theory through maintaining both, isolated perspectives on the development knowledge (either specific to phases or models), and their mutual context. Enablers are, again, the unifying notation as well as the set of additional semantic relationships to object-oriented specification that is supported through a corresponding set of algorithms. Thus, the consistency and task completeness of development knowledge can be ensured.

These enablers also capture the already addressed understanding of systems dynamics as a process of co-construction. Analysts and designers, in cooperation with users, accumulate knowledge along the development process. As recognized by Wehner et al. [21] this accumulation process empowers developers to question proposed or existing solutions, and to develop new ones. Since software design is also work design (addressing the work spaces of users), the common redefinition of roles, work objectives, and patterns of interaction requires a common space for (re)design and communication for mutual understanding. Although TADEUS provides the technical means for this type of collaboration, it cannot ensure the required social and project setting to accomplish this task properly.

5. CONCLUSION

Activity theory helps to facilitate the development of task- and user-centred software systems. In this contribution a particular approach, namely the model-based TADEUS (Task Analysis / Design / End User Systems) technique, has been revisited. The findings indicate that activity theory facilitates the understanding of the development process. Hereby, the crucial issues are:

- The co-construction and maintenance of development knowledge,
- The intelligibility of design representation for different user groups (developers and workers), and
- The recognition of dynamics of development, such as switching between perspectives, and proceeding from analysis to design.

In contrast to other development techniques for designing user interfaces and prototyping, TADEUS keeps the context of development throughout the different phases of development. Hence, it maintains knowledge about the context of use, i.e. work actors, tasks etc. This way, TADEUS provides the required support of designers, namely, a frame of reference and relevant design entities.

Activity theory does not only help to understand the development process, but also the conditions under which the development activities are performed. It helps to model human activities in their organizational and societal context for user interface development. Its elements have been instantiated through TADEUS, according to the dynamics of interactive system development.

The next step in research will be to further detail the process and to address the content level through discussing the co-construction at the method level. A candidate under methodological investigation is the repertory grid technique for work-task acquisition. This technique is based on Kelly's theory of personal constructs [13] and has been used successfully for knowledge acquisition by Gaines et al. [9]. Subjectively perceived similarities can be verified for the sake of a common understanding of a work space. In addition, knowledge externalisation can be facilitated, since items describing a universe of discourse have to be set up in the course of knowledge elicitation. The use of such a technique could increase the quality of analysis, and thus the embodiment of task and user knowledge into design knowledge.

REFERENCES

[1] Bannon, L.J. and Bødker, S., *Constructing Common Information Spaces*, in Proc. of Fifth European Conf. on Computer Supported Cooperative Work ECSCW'97 (Lancaster, 7-11 September 1997), Kluwer Academics Pub., Dordrecht, 1997, pp. 81-96.

[2] Bannon, L.J. and Kuuti, K., *Shifting Perspectives on Organizational Memory: From Storage to Active Remembering*, in Proc. of 29th Hawaii Int. Conf. on System Sciences HICSS'96 (Maui, 3-6 January 1996), IEEE Press, Los Alamitos, 1996, pp. 156-167.

[3] Bedny, G.Z., Karwowski, W., and Seglin, M.H., *Activity Theory as a Basis for the Study and Redesign of computer-based Task*, in "Usability Evaluation and Interface Design", Smith, M.J. et al. (eds.), Vol. 1, Lawrence Erlbaum, Mahwah, 2001, pp. 342-346.

[4] Blackler, F., *Knowledge, Knowledge Work and Organizations. An Overview and Interpretation*, Organization Studies, Vol. 16, No. 4, 1995, pp. 1021-1046.

[5] Cyert, R.M. and March, J.G., Eine verhaltenswissenschaftliche Theorie der Unternehmung, Stuttgart, 1995.

[6] Diaper, D. (ed.), *Task Analysis for Human-Computer Interaction*, Ellis Horwood, Chicester, 1990.

[7] Embley, D.W., Kurtz, B.D., and Woodfield, S.N., *Object-Oriented Systems Analysis. A Model-Driven Approach*, Yourdon Press, Englewood Cliffs, 1992.

[8] Engeström, Y., *Learning by Expanding, An Activity-Theoretical Approach to Developmental Resarch*, PhD thesis, Orienta-Konsultit Oy, Helsinki, 1987.

[9] Gaines, B.R. and Shaw, M.L.G., *Knowledge Acquisition Tools Based on Personal Construct Psychology*, in Knowledge Engineering Review, Special Issue on Automated Knowledge Acquisition Tools, Vol. 8, 1992, pp. 49-85.

[10] Johnson, P., *Human-Computer Interaction: Psychology, Task Analysis, and Software Engineering*, McGraw Hill, London, 1992.

[11] Kaptelinin, V., *Computer-mediated Activity: Functional Organs in Social and Developmental Contexts*, in [15], pp. 45-67.

[12] Kaptelinin, V., *Activity Theory: Implications for Human-Computer Interaction*, in [15], pp. 103-114.

[13] Kelly, G.A., *The Psychology of Personal Constructs: A Theory of Personality*, New York, 1955.
[14] Kuutti, K., *Activity Theory as a Potential Framework for Human-Computer Interaction*, in [15], pp. 17-44.
[15] Nardi, B. (ed.), *Context and Consciousness. Activity Theory and Human-Computer Interaction*, MIT Press, 1996.
[16] Preece, J. (ed.): *A Guide to Usability: Human Factors in Computing*, Addison-Wesley, New York, 1993.
[17] Raithel, A. and Velichkovsky, B., *Joint Attention and Co-Construction. New Ways to Foster User-Designer Collaboration*, in [16], pp. 199-233.
[18] Raithel, A., *Semiotic Self-Regulation and Work. An Activity-theoretical Foundation for Design*, in Software Development and Reality Construction, Cambridge, 1992, pp. 391-415.
[19] Stary, Ch., *TADEUS: Seamless Development of Task-Based and User-Oriented Interfaces*, IEEE Trans. on Systems, Man, and Cybernetics, Vol. 30, 2000, pp. 509-525.
[20] Vanderdonckt, J. and Puerta, A. (eds.), *Computer-Aided Design II*, Proc. of the 3rd Int. Conf. on Computer-Aided Design of User Interfaces CADUI'99 (Louvain-la-Neuve, 25-27 October 1999), Kluwer Academics Pub., Dordrecht, 1999.
[21] Wehner, T. and Endres, E. (eds.), *Zwischenbetriebliche Kooperation,* Weinheim, 1996.
[22] Wehner, Th., Clases, Ch., and Bachmann: *Cooperation at Work: A Process-Oriented Perspective on Joint Activity in Inter-organizational Relations*, Ergonomics, Vol. 43, No. 7, 2000, pp. 983-998.
[23] Wilson, S. and Johnson, P., *Bridging the Generation Gap: From Work Tasks to User Interface Design*, in J. Vanderdonckt (ed.), Proc. of 2nd Int. Workshop on Computer-Aided Design of User Interfaces CADUI'96 (Namur, 5-7 June 1996), Presses Universitaires de Namur, Namur, 1996, pp. 77-94.

Chapter 18

MODEL-BASED INTERACTIVE PROTOTYPING OF HIGHLY INTERACTIVE APPLICATIONS

David Navarre[1], Philippe Palanque[1,2] & Rémi Bastide[1]
[1] *LIHS-IRIT, University Toulouse 1, Place Anatole France, F-31042 Toulouse (France).*
E-mail: {navarre, bastide}@univ-tlse1.fr - URL: http://lihs.univ-tlse1.fr/navarre, bastide
[2] *LIHS-IRIT, Univ. Toulouse 3, 118, route de Narbonne, F-31062 Toulouse Cedex 4 (France).*
E-mail: palanque@irit.fr – URL: http://lihs.univ-tlse1.fr/palanque
Tel: +33-561-556 965 – Fax: +33-561-556 258

Abstract This paper presents a case tool supporting the ICO (Interactive Cooperative Object) formalism. This formalism allows for describing, in a formal way, highly interactive applications (also called post-WIMP). The first section describes both why such user interfaces are challenging for most description techniques and the state of the art in this field. Then, we use a case study in order to recall the basic concepts of the ICO formalism and the recent extensions added in order to take into account post-WIMP interfaces' specificities. The next section introduces PetShop a case tool supporting the edition and the execution of ICOs specifications. Lastly, we present how the underlying architecture of PetShop and the executable nature of the ICOs support efficiently iterative development of highly interactive applications through interactive prototyping.

Keywords: Formal Description Techniques, Model-Based UI Design, Prototyping.

1. INTRODUCTION

Being able to fully specify interactive application is nowadays mandatory due, for instance, to the arrival of such applications in the control system of safety critical applications. The reason for putting some effort in the use and the deployment of formal description techniques lies in the fact that they are the only means for both modelling in a precise and unambiguous way all the components of an interactive application (presentation, dialogue and func-

C. Kolski and J. Vanderdonckt (eds.), Computer-Aided Design of User Interfaces III, 205–216.
© 2002 *Kluwer Academic Publishers.*

tional core) and to propose techniques for reasoning about (and also verifying) the models.

Formal description techniques are usually applied to early phases in the development process (requirements analysis and elicitation) and clearly show their limits when it comes to evaluation (testing).

When the emphasis is on validation, iterative design processes are generally put forward with the support of prototyping as a critical tool [11]. However, if used in a non-structured way, and without links to the classical phases of the development process, results produced using such iterative processes are usually weak in terms of reliability. They also can be unacceptable when interfaces for safety critical applications are concerned.

Several approaches propose solutions for the reconciliation of the specification and the validation phases in the field of interactive applications, but these solutions are often incomplete.

***Interaction style* viewpoint:** post-WIMP user interfaces are not yet widely developed. For this reason, most of the approaches (see for instance 0) only deal with WIMP interfaces (Window Icon Menu and Pointing), i.e. static interfaces for which the set and the number of interactors is known beforehand. The behaviour and the role of these interactors is standardised (typically windows and buttons belong to this category).

***Development phase* viewpoint:** one can often find disparate solutions that do not integrate the various phases in a consistent manner [8]. So, most often several gaps remain to be bridged manually by the teams involved in the development process.

***Reliability of results* viewpoint:** several integrated approaches have been proposed for WIMP interactive applications. Among them we find TRIDENT [3] which is the most successful one as it handles both data and dialogue description and as it also incorporates ergonomic evaluation by means of embedded ergonomic rules. However, specification techniques used in the project have not been provided with analysis techniques for verifying models and the consistency between models.

The paper is structured as follows. Section 2 describes the differences between “classical user interfaces” and “highly interactive” ones. Section 3 introduces a case study from the Air Traffic Control domain. This case study is used for describing the concepts of the ICO formalism. Section 4 describes PetShop, the case tool supporting the formalism. In this section we present in detail how an ICO model can be edited and executed using this environment. In section 5 we show how PetShop can be used for prototyping interactive applications. In this section several scenarios are described and we present how they can be performed interactively with PetShop.

2. HIGHLY INTERACTIVE USER INTERFACES

Interfaces are usually called highly interactive (or post-WIMP) when the dialogue is directly driven by the user and when the interaction style is direct manipulation [12]. This type of interaction allows the user manipulating domain objects directly i.e. without using standardized, predefined interactors [6] as for WIMP interfaces. Papers dealing with this kind of interfaces usually put the emphasis on the novelty of their interaction style [14] (use of new input devices and new visualization techniques). The parallel and asynchronous nature of their handling of inputs and outputs make their behaviour too complex to be described by means of classical description techniques [7]. Description techniques used for modelling such interaction styles and techniques must be able [2] to take into account existing as well as new applications, to compare various design alternatives and to make easier the identification and the definition of new interaction techniques.

If we consider interfaces such as the ones developed in the field of Air Traffic Control for instance, a new characteristic appears which is the dynamicity of interaction objects in terms of existence, reactivity and interrelations [4]. At the opposite of WIMP interfaces, where the interaction space is predetermined, these interfaces may include new interactors (for instance graphical representations of planes) at any time during the use of the application. Even though this kind of problem is easily mastered by programming languages it is hard to tackle in terms of modelling. This is why classical description techniques must be improved in order to be able to describe in a complete way highly interactive application.

3. A CASE STUDY

The ICO (Interactive Cooperative Object) formalism aims at describing in a formal way the dialog part of an interactive application in order to validate models through specific verification techniques. The formalism uses concepts borrowed to Object-Oriented approaches (such as classification, dynamic instanciation, encapsulation, inheritance and client-server relationship) for describing data or static aspects of the interactive system. Behavioural aspects are described using High-Level Petri nets.

3.1 Informal Description of the Example

The example presented in this section comes from a more complex application studied in the context of the European project Mefisto. This project is dedicated to formal description techniques and focuses on the field of Air Traffic Control. This example comes from an En-route Air Traffic Control application focusing on the impact of data-link technologies in the ATC field. Using such applications air traffic controllers can direct pilots in a sector (a decomposition of the airspace). The radar image is shown on Fig. 1. On the radar image each plane is represented by a graphical element providing air traffic controllers with useful information for handling air traffic in a sector. In the simplified version of the radar image we are considering, each graphical representation of a plane is made up of three components: a label (providing precise information about the plane such as ID, speed, cleared flight level,...), a dot (representing the current position of the plane in the sector) and a speed vector (a graphical line from the dot which represent the envisioned position of the plane in 3 minutes).

On the top of the window a button named (New Plane) allows for introducing new plane in the sector. This button allows for simulating the arrival of new planes in the sector while in reality they would be instantiated on the user interface by calls from the functional core of the application processing information provided by physical radars.

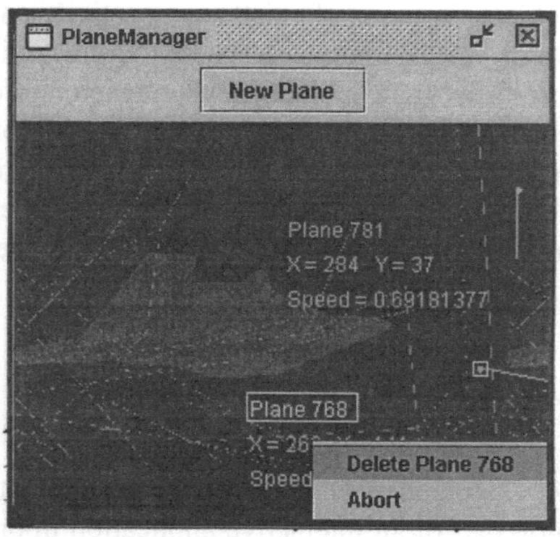

Figure 1. A menu opened on the radar for the selected plane.

Initially the radar image is empty. Each time the button is pressed, a new plane is randomly generated. It is possible for the user to select planes by *shift-clicking* on its graphical representation. A *right-click* on a selected plane opens a menu made up of two elements (this is only for sake of simplicity): *Abort*, for closing the menu and *Delete*, for deleting the plane (removing its graphical representation from the radar image).

At a time only one plane can be selected and the menu can only be opened for a selected plane. Planes are automatically removed when leaving the sector.

3.2 Formal Description of the Example

This section presents both the formal specification of the case study introduced in the previous section and the main concepts of the ICO formalism.

Behaviour of the application. The first step in the modelling process is to identify the objects of the application. Then for each object we have to describe the set of services offered by this object to its environment (i.e. the other objects of the application). For this purpose we use the Interface Description Language (IDL) promoted by the Object Management Group in CORBA [10]. For modelling the case study we have identified three classes: a class PlaneManager managing all the planes in a sector, a class Plane (one instance of this class is created each time the user clicks on the New Plane button) and a class menu (for which only one instance exists at a time). Fig. 2 contains the IDL description of the three classes.

```
module PlaneManager {
    interface IPlaneManager {
            void openPlane(in Plane) ;
            void closePlane(in Plane) ;
            void removePlane(in Plane) ;
    };
    interface IPlane {
            void select() ;
            void deselect() ;
            void openMenu() ;
            void closeMenu() ;
            void remove() ;
    };
    interface IMenu {
            void open() ;
    };
};
```

Figure 2. IDL interfaces of the application.

When the IDL is defined for each class it is important to describe more precisely the behaviour of each class. This behaviour defines according to the internal state of each object of a class what services are currently available. It also defines what state changes occur when a service is performed. Left-hand side of Fig. 2 presents the behaviour of the class PlaneManager modelled by high-level Petri nets [1]. For space reasons the description of the behaviour of the other classes is not presented here.

This Object Control Structures (ObCS) defines in a complete and unambiguous way the behaviour of the class. The aim of this paper is not to focus on this modelling technique but on the use of the environment supporting this formalism for prototyping interactive application. For this reason the model is not presented in details here but the interested reader can find more detail in [9]. As this class is in charge of creating and managing planes in a sector it is in charge of instantiating objects from the Plane class. This functionality is modelled by the transition newPlane in the model and the reference to the newly created plane is stored in the outgoing place of this transition, i.e. the place Plane.

This is one of the arguments for using high-level Petri nets as they allows for representing in a graphical and formal way dynamic instanciation of objects which is a mandatory requirement for modelling highly interactive applications as introduced in section 2.

widget PlaneManager
//No rendering method.

widget Plane

void show() {
//Display plane as a graphical point, a speed vector and a label. The plane is shown as unselected. }
void hide() {
//Remove plane from the screen.}
void showSelected() {
//show the Id of the plane surrounded by a green rectangle and the dot circled by a green circle. }

Figure 3. Rendering methods for the case study.

Description of the presentation part. In this step of the specification process, information is added to the behavioural specification for describing the user interface part of the application. Three different elements have to be defined:

- The *rendering methods* (i.e. for this case study the set of methods dedicated to displaying graphical information on the screen). They are represented in Fig. 3 for classes PlaneManager and Plane.
- The *activation function.* As for the behavioural part, an activation function must be defined for each class. The class PlaneManager one is presented in Fig. 4. For each couple (Object, event) this function associates a user service. A user service is defined by a set of transitions in the ObCS. These transitions can only be fired if they are available (according to the current state of the application) and the event has been triggered through user action on the input device. Graphically, each transition of this set is represented in the ObCS with an incoming broken arrow with an oval labelled by the name of the event. Managing dynamically instantiated objects requires the referencing of the objects within the activation function. This is modelled by the inclusion of a variable to which the event is asso-

ciated (see for instance the definition of the selection of a plane in line 2 of the array in Fig. 4) and of course the place in which this information is stored.

- The *rendering function* aims at representing the reaction of the system when a state change occurs. In Petri nets, a state change can only occur when tokens are removed or added to a place. Thus the rendering function associates, to each of these possible state changes, a previously defined rendering method. Fig. 5 shows for each place of the ObCS of the class PlaneManager which rendering method is triggered when a token is removed or added to a place.

PlaneManager			
Place	**Object type**	**Event**	**Service**
	ButtonNewPlane	Click	newPlane
Planes	Plane	Shift Left Click <x>	select
Selected Plane	Plane	Left Click <x>	deselect

Figure 4. Activation function of class PlaneManager.

PlaneManager		
Element of the ObCS		Rendering method
Type	State changing	
Place Planes	Token <x> enters	x.show()
Place RemovedPlanes	Token <x> enters	x.hide()

Figure 5. Rendering function of the case study.

4. PETSHOP ENVIRONMENT

In this section we present the PetShop environment and the design process it supports. Some screen dumps are included in order to show what is currently available.

Fig. 6 presents the general architecture of PetShop. It is composed of a set of rectangles and documents-like shapes. The rectangles represent the functional modules of PetShop. The documents-like shapes represent the models produced and used by the modules.

4.1 Editing the ObCS

PetShop features an Object Petri net editor that allows for editing and executing the ObCSs of the classes (see left-hand side). All the components of the ObCS can be interactively built using PetShop. PetShop also automatically generates an Object Petri net from the IDL description [15]. This Object Petri net is not the final ObCS of the class but only the minimal set of places and transitions corresponding to the IDL description. The editing of the Object Petri net is done graphically using the Palette in the centre of the toolbar. The left part of the toolbar is used for generic functions such as load, save, cut-copy and paste. The right hand side of the toolbar drives the execution of the specification.

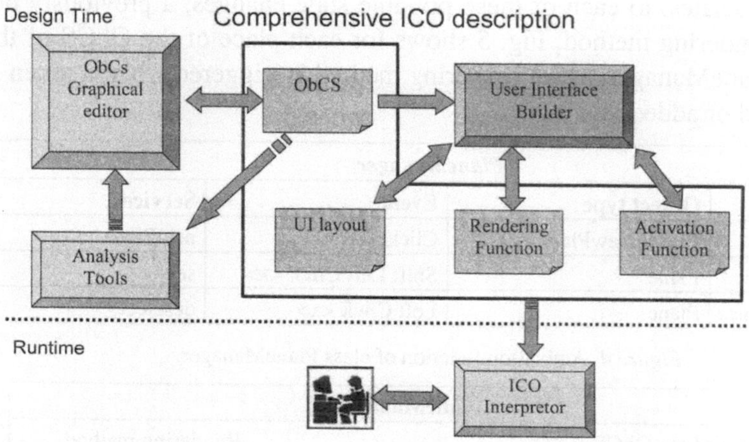

Figure 6. Architecture of the PetShop Environment.

4.2 Editing the Presentation

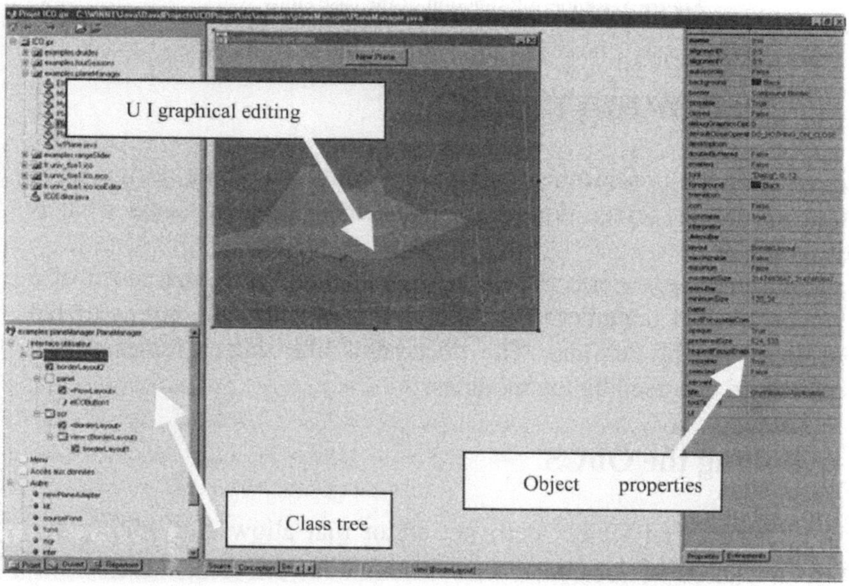

Figure 7. Editing of the presentation part using JBuilder Interface builder.

Currently, PetShop is linked to JBuilder™ environment for the creation of the presentation part of the ICOs. Thus creation of widgets is done by means of JBuilder interface builder (Fig. 7). This figure shows how the PlaneManager components are created using the interface builder. However, we have not yet created a visual tool for editing the rendering and the activation function that still have to be typed in Java.

4.3 Execution

A well-known advantage of Petri nets is their executability. This is highly beneficial to our approach, since as soon as a behavioural specification is provided in term of ObCS, this specification can be executed to provide additional insights on the possible evolutions of the system.

Fig. 8 shows the execution of the specification of the Range Slider in Petshop. The ICO specification is embedded at run time according to the interpreted execution of the ICO (see [1] for more details about it: both data structures and execution algorithms).

At run time, the user can both look at the specification and the actual application. They are in two different windows overlapping in Fig. 8. The window PlaneManager corresponds to the execution of the window with the Object Petri net underneath.

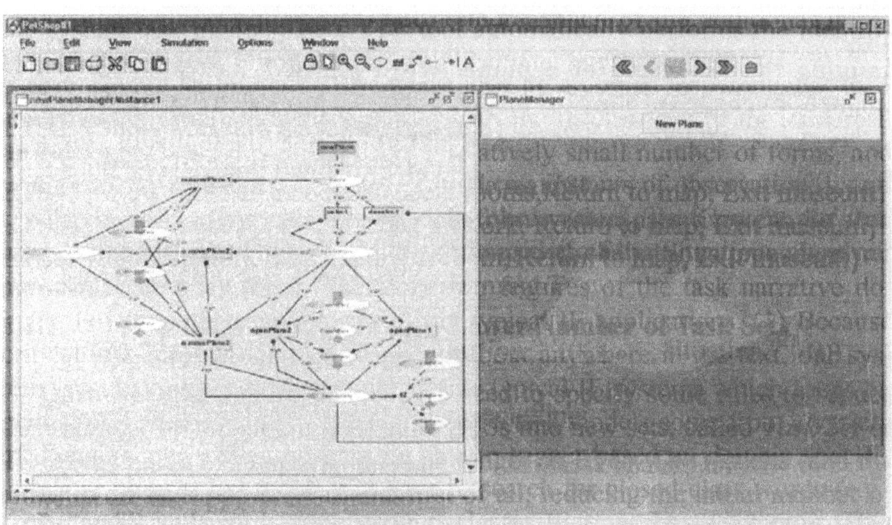

Figure 8. The execution of ICO specification in PetShop.

In this window we can see the set of transition that are currently enabled (represented in dark grey and the other ones in light grey). This is automatically calculated from the current marking of the Object Petri net.

Each time the user acts on the PlaneManager the event is passed onto the interpreter. If the corresponding transition is enabled then the interpreter fires it, performs its action (if any), changes the marking of the input and output places and perform the rendering associated (if any).

5. INTERACTIVE PROTOTYPING

Within PetShop, prototyping from specification is performed in an interactive way. At anytime during the design process it is possible to introduce modifications either in order to make the specification more precise or to change it. The advantage of model-based prototyping is that it allows designers to immediately evaluate the impact of a modification.

We have identified two different kinds of modifications that can be performed using Petshop, namely : lexical and syntactic.

5.1 Lexical Modifications

Lexical part of the user interface gathers elementary elements of the presentation (for instance the drawing of a button) and all the elementary actions offered to the user (such as clicking on a button). Lexical modifications concern the addition, the removal or the modification of this kind of elements.

Changing the rendering of a plane. When selected, the colour of a plane changes to green. As a lexical modification, we propose to change it to red. *At the specification level*: nothing changes in the specification. Only the content of the method *showSelected* must be modified and this must be done using the Jbuilder environment.

Changing the event triggering the selection of a plane. The currently used event (as defined in 3.1) is Left Button Shift Click. We propose to use instead the event Left Button Click. Therefore we modify:

- At the specification level: the corresponding event must be changed in the activation function.
- At the code level: the Java code must be modified to change the adapter (representing the activation function) of the widget plane.

5.2 Syntactic Modifications

The syntactic part of the user interface describes the links and relationships between the lexical elements (for instance shift clicking on a plane then right clicking on the plane to open the menu and then deleting the plane).

Modification of the selection mechanism. Currently only one plane can be selected at a time. In order to allow multiple selection the following modifications must be performed:

- at the specification level: the inhibitor arc (the arc terminated by a black circle) linking the transition select to the place SelectedPlane (Fig. 8) must be removed,
- at the code level: no modification.

Defining a upper limit for the number of planes in the sector. In the initial informal specification there is no limit on the number of planes. Adding a maximum limit to 20 planes (number of planes normally controlled by a controller) requires the following modifications:

- At the specification level: A new place must be added in the PlaneManager ObCS. Initially this place will hold 20 tokens. This place has to be connected by an arc to the transition NewPlane of the same ObCS. When a plane leaves a sector (or is deleted using the menu) the corresponding transition must add a new token to this place.
- At *the code level:* no modification.

6. CONCLUSION

Prototyping is now recognised as a cornerstone of the successful construction of interactive systems as it allows making users at the centre of the development process. However, prototyping tends to produce low quality software as no specification or global design is undertaken. We have shown in this paper how formal specification techniques can contribute to the development process of interactive systems through prototyping activities.

While the ICO formal specification technique has reached a maturity level allowing coping with real size dynamic interactive applications, the Petshop environment is still under development. A real size application has been completely specified in the field of the European project MEFISTO (http://giove.cnuce.cnr.it/mefisto.html). More information about PetShop can be found on PetShop's web site: http://lis.univ-tlse1.fr/petshop/

However, the work done on this Air Traffic Control application has also shown the amount of work that is still required before the environment can be used by other people than the ones that took part in its development.

In order to make it attractive to developers we are integrating additional features such as:

- Tool-supported verification of properties,
- Analysis of conformance with other representations such as tasks models

- Performance analysis in order to support widgets selection and structuring

Another stream of research we are investigating is the generation of test cases from the formal specification in order to help developers checking whether an implementation is conformant with respect to the specification. This will allow development teams to take the specifications, still use their favourite programming environment and later check whether their implementation is conformant with it.

REFERENCES

[1] Bastide, R. and Palanque, Ph., *A Visual and Formal Glue Between Application and Interaction*, J. of Visual Language and Computing, Vol. 10, No. 5, 1999, pp. 481-507.

[2] Beaudouin-Lafon, M.,. *Instrumental Interaction: An Interaction Model for Designing Post-WIMP User Interfaces*, in Proc. of ACM Conf. on Human Factors in Computing Systems CHI'2000, ACM Press, New York, 2000, pp. 446-453.

[3] Bodart, F. and Vanderdonckt, J., *Encapsulating Knowledge for Intelligent Automatic Interaction Objects Selection*, in Proc. of ACM Conf. of Human Factors in Computing Systems InterCHI'93, ACM Press, New York, 1993, pp. 424-429.

[4] Esteban, O., Chatty, S. and Palanque, Ph., *Visual Construction of Highly Interactive Applications*, in Proc. of IFIP 2.8 Conference on Management of Visual Data, Chapman & Hall, London, 1998, pp. 304-316.

[5] Hussey, A. and Carrington, D., *Model-Based Design of User Interfaces Using Object-Z*, in J. Vanderdonckt and A. Puerta (eds.), Proc. of 3rd Conf. on Computer-Aided Design of User Interfaces CADUI'99, Kluwer Academics Pub., Dordrecht, 1999, pp. 43-53.

[6] IBM, *Common User Access Guidelines, Object-Oriented Interface Design*, Document SC34-4399, IBM Corporation, 1993.

[7] Jacob, R.J.K., Deligiannidis, L. and Morrison, S., *A Software Model and Specification Language for Non-WIMP User Interfaces*, ACM Transactions on Computer-Human Interaction, Vol. 6, No. 1, March 1999, pp. 1-46.

[8] Märtin, Ch., *A Method Engineering Framework for Modelling and Generating Interactive Applications*, in Proc. of 3rd Conf. on Computer-Aided Design of User Interfaces CADUI'99, Kluwer Academics Pub., Dordrecht, 1999, pp. 55-60.

[9] Navarre D., Palanque P., Bastide R., and Sy, O., *Structuring Interactive Systems Specifications for Executability and Prototypability*, in Proc. of 7th Eurographics Workshop on Design, Specification and Verification of Interactive Systems DSV-IS'2000 (Limerick, 5-6 June 2000), LNCS Vol. 1946, Springer-Verlag, Berlin, 2000, pp. 97-119.

[10] OMG. *The Common Object Request Broker: Architecture and Specification. CORBA IIOP 2.2 /98-02-01*, Framingham, 1998.

[11] Rettig, M., *Prototyping for Tiny Fingers*, Communication of the ACM, Vol. 37, No. 4, 1994, pp. 21-27.

[8] Shneiderman, B., *Direct Manipulations: a Step Beyond Programming Languages*, IEEE Computer, 1983, pp. 27-69.

[13] Sy, O., Bastide, R., Palanque, P., Le Duc, H., and Navarre, D., *PetShop: a CASE Tool for the Petri Net Based Specification and Prototyping of CORBA Systems*, in Proc. of 20th Conference on Applications and Theory of Petri Nets ICATPN'99, 1999.

[14] van Dam, A., *Post-WIMP User Interfaces*, Communications of the ACM, Vol. 40, No. 2, 1997, pp. 63-67.

Chapter 19

MODELING STYLE OF WORK AS AN AID TO THE DESIGN AND EVALUATION OF INTERACTIVE SYSTEMS

James Wu, T.C. Nicholas Graham, Katherine Everitt, Dorothea Blostein, and Edward Lank
Department of Computing and Information Science, Queen's University
Kingston, Ontario, K7L 3N6 (Canada)
E-mail: {wuj, graham}@cs.queensu.ca – URL: http://www.cs.queensu.ca/home/graham/
Tel.: +1-613-533-6526 – Fax: +1-613-533-6513

Abstract This paper presents the *workstyle model*, a novel technique for recording the working style of people using an interactive system. Workstyle complements task modeling by providing information on how people communicate and co-ordinate their activities, and by showing what style of artifact the work is to produce. We have applied the workstyle model to the evaluation of UML design tools and the design of a new tool, the Software Design Board. The design of the model itself was informed by studies of tools and designers both at Queen's University and at a large software development organization.

Keywords: Model-based design, Software design tools, UML, Work style.

1. INTRODUCTION

Task models [5] help in understanding the goals and activities of users of a software system. Through this understanding, the designer of a system can ensure that users' tasks are supported. Techniques such as cognitive walk-through [25], task simulation and model checking [18] allow user interface designs to be checked versus task models, exposing areas where the system fails to adequately support user tasks, or where user tasks are supported in an inconvenient manner. Task models therefore help to ensure that software systems meet users' needs.

C. Kolski and J. Vanderdonckt (eds.), Computer-Aided Design of User Interfaces III, 217–228.
© 2002 *Kluwer Academic Publishers.*

Figure 1. Different tools (e.g. a whiteboard and a PC) may support the same tasks, while affording different styles of work.

Task models are less successful, however, in capturing what it means for a task to be supported in a usable manner. To address this problem, we present the *Workstyle Model,* a novel model capturing some aspects of users' preferred style of work. This allows analysis of whether an interactive system design supports users in performing their tasks, and of whether this support is consistent with the users' working style. The model concentrates on users' preferred collaboration styles and on the desired properties of artifacts developed through this collaboration.

The workstyle model was developed in the context of the Software Design Board project, a project aiming to provide better tools for software design. The model has been validated through evaluation of existing design tools, and has motivated the design of a new software design tool.

The paper is organized as follows. In sections 2 and 3, we motivate and introduce the model. In section 4, we present the Software Design Board as a case study of the use of the model. The Software Design Board is an electronic whiteboard-based tool supporting the collaborative creation of design diagrams in the Unified Modeling Language (UML) [20].

2. MOTIVATION

In order to motivate the workstyle model, we consider the task of creating a design diagram in the UML notation. A task model can help us understand the activities involved in creating such a diagram: drawing and labeling nodes, connecting them with relations, editing and reformatting diagram elements, and so forth. Such a model of design activities might lead us to develop a tool similar to Rational Rose, permitting mouse-based structural editing of design diagrams.

However, before committing to such a design, it is important to understand the users' preferred workstyle in addition to the tasks they need to perform. For example, designers may be working in a brainstorming style, or may be recording precise documentation from which the system is to be built.

As illustrated by Fig. 1, the brainstorming style is well supported by a whiteboard. A whiteboard provides sufficient space for small groups to work, and supports a fluid style of interaction where multiple designers may interact with the design artifact in parallel. The designers are also not restricted to following a precise design syntax.

Alternatively, the precise design style is well supported by a traditional Computer-Aided Software Engineering (CASE) tool. Both tools support the activities identified through the task model. However, they support the tasks in different ways, appropriate to either the brainstorming or precise design styles of work. As we shall see in the following section, the workstyle model helps in the analysis of peoples' goals and tasks by helping to understand their preferred style of work.

3. THE WORKSTYLE MODEL

As motivated by the above example, we characterize the workstyle of a group in terms of how the group chooses to collaborate, as well as the kinds of artifacts the group chooses to create. As shown in Fig. 2, the workstyle model characterizes working style as a space of eight continuous dimensions.

The first four describe collaboration style; the remaining four describe the properties of artifacts being created. A particular workstyle can then be represented as a point in this space. A particular tool may support a set of workstyles, which can be represented as a region in this space. As will be shown in section 4, it is then possible to compare peoples' desired workstyles to those supported by tools, helping to identify potential tool mismatches.

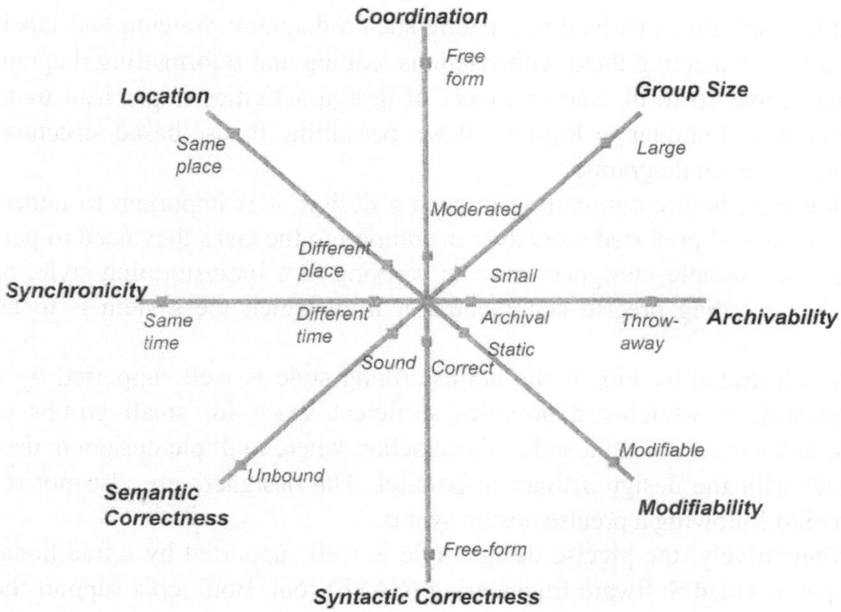

Figure 1. The workstyle model presents an eight-dimensional space on which working styles can be plotted. Workstyles are decomposed into collaboration style, and style of artifact being produced.

3.1 Dimensions Describing Collaboration Style

The first four dimensions describe how people choose to collaborate while performing their tasks. These are:

- **Location** – The location axis refers to the location of the people involved in the collaboration. People may be in the same place (*co-located*) or in different places (*distributed.*) In general, collaboration becomes more difficult at a distance [21], and requires more support from tools.
- **Synchronicity** – The synchronicity axis captures temporal aspects of the collaboration. People may work together at the same time (*synchronously*) or at different times (*asynchronously*). Face-to-face or telephone conversations are examples of same-time interaction; email conversations or information sharing through a Lotus Notes database are examples of different-time interaction, while a rapid exchange of emails falls between the two.
- **Group Size** – The group size axis captures the number of people involved in the collaboration. Group size influences what styles of interaction are practical. For example, brainstorming may work in small groups, whereas larger groups require support of tools or communication processes.

- **Coordination** – This axis represents the model used to coordinate [16] the group's activities. For example, in a brainstorming session, free-form coordination is typical. Social protocols can determine the order of speaking or modifying shared artifacts. In meeting situations, more rigid coordination is typical, relying on a chair or even formal rules of order. Asynchronous tools typically rely on moderated coordination, such as check-in/check-out protocols, while synchronous tools like telephone or chat support more free-form interaction.

3.2 Dimensions Describing Artifact Style

The remaining four dimensions describe the properties of artifacts that result from the users' tasks. The properties are:

- **Syntactic Correctness** – This axis represents the degree to which the production of an artifact is required to follow a precise syntax. For example, a programmer must follow the rules of the programming language being used, while a designer may choose to follow the precise rules of a notation such as UML. However, in the early stages of design, a requirement to adhere to precise syntax may hinder creativity by diverting designers from the global concepts of design [13,22].
- **Semantic Correctness** – This axis represents the clarity of meaning of produced artifacts: that is, the degree to which they are ambiguous or contradictory. The production of semantically sound artifacts may be impractical and unnecessary. For example, design documents often contain contradictions, inconsistencies and missing information; humans can often work effectively in the presence of such contradiction [7].
- **Archivability** – Archivability represents the difficulty of saving an artifact so that it can be used at a later time. For example, word processing documents have high archivability, as they can be saved to disk and retrieved later. A whiteboard has poor archivability, as once it is erased, its contents are lost. Archiving is considered more difficult if an archived version cannot be used in the same way as the original. For example, a whiteboard drawing can be archived by photographing it; however, the photograph can no longer be manipulated on the whiteboard.
- **Modifiability** – This axis represents the ease with which an artifact can be modified. Modifiability is closely tied to the modification task. For example, small modifications to a whiteboard drawing are simply performed by erasing and redrawing. A modification such as reformatting a complex diagram is, however, difficult. Modifications to a diagram produced using a drawing program are more completely supported, but may require complex editing operations.

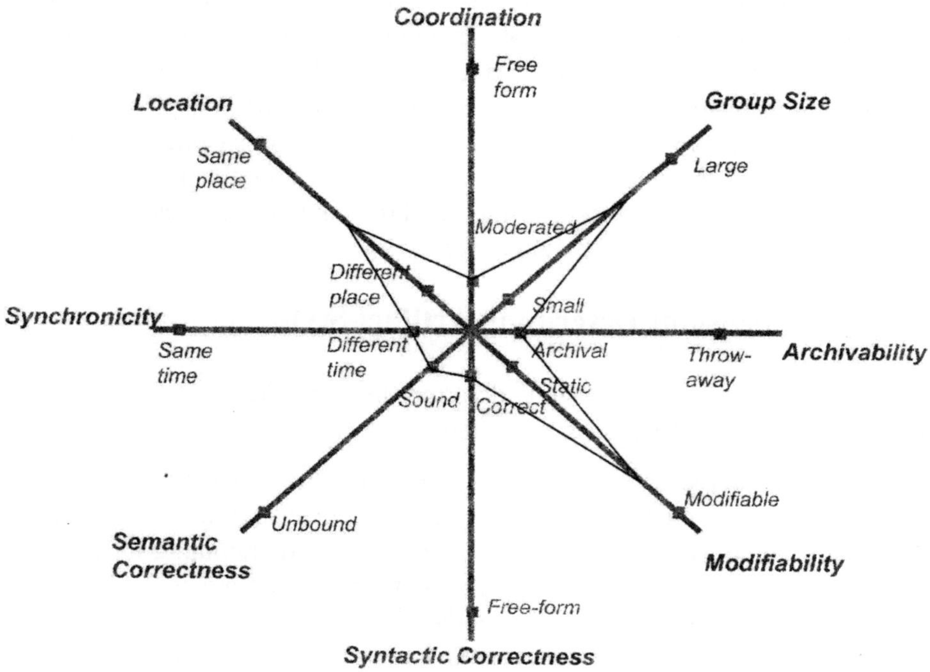

Figure 3. Workstyle supported by popular UML design tools, plotted using the workstyle model.

4. APPLICATION OF THE MODEL

The model presented in section 3 has been applied to the development of a UML design tool. We first used the model to show how existing UML design tools fail to match the work style of software developers. We then used the model to help motivate the design of a new tool.

It is useful to consider the workstyle supported by popular UML design tools such as Rational Rose, Aonix Software through Pictures (STP) and Together Control Center. As shown in Fig. 3, these tools support small-to-medium groups. The activities of different designers are coordinated through a repository, using locking and merging to support concurrent work. Designers can work in different places. Communication is different-time, through the contents of the repository. The tools provide structure editing that guarantees that designs will be syntactically correct and semantically sound. Since the tools provide structure editing and the ability to save and restore designs, designs are highly modifiable and easily archived.

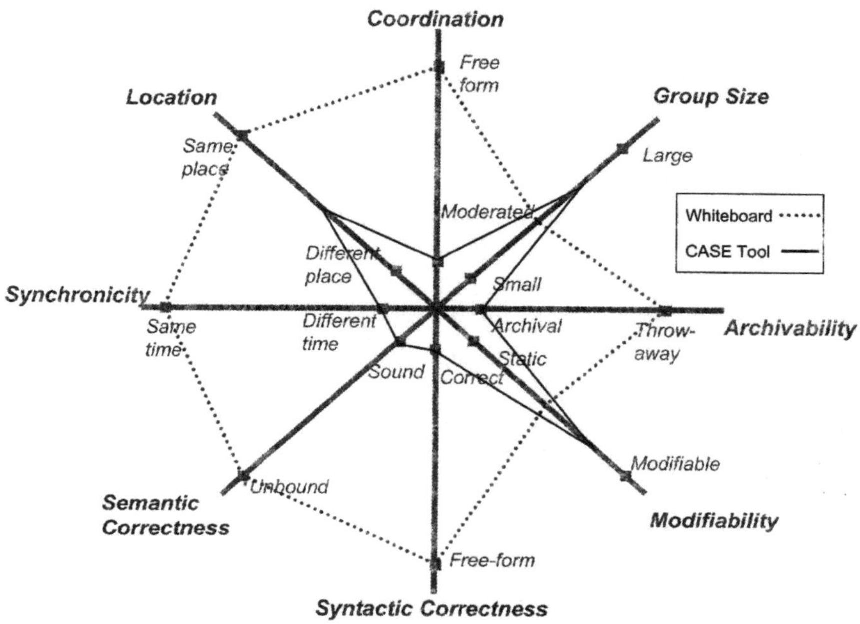

Figure 4. Ideal workstyle for brainstorming a software design overlaid with workstyle supported by existing UML CASE design tools.

4.1 Tools for UML Design

UML design tools such as described above are a good fit with workstyles where relatively little communication with other designers is required, and where the goal is to create precise, archival designs. The tools are particularly helpful in enforcing UML syntactic and semantic rules, and provide good support for editing and archiving documents.

However, as discussed in section 2, traditional UML design tools provide poor support for the early stages of design, such as brainstorming. During these phases, designers spend large percentages of their time on communications tasks. For example, two studies show communication activities as requiring between 70% [4] and 85% [11] of software developers' time.

This communication is largely informal in nature: Kraut and Streeter [12] report that software developers report "discussion with peers" as their most important method of coordinating their activities. Following a large study of a software development project in the U.S. Navy, Norcio and Chmura report that informal discussion is correlated with progress in design, and that the more complex the design problem, the larger the percentage of designers' time is spent on discussion [2]. Studies of design tasks in general have shown that in brainstorming sessions, the majority of time is spent talking and gesturing at the artifact being produced [1,22]. In simple activity analysis of brainstorming tasks, we have observed that as little as 5% of brainstorming time is spent actually producing the design artifact, while the remaining 95% is spent discussing it.

At the same time, it has been observed that traditional design tools provide poor support for informal communication [24], and this lack of support has been linked to low adoption rates of these tools [9,10]. In studies of designers in a large software company, we observed that the use of UML design tools was low, and that much design was performed with informal media such as paper or whiteboards.

The inappropriateness of UML design tools for early stages of design can be clearly shown by examining the brainstorming workstyle. As shown in Fig. 4, brainstorming is typically carried out by small groups working face to face. These groups typically use free-form coordination, using social protocols to determine who gets to speak or write next. In brainstorming, designers do not wish to be distracted by requirements to be syntactically correct, or even semantically sound [1,22]. Modifiability is important as early designs evolve rapidly. Archivability is important to allow early designs to be migrated to more formal designs.

Fig. 4 shows that while UML design tools support the core tasks of the early stages of design, they do not support the workstyle of early design. The emphasis on asynchronous, moderated work with strong emphasis on syntactic correctness and semantic soundness is thoroughly incompatible with the free-form brainstorming workstyle. Ivarii's study shows that once designers move beyond this early design stage, they tend not to record the designs in a CASE tool unless management requires it. We therefore believe that Fig. 4 demonstrates a large part of the problem with current UML design tools.

4.2 The Software Design Board

To address these problems, we have developed the Software Design Board, a prototype UML design tool that supports a variety of workstyles appropriate to the early stages of design. As can be seen in Fig. 1, the software design board is physically based on an electronic whiteboard. This whiteboard is a touch-sensitive membrane allowing drawings with a plastic stylus to be captured. The drawings are then projected onto the whiteboard display using a projector.

Using the Software Design Board, designers can create UML designs simply by drawing them, similarly to the free-style drawing of the Tivoli system [19]. This gives the full flexibility of media such as paper or standard whiteboards. This contrasts with other whiteboard-based UML tools such as Knight [3], which is a structure-editor using a gesture language to specify editing operations. Once designs have been drawn, an experimental UML recognizer tool [14] can be used to turn them into structured drawings, reformat them, and export them in XML format suitable for use in a UML CASE tool.

The Software Design Board supports collaborative work in a variety of ways. Small groups can work together at the whiteboard, similarly to working with a standard whiteboard. Different-time work is supported (as with a traditional whiteboard), by leaving board contents available for others to look at. Different-place work is also supported, by allowing the whiteboard contents to be shared in real-time. I.e., shared drawing artifacts can be shared amongst two or more Software Design Boards, so that changes to one board are immediately reflected on the others.

Since not all users may have electronic whiteboards available, the Software Design Board can also be hosted on a standard PC. For same-time, different-place work, gestural information (pointing, circling, etc.) is also communicated (as motivated by the VideoWhiteboard [23].) On a PC, designers gesture using the mouse; on an electronic whiteboard, a camera is used to capture gestures.

The implementation of the Software Design Board is an ongoing project. The UML recognizer is robust, but does not yet have sufficient accuracy for production use. A first prototype of the collaborative aspects of the design tool has been produced, and is being extended.

The Software Design Board supports the transition between a number of different workstyles:

- *Same-place to different-place interaction:* designers may share a single whiteboard, or dynamically connect to remote whiteboards or PC's.
- *Free-form to moderated coordination:* by exporting the design to a CASE tool, designers may take advantage of design repositories with check-in/check-out functionality. Exported designs can also take advantage of superior archivability and modifiability provided by CASE tools.
- *Syntactic/semantic freedom to syntactic/semantic correctness:* applying the UML recognizer requires the design to be made syntactically correct, and encourages semantic refinement.
- *Same-time to different-time interaction:* once a same-time brainstorming session is complete, designs may be exported to a CASE tool for asynchronous access, or may be left on the whiteboard as a reference.

4.3 Analysis

As shown in Fig. 5, the Software Design Board supports a broad range of working styles. These styles are a better fit with the early design workstyle (Fig. 4) than the style supported by traditional UML design tools (Fig. 3). Understanding work styles therefore helps us design tools that will better support the tasks to be performed.

The workstyle model complements a number other techniques for interactive system evaluation and design. For example, Lumsden has developed a sophisticated tool for matching CASE tools to their use [15]. Design notations such as OPAS [6] and our own dimension space [8] help in understanding the context of use of interactive systems, particularly how they fit within their physical environments. The Questions-Options-Criteria (QOC) method [17] helps evaluate design choices. While complementing these approaches, the workstyle model has the contribution of being simple to apply, and clearly showing where interactive system designs match or fail to match their intended work context.

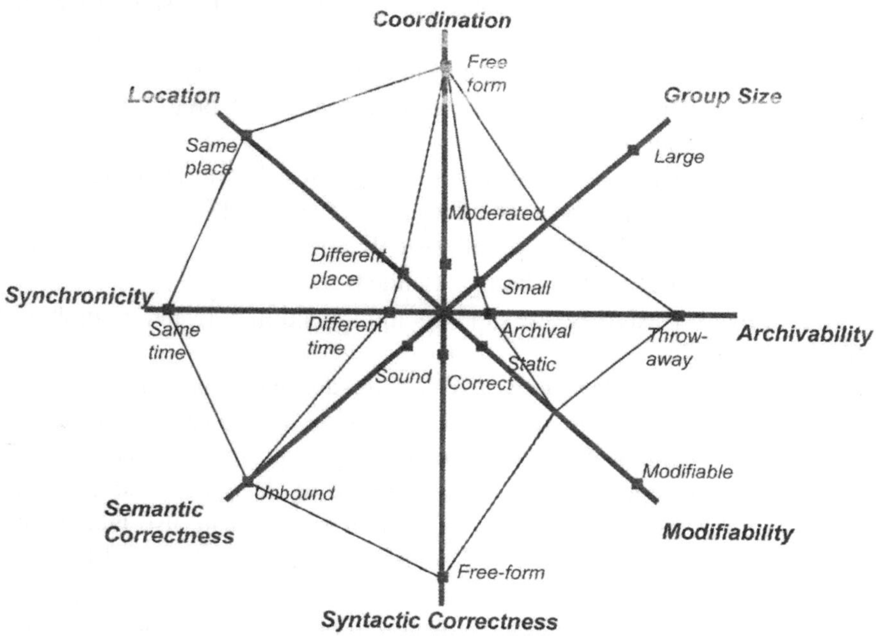

Figure 5. Workstyles supported by the Software Design Board. These range over same-place and different-place, same-time and different time, small to medium groups. Consistently with early stages of design, coordination is free-form, with no restrictions on syntactic correctness or semantic soundness. Designs are somewhat modifiable through standard whiteboard erasing and redrawing. Designs can be archived by exporting them in XML to a standard UML CASE tool.

5. CONCLUSIONS

In this paper, we have presented the *workstyle model*, a model capturing aspects of the style in which people carry out their tasks. The workstyle model complements task modeling by helping to develop deeper understanding of how tasks are to be performed. The model illustrates the ways in which people communicate during their work, and the properties of the artifacts that people produce.

We have shown that the workstyle model can be used to evaluate existing tools, and to help in the design of new tools. By examining the work styles supported by a tool, we can better understand how the tool can be effectively deployed, or identify mismatches between a tool and its intended use. By understanding the workstyles that a tool is to support, we can build tools that will be more effective in their deployment.

ACKNOWLEDGEMENTS

This work was partially supported by the Communications and Information Technology Ontario (CITO) Software Design Technology project and IBM's Centre for Advanced Studies. We gratefully acknowledge the donation by SMART Technologies Inc. of the SMART Board shown in Fig. 5.

REFERENCES

[1] Bly, S.A., *A Use of Drawing Surfaces in Different Collaborative Settings*, in Proceedings of the ACM Conference on Computer-Supported Cooperative Work CSCW'88 (Portland, 26-28 September 1988), ACM Press, New York, 1988, pp. 250-256.

[2] Chmura, L. and Norcio, A., *Design Activity in Developing Modules for Complex Software,* in E. Soloway and S. Iyengar (eds.), Proceedings of Empirical Studies of Programmers, Ablex Publishing Corporation, Norwood, 1986, pp. 99-116.

[3] Damm, C.H., Hansen, K.M., and Thomsen, M., *Tool Support for Object-Oriented Cooperative Design: Gesture-Based Modelling on an Electronic Whiteboard*, in Proceedings of ACM Conf. on Human Aspects in Computing Systems CHI'2000 (The Hague, 1-6 April 2000), ACM Press, New York, 2000, pp. 518-525.

[4] DeMarco, T. and Lister, T., *Peopleware*, Dorset House, New York, 1987.

[5] Diaper , D., *Task analysis for human computer interaction*, Ellis Horwood, 1989.

[6] Dubois, E., Nigay, L., Troccaz, J., Chavanon, O., and Carrat., L., *Classification space for augmented surgery, an augmented reality case study*, in Proc. of 7th IFIP International Conference on Human-Computer Interaction Interact'99 (Edinburgh, 30 August–3 September 1999), Kluwer Academics, Dordrecht, 1999, pp. 353-359.

[7] Finkelstein, A., Gabbay, D., Hunter, A., Kramer, J., and Nuseibeh, B., *Inconsistency Handling In Multi-Perspective Specifications*, IEEE Transactions on Software Engineering, Vol. 20, No. 8, 1994, pp. 569-578.

[8] Graham, T.C.N., Watts, L., Calvary, G., Coutaz, J., Dubois, E., and Nigay, L., *A Dimension Space for the Design of Interactive Systems within their Physical Environments*, in Proc. of ACM Conf. on Designing Interactive Systems DIS'2000, ACM Press, New York, 2000, pp. 406-416.

[9] Iivari, J., *Why are CASE Tools Not Used?*, Communications of the ACM, Vol. 39, No. 10, October 1996, pp. 94-103.

[10] Jarzabek, S. and Huang, R., *The Case for User-Centered CASE Tools,* Communications of the ACM, Vol. 41, No. 8, August 1998, pp. 93-99.

[11] Jones, T.C. *Programming Productivity*. McGraw-Hill, New York, 1986.

[12] Kraut, R. E. and Streeter, L., *Coordination in Software Development*, Communications of the ACM, Vol. 38, No. 3, 1995, pp. 69-81.

[13] Landay, J.A. and Myers, B.A., *Interactive sketching for the early stages of user interface design*, in Proceedings of ACM Conf. on Human Factors in Computing Systems CHI'95 (Denver, 7-11 May 1995), ACM Press, New York, 1995, pp. 43-50.

[14] Lank, E., Thorley, J., Chen, S., and Blostein, D., *On-line Recognition of UML Diagrams*, in Proc. of 6th Int. Conf. on Document Analysis and Recognition ICDAR'2001 (Seattle, September 2001), IEEE Computer Society Press, Los Alamitos, 2001, pp. 356-360.

[15] Lumsden, J. and Gray, P., *SUIT - Context Sensitive Evaluation of User Interface Development Tools*, in Proc. of DSV-IS'2000, LNCS, Springer-Verlag, Berlin, 2000, pp. 79-95.

[16] Malone, T.W. and Crowston, K., *What is coordination theory and how can it help design cooperative work systems?*, in Proceedings of the ACM Conf. on Computer-Supported Cooperative Work CSCW'90 (Los Angeles, 7-10 October 1990), ACM Press, New York, 1990, pp. 357-370.

[17] McLean, A., Young, R.M., Bellotti, V.M.E., and Moran, T.P., Questions, options and criteria: Elements of design space analysis, Human-Computer Interaction, Vol. 6, 1991, pp. 201-250.

[18] Paternò, F. and Santoro, C., *Integrating Model Checking and HCI Tools to Support Designers in Verification of User Interfaces Properties*, in Proceedings of DSV-IS'2000, LNCS, Springer-Verlag, Berlin, 2000, pp. 135-150.

[19] Pederson, E.R, McCall, K., Moran, T.P., and Halasz, F.G., *Tivoli: An Electronic Whiteboard for Informal Workgroup Meetings*, in Proc. of InterCHI'93, 1993, pp. 391-398.

[20] Rumbaugh, J., Booch, G., and Jakobsen, I., *The Unified Modeling Language Reference Manual*. Addison Wesley, New York, 1999.

[21] Seaman, C.B. and Basili, V.R., *Communication and Organization in Software Development: An Empirical Study*, IBM Systems Journal, Vol. 36, No. 4, 1997, pp. 550-563.

[22] Tang, J.C., *Findings from Observational Studies of Collaborative Work*, International Journal of Man-Machine Studies, Vol. 34, No. 2, 1991, pp.143-160.

[23] Tang, J.C and Minneman, S., *VideoWhiteboard: video shadows to support remote collaboration*, in Proc. of CHI'91, ACM Press, New York, 1991, pp. 391-398.

[24] Vessey, I. and Sravandapudi, A.P., *CASE Tools as Collaborative Support Technologies*, Communications of the ACM, Vol. 38, No. 1, 1995, pp. 83-95.

[25] Wharton, C., Rieman, J., Lewis, C., and Polson, P., *The Cognitive Walkthrough Method: A Practitioner's Guide*, in J. Nielsen and R.L. Mack (eds.), Usability Inspection Methods, John Wiley & Sons, New York, 1994, pp.105-141.

Chapter 20

AN ONLINE MULTIMEDIA SYSTEM FOR LEARNING TO DESIGN USER INTERFACES

Elizabeth Furtado, Vasco Furtado, Kenia Sousa, and Arnaldo Belchior
Universidade de Fortaleza (UNIFOR)
Av. Washington Soares, 1321 – Bairro Edson Queiroz - Fortaleza (CE), (Brazil)
E-mail: elizabet@feq.unifor.br, vasco@feq.unifor.br, kenia@unifor.br, belchior@unifor.br
URL: http://www2.unifor.br/elizabeth/main.htm – Tel.: +55-85-476 30 79

Abstract This work addresses the problem of learning how to (i) design user interfaces (UIs) and (ii) evaluate their quality. We present an online collaborative multimedia system, the TELE-environment, to help UI designers and software engineers solve problems of modeling, usability and acceptability during the entire development process. The developer accesses the environment as a tool for assistance, aiming at learning design concepts, guidelines and activities. During the interaction, the environment provides assistance with textual descriptions, examples and similar solution cases in different media. Moreover, the environment provides a collaborative support that allows the interaction among developers in a synchronous or asynchronous way.

Keywords: Collaborative learning, Learning by cases, On line learning, Scenario, UI design, Use case.

1. INTRODUCTION

Problems of designing usable UIs are mainly due to the necessity that the developers, i.e., designers and software engineers, have to learn different models (task model, implementation model, etc.) with different formalisms [4] in an autonomous and quick way. In addition, they have to follow many guidelines to improve the ways humans interact with computers. For instance, the UI should not display unnecessary information, and the dialogs should be simple enough for end-users to gain control of the system. Moreover, development methods do not provide efficient ways for developers to learn models and guidelines. A method description generally is a guide to

C. Kolski and J. Vanderdonckt (eds.), Computer-Aided Design of User Interfaces III, 229–242.
© 2002 *Kluwer Academic Publishers.*

help the developers create models [6] and to get a great amount of written guidelines [3]. They are also true because computer-based tools which implement these methods and generate interfaces automatically are generally difficult to use. Using these tools, the developers have to write specifications on the domain classes and tasks to be performed by the end-user. Other models used during the design of the interactive system can be derived from these specifications. However, it is important to point out that the quality of these specifications is a key issue. Some of the problems that can happen with these specifications and their validations are the difficulty in identifying potential end-users, inconsistency in the terminology used, and inadequacy to the end-users' needs.

Instead of giving solutions to the developers, several educational theories claim that a person learns better when reflecting about difficulties and discussing solutions with others [5]. In addition, a person learns better by actually doing [19] and understanding the context and its relationships [18]. In contrast, using UI generator tools, developers generally have a passive role in the design process. They depend on the tool, where most of the design knowledge resides. This verifies the importance of regarding developers as active participants in the process, making all the important decisions related to design and evaluation.

With the learning system described here, called TELE-environment [8], developers control their own learning process. The system consists of a multimedia learning environment for the web with different assistances (interactive examples, texts and cases) associated to UI design themes. Themes correspond to concepts and activities existing in any method of UI design, but a specific method was used in this study. Although themes are correlated, the developer can access texts and interactive examples in any sequence. An interactive example consists of: (i) presenting a problem related to modeling, usability and acceptability which should be analyzed, then (ii) requiring developers to build possible solutions using UI design tools or CASE tools. These problems are represented in cases (called problem-cases). Cases represent situations that either comply with or violate several guidelines in a system specification, dialogue design and information presentation. The objective is to help developers understand and apply guidelines during the entire design process. In addition, the environment implements a collaborative resolution strategy that allows developers to discuss their design problems with others on-line.

The remainder of this paper is structured as follows: section 2 provides an overview of state-of-the-art tools to support learning and designing UIs. Section 3 provides the basic concepts used in TELE-environment focusing on the method that developers need to learn.

The TELE-environment architecture is described in section 4. Section 5 describes the process of the user interaction. Section 6 summarizes the main points of the paper.

2. APPROACHES TO USER INTERFACE DESIGN

There are some methodological frameworks and tools for UI development [10, 6], called Tools for Working with Guidelines (TFWWG approach), which enable developers to integrate usability issues into the software development process. The main point of this approach is to design usable UIs that optimize the performance of tasks, through error reduction, higher throughput, and higher user satisfaction, and comfort [17]. An important research goal of the TFWWG approach is to discover ways to integrate guidelines into the development process without stifling creativity [17]. These research studies include methods and tools that help the developers understand, search and apply design principles, guidelines and standards from the beginning of the design process. Therefore, it is necessary to use notations that are familiar to UI developers and tools that are simple to use. For example, the JANUS system [2] is a CASE-based approach for UI development. It employs UML (Unified Modeling Language) with the help of the CASE tool Rational Rose [15] to allow an automatic transformation of the formal specification into a preliminary UI.

A complementary approach to the automatic generation approach is the use of design aid tools to support learning and designing. Some of these tools are: i) SIERRA [16], which offers the developer a detailed computer-based description of many guidelines; ii) Sherlock [10], which allows evaluating the generated UIs by offering the developer some advice about how to solve detected design problems, and iii) GUIDE [13], which offers the developers a CASE-based decision support system. The developers define their current design context and the system will find existing similar cases. New cases can be added to the tool database in order to help with future projects.

These tools support developers with learning and designing, but they do not require the developer to think about UI design problems through practice on the collective experience. One way to help developers in solving a real problem is to understand it very well and visualize its consequences. During the examination of a problem, the developer can access a set of cases that describe similar problem situations. These will induce developers to ask themselves question like "what caused this problem?". Another way is to create a virtual situation through the use of graphical tools. The graphical tool approach can help developers perform operations that can be illustrated through images, which can represent a problematic situation or depict a possible solution to a problem. The operations can be the following: contemplate alternatives, anticipate the implications of a given decision, follow a discourse while commenting on what is being shown, identify guidelines and evaluate designs for usability and conformance to applicable guidelines.

3. THE TELE-ENVIRONMENT FOR LEARNING: GROUND CONCEPTS

In this section, we describe basic concepts related to assistance provided by the TELE-environment, such as the method of UI design and the situations which developers face during the development process, and concepts related to its usability.

3.1 The UI Design Method

The simplified UI design method studied here [7], inspired from [6], is user centered, object-oriented, iterative and incremental (composed of many development cycles, where the results of a cycle can feed into the beginning of the next one). Each development cycle is mainly composed of the following phases: analysis, design, construction and test. In the analysis phase, requirements are captured in order to specify what the system must do (its business process expressed in use cases), and who the end-users are (user model). Tests are also applied to validate information from the diagrams[1] and requirements captured according to guidelines. Techniques, such as prototype, are used to obtain feedback from the end-user to assure the system usability. The design phase can be divided into logical and physical. In the logical design phase, generic specifications are done and in the physical design phase, these specifications are detailed and approximated to the implementation (construction phase).

To make it easier to build prototypes, the design phase of this method emphasizes the separation between the application and the UI [12]. Concerning the UI, the *interface logical design* phase consists of specifying interactive objects from the end-users' perspective taking into account guidelines for semantic functions of the UI, such as the treatment of errors, feedback, and memory overflow. In this phase, classes representing these interactive objects are modeled and the initial prototype can be presented. The *interface physical design* phase consists of specifying interactive objects from the system's perspective taking into account guidelines for syntactic

[1] To improve the method acceptability, we use UML diagrams, which have been studied by a large population of developers.

functions of the UI, such as, choosing the best interactive object to activate a task and the spatial organization of the objects.

As for the application part, the *application logical design* phase consists of specifying objects (attributes and relationships) of the domain and their methods taking into account the end-users' needs. In this phase, a class diagram with classes representing these interactive objects is prepared. In the *application physical design* phase, technical decisions are taken such as the treatment of object persistence and message exchanging among objects.

3.2 The Use Cases on UI Design

As mentioned before, cases are specific situations related to UI design, which developers face when using the method described previously. One example of a case may be the following: A developer validated a prototype with two end-users after they checked the conformity with their needs and the usability. Cases must be organized in the UI design method context [1] in order to be provided to the developers when solving a design problem.

To increase the effectiveness of representations, and recovery, we have associated cases with generic situations, such as "validating prototype" and "identifying the end-users' needs". These generic situations are associated with the UML notion of "use case". Cases are therefore variations (instances) of a use case type that happens on UI design. Fig. 1 is a simplified diagram of a use case organization for the UI design method. A use case may be split up into several specific use cases existing in a relationship of generalization, where each specific use case is a derivative of a generic use case. Generic and specific use cases form a hierarchy, where a use case may be linked to others from anywhere in the hierarchy.

Thus, the use case hierarchy described is not a strict one. In the situation presented in Fig. 1, there is the relationship **use**, which means that if A uses B, then B can happen during the realization of A and the problems of A can be caused by problems of B. In some levels of the hierarchy, problem-cases can be found. A problem-case is a description of a real situation, including characteristics of the context and of the participants.

Its main goal is to make the developer think about the problem and possible solutions. An analysis-case is a problem-case with the solution already defined. Its main goal is to make the developer think about the proposed solution and discuss about other possible solutions with other developers.

Figure 1. Use case organization and UI design problems.

3.3 Usability of the Learning System

Many concepts studied in different areas (HCI, cognitive sciences, ergonomic, AI and pedagogy) have been considered in order to assure TELE-environment´s usability. We associate these concepts with some components related to the development of the overall TELE-environment (such as the UI, the application and the end-user) (Fig. 2):

<table>
<tr><td rowspan="2">Quality of the User
(e.g., Allowing the user to collaborate and communicate with other users)</td><td>Usability through Interaction Devices</td><td>Usability of the User Interface
Guidelines
Multimedia
Interaction</td><td>Quality of the Learning Application
Cases
Ontology
Related Themes</td></tr>
<tr><td colspan="3">Usability of the Computer-Based System</td></tr>
<tr><td colspan="4">Usability of the Overall On-Line Learning System</td></tr>
</table>

Figure 2. Usability in the TELE-environment (modified from [12]).

i) *Using collaboration and communication mechanism to assure the quality of the end-user* – TELE-environment implements the collaborative aspect by allowing a developer to share knowledge (obtained by practice) with other developers by sharing any application. In addition, it enables developers to interact with others by means of a forum and chats.

ii) *Using interactive devices to assure the usability* – The developers need to choose the appropriate devices to facilitate the use of the system by the end-users, taking into account any kind of physical disability. The end-user can use the camera and the microphone to communicate with other end-users.

iii) *Using guidelines to assure the usability with multimedia interaction* – To determine how a case should be shown on the screen, guidelines related to graphical aspects and characteristics about the end-user and the context of use are considered. It allows us to determine the best way a case must be given to the developer during the interaction with this system.

iv) *Using ontology and hypertext to assure the quality of the learning application* – Cases are represented in a natural way through ontology. The ontology notion comes from the AI context where it is identified as the set of formal terms with representation knowledge, since the representation completely determines what "exists" in the system [11]. In addition, to facilitate the learning process during the exploration of concepts about UI design, themes are related through a hypertext structure, obtained from the use-case organization.

4. GENERAL ARCHITECTURE OF THE TELE-ENVIRONMENT

Fig. 3 depicts the architecture of the TELE-environment on three levels (presentation, management and information storage) including five main components:

- CADI, which implements the problem-based resolution strategy. It has an Assistance module, which coordinates the recovering and presentation of cases. A case can be shown on the screen in different ways, such as image, audio or text. Details are provided in [20].
- TELE, which allows the collaboration and communication over the web by chat and by sharing any application, such as a User Interface Design Tool. This component is described in [14].
- CADInet, which offers a UI Design course and assistance with texts and links. This component is described in [9].
- User interface, which is used by developers to interact with the environment.
- The knowledge base, which will give support to most of the problem-solution-based process. This base contains the frequently encountered

problem-cases (associated to scenarios, text and audio files), the use case organization, themes and rules.

The cooperation between the components is the following: the developer who is taking a UI Design course at CADInet, identifies a problem and requests the analysis of it. The UI component, during this analysis, gives the developer some assistance through CADI. The developer is assisted by cases, shown in different ways, which are recovered from the knowledge base by the assistance module. If the developer wants to communicate with other developers who have ecountered similar problem-cases, and/or create an analysis-case for the problem, the UI component calls TELE module. The developer's solutions are validated by an expert before being effectively stored and made available to others.

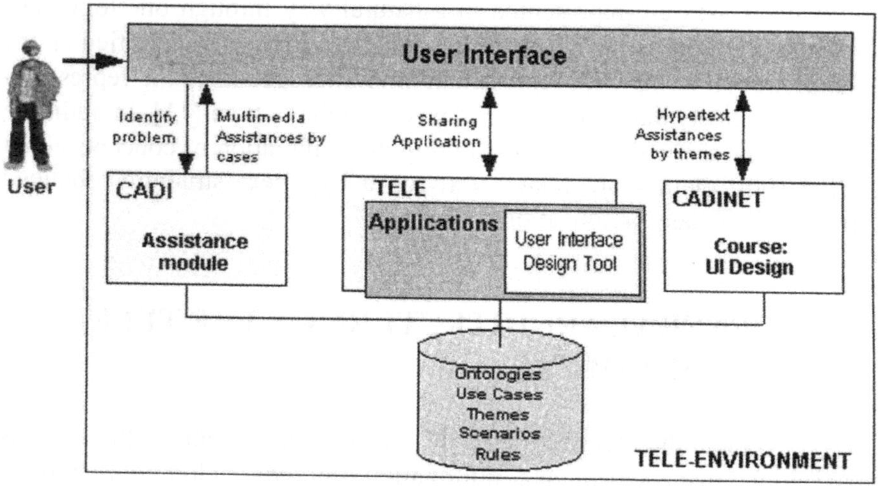

Figure 3. TELE-environment architecture.

The knowledge base is mainly built by the use of three editors: use case editor, ontology editor and graphic scenario editor. The *use case editor* is used to organize use cases according to Fig. 1. When a problem-case or analysis-case has to be defined, the ontology editor is called.

The *ontology editor* is used to represent cases[2]. A case model is represented as a collection of scenes. Scenes are tasks which are represented using parameters. Each parameter has a set of values, possibly enumerated. For instance, the parameters of a scene and their values can be the following: actors (such as end-users, engineers), actions (saying, showing, complaining),

[2] For the simplicity of this paper, we focused on describing the ontology of a case model, but the ontology editor is also used to describe the ontology of a user model, for instance, in order to control the adaptive assistance process.

objects (forms, prototype and diagram where the problem is found), and context of use (place: classroom, office; time: day, night; interactive application: bank application, e-commerce; and interactive objects: icon, window). The parameters have relationships, such as: *is-a* relationship, which denotes generalization, or *has* relationship, which denotes properties. Each scene can be presented in different media: *text*, describing the problem situation; *graphics*, showing a problem in a diagram or in a GUI; *image* (scenario), illustrating a problem related to the context of use and/or *sound*, to tell a story associated to the problem.

Fig. 4 depicts how the ontology graphic editor can be used to specify a scene. The graphical nature of the editor improves the legibility and the communicability of the information. On the left side of Fig. 4, parameters are instantiated with the values of the scene being specified in the right side. In the pop-up window, multimedia files, generated by the graphic scenario editor, can be associated to a scene.

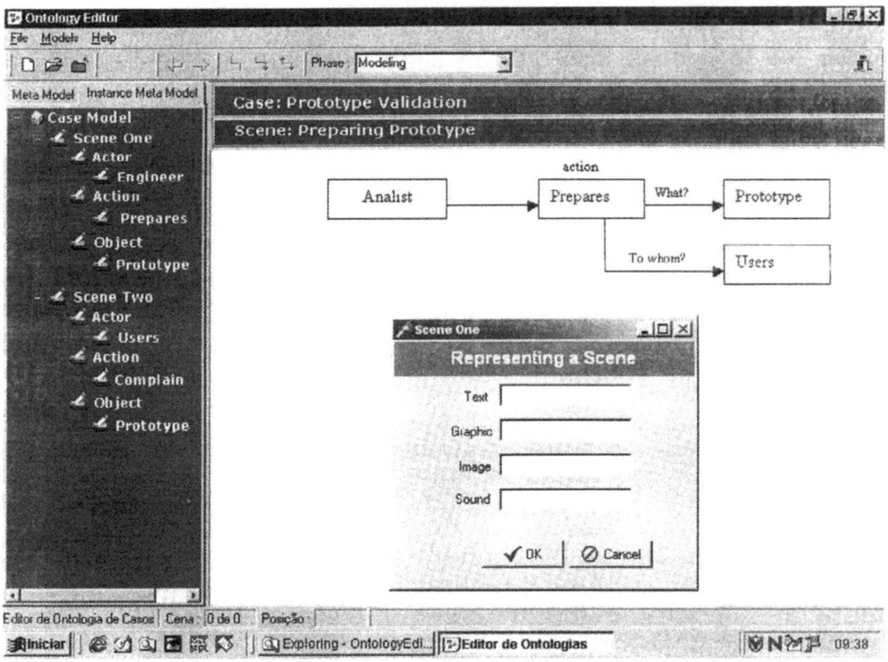

Figure 4. A scene modeling.

The need for modeling different media has led us to develop a *graphic scenario editor,* described in [8]. A scenario about a usability problem could be, for instance, a picture illustrating an end-user entering data and, accidentally, selecting a function, which closes the data input window. Mainly, scenarios are used to graphically express human factors (e.g., end-users' characteristics, position and expression, tasks and context). These factors are crucial for knowing which guidelines to use and why to use them. For example, in noisy environments such as shopping malls during holiday time, we must create a UI that works well for the hearing impaired.

In the next section, we will describe CADI's assistance process, taking into account the knowledge represented in the ontology, use case organization and developers' characteristics.

5. INTERACTING WITH THE SYSTEM TO LEARN THE UI DESIGN METHOD

Case study. Fig. 5 illustrates an interactive example, which developers take when navigating in the interface logical design theme available in CADInet. In this example, developers have to solve the following problem related to a prototype usability: *during the initial prototype validation, the end-users complain that they cannot find the most relevant information on the screen.* What must the developer do? Next, we will show how CADI can help them reflect about a possible solution.

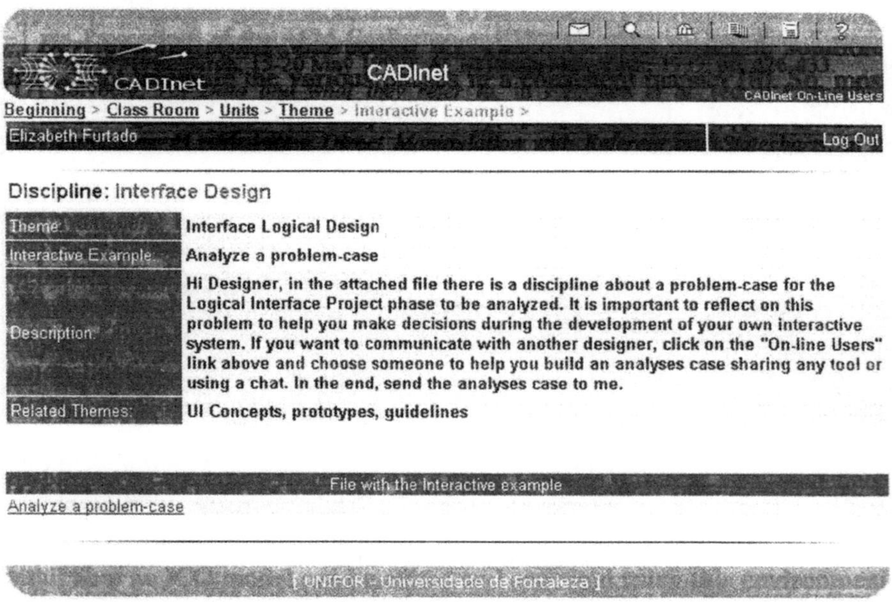

Figure 5. An interactive example on the WEB.

Case Identifying. Using CADI, developers must at first identify the problem. After identifying it, developers have two options: i) choose a use case which defines the context of the problem and subsequently the problem itself by selecting a problem-case, and/or ii) specify scenes, which express the situation, using the ontology structure defined in Fig. 4. Once the problem-case has been accurately defined, the assistance module starts to work, retrieving and showing similar cases stored in the database of cases.

Case Retrieving. The assistance module asks developers some questions and applies algorithms and rules in order to retrieve already existing cases from the database. There are two algorithms for case retrieval.

One of the algorithms allows the cross-contextual retrieving. If the developer chooses use cases, then problem-cases are retrieved by taking into account the relationship *use* between the use cases. This happens because developers may initially choose a problem-case thinking they know the problem well and, after answering questions about related use cases, the assistance module may determine that the problem in question is not the problem selected, but a consequence of a problem related to the one selected. This may happen because of the cross-contextual retrieval algorithm, and the non-strict hierarchical nature of the use case organization. In this example, the developer may choose the following use cases: *evaluating* then *integrating guidelines*. The assistance module asks about some graphical aspects of the UI, for instance, if the most important information is already on the top left corner of the window. If any problem is found in the guidelines, the module tries to retrieve problems related to other use cases. Taking into account the relationship between *evaluating* and *identifying end-user needs*, some questions about the end-user's characteristics are asked. If the end-user has visual impairments, for instance, a problem-case related to end-users' disabilities can be retrieved, if not, problem-cases related to inadequate end-users' needs can be retrieved.

The other algorithm allows for similarity retrieving. This search considers concepts represented in the ontology in order to improve the heuristic function used by the algorithm. This function computes the similarity between cases by measuring the distance of the case's characteristic to the cases in the database. During this computation, it navigates in the ontology in order to identify generic concepts which are common to the characteristics being compared, allowing it to compute a distance based on the characteristic hierarchical position. In this example, the assistance module can retrieve cases related to the usability of the final prototype. This is possible because the initial and final prototypes are represented in the ontology as being a prototype type, then the algorithm assigns some degree of similarity to them.

In addition to the use of the ontology and use case relationships, the assistance module takes into account the base of rules representing the beliefs of the developers. This module instantiates the conditions of the belief rules with the characteristics of the problem-case in order to obtain new characteristics to the problem-case or to increase the relevance of the existing ones which are associated to implicit beliefs that the developer can have. In this example, if the developer informs that the end-user never *indicated the most relevant information*, the assistance module can recover from the base of rules the following belief: "developers believe that the end-user participation during the development process causes a delay in the work". This way, the assistance module can retrieve past similar cases where this belief is presented.

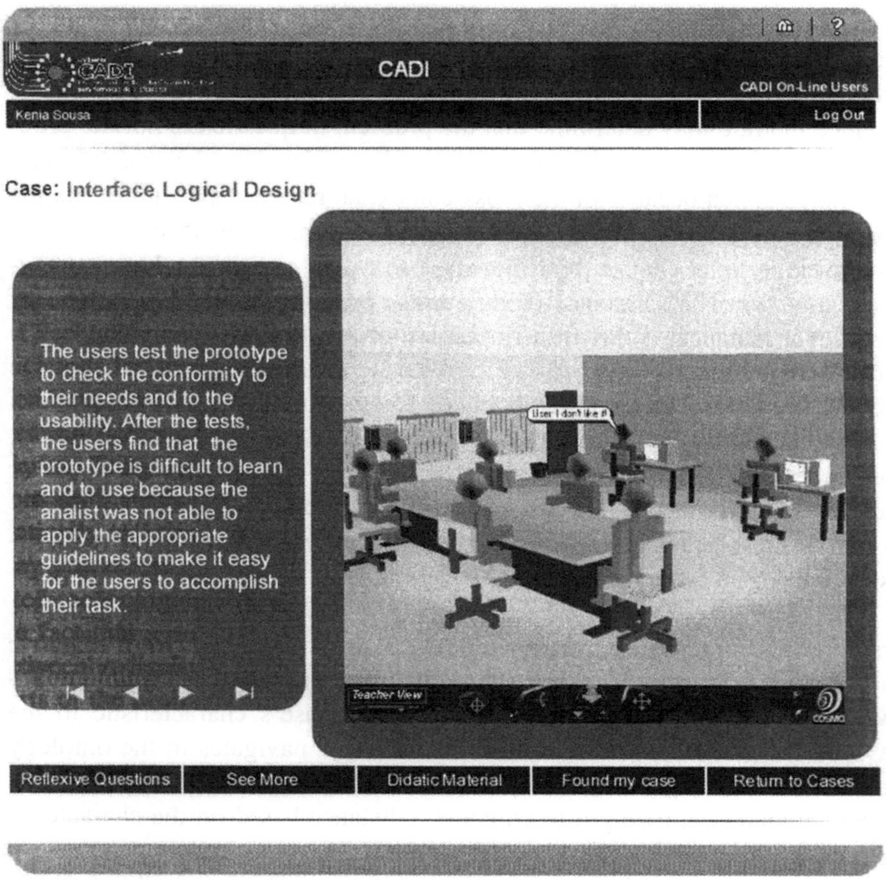

Figure 6. A problem-case being analyzed.

Case showing. To define how a case must be shown, this module takes into account the characteristics of the developer and of the context of use. After these characteristics are identified, it chooses the best view to show a case. For instance, a view having a combination of sound and image of a case is not appropriate for a very noisy context (a laboratory, for instance). The views are predefined according to guidelines. These guidelines helped us to define the best way to divide a screen, to show many media at the same time, and to hear a story about a case. Fig. 6 shows a view combining a graphical scenario and a textual story of a similar case to the problem-case in question. It is a picture of an end-user not satisfied with a prototype, because it is difficult to accomplish a certain interactive task and the prototype is not in conformity with the requirements. Other end-users are also waiting to validate this prototype. Then, they will work together to solve the problems found.

6. CONCLUSION

The TELE-environment described here is considered essential for a developer to make a usable UI system. To assure UI usability, guideline rules, developer's beliefs and preferences have been defined, providing hypertext and multimedia assistance. To assure the quality of the learning process, the use case organization allows for UI themes to be related giving more autonomy to the developer and to associate cases in order to contextualize design and evaluation problems. In addition, cases are expressed in a natural and graphical way through an ontological structure. To assure the quality of the developer's task, a collaborative process is provided.

Our work is still in early stages; however some evidences make us believe that the overall environment has effective possibilities. The knowledge base is based on concrete experiences, obtained from discussions in group with designers. During these discussions, the groups discovered 20 believes and 70 cases. At this point, we are examining these solutions that fit the new educational paradigm, which we believe is raising nowadays.

REFERENCES

[1] Aamodt, A. and Plaza, E., *Case-Based Reasoning: Foundation Issues, Methodological Variations and System Approach*, AI Com. Artificial Intelligence Communications, Vol. 7, No. 11, 1994.

[2] Balzert, H., *From OOA to GUIs – the JANUS system*, in Proc. of IFIP Conf. on Human-Computer Interaction Interact'95 (Lillehammer, 27-29 June 1995), Kluwer Academics, Dordrecht, 1995, pp. 319-324.

[3] Bastien, J.M.C. and Scapin, D.L., *Ergonomic criteria for the evaluation of user interfaces*, INRIA, Research report No.156, Rocquencourt, 1993.

[4] Bodart, F. and Vanderdonckt, J., *Expressing Guidelines into an Ergonomical Style-Guide for highly Interactive Applications*, in S. Ashlundn, K. Mullet, A. Henderson, E. Hollnagel, and T. White (eds.), Proceedings of ACM Conf. on Human Aspects in Computing Systems InterCHI'93 (Amsterdam, 24-29 April 1993), ACM Press, New York, 1993, pp. 35-36.

[5] Dewey, J., *Como Pensamos*, Companhia Editora Nacional, São Paulo, 1959.

[6] Furtado, E., *Mise en œuvre d'une méthode de conception d'interfaces adaptatives pour des systèmes de supervision à partir des Spécifications Conceptuelles*, Ph.D. thesis, Université d'Aix Marseille III, March 1997.

[7] Furtado, E. and Simao, R. *A method of UI design respecting the principle of IHC dialog*, in Proc. of Workshop on Human Factors IHC'2001 (Florianopolis, October 2001), in press.

[8] Furtado, E., Mattos, F.L., Furtado, J.J.V., and Holanda, R., *Um Sistema de Aprendizagem Colaborativa de Didática Utilizando Cenários*, Brazilian Review of Learning Systems, Vol. 8, April 2001.

[9] Furtado, E., Silva, W., Alves, J.J., and Távora, F., *CADINET: Um Ambiente de Ensino e Colaboração a Distância para Formação e Atualização de Professores da UNIFOR*, in Proceedings of International Conference on Distance Learning, August 2001, in press.

[10] Grammenos, D., Akoumianakis, D., and Stephanidis, C., *Integrated support for working with guidelines: the Sherlock guidelines management system*, Interacting with Computers Vol. 12, No. 3, 2000, pp. 281-311.

[11] Gruber, T.R., *Toward Principles for the design of Ontologies Used for Knowledge Sharing*, Technical Report, Stanford University, Stanford, 1993.

[12] Hix, D. and Hartson, R., *Developing user interfaces*, John Wiley & Sons, New York, 1993.

[13] Henninger, S., *A methodology and tools for applying context-specific usability guidelines to interface design*, Interacting with Computers, Vol. 12, No. 3, 2000, pp. 225-243.

[14] Neto, H., Raimir, H., Bezerra, W., and Sarquis, O., *Especificando o Tele-Ambiente no Contexto da Educação a Distância*, in Proc. of SBIE'2000 (Alagoas, November 2000).

[15] Rational Rose, accessible at http://www.rational.com/products/rose/index.jtmpl

[16] Vanderdonckt, J., *Accessing Guidelines Information with SIERRA*, in Proc. of IFIP Conf. on Human-Computer Interaction Interact'95 (Lillehammer, 27-29 June 1995), Chapman & Hall, London, 1995, pp. 311-316, accessible at http://www.info.fundp.ac.be/cgi-publi/pub-spec-paper?RP-95-020

[17] Reiterer, H., *Tools for Working with Guidelines in Different Interface Design Approaches,* in J. Vanderdonckt and Ch. Farenc (eds.), Tools For Working With Guidelines, Proc. of the Annual Meeting of the Special Interest Group TFWWG'2000 (Biarritz, 7-8 October 2000), Springer-Verlag, London, 2000, pp. 225-254.

[18] Schank, R., *Dynamic Memory: a Theory of Learning in Computers and People*, Cambridge University Press, Cambridge, 1994.

[19] Schank, R. and Cleary, C., *Engines for Education*, Paperback, 1995.

[20] Silva, M.M. and Furtado, E., *Incorporando aspectos adaptativos em um ambiente de educação a distância*, Graduate course monography, University of Fortaleza, 2001.

Chapter 21

UML AND INTERACTIVE SYSTEMS, ANOTHER STEP FORWARD

Jean René Ruault
Consultant, 11 rue Ernoult, F-92260 Fontenay aux Roses (France)
E-mail: ruault@club-internet.fr

Abstract Primary UML notation does not model the HCI part neither the difference between requirements and design, nor that between information model and interface dependent objects. Recent works, such as OVID, Wisdom, or TUPIS (Toward a UML Profile for Interaction Systems) suggest enhancing UML and using it to model tasks, user representation, and dialogue. In accordance with OVID and Wisdom, this article suggests improving UML notation, with additional objects to support various user mental models and events driven systems. We define the adapter and view filter stereotypes in the interaction space, while publisher and listener are included in the task model.

Keywords: OVID, UML profile, User centred design, User mental representation, Wisdom.

1. INTRODUCTION

40 to 50 % of the interactive systems design lays in the human-computer interface part. Most of the methods used to design this part are not linked with software engineering methods and are rather specific methods. Today UML the Unified Modeling Language used to visualize, specify, design and document the artefacts of a software system is a standard, is used more and more frequently. UML is a system centred method and is not compatible with interactive system design. OVID [10], the first method based upon UML, enhances the semantics of UML to support the design of interactive systems. Recently, other works, like UML*i* [4] and Wisdom [8], for instance have reached the same goal. The main features deal with user properties, task models, navigation models and layout models. Most of these articles deal with use case diagrams and state chart diagrams in order to adapt to task

C. Kolski and J. Vanderdonckt (eds.), Computer-Aided Design of User Interfaces III, 243–254.
© 2002 *Kluwer Academic Publishers.*

models. Few of them deal with user representation or additional objects induced by analysis or design. The first part of this article presents these recent publications on task models and UML. We focus on OVID which allows various user viewpoints and Wisdom which enhances UML notation by using constraints, tagged values and stereotypes. Then the second section shows how additional objects are used in three contexts : domain dependent additional objects in complex systems, subscription additional objects in events driven systems, and adapter additional objects which supports various user profiles.

2. USER CENTRED DESIGN WITH UML – STATE OF THE ART

Task analysis [12] is one of the main methods for user centred design, describing user's characteristics (novice, expert...), task properties (sequential, parallel, mandatory, optional), and user's conceptual models. The display content and layout are designed from the user conceptual model, and the dialogue or navigation is designed from the task model. We summarize UML improvements that have be made in order to support these features of user interface (UI) design.

OVID -Object, View and Interaction Design-[10] and, Wisdom [8] are methods that enhance UML semantics to support UI design. TUPIS (Toward a UML Profile for Interaction Systems) is a program that sets up a UML profile adapted to UI design.

One part of these works deals with user's characteristics relevant to interface design (kind of user: novice, expert, role, age, direct users and indirect users...). They model the user as an actor in the use case diagram and suggest enriching the actor with user's characteristics. There is no semantics to model the impact of the user's characteristics on the interface. For instance, one attribute is visible for one role, but not for the other. The other part deals with task modelling, mostly with hierarchical task analysis. [11] suggests improving OOSE use cases notation (UML use cases, today) to support a task modelling (temporal and logical aspects, abstraction and aggregation relationship...) based upon MAD (Méthode Analytique de Description [12]). They exploit the same kinds of objects as OOSE (interface, entity, control) to support the interface model, the information model and the dialogue.

Roberts *et al.* [10] exploit use cases at the requirements stage in order to model hierarchical task analysis, but does not reduce the gap between task modelling (temporal and logical aspects, goals/sub-goals decomposition, frequency, errors, time critical task, unusual circumstances...) and use cases. Task modelling deals with the user's work, while use cases are about functional requirements. State diagrams are used to design interface control. Depending on the state of an object's attribute, one can allow or forbid a user's action.

Nunes and Cunha [8] suggest a light process development method, close to the Unified Process, and improves UML in order to support task analysis, dialogue and presentation modelling. The authors define the "Task" class stereotype that "models the structure of the dialogue between the user and the system" (p. 216). «Interaction space» stereotype class models the interaction between the system and the user. This architecture is in keeping with the MVC or PAC [3]. They use UML constraint extension and stereotyped dependency to express logical and temporal operators for this task class (p. 221-222): independent concurrency, choice, concurrence with information exchange, iteration, deactivation, enabling, enabling with information passing, finite iteration, optional tasks. Tag values are applied to the various task classes: abstract task, user task, application task, interaction task. Activity diagrams show the navigational structure of the application, while class diagrams show static relationships, and state diagrams show the internal dynamic behaviour of each view.

The last part deals with user's mental representations modelling. Norman [7] differentiates the user's and the designer's conceptual models. Collins [2] describes three areas as objects oriented models. The first one the conceptual model may be either in the user's head or in the designer's head. The second one the UI model is the look and feel of the interface, visible to the user. The third includes the underlying functional objects of the system, and the software structure that implements the visible UI. The structure of the analysis model is mirrored in each area. Collins [2] advocates isomorphism between the user's conceptual model, the information model and the UI model.

On the other hand, [11] does not suggest any isomorphism between the user's conceptual model (supported by the interface model) and the information model. Such isomorphism is not able to deal with different kinds of users, having different levels of expertise and different modes of representation (analytic versus global, accounting versus management). They suggest drawing relationship between actors and use cases to highlight the context in which the system is used.

Basing their method on Norman [7], Roberts *et al.* [10] differentiate between: the user's conceptual model of the system (i.e. the user's model in Norman) that the user forms as he or she interacts with the system ; the designer's model (the designer's model in Norman) which represents the designer's intent in terms of objects users will see and how they will use the objects to accomplish their tasks ; and the implementer's model, describing the internal system used to implement the design model. The interaction space stereotype [8] is a class with stereotype attributes and operations. Input elements denote information received from the user, while output elements denote information presented to the user. Action elements denote things a user can do.

UML proposes the "communicate" and "subscribe" stereotype associations. To these native associations, Nunes and Cunha [8] add new stereotype associations between task and interaction space: "refine task" denotes the hierarchical relationship between tasks ; "navigate" is an association between two interaction space classes denoting a user moving from one interaction space to another ; and "contains" is an association between two interaction space classes denoting that the source (container) contains the target class (content).

Anderson [1] puts forward the "Domain Adapter layer", between the information model (domain model) and the interaction space. Each interaction space requires a domain adapter layer. This layer avoids normalizing the interaction space. It encapsulates a notification mechanism, notifying any change in the underlying system state to the interaction space.

Table 1. UML diagrams used in methods.

UML diagram	Used	Method	Rationale
Class	Yes	Ovid, Wisdom	Class diagram makes it possible to model user mental representation
Object	No		Methods use more abstract classes than concrete and instance objects
Use cases	Yes	Ovid, Wisdom	Use cases diagram makes it possible to map with user's task
Interaction	Yes	Ovid	Sequence diagram models the sequence of actions between the user and the system, when the duration is important
State chart	Yes	Ovid	State chart models dynamic aspects of workflow (state and transition, such as the transition from user's action)
Activity	Yes	Wisdom	Activity diagram models the workflow and the internal view of the system
Component	No		These diagrams deal with physical and logical architectures.
Deployment	No		

3. SYNTHESIS

While OVID deals with the user's model, Wisdom is concerned with the task. However, both methods model office automation tasks with a user driving the interface, but not tasks in the context of an event oriented system.

Both works suggest a linear mapping between task model and navigation model. These models must be improved in order to take into account the information proved by the system, such as alarms and state messages, objects (version flag) and tasks (database administration) induced by the artefact. In a business, everyone has a job and a role, is skilled or not (novice, expert). According to these roles and skills, one can, or cannot, get access to a specific kind of information. Everybody sees some information, while other information is confidential or private. We must be able to differentiate between the main roles and to identify the parts of the objects seen in each case. The next section of this article deals with UML improvement in order to match various user profiles and events oriented systems.

Table 2 traces the propositions of each method (OVID, Wisdom, this article) with regard to the main propositions (additional objects, events management and alternates models).

Table 2. Position statement of this article.

Methods / Propositions	OVID	Wisdom	This article
Additional objects	OVID uses additional objects, like association objects, but merely to explain and detail cardinality and other design features.	Wisdom specifies task stereotype classes, but without defining them as additional objects with business features.	This article uses an additional object to design smart UI. This object, a task stereotype one, integrates business rules
Events management	These methods are user driven and do not take system events into account.		Proposes a solution to design UI for events driven systems.
Alternate models	OVID proposes alternate models, creating copies and subsets of diagrams in order to do this.	Wisdom does not explicit the relationship between information model and interaction in the case of alternate models.	The alternate models are based upon various UI and upon one information model, with adapter stereotype class.

4. UML, A STEP FORWARD

In this section, we offer three types of improvement based upon additional objects. The first is a domain dependent additional object which resolves the heterogeneity of devices. The second allows notification between the information model and the interaction space. The third supports various user profiles.

4.1 Domain Dependent Additional Objects

Some additional objects are induced by analysis and implementation, but either they have little impact on the user's conceptual model (the relationship object of Collins), or they do not reduce the complexity of the underlying system. Here, we make a strong modifications of the model.

The example domain deals with publiphone supervision and management. The publiphone supervisor is used to load software and data (configuration, fees...) on the publiphones, and to get information from the publiphones (alarms, breakdown, turnover). There are three kinds of publiphones, with various data and data formats, with one supervisor for each kind of publiphone. The three publiphones are: the “OldVersionPubliphone”, rather simple and not manageable; the “MediumVersionPubliphone”, little manageable ; and the “NewVersionPubliphone”, easily updated and manageable. The marketing team's goal is to increase the turnover of the telecommunication operators. They get and exploit information coming from the publiphones' counters, that indicates the traffic and the reliability of the publiphones (hourly call counter, hourly turnover counter...). Then, they can update the tariff configuration. To do that, they must input these data into every single supervisor. It is time consuming and increases error rates. The main requirement of the new supervisor is that it merges all the supervisors into one big supervisor, to support all kinds of publiphones. This aims at reducing the user’s workload. But the heterogeneity of the publiphones remains. The designer is confronted with this heterogeneity when he wants to design information models, suitable and usable interface models. The task is quite difficult, as he needs to hide this heterogeneity from the end user.

Such an analysis does not enable us to select various kinds of publiphones, highlighting the common attributes. That implies additional objects and rules designed to reduce the complexity of the model shown to the user. The proposed solution defines a “virtual” publiphone that shows the relevant attributes of the selected publiphones dynamically.

When the user selects a set of publiphones (for instance, four new publiphones, three medium and one old), it is necessary to define the most relevant properties that can be updated for this set of “real” publiphones. The set of attributes is not defined a priori. It depends on the properties of the selected publiphones. Therefore, the transient virtual publiphone has no attributes, but only operations that make it possible to build the relevant attributes. When these attributes are specified, it is possible to define a transient virtual publiphone that matches these attributes. Then the user can fill this transient virtual publiphone with data. The new configuration is applied to this set of selected publiphones. They are updated. After checking the data, the transient virtual publiphone is deleted.

This transient virtual publiphone is not an entity class which is a persistent object of the application. Rather, one can define it as a task class, which "encapsulates complex behaviour that cannot be related to specific entity classes" [8].

Fig. 1 shows this Virtual Publiphone using Wisdom representation with the task and entity graphical models.

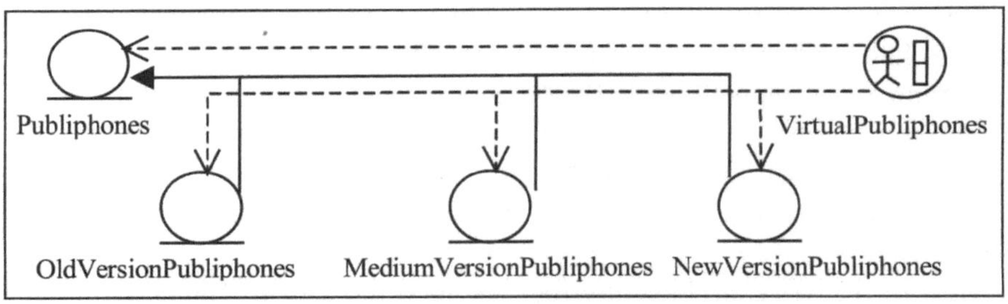

Figure 1. VirtualPubliphone as a task class.

Fig. 2 shows a model with task and entity stereotypes.

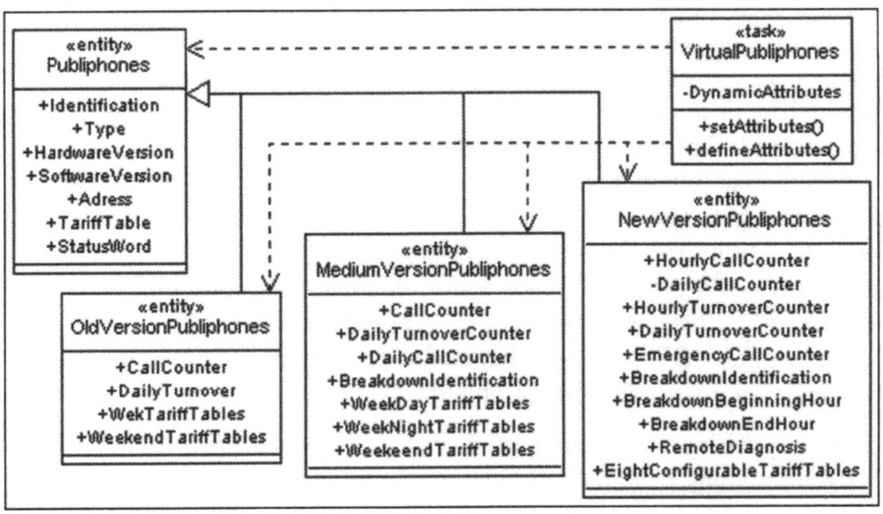

Figure 2. Publiphones' supervisor model with task class stereotype.

4.2 Subscription Additional Objects

In the context of events driven system (telecommunication, nuclear plant, railways supervision, air traffic control), the user acts upon the system via the interaction space and the information model, while the information (status, alarms, functional events) coming from the system via the information model and the interaction space must be presented to the user.

Events happen in the information model, coming from the underlying system. Then, the information model must publish these events and broadcast them to subscribers. The task could subscribe to these events. The information model must maintain a list of public events that may be subscribed to and a list of the tasks that subscribe to these events. The information model alerts the tasks that subscribe to specific events.

Here is the supervision of ticket vending machines. There are two user profiles, a maintenance agent and an operation one. The maintenance agent wants to know when the «ticket printer breakdown» event or the «computer shutdown» event happen, while the operation agent wants to be informed of the «printer empty» event and «vault full» event. Each agent should subscribe to events that are relevant to him. The use case diagram and view-object additional object enable us to make sure that each agent can get access to these data.

Most of the MVC architecture focuses upon the user's actions, not upon the system's events. In this context, there are few means to inform the user from the information model. [8] suggests using the subscribe association between task and entity, that is, between publisher and subscriber (p. 219).

Does each « task » class subscribe to each « entity » class which is relevant to it? Does each « entity » class maintain a list of all its subscribers? When there are many tasks that subscribe to many entities, this solution seems difficult to design and reuse. It mixes business objects and architecture dependent objects. It is irrelevant.

In this case, interaction space and task and information models are both UML packages. The operation agent and the maintenance agent have their own interaction spaces and tasks. The task package encapsulates the specific operations and attributes of each agent. Among these attributes and operations, there are the specific subscriptions of each agent.

We suggest adding objects that enable us to notify the interaction space from the system via the information model (Fig. 3):

- In the task package, an eventsListener, that subscribes to the relevant events coming from the information model, and listens to these events,
- In the information model, an EventsManager, that manages the subscribers of the information model events.

In accordance with [8], we define «publisher» and «subscriber» stereotype classes as new additional objects.

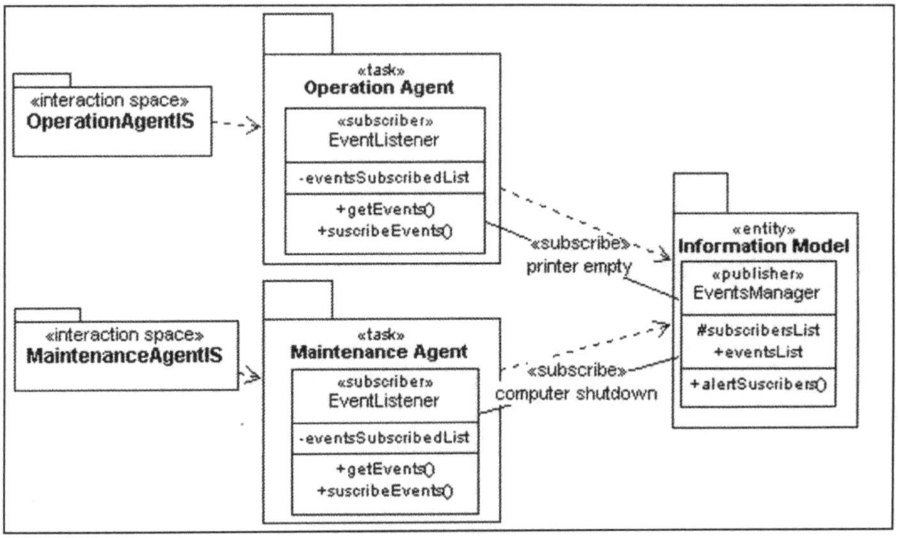

Figure 3. Subscription, with publisher, subscriber and subscribe association.

The EventsManager object, a publisher stereotype class, is a proxy for tasks in the information model. It makes it possible to centralize the events management and to avoid polluting the information model. The EventsManager maintains the list of public events, which may be subscribed to by tasks, and the list of the tasks that subscribe to some of these events.

The EventsListener object, a subscriber stereotype class, is the only partner of the EventsManager in each task. It maintains the list of the events relevant to the task. To do that, it asks the EventsManager to get the list of public events. Then, it selects a set of events and sends this set of subscribed events to the EventsManager.

For instance, the Operation Agent's task selects the "printer empty" and "vault full" events. So, it sends this set to the EventsManager, while the Maintenance Agent's task sends the "ticket printer breakdown" and the "computer shutdown" events set. The "subscribe" stereotype association is the same as the Wisdom one.

These additional objects are characterized as follows:

- EventsListener:

Attributes	Operations	Stereotype
eventsSubscribedList,	getEvents, subscribesEvents,	subscriber,

- EventsManager:

Attributes	Operations	Stereotype
subscibersList eventsList	alertSubscribers	publisher,

These additional objects are not business objects: they are induced by the design. It may be relevant to specify these recurrent objects and to put them among the software engineering tools.

4.3 Alternate User's Models with UML

Most applications have many users with various profiles. It is necessary to design a relevant interface for each profile. For instance, a marketing agent needs analytical information about turnover and traffic while a manager needs synthetic information about turnover and statistics. Some information is common to these two profiles, while other information is specific to one of them.

We suggest adding objects that filter information models, according to user profiles. In each user profile interaction space, this adapter stereotype class maps the interface with the entity. The mapping is not isomorphic. The adapter maps only part of the corresponding entity class. The marketing manager sees only the turnover counters, and not the call counters of the Results entity class. The adapter maps two different entity classes. The marketing manager reaches information both from publiphones turnover counters (Results) and from statistics (ResultsBoard). The same adapter stereotype class gathers this information and presents it to the marketing manager.

This operation works together with a view filter stereotype dependency relationship between this adapter class and the entity class. This dependency checks only the relevant entity class attributes among all the attributes. It allows a smart mapping between the interaction space adapter classes and the entity classes. There is one check operation per entity class, so that when an adapter class maps two entity classes, it has two check operations.

We use the input or/and output stereotype attributes to specify each relevant attribute [8]. For instance, the marketing agent can only see the counter, and not change it (output), while he fills the tariff tables with data (input). We use the OVID note to detail the view (i.e. graphs are better than spreadsheets).

These additional objects (adapter stereotype class, input or output stereotype attributes, view filter stereotype dependency relationship) enable us to create a non isomorphic relationship between information model and interaction space, and to design UI for many user profiles.

Fig. 4 shows these additional objects in the publiphone context.

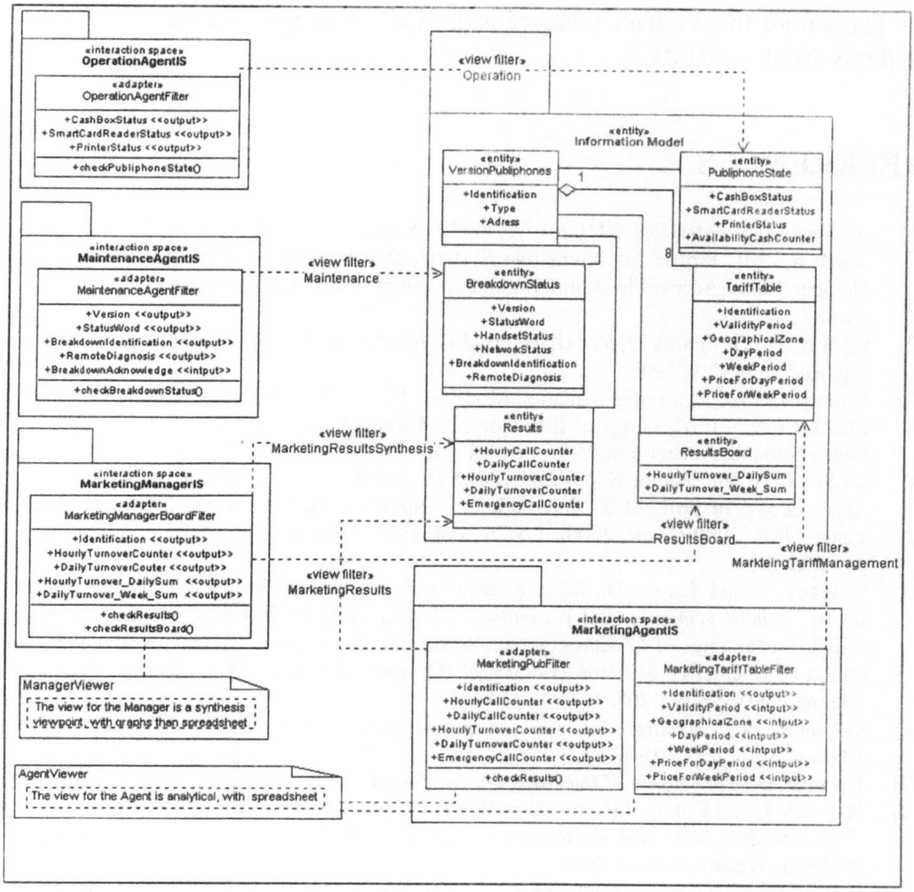

Figure 4. Adapter, view filter and stereotype attributes to support many user profiles.

5. CONCLUSION AND PERSPECTIVES

This article suggests improving UML with adapter, publisher and subscriber stereotype classes, input and output stereotype attributes, subscribe and view filter stereotype relationships to support events driven systems and various user profiles. Evolving CASE tools with this UI profile would enable software engineers to properly design genuine user-centred systems.

ACKNOWLEDGEMENT

The author thanks Jean Vanderdonckt and Christophe Kolski, who initiated this article on UML.

REFERENCES

[1] Anderson, D., *Extending UML for UI*, in N.J. Nunes (ed.), Proc. of Workshop on "Towards a UML Profile for Interactive Systems Development TUPIS'2000 (York, 2-3 October 2000), Accessible at http://math.uma.pt/tupis00/submissions/anderson/anderson .html.

[2] Collins, D., *Designing Object-Oriented User Interfaces*, Benjamin/Cummings Publishing, Redwood City, 1995.

[3] Coutaz, J., PAC, An Implementation Model for Dialog Design, in H.J. Bullinger and B. Shackel (eds.), Proceedings of IFIP Conf. on Human-Computer Interaction Interact'87, North Holland, Amsterdam, 1987, pp. 431-436.

[4] da Silva P.P. and Paton, N.W., *UMLi: The Unified Modeling Language for Interactive Applications*, in Proc. of 3rd International Conference on the Unified Modeling Language UML'2000 (York, 2000), LNCS, Vol. 1938, Springer-Verlag, Berlin, 2000, pp. 117-132.

[5] Gamboa, F. and Scapin, D., *Editing MAD* task descriptions for specifying user interfaces, at both semantic and presentation levels*, in M.D. Harrison and J.C. Torres (eds.), Proceedings of 4th Eurographics Workshop on Design, Specification and Verification of Interactive Systems DSV-IS'97 (Granada, 4-6 June 1997), Springer-Verlag, Vienna, 1997, pp.193-208.

[6] Goldberg, A., *Smalltalk-80, the interactive programming environment*, Addison-Wesley, New York, 1984.

[7] Norman, D., *The Design of Everyday Things, New York*, Doubleday, Currency, 1989.

[8] Nunes N.J. and Cunha, J.F., *Wisdom- Whitewater Interactive System Development with Object Models*, in M. van Harmelen (ed.), Object Modeling and User Interface Design, Addison -Wesley, Boston, 2001.

[9] Paternò, F., *Towards a UML for Interactive Systems*, in Proc. of EHCI'01, Lecture Notes Computer Science, Springer-Verlag, Berlin, 2001.

[10] Roberts, D., Berry, D., Isensee, S., and Mullaly, J., *Designing for the User with OVID: Bridging User Interface Design and Software Engineering*, Macmillan Technical Publishing, Indianapolis, 1998.

[11] Ruault J.-R. and Van Heylen, H., *Convergence entre cas d'utilisation (OOSE) et notion de tâche en ergonomie des IHM*, in Proceedings of IHM'97, Cépaduès-Editions, Toulouse, 1997.

[12] Sébillotte, S. and Scapin, D.L., *From users' task knowledge to high level interface specification*, International Journal of Human-computer Interaction, Vol. 6, 1994, pp. 1-15.

Chapter 22

BUILDING MULTI-PLATFORM USER INTERFACES WITH UIML

Mir Farooq Ali[1], Manuel A. Pérez-Quiñones[1], Marc Abrams[2], and Eric Shell[1]
[1]*Department of Computer Science, Virginia Tech,*
660, 621, 508, McBryde Hall, Blacksburg, VA 24061 (USA)
E-mail: mfali@csgrad.cs.vt.edu, {perez, ershell}@cs.vt.edu
URL: http://www.cs.vt.edu/uiml/, csgrad.cs.vt.edu/~mfali/, people.cs.vt.edu/~perez/
Tel.: +1-540-231-2646, +1-540-231-8457 – Fax: +1-540- 231-6075

[2]*Harmonia, Inc., PO Box 11282, Blacksburg, VA 24062 (USA)*
Development Offices, Virginia Tech Corporate Research Center,
1715 Pratt Drive, Suite 3100, Blacksburg, VA 24060 (USA)
E-mail: marc@harmonia.com – URL: www.harmonia.com or
http://www.cs.vt.edu/info/people/vitae/Abrams.html
Tel.: +1-540-951-5900 – Fax: +1-540-951-5911

Abstract There has been a widespread emergence of computing devices in the past few years that go beyond the capabilities of traditional desktop computers. However, users want to use the same kinds of applications and access the same data and information on these appliances that they can access on their desktop computers. The user interfaces (UI) for these platforms go beyond the traditional interaction metaphors. It is a challenge to build UIs for these devices of differing capabilities that allow the end users to perform the same kinds of tasks. The User Interface Markup Language (UIML) is an XML-based language that allows the canonical description of UIs for different platforms. We describe the key aspects of our approach that makes UIML successful in building multi-platform UIs, namely the division in the representation of a UI, the use of a generic vocabulary, a process of transformations and an integrated development environment specifically designed for transformation-based UI development. Finally we describe the initial details of a multi-step usability engineering process for building multi-platform UI using UIML.

Keywords: Logical Model, Multi-Platform User Interfaces, Physical Model, Transformations, UIML, Usability Engineering.

C. Kolski and J. Vanderdonckt (eds.), Computer-Aided Design of User Interfaces III, 255–266.
© 2002 *Kluwer Academic Publishers.*

1. INTRODUCTION

Advances in electronics, communications, and the fast growth of the Internet have made the use of a wide variety of computing devices an everyday occurrence. These computing devices have different interaction styles, input/output techniques, modalities, characteristics, and contexts of use. Furthermore, users expect to access their data and run the same application from any of these devices. Two of the problems we encountered in our own work [2] in building UIs for different platforms were the different layout features and screen sizes associated with each platform and device. Dan Olsen [13], Peter Johnson [9], and Stephen Brewster, et al. [4] all talk about problems in interaction due to the diversity of interactive platforms, devices, network services and applications. They also talk about the problems associated with the small screen size of hand-held devices. In comparison to desktop computers, hand-held devices will always suffer from a lack of screen real estate, so new metaphors of interaction have to be devised for such devices. It is difficult to develop a multi-platform user interface (UI) without duplicating development effort. Developers now face the daunting task to build UIs that must work across multiple devices. There have been some approaches towards solving this problem of multi-platform UI development including XWeb [14]. Building "plastic interfaces" [5,20] is one such method in which the UIs are designed to "withstand variations of context of use while preserving usability".

We developed the User Interface Markup Language (UIML) to address the need for a uniform language for building multi-platform applications. We discuss our research in creating such language, some of the support tools available, and describe our approach towards creating a new UI design methodology to build multi-platform user interfaces.

UIML is a single language for building user interfaces for any device. UIML emphasizes the separation of concerns of an interactive application in such a way that moving one program from one platform to another (see our definition of platform later) is relatively easy. Furthermore, because it is based on XML, it is easy to write transformations using a tool like XSLT [6] that take the language from one abstract representation to a more concrete representation. The tools built around UIML extend the language with the use of transformations that afford the developer the creation of user interfaces with a single language that executes on multiple platforms.

The approach taken with UIML is that of building an application using a *generic vocabulary* that could then be *rendered* for multiple platforms. Using a generic vocabulary for desktop applications, for example, the developer can write a program in UIML only once and have it be rendered for Java or HTML. And, within HTML, it can be rendered to different versions of HTML and/or browsers. We present some details of the generic vocabulary and the advantages of this approach in this paper.

Based on our experience with UIML, we have learned that one generic vocabulary is not sufficient to build interfaces for widely varying platforms, such as VoiceXML, handhelds (e.g. Palm PDAs) and desktops. In this paper, we describe the preliminary results of a multi-step process of building multi-platform user interfaces. It involves programming in UIML at different levels of abstractions with the support of transformations that move the developer's work from one representation to the next. This paper presents our initial results on this area.

Some terminology that is used in the paper is defined next. A *device* is a physical object with which an end-user interacts using a user interface, such as a Personal Computer (PC), a hand-held computer (like Palm), a cell-phone, an ordinary desktop telephone or a pager. A *toolkit* is the library or markup language used by the application program to build its UI. Unlike its traditional definition, the term *toolkit* implies both markup languages and more traditional APIs for imperative or object-oriented languages. A *Vocabulary* is the set of names, properties and associated behaviour for UI elements available in any toolkit. A *platform* is a combination of device, operating system and toolkit. An example of a platform is a PC running Windows 2000 on which applications use the Java Swing toolkit. This definition has to be expanded in the case of HTML to include the version of HTML and the particular web browser being used. For example, Internet Explorer 5.5 running on a PC with Windows NT would be a different platform than Netscape Communicator 6.0 running on the same PC with the same OS since they implement various features of HTML differently. A related term we use in this paper is *family*, which indicates a group of platforms that have similar layout features. A *Generic Vocabulary* is the vocabulary shared by all platforms of a family.

2. RELATED WORK

Transcoding [3,8] is a technique used in the World Wide Web for adaptively converting web-content, i.e. HTML page, for the increasingly diverse kinds of devices that are being used these days to access web pages. This process also requires some kind of transformation that occurs on the HTML web page to convert it to the desired format. In its simplest form, semantic meaning is inferred from the structure of the web page and the page is transformed using this semantic information. A more sophisticated version of transcoding annotates the structural elements of the web page and the transformation occurs based on these annotations. The transcoding approach is limited in the amount of semantic inferencing that can be made automatically from structural elements of web pages and because annotations are done by hand and are often tied to the structure of existing web pages. If these pages are modified, the annotations have to be modified.

It is useful to revisit some of the concepts behind model-based UI development tools since these concepts have to be utilized for generating multi-platform UIs [12]. Model-based user interface development tools use high-level specifications of different aspects of the UI and automatically generate some parts or the complete UI [11]. One of the central ideas behind model-based tools is to achieve balance between the detailed control of the design of the UI and automation. Many model-based tools built in the late 80's and early 90's include UIDE [18], HUMANOID [10], MASTERMIND [19], ITS [21], Mecano [17], and Mobi-D [16].

The central component in a model-based tool is an abstract model representing the UI. Different types of models have been used in different systems including task models, dialogue models, domain models, and application models. All these models represent the UI at a higher level of abstraction than what is possible with a more concrete representation. The UI developer builds these models that are transformed either automatically or semi-automatically to generate the final UI. The generation of the interface was often done via an automated tool that included a set of rules for generation of the interface components and the interface style.

Although model-based tools provide many advantages over other user interface development tools, one of the main drawbacks of these systems was that the automatically generated interfaces were not of very good quality. One more limitation of some of the earlier systems was the lack of developer control over the process of UI generation. Having more developer-control over the UI development process and having more usable models could rectify some of the deficiencies of the model-based approaches.

3. UIML, GENERIC VOCABULARY AND TRANSFORMATIONS

UIML is a declarative XML-based language that can be used to define user interfaces. More details about the language itself can be found in other references [1,15]. The mechanism that is currently employed for creating UIs with UIML is to render a UIML document created by a UI developer using a platform-specific vocabulary for the target platform. These renderers can be downloaded from http://www.harmonia.com. Currently, there are platform-specific renderers available for UIML for a number of different platforms. These include Java, HTML, WML, and VoiceXML. Each of these renderers has a platform-specific vocabulary associated with it to describe the UI elements, their behavior and layout. The formal definition of each vocabulary is available at http://www.uiml.org/toolkits. Table 1 shows five out of eleven vocabularies publicly available at the time of publication.

Table 1. UIML Vocabularies available from http://www.uiml.org/toolkits as of August 2001.

Generic Vocabulary Available for Platform
W3C's HTML v4.01 with the frameset DTD and CSS Level 1
Java™ 2 SDK (J2SE) v1.3, specifying AWT and Swing toolkits
A single, generic vocabulary for creating Java *and* HTML user interfaces
VoiceXML Forum's VoiceXML v1.0
WAP Forum's Wireless Markup Language (WML) v1.3

The platform-specific vocabulary for Java, HTML, WML, and VoiceXML uses AWT/Swing, HTML, WML, and VoiceXML tags as UIML part names, respectively. This enables the UIML author to create a UI in UIML that is equivalent to a UI that is possible in Java, HTML, WML, and VoiceXML. However, the platform-specific vocabularies are not suitable for UIML documents to be mapped to multiple target platforms. For this a *generic* vocabulary is needed. To date, one generic vocabulary has been defined, *GenericJH*, which maps to both Java Swing and HTML 4.0. The next section describes how a generic vocabulary is used with UIML

From Section 1, we recall that the definition of family refers to multiple platforms that share common layout capabilities. Different platforms within a family often differ on the toolkit used to build the interface. Consider for example, a Windows OS machine capable of displaying HTML using some browser and capable also of running Java applications. Both of these use different toolkits, thus making it impossible to write an application in one and have it execute in the other, even though they both run on the same hardware device using the same operating system. For these particular cases, we have built into UIML support for generic vocabularies. A generic vocabulary of UI elements for UIML, can describe any UI for any platform within its family. The vocabulary has two objectives: to be powerful enough to accommodate a family of devices, and, to be generic enough to be used without having expertise in all the various platforms and toolkits within the family.

We have identified and defined a set of generic UI elements including their properties and events for desktop applications. Ali *et al.* provide a more detailed description of this generic vocabulary in [2]. Table 2 shows some of the part classes in this vocabulary for the desktop family that includes HTML 4 and Java Swing. A generic vocabulary is useless without a corresponding set of transformations that convert the user interface from the generic terms to a particular toolkit. These transformations are basically a conversion from generic UIML to platform-specific UIML. Both of these representations are be represented as trees since they are XML-based. The platform specific UIML is then rendered using an existing UIML renderer.

Table 2. Example of a Generic Vocabulary.

Generic Part	UIML Class Name	Generic Part	UIML Class
Generic top container	G:TopContainer	Generic Label	G:Label
Generic area	G:Area	Generic Button	G:Button
Generic Internal	G:InternalFrame	Generic Icon	G:Icon
Generic Menu Item	G:Menu	Generic Radio Button	G:RadioButton
Generic Menubar	G:MenuBar	Generic File Chooser	G:FileChooser

There are several types of transformations that are performed:

- Map a generic class name to one or more parts in the target platform. For example, a G:TopContainer is mapped to the following sequence of parts in HTML:

```
<html>
  <head>...
    <title>...
    <base>...
    <style>...
    <link>...
    <meta>...
  <body>...
```

  In contrast, G:TopContainer is mapped simply to one part, JFrame, in Java.
- Map properties of the generic part to the proper platform-specific part.
- Map generic events to the proper platform-specific events.

In order to allow a UI designer to fine-tune the UI to a particular platform, the generic vocabulary contains platform-specific properties. These are used when one platform has a property that has no equivalent on another platform. In the generic vocabulary, these property names are prefixed by J: or H: for mapping to Java or HTML only. The transform engine automatically identifies which target part to associate the property with, in the event that a generic part (e.g., G:TopContainer) maps to several parts (e.g., 7 parts for HTML). This is also done for events that are specific to one platform. In this way, the generic vocabulary is not a lowest-common-denominator approach. The generic UIML file would then contain three <style> elements. One is for cross-platform style, one for HTML, and one for Java UIs:

```
<uiml>
...
 <style id="allPlatforms">
   <property id="g:title">My User Interface</property>
 </style>
 <style id="onlyHTML" source="allPlatforms">
   <property id="h:link-color">red</property>
 </style>
 <style id="onlyJava" source="allPlatforms">
   <property id="j:resizable">red</property>
 </style>
</uiml>
```

In the example above, both a web browser and a Java frame have a title, which is "`My User Interface`". However, only web browsers can have the color of their links set, so property h:link-color is used only for HTML UIs. Similarly, only Java UIs can make themselves non-resizable, so the j:resizable property applies only to Java UIs. When the UI is rendered, the renderer chooses exactly one <style> element. For example, an HTML UI would use *onlyHTML*. This <style> element specifies in its *source* attribute the name of the common, shared *allPlatforms* style, so the *allPlatforms* style is shared by both the HTML and Java style elements.

Fig. 1 illustrates two interfaces generated from generic UIML for Java Swing and HTML through a process of transformation. Fig. 3 illustrates a complex application for Java Swing. For economy of space, the corresponding HTML interface is not shown.

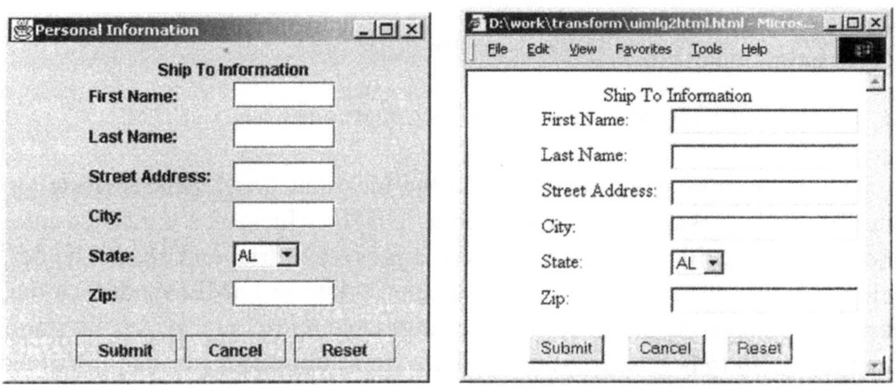

Figure 1. Screen-shots of a sample form in Java Swing (left) and HTML (right).

4. TRANSFORMATION-BASED DEVELOPMENT

A transformation-based UI development places the developer in unfamiliar territory. Developers are accustomed to having total control over the language and the specification of the user interface elements. A transformation-based environment asks the developer to provide a high-level description of the interface and to "trust" the result. This is one of the common limitations of code-generators and model-based UI systems. To address this limitation, we have developed a Transformation-based Integrated Development Environment (TIDE) at Virginia Tech for UIML. In TIDE, the developer writes UIML code and the IDE generates the interface, as expected. However, the relationship between UIML code and its resulting interface component is explicitly shown. This section briefly shows how TIDE works.

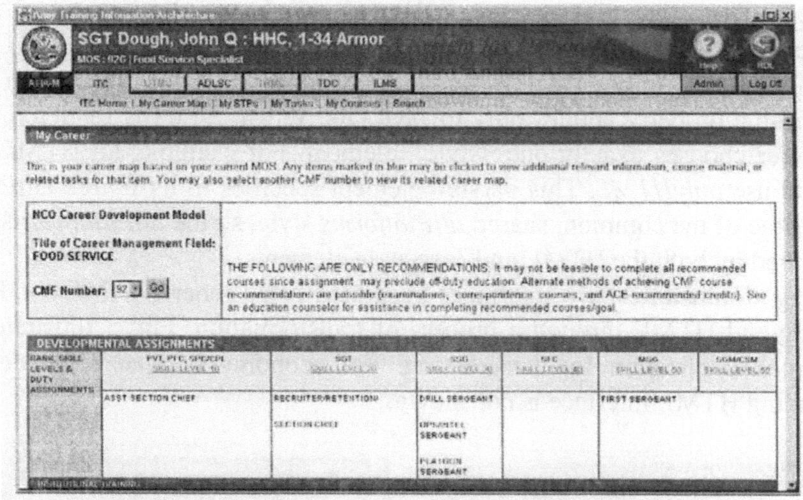

Figure 2. Screen-shots of a complex application for Java built with UIML.

The TIDE application was built on the idea that developers creating an interface in an abstract language, such as UIML, which gets translated into one or more specific languages, undergo a process of trial and error. The developer builds what he or she thinks is appropriate in UIML, renders to the desired language(s), and then makes changes as appropriate. As an environment designed to help support this process, this application shows the developer three things: the original, abstract interface (in source code form), the resultant interface after rendering, and the relationship between elements in the two. Fig. 3 shows two pictures of the TIDE environment.

The application uses Harmonia's LiquidUI product suite, version 1.0c. Harmonia's product was not changed in any way, and was used by the application to render from the original UIML to Java. The developer may open and close files, view the original UIML source code as plain text or as a tree, and make changes from the tree view. The developer can also re-render at any time (by pressing the red arrow in the center of the window).

The relationship between UIML code and the generated interface is made explicit as shown in Fig. 3. The developer may click on a node in the UIML tree view and the corresponding element on the graphical user interface is highlighted on the right side. The same is true if the developer clicks on a component of the graphical user interface. In the right hand side of Fig. 3, the developer has clicked on the cancel button (middle of the three buttons) and the corresponding code is highlighted on the UIML tree-view.

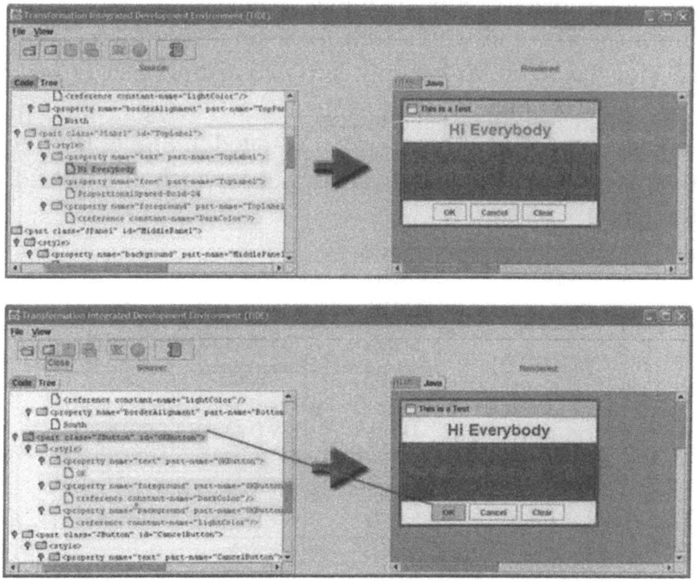

Figure 3. Selection in UIML Code.

TIDE makes it very easy to explore the different UIML elements and the effect they have on the generation of the interface. A UIML element's property (e.g. the color of a button) can be edited in place within the tree view.

5. FRAMEWORK FOR MULTI-PLATFORM UI DEVELOPMENT

UIML and the tools presented above are not sufficient to properly address the problem of interface development for multiple platforms. Therefore, we are adding a more abstract layer to support development of interfaces for a wide variety of platforms. This section describes preliminary work on how this higher-abstraction layer would work with UIML.

The concept of building multi-platform UIs is relatively new. To envision the development process, we followed an existing approach from the usability engineering (UE) literature. One such approach [7] identifies three different phases in the UI development process: *interaction design*, *interaction software design* and *interaction software implementation*. Interaction design is the phase of the usability engineering cycle in which the "look and feel" and behaviour of an UI is designed. In current Usability Engineering practices, this phase is highly platform-specific. Once the interaction design is done, the interaction software is designed, which involves making decisions about the UI toolkit(s), widgets, etc. Once this design is done, the software is implemented Unfortunately, this traditional view of interaction design is highly platform-specific and works well for a single platform. The stage of interaction design has to be further split into two distinct phases for multiple platforms: a platform-independent interaction design and platform-dependent interaction design. This phase, illustrated in Fig. 4, leads to different platform-specific interaction software designs, which in turn lead to platform-specific UIs.

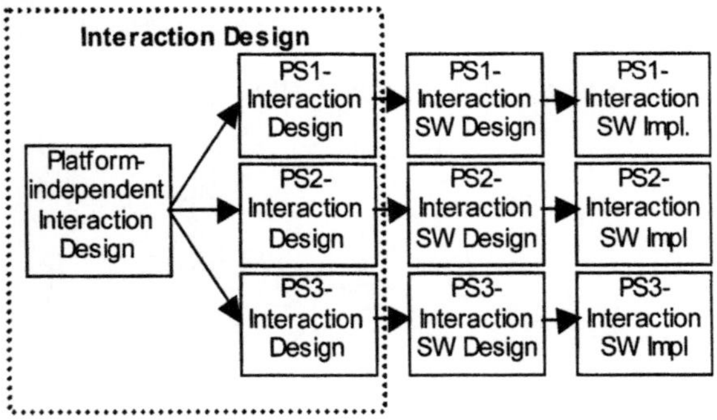

Figure 4. Usability Engineering process for multiple platforms.

6. UIML-BASED USABILITY ENGINEERING PROCESS

We have developed a framework that is very closely related to the UE process discussed above. The main building blocks within this framework are the *Logical Model, Family Model* and the *Platform-Specific Model.* The *logical model* is the new model that we are creating, and it is briefly described below. We described the *family* and *platform-specific models* in earlier sections. There is also a new set of transformations needed to convert the *logical model* to different *family models*. Thus, we have one new level of representation, the *logical model*, and one new process of transformations. The resulting diagram is shown in Fig. 5.

The main objective of the *logical model* is to capture the UI description at a high level of abstraction. The logical model is a collection of logical constructs that represent the UI in some abstract fashion. We are considering using a hybrid task/domain model that can be transformed to the physical model. Research on this representation is underway.

The transformation from the *logical model* to a particular *family model* has to be developer-guided and cannot be fully automated. By allowing the UI developer to intervene in the transformation and mapping process, it is easier to ensure usability. Once the developer had identified the mappings, the system generates a *family model* based on the target family mappings.

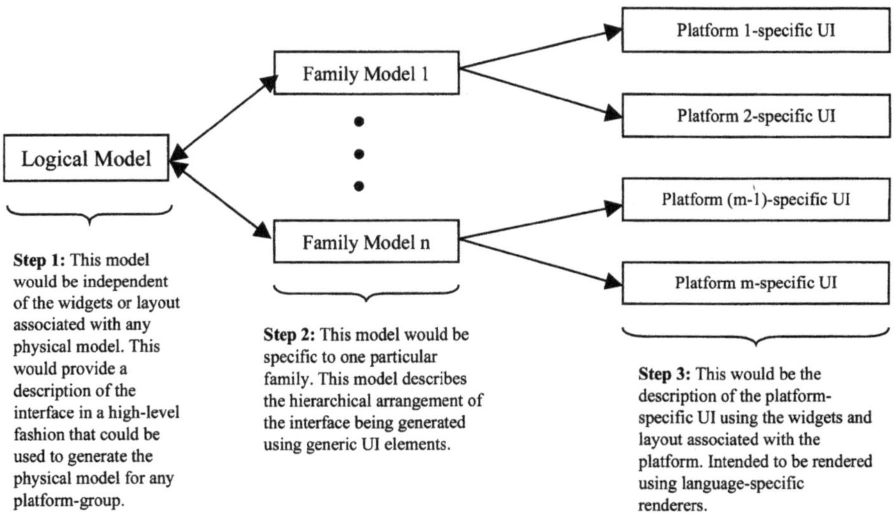

Figure 5. The overall framework for building multi-platform UIs using UIML.

7. CONCLUSIONS

In this paper we have shown some of our research in extending and utilizing UIML to generate multi-platform user interfaces. We are using a single language, UIML, to provide the multi-platform development support needed. This language is extended via the use of a logical model, alternate vocabularies and transformation algorithms. Our approach allows the developer to build a single specification for a *family* of devices. UIML and its associated tools transform this single representation to multiple platform-specific representations that can then be rendered in each device. We have presented our current research in extending UIML to allow building of interfaces for very-different platforms, such as VoiceXML, WML and desktop computers.

REFERENCES

[1] Abrams, M., Phanouriou, C., Batongbacal, A. and Shuster, J., *UIML: An Appliance-Independent XML User Interface Language*, in Proc. of 8th World Wide Web Conference WWW'8 (Toronto, 11-14 May 1999), accessible at http://www.harmonia.com/resources/papers/www8_0599/index.htm

[2] Ali, M.F. and Abrams, M., *Simplifying Construction of Multi-Platform User Interfaces Using UIML*, in Proceedings of UIML'2001 Europe (Paris, March 2001), accessible at http://www.harmonia.com/resources/papers/FarooqAli_finaldraft.pdf

[3] Asakawa, C. and Takagi, H., *Annotation-Based Transcoding for Nonvisual Web Access*. in Proc. of 4th ACM SIGCAPH Conf. on Assistive Technologies ASSETS'2000 (Arlington, 13-15 November 2000), ACM Press, New York, 2000, pp. 172-179.

[4] Brewster, S., Leplâtre, G., and Crease, M., *Using Non-Speech Sounds in Mobile Computing Devices*, in Ch. Johnson (ed.), Proceedings of First Workshop on Human Computer Interaction of Mobile Devices MobileHCI'98 (Glasgow, 21-23 May 1998), GIST Technical Report G98-1, Department of Computing Science, University of Glasgow, Scotland, accessible at http://www.dcs.gla.ac.uk/~johnson/papers/mobile/HCIMD1.html

[5] Calvary, G., Coutaz, J., and Thevenin, D., *Embedding Plasticity in the Development Process of Interactive Systems*, in P.L. Emiliani and C. Stephanidis (eds.), Proc. of 6th ERCIM Workshop "User Interfaces for All" UI4ALL'00 (Florence, 25-26 Oct. 2000), accessible at http://ui4all.ics.forth.gr/UI4ALL-2000/files/Short_papers/Calvary.pdf

[6] Clark, J., *XSL Transformations (Version 1.0)*, 1999, http://www.w3.org/TR/xslt.

[7] Hix, D. and Hartson, R., *Developing User Interfaces: Ensuring Usability Through Product and Process*, John Wiley and Sons, New York, 1993.

[8] Huang, A. and Sundaresan, N., *Aurora: A Conceptual Model for Web-Content Adaptation to Support the Universal Usability of Web-based Services*, in Proc. of ACM Conference on Universal Usability CUU'2000 (Arlington, 16-17 November 2000), ACM Press, New York, pp. 124-131.

[9] Johnson, P., *Usability and Mobility: Interactions on the move*, in Ch. Johnson (ed.), Proceedings of First Workshop on Human Computer Interaction of Mobile Devices MobileHCI'98 (Glasgow, 21-23 May 1998), GIST Technical Report G98-1, Department of Computing Science, University of Glasgow, Scotland, 1998.

[10] Luo, P., Szekely, P. and Neches, R., *Management of Interface Design in Humanoid*, in Proc. of ACM Conf. on Human Aspects in Computing Systems InterCHI'93 (Amsterdam, 24-29 April 1993), ACM Press, New York, 1993, pp. 107-114.

[11] Myers, B., *User Interface Software Tools*, ACM Transactions on Computer-Human Interaction, Vol. 2, No. 1, 1995, pp. 64-103.

[12] Myers, B., Hudson, S., and Pausch, R., *Past, Present, and Future of User Interface Software Tools*, ACM Trans. on Computer-Human Interaction, Vol. 7, No. 1, 2000, pp. 3-28.

[13] Olsen, D., *Interacting in Chaos*, Interactions, Vol. 6, No. 5, 1999, pp. 42-54.

[14] Olsen, D., Jeffries, S., Nielsen, T., Moyes, W. and Fredrickson, P., *Cross-modal Interaction using Xweb*, in Proc. of ACM Conf. on User Interface Soft. Technology UIST'2000 (San Diego, 5-8 November 2000), ACM Press, New York, 2000, pp. 191-200.

[15] Phanouri, C., *UIML: An Appliance Independent XML User Interface Language*, Ph.D. thesis, Computer Science Dept., Virginia Tech, 2000.

[16] Puerta, A. and Eisenstein, J., *Towards a General Computational Framework for Model-Based Interface Development Systems*, in Proc. of ACM Conf. on Int. User Interfaces IUI'99 (Los Angeles , 5-8 January 1999), ACM Press, New York, 1999, pp. 171-178.

[17] Puerta, A., Eriksson, H., Gennari, J.H. and Musen, M.A., *Model-Based Automated Generation of User Interfaces*, in Proc. of National Conference on Artificial Intelligence AAAI'94 (Seattle, August 1994), pp. 471-477.

[18] Sukaviriya, P. and Foley, J., *Supporting Adaptive Interfaces in a Knowledge-Based User Interface Environment*, in Proc. of International Workshop on Intelligent User Interfaces IWIUI'93 (Orlando, 4-7 January 1993), ACM Press, New York, 1993, pp. 107-113.

[19] Szekely, P., Sukaviriya, P.N., Castells, P., Mukthukumarasamy, J., and Salcher, E., *Declarative Interface Models for User Interface Construction Tools: The MASTERMIND Approach*, in Proc. of 6th IFIP Working Conference on Engineering for HCI EHCI'95, (Grand Targhee Resort, 14-18 August 1995), Kluwer Academics, 1995.

[20] Thevenin, D. and Coutaz, J., *Plasticity of User Interfaces: Framework and Research Agenda*, in A. Sasse and C. Johnson (eds.), Proc. of Interact'99 (Edinburgh, August 1999), IOS Press Publ., 1999, pp. 110-117.

[21] Wiecha, C., Bennett, W., Boies, S., Gould, J., and Greene, S., *ITS: A Tool for Rapidly Deveoping Interactive Applications*, ACM Transactions on Information Systems, Vol. 8, No. 3, 1990, pp. 204-236.

Chapter 23

DEVELOPMENT OF A UIML RENDERER FOR DIFFERENT TARGET LANGUAGES: EXPERIENCES AND DESIGN DECISIONS

Carsten Binnig and Andreas Schmidt
Institute for Applied Computer Science, Forschungszentrum Karlsruhe
Institut für Angewandte Informatik, Abt. Steuerungssysteme und Kommunikation (SK)
Postfach 3640, D-76021 Karlruhe (Germany)
E-mail: {binnig,schmidt}@iai.fzk.de
Tel.:. +49-7247-82 5714, 5774 – Fax: +49-7247-82 5786

Abstract Generic development of user interfaces allows to considerably reduce the time consuming manual coding expenditure that may reach up to 50% of the development work. With UIML, the specification of an XML meta language was made available recently, which claims to define user interfaces independently of the platform and target language. The present article describes our experience gained from the development of a UIML renderer for various target languages. Division into target language-dependent and independent generation steps as well as various types of final target code generation play an important role in minimizing the expenditure of incorporating new target languages.

Keywords: Abstract user interface description, Automatic code generation, UIML, User interface development.

1. INTRODUCTION

In the past years, development of user interfaces has gained importance [5]. Wide use of high-performance platforms and the associated high acceptance of graphical user interfaces caused the users to make ever increasing requirements on the quality and ergonomics of interactive application systems.

To meet these requirements, efforts were taken very early to separate development activities in both areas, graphical user interface and the applica-

C. Kolski and J. Vanderdonckt (eds.), Computer-Aided Design of User Interfaces III, 267–274.
© 2002 *Kluwer Academic Publishers.*

tion/data source logic, from each other. This separation has the advantage that the expenditure required for the development of application software can be shared. It is possible to employ specially trained personnel in each area. Consulting of experts in software ergonomics during the development of the graphical user interface results in a very user-friendly software. As a drawback, however, the total expenditure required for the development of the application software is not reduced, but rather increased, since the graphical user interface still has to be linked manually to the application/data source logic on the program code level.

Another increase in the development expenditure results from today's frequently made requirement of the application having to offer the same user interfaces for several platforms. This implies that the developers should know several programming languages and various methods. Furthermore, extensions of the application result in the interfaces having to be maintained in parallel.

To counteract this increasing development expenditure resulting from the requirements mentioned above and simultaneously ensure the required quality, interface development is often accomplished using special tools [5] (e.g. UI-builder). However, these tools mostly do not support the separate development process, as the graphical user interface is automatically linked to the application/data source logic. They often generate a code for a certain target language only. To avoid parallel development and maintenance of several platforms or target languages, various approaches to describing the graphical user interfaces in a platform-independent and abstract manner were conceived recently. An example is the User Interface Markup Language (UIML). Current implementations of the renderers that map the UIML onto concrete target languages, however, generate a code for a certain target language only.

The present article summarizes the design decisions and results of a diploma thesis focusing on the development of a concept for a UIML renderer for easy integration of mapping onto further target languages. The concept was also implemented.

2. UIML - THE LANGUAGE

The User Interface Markup Language (UIML) represents a markup language that is completely based on the Extensible Markup Language (XML) [9]. UIML serves to describe user interfaces for various platforms, i.e. for various combinations of an output device with a certain operation system and a toolkit (the toolkit supplies a set of ready surface elements). As any other markup languages, UIML is a declarative language. It allows for a relatively simple generation of user interfaces and supports the principle of separating the user interface from the application/data source logic. UIML is based on an own Meta Interface Model (MIM) [8]. This, in turn, is based on experience gained from the use of existing models, such as the "Seeheim layer model" and the "Model View Controller Paradigm" [8]. The basic idea of these different models is to separate the user interface from the application/data source logic, as a result of which reusability and maintainability of the individual components are improved. However, existing models suffer from weaknesses in terms of reusability for various output devices, as it is not taken into account, for instance, that surface elements on variable platforms may possess variable properties. To bypass these weaknesses, a catalogue of criteria was proposed in [8]. It contains five aspects to be described by a model for user interfaces to be specified completely and independently of the platform:

1. User interface and structure of the surface elements,
2. Their properties and concrete representation,
3. The contents of the individual surface elements,
4. The behavior of the individual surface elements, and
5. The linking to the application/data source logic.

Figure 1. The Meta Interface Model (MIM).

For this purpose, the MIM is divided into several components (Fig. 1):

1. The presentation component describes the mapping of the abstract surface elements and events onto a concrete toolkit.
2. The logic component supplies an abstract representation of the application logic to the interface component.
3. The interface component describes various aspects of a user interface. For this purpose, it is divided into the following sub-components:
   a. ***Structure***: Describes the structure of the surface elements (part elements).

   b. ***Content*:** Describes the contents (constant elements) represented by the part elements.
   c. ***Style*:** Describes the properties (property elements) of the part elements.
   d. ***Behavior*:** Describes the runtime behavior (rule elements) by means of conditions and actions.
4. Other components: Apart from the MIM components, two other elements exist in UIML documents. The ***head*** element contains meta data of the user interface, such as the version number. The ***template*** element allows defining reusable UIML fragments.

3. THE UIML2ALL RENDERER

In UIML, rendering means the mapping of the UIML document that describes a user interface independently of the platform onto a concrete representation for a certain platform. Rendering may take place in two ways:

1. As in ***compilation***, the UIML document is translated into a target language that uses a certain toolkit.
2. The UIML document is ***interpreted*** at runtime and represented.

Below, the compiler variant shall be dealt with only. In terms of functioning, a renderer that generates a code corresponds to a code generator. Code generators are made up of three partial areas. They shall be explained below with reference to the tasks of a UIML renderer [1].

- ***Read-in*** of the UIML document into the corresponding meta object model of the implementation language of the renderer.
- ***Analysis/transformation*** of the meta object model. During analysis, the information is checked for correctness and completeness. The trasformation supplies a data structure that is optimized for code generation.
- ***Code generation*** from the information of the transformed meta object model.

It is the advantage of this division into partial areas that only those partial areas which are dependent on the target language have to be implemented several times for several target languages to be supported. As evident, *read-in* and *analysis/transformation* are independent of a target language, as no syntactic constructs of the target language are generated in these partial areas. Contrary to them, *code generation* depends on the target language. Further division of this partial area results in sub-areas which are also independent of the target language. Code generation may be divided into:

- ***Initialization*** of the values required for code generation from the transformed meta object model, e.g. mapping of an abstract surface element onto a concrete widget. This process does not depend on the target language.
- ***Generation*** of language-dependent *code fragments* from the initialized values for all *part* elements of the user interface as well as for the corresponding *style* and *behavior*. This process depends on the target language.
- ***Assembly*** of the code fragments generated. This process is also dependent on the target language.

The tasks of the renderer are represented schematically in Fig. 2 with those depending on the target language being colored white and those independent of the target language being shaded gray.

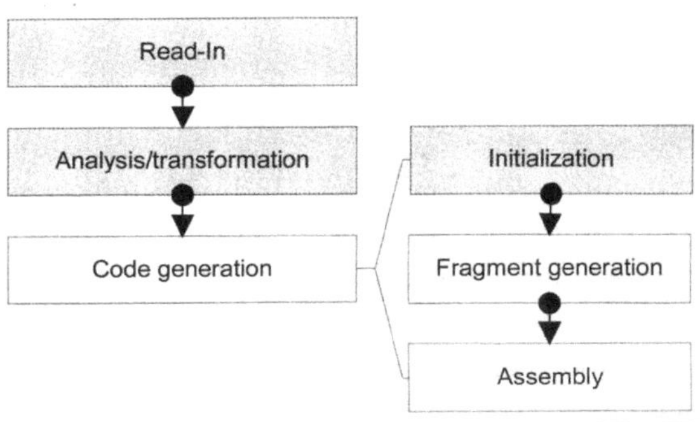

Figure 2. Tasks of the renderer.

The general statements obtained in the previous sections with regard to implementation allow to derive an architecture of the *renderer*. Based on the three tasks of the *renderer* (*read-in, transformation*, and *code generation*), the individual features of the architecture selected shall be listed and the methods applied shall be presented. Concrete implementation of the *renderer* was accomplished using the Java language [7], as mature APIs exist for access to or processing of XML documents. Furthermore, the combination of Java and XML represents a platform-independent solution for the *renderer*. Fig. 3 shows the *rendering process* for the two target languages of Java and HTML [6]. These languages were selected, since they represent two different concepts, i.e. an imperative language of the third generation and a markup language, and, thus, illustrate the flexibility of the renderer. Minimization of the expenditure required for the integration of a new target language is obvious. It results from the reuse of those components that are independent of the target language to be generated (shaded gray). Only those components that are dependent on the target language (colored white) have to be implemented several times.

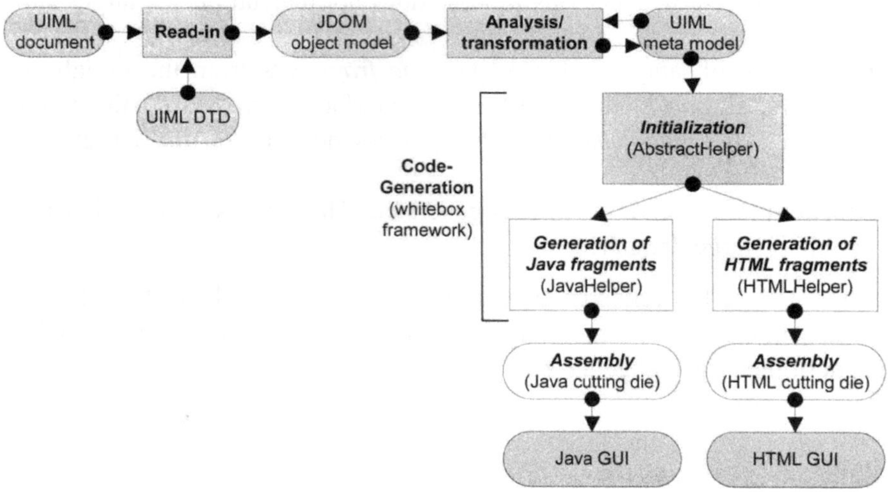

Figure 3. Architecture of the renderer.

Read-in: The data are *read-in* with the help of the JDOM-API [3]. By the read-in process, the data are mapped into the JDOM object model and may be validated in terms of their *document type definition* (DTD) [9]. It is an advantage of this document validation that the UIML document may be assumed to be syntactically correct in terms of DTD during the subsequent analysis and transformation phase.

Analysis/transformation: *Analysis and transformation* of the data are based on the JDOM object model. In a first step, the information of the JDOM object model is mapped onto an individual object model (*UIML meta model*). The *UIML meta model* consists of individual classes that reflect the elements of a UIML document. As soon as the *UIML meta model* has been initialized, the data are analyzed and transformed.

Code generation: *Code generation* is based on a combination of the template method [2] with so-called cutting dies [4]. To explain this in further detail, each sub-area of *code generation* and the methods applied shall be dealt with separately.

Initialization: As known from the investigation of the dependence of the sub-areas on the target language, *initialization* is independent of the target language. Therefore, it is recommended to summarize its implementation in an abstract parent class (*AbstractHelper*).

Generation: As the code varies syntactically for different target languages, the code generation methods are implemented in classes that are derived from *AbstractHelper* (*JavaHelper*, *HTMLHelper*). This code generation function corresponds to the above *template method* and represents a whitebox framework. Actually, code fragments are generated, which are responsible e.g. for the implementation of the corresponding surface elements (widgets) or the setting of properties in the target language.

Assembly: *Assembly* of the individual code fragments is also dependent on the target language and takes place in a cutting die. It uses the code fragments generated by the derived helper class for individual *parts* elements, their *style*, and *behavior* (Fig. 4).

```
import java.awt.*;
<%
  uiml2all.codegenerators.helpers.JavaHelper helper =
  new uiml2all.codegenerators.helpers.JavaHelper(uimlAdapter);
%>
public class SimpleGUI extends <%=helper.rootPartCodeOut.toString()%> {
  public Template(){
  <%=helper.PartCodeOut.toString()   %>
  <%=helper.PropCodeOut.toString()   %>
  <%=helper.BehaveCodeOut.toString()%>
  show();
  }
  public static void main(String[] args){
    new SimpleGUI();
  }
}
```

Figure 4. Cutting die for the assembly of language-dependent (Java) code sections.

4. CONCLUSION

The present article focuses on the results of the conception and implementation of a *UIML renderer* that generates a code for various target languages from an abstract user interface description (UIML). It was found out that the *renderer* consists of three partial areas: *Read-in* of the UIML document, *analysis/transformation* of the read-in information, and *code generation* for a certain target language. Investigation of the dependence of these partial areas of the *renderer* on the target language demonstrated that only sub-areas of *code generation* have to be implemented for each target language. On the basis of this finding, a *code generation* concept was developed. By encapsulating the language-dependent areas, the expenditure needed for mapping onto a new target language is minimized. Implementation of a final *code generation* concept was started by combining cutting dies with a whitebox framework.

The current state of development is considered to be promising, although several assumptions made in the overall approach, such as general applicability to all target languages, still need to be verified.

REFERENCES

[1] Cleaveland, J.C., *Program Generators with XML and Java*, Prentice Hall, Upper Saddle River, 2001.

[2] Gamma, E., Helm, R., Johnson, R., and Vlissides, J., *Design patterns: elements of reusable object-oriented software,* Addison-Wesley, New York, 1994.

[3] McLaughlin, B., *Java & XML,* O'Reilly, September 2001.

[4] Metzen, P. and Szallies, C., *Architekturgetriebene Entwicklung für objektorientierte Softwaresysteme*, OBJEKTspektrum, February 2000, pp. 73-78.

[5] Myers; B.A., *User Interface Software Tools*, ACM Transactions on Computer-Human Interaction, Vol. 2, No. 1, 1995, pp. 64-103.

[6] Niederst, J., *HTML Pocket Reference*, O'Reilly, December 1999.

[7] Niemeyer, P. and Knudsen, J., *Learning Java*, O'Reilly, June 2000.

[8] Phanouriou, C., *UIML: A Device-Independent User Interface Markup Language*, Ph.D. thesis, Blacksburg, Virginia, September 2000.

[9] Ray; E.T., *Learning XML*, O'Reilly, 2001.

Chapter 24

GENERIC INTERFACE DESCRIPTIONS USING XML

Kai Richter
Zentrum für Graphische Datenverarbeitung e.V.
Rundeturmstr. 6, D-64283 Darmstadt (Germany)
E-mail: Kai.Richter@ZGDV.de – URL:http://www.zgdv.de/zgdv/departments/z4/Z4Staff/krichter
Tel.: +49-6151-155609 – Fax: +49-6151-155450

Abstract Universal access and accessibility for all require a certain flexibility of technical devices. Some technical applications have only limited and very static interfaces as there are public kiosk systems (e.g. banking terminals or ticket machines). Interfaces of such machines are designed for the average user. This paper presents a remote access platform for mobile devices allowing every user to interact with common kiosks through their own customised mobile device. The user interface of the original terminal application is represented in a generic XML-based description which then is interpreted on the user device. The work is currently supported by the project EMBASSI, which is co-funded by the German Ministry of Education and Research (BMBF).

Keywords: Human Computer Interaction, Multimodal User Interfaces, Remote Access, UIML, XML.

1. INTRODUCTION

Ubiquitous computing, every time and every place access to information resided in global networks is one of the central topics of today's information society. Mobile information technology might also serve as a personalised gateway to information resided in our nearby environment.

In the case of users with special needs mobile assistants could provide an alternative, if not the only possible access to information and services. Public kiosk systems for instance represent an application of information technology which is present and indispensable in our everyday life. Nevertheless accessibility of those systems tends to be very limited. Being confronted

C. Kolski and J. Vanderdonckt (eds.), Computer-Aided Design of User Interfaces III, 275–282.
© 2002 *Kluwer Academic Publishers.*

with numerous requirements like cost-efficiency, data and physical security public kiosk systems represent something like the least common denominator. Disabled or even only cognitively challenged persons often are excluded from the use of such systems.

In this work we will introduce an agent-based platform for remote access to public kiosk systems (e.g. ATM, ticket machines). This approach provides the user of such systems with the possibility to access and interact with an ordinary kiosk through a personalised mobile device (e.g. mobile personal computer, PDA, etc.) with exactly those in- and output facilities that the user prefers. A mobile device also can serve as a more intelligent front-end to an enhanced kiosk software that could make use of user-specific information in order to alleviate interaction and provide customised services [10,13].

The user interface itself plays a central role in this scenario as it should allow dynamic customisation of a presentation held in one resource. Customisation in this case means not only the modification of the interfaces look and feel or the enabling of certain features but also the entire adaptation of the in- and output modality to the users needs. This also comprises the ability to switch modality and the possibility to change interaction paths.

2. THE REMOTE ACCESS PLATFORM

The remote access platform is designed to allow the provider of kiosk system services to extend existing kiosks by simply plugging in a module that establishes the connection to our platform. A narrow and well-defined interface is specified. The module is monitoring the state of the kiosk interface and reports changes to the platform. In the other direction user input from the remote user is being applied to the kiosk software. What is reported from the user-input is just the kind of interaction and the name of the element involved. No method bindings are defined in the interface.

Based on the generic EMBASSI [6] architecture for multimodal interactive assistant systems [9] the remote access platform consists of a set of independent software agents. On top of the TCP/IP protocol (e.g., ISO OSI layer 5) agent communication is realised by means of the Knowledge Query and Manipulation Language (KQML [7]) and a KQML-router also serving as name service. This highly flexible framework allows dynamic configuration of application components of different classes as outlined in Fig. 1:

- Device Manager: components that are connected directly to a legacy device, not communicating through KQML framework.
- Assistants: components that provide any kind of assistance to the user, e.g., including sentence completion, input assistance, etc.

- Dialog Manager: components that translate and interpret user input by assigning it to a possible intention. In the case of the application presented here this component is rather limited to the administration of the user interface description as user input is not expected to be ambiguous as being limited to the interaction with a well-defined interface.
- Context Manager: component that represents a shared memory containing context information.
- Interface Player: component that administers one or many input (Filter) and output (Renderer) components and plans and integrates them.
- Filter and Renderer: components that gather input (Filter) from the user and that generate the output derived from the interface description (Renderer) in different modalities.

In a mobile environment part of this platform is located on the mobile device and can be removed and added dynamically. Communication is established through a wireless LAN peer-to-peer network connection.

Several security issues have to be taken into account when offering confidential services like banking and shopping to an open and unattended ambience as there are identification, prevention from unauthorised access and session management. Those issues are beyond the scope of this paper and will therefore not be discussed here.

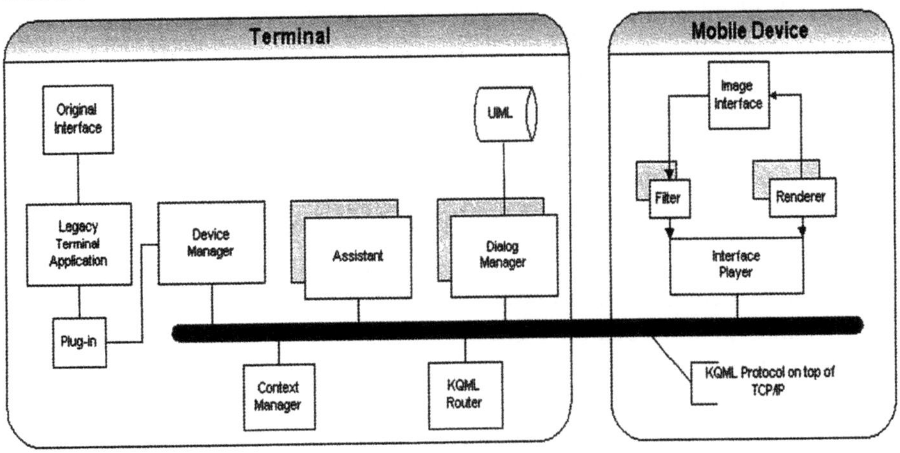

Figure 1. Architecture of the remote access platform to public kiosk systems. On the left the legacy terminal application is shown which is connected to the platform over a plug-in reporting and changing the state of the interface to the platform. The description of the interface presentation in UIML is stored as static resource.

Such a flexible and dynamic architecture provides a framework for personalised and context-sensitive multimodal assistance. Distributed processing can be considered as especially relevant in the mobile domain allowing weaker devices to demand complex calculations from the terminal.

It is also an important feature that application logic of the kiosk software is not revealed. The supplier of the kiosk software only has to provide a shallow generic description of the interfaces of the kiosk software, limited to the mere presentational level which will then be stored as a static resource. The interface description then is retrieved and send to the remote device when the kiosk software reports to be switched to the corresponding interface. The main part of the platform is universally applicable.

3. USER INTERFACE CONCEPT

3.1 Requirements

In order to allow the user to interact with the kiosk system a user interface representation has to be transported to the remote, mobile client. During the conceptual stage of the development we detected the following requirements for such a representation:

- The interface representation has to be transported over the platform protocol, which means it should be as small as possible.
- The interface representation should be configurable, not only on kiosk side, but also on the remote device. This requirement excludes binary precompiled interface representations.
- The interface representation should not be limited to one specific modality, but should allow the mapping on other singular or multiple modalities.

Taking into consideration these requirements we decided to use an XML-based interface definition called User Interface Mark-up Language (UIML, [1,2]) which seemed an appropriate solution for us. In UIML an interface representation is described on a generic level using the four dimensions [12]: structure (which elements exist and how are they structured), style (how are the elements realised), content (textual content) and behaviour (what happens if e.g. a button is pressed).

Fig. 2 shows how in the so-called peers part, the generic interface description then could be mapped to a concrete toolkit and to concrete method-calls. UIML therefore not only represents the first two layers of a three tier concept but also allows a modularization in the definition of interface presentations.

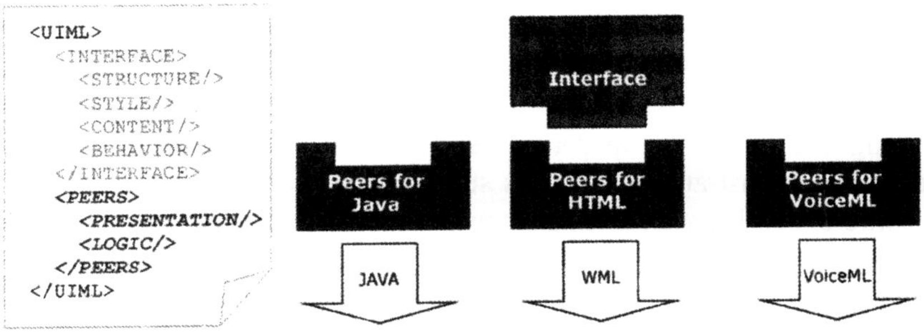

Figure 2. Concept of different bindings for one generic interface description in the User Interface Mark-up Language (UIML).

3.2 Realisation

In a first step we created UIML interface descriptions for our two scenarios (an ATM and a shopping terminal) with two different styles each, which could then be rendered into a Java-Swing interface. As shown in Fig. 3 we decided to create one generic style, which contained minimal data concerning presentation and maximum accessibility and one rich style that should prove the possibility to create a 1:1 copy of the original interface.

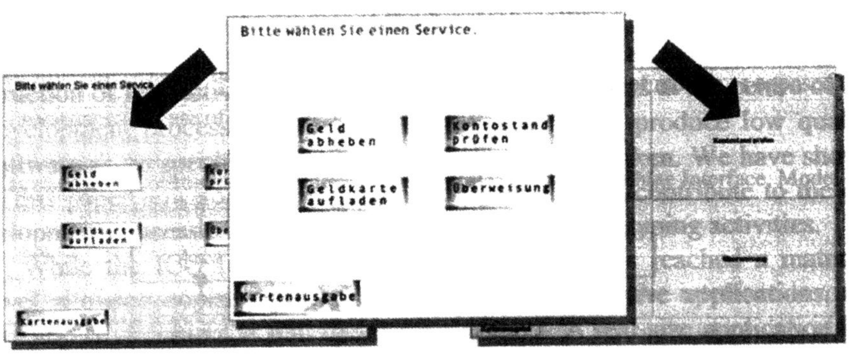

Figure 3. Original kiosk interface from the ATM application (centre) and the remote instances rendered with the Harmonia UIML to Java renderer. The right instance shows the rich styled, and the left shows the generic styled image.

User Input to the Interface is mapped into control-specific events that are parameterised with the name of the control. Events are fed through to the Device Manager and the Plug-in which then translates the events into application-specific commands taking the name parameter as identifier. No bindings and dynamic Interface structures are needed as the interface is built through the response of the application. No application logic has to be duplicated.

4. DISCUSSION

4.1 UIML

Using UIML and the approach discribed above we implemented a fully functional demonstrator which was successfully presented to the public on the conference "Mensch und Computer 2001" in Bad Honnef, Germany. Through this first iteration in our development cycle amongst others the following shortcomings of our interface concept emerged:

Although representing a very sophisticated concept of interface description with a high degree of modularization, UIML did not fully meet our requirements. UIML gives a generic description of interfaces, but it does not provide the developer with a set of generic interface elements which then could be mapped into different modalities. At present the elements defined in the interface part are already bound to a special target representation (e.g. Java, HTML, VXML,...). There is no toolkit covering all of them (the toolkit which is announced to be developed presently seems to target HTML and Java).

The concept of different peer elements for different renderers seems practical, but in realisation writing the peer-part is complicated and error-prone. Further if the target representation is another text-based format, as for instance HTML, the rendering process is rather an XML Style sheet Transformation (XSLT) than a rendering, and thus should be controlled by an appropriate style sheet. Using UIML-to-? renderers therefore results in a heterogeneous process chain.

Due to the modularization of the four interface dimensions mentioned above (e.g. structure, style, content and behaviour) elements have to be referenced through the name-attribute of an element. This has deep implications on subsequent XML processes like XSLT [3]. Information about an interface control has to be collected from several sections of the description where it can be identified only by the element name, or even worse by element class. The fact that all the four dimensions of the interface element can either be defined within the structure or within separate elements still aggravates this. The document structure of UIML description as it is implicated by the UIML concept is not appropriate for such kind of processes.

Summarising all said above leads to the conclusion that the UIML concept might be advantageous when using a certain modality and a similar platform (e.g. a graphical UI for Java or HTML). However a really generic and therefore cross-modality still must be designed. Application of XSLT-processes requires the UIML-resources to be structured in a certain manner namely nested thus giving up the modularity and still remaining complicated.

4.2 Alternatives

As alternative concepts there seems to be three main competitors. First, the common HTML form extensions [14], that allow to define a basic set of interface controls for form interactions on the web. Anyway HTML forms are not suitable for our approach, as they define a purely graphical toolkit. Further one of the general shortcomings of HTML, which is the mixing of structure and style.

Second, the Mozilla project [11] presented another example how to realise a platform-independent interface description with their Cross Platform Front End (XPFE) described in the XML-based User Interface Language (XUL) integrated in their browser. The toolkit developed here is designed for window based systems and does not offer the flexibility required for the translation to other interface concepts.

Third, XForms [5] a new standard currently developed by the W3C which is thought as a successor of the above mentioned HTML Forms within the new XHTML-framework. XForms comprises a generic description of interface elements classified in input and output elements. Extending those basic types all other elements can be derived on a still very generic level (e.g. the element selected can be instantiated as a list, a radio button or a combo box). This concept seems to been very promising even though its conception as such for our use is bound too strictly to HTML and a form-based mechanism.

Several other approaches are being developed to date (e.g. [8]) and there are also efforts to integrate existing standards like XForms into a broader framework [4].

5. OUTLOOK

Based on the XForms concept of input and output elements we presently develop a generic toolkit which defines a set of modality independent controls. As an extension to this, we define higher-level elements that serve as containers for those basic elements in this way not only allowing a form mechanism, but also the possibility of serialising the interface into an acoustic presentation through the dialog element.

Interaction with the computer thus is being regarded from a hybrid point of view, same acoustic and visual. It is considered as a dialog, where the machine poses questions, prompts user input and gives answers to this. A resource defined in a such presentation then should provide an appropriate resource for transformations into several target representations, such as Java-UIML, VXML, HTML, SVG and so forth. Further it will provide the means for customisations and adaptations during runtime that allow a change in the interaction with the interface. In the new platform UIML as it has been used to date, is thus already a concrete instantiation rather than a generic description

REFERENCES

[1] Abrams, M., Phanouri, C., Batongbacal, A. and Shuster, J., *UIML: An Appliance-Independent XML User Interface Language*, in Proc. of 8th World Wide Web Conference WWW'8 (Toronto, 11-14 May 1999), accessible at http://www.harmonia.com/resources/papers/www8_0599/index.htm

[2] Abrams, M. User Interface Markup Language (UIML) - Draft Specification, Version 2.0a, Harmonia, Inc., 2000, accessible at www.harmonia.com

[3] Clark, J., *XSL Transformations (XSLT)*, Version 1.0, W3Consortium, 1999.

[4] Diaz, A., Lucassen, J., and Wiecha, C.F., *Web Services Experience Language*, Vol. 2001, IBM Alphaworks, 2001.

[5] Dubinko, M., Dietl, J., Merrick, R., Raggett, D., Raman, T.V., and Welsh, L.B., *XForms 1.0*, W3C Working Draft, W3C, 2001.

[6] EMBASSI, accessible at http://www.embassi.de

[7] Finn, T., Wber, J., Wiederhold, G., Genesereth, M. Fritzson, R., McKay, D., McGuire, J. Pelavin, R., and Beck, C., *DRAFT Specification of the KQML Agent-Communication Language*, The DARPA Knowledge Sharing Initiative External Interfaces Working Group, 1993.

[8] Forbrig, P., Müller, A., and Cap, C.H., *Appliance independent specification of User Intefaces by XML - A model based view*, in C. Stephanidis (ed.), Proc. of 1st International Conference on Universal Access in Human-Computer Interaction UAHCI'2001 (New Orleans, 5-10 August 2001), Lawrence Erlbaum Associates, Mahwah, 2001, pp. 170-174.

[9] Kirste, T. and Rapp, S., *Architecture for Multimodal Interactive Assistant Systems*, Statustagung der Leitprojekte "Mensch-Technik-Interaktion" (Saarbrücken, 2001).

[10] Malkewitz, R. and Richter, K., *XML used for Remote Control of Public Kiosk Systems (POI, POS)*, in Proc. of E-Business and E-Work (Venice, 2001).

[11] Mozilla.org, *XPToolkit Project*, 1999, accessible at http://www.mozilla.org

[12] Phanouriou, C., *UIML: A Device-Independent User Interface Markup Language*, in *Computer Science and Applications*, Virginia Polytechnic Institute and State University, Blacksburg, 2000, pp. 158.

[13] Richter, K., *Remote Access to Public Kiosk Systems*, in C. Stephanidis (ed.), Proc. of 1st International Conference on Universal Access in Human-Computer Interaction UA-HCI'2001 (New Orleans, 5-10 August 2001), Lawrence Erlbaum Associates, Mahwah, 2001, pp. 195-199.

[14] W3C, accessible at http://www.w3.org.

Chapter 25

SPECIFYING USER INTERFACES FOR RUNTIME MODAL INDEPENDENT MIGRATION

Kris Luyten, Tom Van Laerhoven, Karin Coninx, and Frank Van Reeth
Expertisecentrum Digitale Media, Limburgs Universitair Centrum
Wetenschapspark 2, B-3590 Diepenbeek (Belgium)
E-mail: {kris.luyten, tom.vanlaerhoven, karin.coninx, frank.vanreeth}@luc.ac.be
URL: http://lumumba.luc.ac.be/kris/
Tel: +32-11-268411 – Fax: +32-11-268400

Abstract The usage of computing systems has evolved dramatically over the last years. Starting from a low level procedural usage, in which a process for executing one or several tasks is carried out, computers now tend to be used in a problem oriented way. Future computer usage will be more centered around particular services, and will not be focused on platforms or applications. These services should be independent of the technology used to interact with them. In this paper an approach will be presented which provides a uniform interface to such services, without any dependence on modality, platform or programming language. Through the usage of general user interface descriptions, presented in XML, and converted using XSLT, a uniform framework is presented for runtime migration of user interfaces. As a consequence, future services will become easily extensible for all kinds of devices and modalities. An implementation serving as a proof of concept, a runtime conversion of a joystick in a 3D virtual environment into a 2D dialog-based user interface, is developed.

Keywords: Modality independence, Model-based approach, Transformation, User interface description, User interface migration, migration, XML, XSLT.

1. INTRODUCTION

Nowadays new computing devices are introduced into the market at a very high rate. A lot of these devices with their own properties and constraints are capable of delivering specialized services. As the technology evolves, more devices will become available with a more general purpose (e.g. Palm) and less constraints. This equipment is capable of presenting dif-

C. Kolski and J. Vanderdonckt (eds.), Computer-Aided Design of User Interfaces III, 283–294.
© 2002 *Kluwer Academic Publishers.*

ferent kinds of services which are available in their environment. One possible service is the usage of a mobile computing device as a remote control.

A transition from an application-oriented view on computing towards a service-oriented view is expected. The last couple of years it has been observed that this approach is not feasible without a reliable framework to support it. This framework should be able to offer support for device-independent migration of services and the user interfaces for these services. It should enable us to create services in a device-independent way, offering the supporting devices the choice of how to present these services. Also, the framework should consider future extensions with new kinds of interaction methods and new possibilities in network communication, memory capacity, processing speed, etc.

This paper presents our ongoing research on the possibility of creating such a framework that will allow for runtime migratable user interfaces, which are independent of the target software platform, the target device and the interaction modalities. These user interfaces are merely considered as a presentation of a single service or of more functionally grouped services. We try to extend the work presented in [3,11,15] which all focus on how to abstract a user interface for a platform- and device-independent usage. At the same time we try to use the work presented in [1,4,10] using markup languages to describe the user interface with the significant difference with our approach that we want the given markup language to describe the user interface to be generated at runtime.

The next section takes a look at how a user interface can be serialized in a user interface description language at runtime. Then we convert this description in a high level description of the user interface, which complies with some rules. In a following paragraph, we consider a possibility for serializing the services and the context these services operate in. An implementation serving as a proof of concept is presented, and finally conclusions with regard to the current work and possible extensions are formulated.

2. RUNTIME GENERATED SPECIFICATION OF THE INTERFACE

The concept of a runtime generated user interface description has been introduced in [7]. At runtime a user interface description is generated by means of eXtensible Markup Language (XML) [17] as a description language. The XML description provides an abstraction of the user interface using *Abstract Interaction Objects* (AIOs) which can be mapped onto *Concrete Interaction Objects* (CIOs) [15]. A more practical view is shown in Fig. 1.

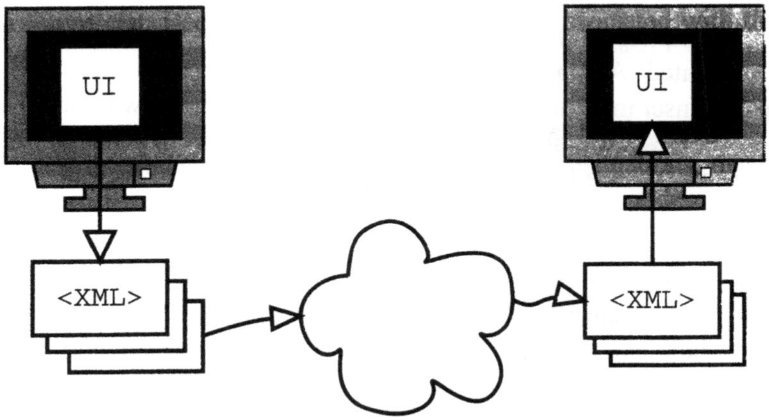

Figure 1. A migrating User Interface.

Notice the similarities with Model-based design [12,13]; the most high-level abstraction of the user interface is a group of tasks. Our work does not aim to extract a Task-based description of the User Interface but merely tries to abstract the "contents" of the user interface, not the presentation. Although we acknowledge the idea of splitting the interface model into a User-task model, a domain model, a user model, a presentation model and a dialog model [13] for getting a better mapping of AIOs on CIOs, we do not consider it to be useful when focusing on runtime migration of *existing* user interfaces.

A working user interface is "serialized" into an XML description at runtime and this description can be transported to another system using for example the Internet or an infrared communication protocol. Once arrived at the target system the XML document can be parsed and converted in a working user interface ("deserialized"). An advantage of this approach can be found in the abstraction of the original user interface that the XML document provides. While parsing the XML document that contains an abstraction of the user interface, the renderer of the target platform is free to choose other ways to present the same functionality in the user interface. Much current research is being conducted on how XML is best structured and used to describe such interfaces.

More information about other approaches and techniques can be found in [1,2,8,10,11]. The most advantageous properties of XML for describing a user interface are enumerated in [7]. The feasibility of this approach depends on how easily an XML description can be generated for a user interface of a working service. For example, when a user interface is written in the programming language Java, it is fairly easy to generate an XML description for this user interface at runtime, even if this possibility was not considered while programming the user interface. Using the reflection mechanism, which allows us to interrogate a Java program about its properties at runtime, an XML description of this structure, and more specific of its user interface, can be generated. Another advantage of this approach is the reusability of existing Java user interfaces which can be incorporated in new systems using new technologies. This should reduce the time-to- market for new versions of systems and reduce the need for reinventing the same user interface over and over again while making use of new technologies.

Unfortunately it is hard or even impossible to add a description of the *context* the user interface is working in at runtime (see section 4 for a more comprehensive explanation). A description of the services it offers should be provided. Those programming languages which do not support a reflection mechanism should provide a framework for the serialization of the user interface in XML at runtime. Section 5.1 shows such a framework currently under development for virtual environments.

3. ABSTRACTING THE USER INTERFACE DESCRIPTION

To allow the user interface to adapt to the constraints of the target system it is important to provide an abstraction of the original user interface. When the user interface description is generated at runtime by the service it is likely to contain system specific elements. To make sure the XML description is sufficiently general the user interface should be abstracted so it becomes independent of how the interaction takes place with the interface. This allows for changes in the interaction modality without a large effort. A great deal of plasticity [14] is gained, allowing us to use system specific data to adapt the user interface to the new constraints.

As an abstraction of the user interface we have defined a DTD [17]. This DTD restricts the possible elements and ordering used in the XML document. Our current DTD is inspired by [10] and enriched by a subset of interactors like the ones presented in [15]. We are planning to replace it with an equivalent XML Schema [16] as soon as there are more mature tools available to use this. The DTD we use to describe the high level user interface description can be found in Fig. 2. The transformation of the original user interface description into a higher level description is realized using the XSLT. Every system or user interface toolkit has to define a conversion providing the appropriate XSLT. Once the higher level description is produced a system specific XML document for the target system has to be produced. For every system a XSLT is defined which maps the AIOs defined in the abstract user interface description to CIOs for that particular system. An overview of this process is given in Fig. 3. Closely related work can be found in AUIML of IBM [9]. However the following difference is to be noticed: in contrast with AUIML our work is mainly focused on runtime migration and adaptation of the user interfaces.

```
<?xml version="1.0"?>
<!ELEMENT interface (aio*)>
<!ELEMENT aio (aio | (input?,output?))+>
<!ATTLIST aio name CDATA #IMPLIED
              type CDATA #REQUIRED>
<!ELEMENT input((input_trigger | input_1-n |
                input_string | input_date | ... ), Icontext)>
<!ATTLIST input name CDATA #REQUIRED>
<!ELEMENT input_trigger (EMPTY)>
<!ATTLIST input_trigger service_name CDATA #REQUIRED>
<!ELEMENT input_1-n (EMPTY)>
<!ATTLIST input_1-n range_min CDATA #IMPLIED
                    range_max CDATA #IMPLIED
                    range_interval CDATA #IMPLIED
                    list_n CDATA #IMPLIED>
...
<!ELEMENT output ((output_1-n | output_string | ...),
          Ocontext)>
<!ATTLIST output name CDATA #REQUIRED>
```

Figure 2. The DTD for the abstract user interface description.

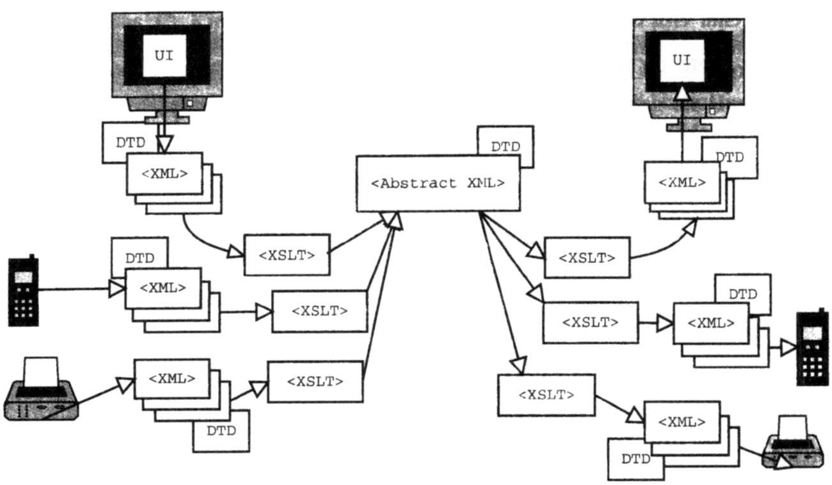

Figure 3. User interface migration.

4. RUNTIME SPECIFICATION OF THE SERVICES

In the previous sections we did not consider how a user interface can be serialized at runtime, taking into account only the *structure* of the user interface but not the *services* it represents. When serializing a user interface at runtime for migration the services these interfaces offer should be accessible through the migrated user interface. On a lower level two different methods give access to the services. Allowing the services (the actual functionality), which are accessed through the interface, to migrate together with the user interface is a first possibility. A second possibility is accessing the services remotely. In this context the user interface actually serves as a remote control to interact with the service it presents. The former can be a reliable approach if the functionality of the service is limited or does not involve a large quantity of data. The latter can be better if the service implies a large and complex application. Another important aspect to take into account is the possible delay, depending on the communication medium. Unlike the user interface, which is entirely migrated, this is not always the case with the services the user interface presents. To make more reasonable decisions on how the user interface can be represented on different systems we feel a need to include the context the interface objects are working in. A context can be defined at several levels: on the lowest level, where some interaction objects are grouped together because they do not have a full meaning on their own. On higher levels, where a context can be hierarchically composed of several other contexts. The context can be divided roughly in two parts: a context for retrieving input and a context for expressing output through the user interface. This enables us to group several AIOs together which have a specific task in common together. For example, consider a 2D user interface for filling in the date composed out of three drop-down boxes. One interactor for the day, another one for the month and one for the year. These three interactors are only meaningful when used in group, otherwise they can not accomplish their original goal: retrieving a date from the operator. When dealing with runtime serialization of the user interface it is very important to remember the context a group of AIOs is working in, so they can be grouped in the same context when they are deserialized. A part of the DTD for describing the context can be found in Fig. 4.

```
...
<!ELEMENT Icontext (Icontext_value)+>
<!ATTLIST Icontext name CDATA #IMPLIED>
<!ELEMENT Ocontext (Ocontext_value)+>
<!ATTLIST Ocontext name CDATA #IMPLIED>
<!ELEMENT Icontext_value (#PCDATA | aio | Icontext_value+ |
Ocontext)>
<!ELEMENT Ocontext_value (#PCDATA | aio | Ocontext_value+ |
Icontext)>
...
```

Figure 4. DTD rules for describing a context.

5. TRANSFORMING MODALITIES

5.1 Description of the Case Study

As a proof of concept we will show how the control for a surveillance camera, presented by a joystick in a virtual environment, can be serialized in XML, processed with XSLT [5], and then deserialized into a 2D control using a Palm device. An operator can change the orientation of the camera in two degrees of freedom: up/down and left/right. The operator must confirm the new orientation with some kind of trigger so the surveillance camera becomes locked in that orientation. This means the input is a position in 2D space with on one axis the vertical orientation and on the other axis the horizontal orientation.

5.2 Description of the Original System

A highly extensible framework for the creation of simulations in a 3D environment has been developed by one of the authors. This framework is used to create a virtual world containing a representation of a control to manipulate a surveillance camera. This control is modeled as a virtual joystick with two buttons providing the user the ability to manipulate the camera. A representation of this joystick is given in Fig. 5. Objects in the environment consist of a collection of modules describing their properties such as shape, state and interactive abilities. The implementation of each of these properties exists in separate modules, which are plugged into the framework. The same modules also provide XML serialization and deserialization.

Figure 5. A joystick in a virtual environment.

The virtual joystick is divided into separate components which in turn can be divided into other components describing its properties. In this case, the lower button consists of a polygon mesh describing its shape, a state module describing its position and orientation, and an interaction module that ensures it the interactive ability to be triggered. Communication between the modules is realised by means of commands, which can also be serialized and deserialized. The button on top of the joystick is modeled in the same way. The handle however requires a different approach. It needs an interaction component that expresses the fact that its container, the handle itself, can give two-dimensional input.

Our framework can serialize this interface in accordance with the XGL [18] specification, a file format designed to capture all 3D information from a system that uses the SGI's OpenGL rendering library. Unfortunately, a DTD for this specification does not exist. The XGL specifications describe their content models by mentioning which elements are required and which are optional, leaving the sequence to the programmer's choice. Defining a content model allowing this kind of freedom, and at the same time expressing the frequency of the elements, is not possible using a DTD. Fortunately, the very few XGL generating applications available seem to agree to some kind of sequence. This is the sequence found in our DTD which is publicly available at http://lumumba.luc.ac.be/tom/xgl/.

The resulting XML document that describes a joystick in a 3D world is shown in Fig. 6. We have limited the example by only depicting the interesting parts of this description.

```
<component type="object" name="button">
  <component type="shape" subtype="tripolymesh">
     <mesh><!-- XGL specific code here --></mesh>
  </component>
  <component type="interaction" subtype="trigger"/>
  <component type="state" subtype="rigidbody">
  <transform><!-- XGL specific code here --></transform>
  </component>
</component>
```

Figure 6. XML document describing part of the joystick.

5.3 Description of the Target System

Our target system is a 2D Java user interface for a Palm device. The user interface operates as a remote control for changing the orientation of a surveillance camera. The description consists of the hierarchy of Java AWT objects which represent the user interface. A subset of Java AWT is used because this Java user interface toolkit is supported by the Palm device. The XML document describing the user interface (Fig. 7) is presented in Fig. 8.

This description is obtained by applying the XSLT in Fig. 9 (only the interesting parts are shown). The XSLT document knows about the constraints the Palm device is subject to, and which the available interaction methods are. The parts of the user interface that cannot be converted, or where too little information is available, could be adapted by a platform specific agent which works on the target XML document for further optimization of the presentation of the AIOs.

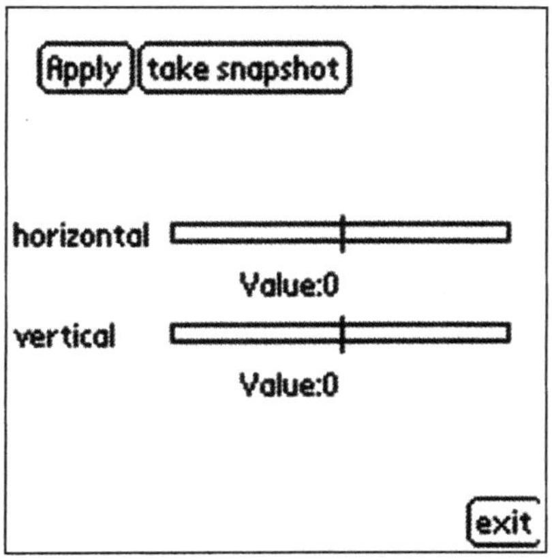

Figure 7. 2D user interface on a Palm device.

```
<Component CLASS="VideoControl">
  <Properties>
   <Property NAME="Apply">
     <Component CLASS="java.awt.Button">
       <Property NAME="label">Apply</Property>
        ...
     </Component>
   </Property>
   <Property Name="HorizontalSlider">
     ...
</Component>
```

Figure 8. XML document describing a Java user interface for the Palm.

```
...
<xsl:template match="interface">
  <xsl:element name="component">
    <xsl:attribute name="CLASS">java.awt.Frame
    </xsl:attribute>
    <xsl:attribute name="NAME"><xsl:value-of
     select="@name"/></xsl:attribute>
    <xsl:apply-templates/>
  </xsl:element>
</xsl:template>

<xsl:template match="aio">
  <xsl:choose>
    <xsl:when test="@type='group'">
```

```
    <xsl:call-template name="grouppanel"/>
  </xsl:when>
  ...
  </xsl:choose>
</xsl:template>

<xsl:template name="push_interact">
  <xsl:element name="Component">
    <xsl:attribute name="CLASS">java.awt.Button
    </xsl:attribute>
      <xsl:attribute name="NAME"><xsl:value-of
       select="@name"/></xsl:attribute>
      <xsl:element name="Properties">
        <xsl:element name="Property">
          <xsl:attribute name="NAME">label</xsl:attribute>
          <xsl:value-of select="@name"/>
...
```

Figure 9. XSLT document for obtaining a Palm user interface.

5.4 A General View on the Migration Process

From the original serialized XML document (Fig. 6) an XML document compliant with the DTD in Fig. 4 should be generated. Each system provides its own XSLT to initiate the conversion. The XSLT document "generalizes" the concrete user interface which was described in the XML document of the original user interface.

Once the high level user interface description is obtained the conversion for the target platform can be initiated. Applying the XSLT document on the high level XML document results in a platform specific user interface description. The XSLT makes sure the AIOs will be mapped on platform specific CIOs, grouping them in a specific context for interaction. Whether the services this user interface represents are invoked remotely or locally is not taken into account here. This should remain transparent for the user whenever possible.

6. CONCLUSIONS AND FUTURE WORK

In this paper we presented the use of a runtime generated user interface description for presenting services on different kind of systems. The user interface description is expressed in XML and we use XSLT to process these descriptions. In a first stage the user interface description is abstracted while the second stage requires the high level user interface to be mapped on a specific GUI toolkit.

We believe the ability to generate a high level user interface description of a service at runtime is a step closer to offering services independent of the system which is used. When the user interface description provides enough information and an abstraction of a sufficiently high level, a user interface becomes almost modeless and switching between modalities can be done automatically. Since a fully automatic conversion of all kinds of user interfaces is unlikely to be successful, a semi-automatic approach is preferred. In the case we have examined here we have shown this approach is feasible and that it provides many opportunities to add extreme extensibility to future user interfaces. One of the consequences is the possibility to adapt a user interface to the target device's constraints. This can be done without forcing the user interface designer to make separate designs for each system. It is even possible to make a user interface for a particular system without considering other, alternative systems with other constraints. This user interface will still be able to migrate to the other systems, adapting to the device's constraints. The context description, explained in section 4, can contribute to a partial solution to overcome this problem. Future work includes a further generalization of the conversion mechanisms and adding user profiling and device constraints to the conversion process. Also, there is a lack of support to describe how several interactor objects are grouped and need each other's data to use certain functionality.

A framework which enables the remote communication or even the migration of services, represented by the migrated user interfaces, is necessary. To make sure that the migrated user interface stays usable when deserialized and that it has the same usability characteristics as the original user interface usability testing would be recommended.

ACKNOWLEDGMENTS

Our research is partly funded by the Flemish government and EFRO (European Fund for Regional Development). The SEESCOA project IWT 980374 is directly funded by the IWT (Flemish subsidy organization). SEESCOA stands for Software Engineering for Embedded Systems using a Component-Oriented Approach, accessible at http://www.cs.kuleuven.ac.be/cwis/research/distrinet/projects/SEESCOA.

REFERENCES

[1] Abrams, M., Phanouriou, C., Batongbacal, A. and Shuster, J., *UIML: An Appliance Independent XML User Interface Language*, in Proc. of 8th World Wide Web Conference WWW'8 (Toronto, 11-14 May 1999), Computer Networks, Vol. 31, No. 11-16, pp.

1695-1708, accessible at http://www.harmonia.com/resources/papers/www8_0599/index.htm.
[2] danm@netscape.com, *Introduction to a XUL Document*, October 1999, accessible at http://www.mozilla.org/xpfe/index.html.
[3] Eisenstein, J., Vanderdonckt, J., and Puerta, A., Applying Model-Based Techniques to the Development of UIs for Mobile Computers, in J. Lester (ed.), Proc. of ACM Conf. on Intelligent User Interfaces IUI'2001 (Santa Fe, 14-17 January 2001), ACM Press, New York, 2001, pp. 69-76.
[4] IBM Corporation, *MoDAL (Mobile Document Application Language*, 2001, accessible at http://www.almaden.ibm.com/cs/TSpaces/MoDAL/
[5] Kay, M., *XSLT Programmer's Reference*, 2nd Edition, Wrox Press, 2001.
[6] Kormann, Th., *The Koala User Interface Language,* 2000, accessible at http://www-sop.inria.fr/koala/kuil/.
[7] Luyten, K. and Coninx, K., *An XML-based runtime user interface description language for mobile computing devices*, in Ch. Johnson (ed.), Proc. of 8th International Workshop on Design, Specification, and Verification of Interactive Systems DSV-IS'2001 (Glasgow, 13-15 June 2001), Lecture Notes in Computer Science, Vol. 2220, Springer-Verlag, Berlin, 2001, pp. 1-15, accessible at http://lumumba.luc.ac.be/kris/publications/dsvis2001/luyten_coninx-dsvis2001.pdf
[8] Luyten, K., Coninx, K., Van den Bergh, J., and Segers, J., *Software engineering for embedded systems using a component oriented approach*, Deliverable 4.2: Implementation of a component based user interface, SEESCOA confidential, Technical report, Expertisecentrum Digitale Media, Limburgs Universitair Centrum, 2001.
[9] Merrick, R.A., *Device Independent User Interfaces in XML*, BelCHI Kickoff meeting, 2001, accessible at http://www.belchi.be/event.htm.
[10] Müller, A., Forbrig, P., and Cap, C., Model-Based User Interface Design Using Markup Concepts, in Ch. Johnson (ed.), Proc. of 8th Int. Workshop on Design, Specification, and Verification of Interactive Systems DSV-IS'2001 (Glasgow, 13-15 June 2001), Lecture Notes in Computer Science, Vol. 2220, Springer-Verlag, Berlin, 2001, pp. 16-27.
[11] Olsen, D.A., Jefferies, S., Nielsen, T., Moyes, W., and Fredrickson, P., *Cross-modal interaction using Xweb*, in Proceedings of the 13th Annual Symposium on User Interface Software and Technology UIST'00 (San Diego, 5-8 November 2000), ACM Press, New York, 2000, pp. 191-200.
[12] Paternò, F., *Model-Based Design and Evaluation of Interactive Applications*, Springer-Verlag, Berlin, 2000.
[13] Puerta, A.R. and Eisenstein, J., *Towards a general computational framework for model-based interface development systems*, in M. Maybury (ed.), Proceedings of the ACM Conf. on Intelligent User Interfaces IUI'99 (Los Angeles, 5-8 January 1999), ACM Press, New York, 1999, pp. 171-180.
[14] Thevenin, D. and Coutaz, J., Adaptation and Plasticity of User Interfaces, in Proc. of i3-spring99 Workshop on Adaptive Design of Interactive Multimedia Presentations for Mobile Users (Sitges, 7-10 March 1999), accessible at http://iihm.imag.fr/thevenin/papiers/I3Workshop99/I3Workshop99.html
[15] Vanderdonckt, J. and Bodart, F., *Encapsulating Knowledge for Intelligent Automatic Interaction Objects Selection*, in Proc. of ACM Conf. on Human Aspects in Computing Systems InterCHI'93 (Amsterdam, 24-29 April 1993), ACM Press, New York, 1993, pp. 424-429.
[16] World Wide Web consortium, *XML Schema*, 2001, accessible at http://www.w3.org/XML/Schema.
[17] World WideWeb consortium, *Extensible Markup Language (XML)*, 2001, accessible at http://www.w3.org/XML/.
[18] XGL Working Group, *XGL File Format Specification*, 2001, accessible at http://www.xglspec.org/.

Chapter 26

REVERSE ENGINEERING INTERACTION PLANS FOR LEGACY INTERFACE MIGRATION

Eleni Stroulia and Rohit V. Kapoor
Department of Computing Science, University of Alberta
259 Computing Science Center, Edmonton, Alberta, T6G 2E8 (Canada)
E-mail: {stroulia, kapoor} @cs.ualberta.ca – URL: http://web.cs.ualberta.ca/~stroulia/
Tel.: +1-780-492 3520 – Fax: +1-780-492-1071
Byte Ryte bv

Abstract Legacy interface migration is becoming an increasingly important IT activity; many organizations are interested in cost effective and low risk processes for making their legacy systems accessible to new, web-based platforms. Most migration techniques proposed to date require a lot of human expertise. In this paper we discuss Mathaino, an intelligent, multi platform, semi-automated, and low risk solution for migrating legacy user interfaces to the web by wrapping them with web-accessible front-ends.

Keywords: Domain specific model-based approaches, Model-based and task-based approaches to UI design, Semi-automated generation of UI, UI modeling language, UI reverse engineering.

1. INTRODUCTION

Legacy systems are antiquated systems that are still in use in spite of their obsolete operation platforms and technology, because their substitution with new systems can be extremely costly and disruptive to the organization's daily operation. As more and more organizations move to delivering their services on the Web, interface migration is becoming a major activity in the Information Technology field and an important research problem in software reengineering.

In general, software-engineering research on legacy application reengineering and migration has followed one of three approaches. First, several methodologies have been proposed to making the legacy mainte-

C. Kolski and J. Vanderdonckt (eds.), Computer-Aided Design of User Interfaces III, 295–310.
© 2002 *Kluwer Academic Publishers.*

nance and evolution practices more principled, measurable and controllable [2,9]. A second line of research [10] has focused on the problem of code understanding for isolating components of the legacy system so that they can be reused in a new environment. Finally, a third line of investigation has focused on the problem of migrating text-based user interfaces to GUIs, by inferring the widgets implied in the interaction provided by the original interface and translating them to corresponding widgets in the target environment [11]. Understanding the user interface from the legacy system's code is a complex and error-prone task. Furthermore it requires a substantial infrastructure for each different programming language that needs to be examined. On the other hand, "translating widgets" from the legacy platform to corresponding widgets in the target platform suffers from two disadvantages. First, the process has to be repeated every time the legacy system needs to migrate to a new platform. Second this migration is likely to result in the interaction model on the target platform being similar to the legacy interaction model, which is undesirable since legacy interfaces are usually difficult to learn.

In our work with the Mathaino system and its precursor, URGenT [8], we have adopted a novel approach to this problem. Our objective is to develop an intelligent system that can declaratively model the current user interface of a legacy system at the user-interaction level and then use this model to simultaneously generate functionally equivalent interfaces simultaneously on a set of other platforms. Mathaino learns a model of the system-user interaction for a particular task from several examples of the task performed by expert users of the legacy system. It uses a set of heuristics to generalize the observed user behavior and constructs a model of how users accomplish this task with the existing interface. This abstract model of the task-specific system-user interaction specifies the pieces of information exchanged between the user and the legacy interface, their inter-dependencies and the elementary interactions that enable this information exchange on the current interface. This abstract model can be executed by a set of platform-specific translators that generate, at run time, an appropriate interface using the widget toolkit available on their own platforms. In our research, we have adopted principles and results of research in model-based user-interface design [4,12,14,15] for selecting and appropriately organizing the graphical interface widgets for the new interface front-end. Furthermore, Mathaino adopts an XML-based syntax for specifying the interaction model of the legacy user interface, similar to other current research efforts [1,16].

In the rest of this paper, we present an overview of the Mathaino legacy-interface migration process (Section 2) and we illustrate it with an example (Section 3). We then discuss its run-time environment (Section 4) and we conclude with our evaluation, a summary of the approach and its main contributions (Section 5).

2. THE MIGRATION PROCESS

Mathaino is part of a larger project, named CelLEST, which is partially supported by Celcorp (http://www.celcorp.com), a company with a decade-long experience in developing intelligent tools to support legacy application integration. The objective of CelLEST (http://www.cs.ualberta.ca/~stroulia/CELLEST) is to develop an environment to support the migration of legacy systems to the web, by (a) reverse engineering their user-interface behavior, based on collected traces of the system-user interaction, (b) constructing web-accessible front-ends for wrapping task-specific legacy interactions, and (c) aggregating the wrapped legacy tasks in integrated consortia that can offer complex services.

The novelty of the CelLEST migration process lies in that it proposes the examination of traces of the actual run-time interaction between the user and the legacy interface, instead of examining the legacy application code. This is because the CelLEST approach aims at understanding the information-exchange behavior of the legacy interface, instead of how it is implemented in the legacy code.

The input to Mathaino is a collection of traces of the interaction between the system and the user while executing several different instances of a particular task. These traces are recorded by specially instrumented terminal emulators, through which the users access the legacy system. Given these traces, Mathaino constructs a model of the underlying interaction plan that accomplishes the demonstrated user task. This involves first, identifying the plan states and plan actions. Mathaino's plan-modeling step is discussed in detail in Section 2.1.

After the reverse engineering of the legacy user interface has been completed, i.e., the interaction plan has been modeled, Mathaino proceeds to generate an abstract specification of a form-based user interface that will act as its front-end. To that end, Mathaino proceeds to specify the forms that the new interface will consist of, based on the inter-dependencies of the pieces of information exchanged through the new interface. Then it decides on the types of widgets that the forms should contain. The abstract GUI design step is discussed in Section 2.2.

The resulting abstract user interface is specified in XML and is executable by Mathaino's run-time interpreters. At this point, we have developed interpreters for translating the abstract specification in XHTML, and thus enabling its access through XHTML-enabled browsers, and in WML to make it available to WAP devices like cell-phones, PDAs etc [7]. These two platforms have widely varying requirements and we have chosen them in order to demonstrate the flexibility of Mathaino's migration processes. The run-time environment responsible for executing this specification is discussed briefly in section 4.

2.1 Plan Modeling

Our view of the purposeful, task-specific system-user as plan execution is motivated by the particular infrastructure we envision for legacy migration. The objective of Mathaino is to model the interaction plan, and to use this model as a proxy between the new interface front-end and the existing legacy user interface. This proxy will receive data provided by the user to the new interface and will use this data to execute the underlying legacy interface. At the same time, it will extract interesting data provided by the legacy interface and will forward it to the interface front-end to be displayed to the user. To be able to correctly interpret and respond to the behavior of the underlying legacy interface, the plan must be able to recognize the individual states of the plan at run-time and to perform the appropriate interactions.

2.1.1 Modeling the Plan States

Mathaino does not have access to the internal behavioral states of the legacy application, i.e., the relevant variables (objects) and their values (states). Instead, it assumes that the distinct, internal, behavioral states that the legacy application goes through during the system-user interaction correspond to the visually distinct screens presented to the user interface. Thus, Mathaino recognizes the different interaction-plan states based on the appearance of their corresponding screens.

Interface screens may be static or dynamic, i.e., they may appear exactly the same every time they are presented to the user or they may differ greatly. Static screens contain little or no application data and their function is to enable navigation or to receive user input. Dynamic screens contain a lot of application and their function is to display information to the user data, such as database query results for example. In the context of CelLEST, we have developed LeNDI [3,13], which, given extensive traces of the system-user interaction, i.e., traces collected over long periods of time involving execution of a variety of tasks, applies a set of clustering algorithms to organize the traces' screen snapshots in clusters. The result of clustering is reviewed and revised by an expert and then LeNDI produces a decision tree for classifying new snapshots at run-time. The run-time classification accuracy of the resulting decision tree is approximately ~90-95%.

However, Mathaino requires 100% classification accuracy. A snapshot classification error at run-time implies an error in the recognition of the current state during execution of the interaction plan. Such an error would imply that the Mathaino plan interpreter would be "lost" and unable to correctly interpret the legacy interface behavior and to interact with it to complete the task.

Mathaino starts by assuming (safely) that LeNDI has accurately clustered the majority of the snapshots contained in the task-specific traces that it examines. Next, Mathaino employs a string-difference algorithm to identify the set of common keywords appearing in the majority of snapshots contained in each cluster. This pattern can be used as the signature for the cluster, and at run-time, it can be used to classify each new snapshot presented to the user in one of the different screens and thus recognize the current plan state. If the learned signature does not apply to some of the cluster snapshots, these snapshots are separated to a new cluster and a new signature is learned to recognize them. This is an automatic process but the user can review and revise the formed clusters, in which case the signatures are re-learned.

At run-time, as each screen is received by the Mathaino run-time subsystem, it is matched against the cluster signature corresponding to the screen that Mathaino expects according to the current plan. In case the incoming snapshot fails to match the required signature, Mathaino tries to recognize it by first switching to an alternate possible plan for carrying out the same task, and then applying the signature of the screen expected according to the new plan. In this way, Mathaino can dynamically adjust its navigation according to different interaction scenarios.

2.1.2 Modeling the Plan Actions

Having learned to recognize the distinct interaction-plan states, i.e., the distinct screens that users have to navigate through to accomplish their task, Mathaino needs to learn to execute the appropriate actions to proceed from one state to another. Mathaino's plan-representation language is called XPDDL, inspired from PDDL [5], and is implemented in XML. In this language, each action involves the input of the value for some type of information by the user, or the acquisition of the value of some type of information from the legacy interface. Each action also has preconditions and effects, in that the action is possible when the system is in a particular state, and when successful, it leaves the system in another state. Given this representation language, to learn the plan actions, Mathaino has to identify

- the distinct pieces of information that are manipulated by the plan actions, that is the information variables, whose values are exchanged between the user and the system,

- the state where each exchange takes place and the state it results in, and
- the syntax of how the exchange occurs, i.e., where in the screen the information is entered or acquired from.

Information-input actions are recorded by the terminal emulator during the task demonstration, since each keystroke is recorded by the legacy interface emulator. However, to be able to learn *information-acquisition* actions, the user demonstrating the task has to highlight, at each state of the interaction plan, the areas of the current interface snapshot that contain information of interest. The location where information acquisition occurs can be static or dynamic. Mathaino's *Display-Information Extraction* subsystem starts by assuming that the coordinates of an information-exchange activity are static, and attempts to learn these coordinates. If this assumption fails because the location of the activity is variable, then it assumes that there must be static landmarks, such as labels for example, surrounding the activity data, and proceeds to learn a pattern for the area surrounding the activity on the interface snapshot.

Having learned where on the interface data is input and displayed, Mathaino examines the specific values of the data exchanged in the individual example traces and generates hypotheses about what are the distinct types of information exchanged during the plan execution. This is the purpose of Mathaino's *Information-Entity Identification* subsystem. Depending on the values input to and acquired from the system during the plan execution, Mathaino hypothesizes the following types of input information:

- *Constants*: an information entity, whose value is the same in all the corresponding actions of all example task traces;
- *Range*: an information entity, whose value varies within a well-defined range for all example traces;
- *Derived*: an information entity, whose value is obtained through an information-acquisition action early in the plan and is subsequently provided to the system through an information-input interaction;
- *Redundant*: an information entity, whose value is provided as input to the system through multiple information-input interactions; and
- *Unpredictable*: an independent information entity that is input by the user.

Mathaino's Information-Entity Identification subsystem categorizes each data element into one of these categories by examining the values of the information in the various example traces. First, if a data item, manipulated at a particular point in the plan, has the same value for all the example traces, Mathaino infers that it is a *constant* entity, and memorizes the particular value for the entity. The run-time environment manipulates these entities automatically, i.e., provides them to the legacy interface without requiring any input from the user performing the task. Usually most of the navigation commands for a system can be grouped under this category, as usually they tend to be constant over all the example traces of a particular task.

In the next phase, Mathaino examines the data items to identify those that are input by the user and have the same value as other data items previously displayed by the system. All such entities are classified as *derived*. The run-time environment automatically acquires the entity values from the legacy interface and enters them on all subsequent states where they are required. Such entities tend to be identification keys that are used to retrieve different pieces of related information from different databases. Similar to derived entities, *redundant* ones are input by the user at some state and have the same value as another input entity in some previous state.

As Mathaino analyzes the given examples, it keeps track of the set of unique values for any particular input entity. In cases where, over a large number of examples, Mathaino detects only a much smaller variation of the set of input, it identifies this entity as a *range* entity and memorizes the set of possible values for it. This is used in the design of the new interface, where this entity can be input using a selection widget as opposed to an entry widget.

The rest of the entities, which can't be categorized into any other set, are marked as *unpredictable*. This set constitutes the minimum set of user input that is actually required for performing the given task on the legacy system. Usually this categorization of input fields leads to a very significant reduction in the actual input required from the user.

For example, for the Harvard University Library Union Catalog (HOLLIS, http://hollis.harvard.edu) that we have been experimenting with, the actual input information for a typical search task reduces from a set of 16 fields to just a single field, i.e., the name of the book to search for. This represents a 93.75% reduction in the actual input information required for performing this particular task.

2.2 Abstract GUI Design

The forward-engineering phase of Mathaino's migration process involves, first, identifying the abstract forms that will be contained in the new interface, and second, selecting abstract interaction widgets, appropriate for supporting the elementary interactions of the underlying interaction plan, in order to produce a new, web-accessible interface that will enable users to accomplish the demonstrated task by executing the underlying interaction plan, modeled in the previous phase.

2.2.1 Identifying the Abstract Forms

The new abstract GUI constructed by Mathaino does not have to, and in fact, should not, contain the same number of interactions that the original legacy interface requires. Since it is intended for web access, the new front-end interface is form based. Each form must then correspond to a set of elementary interactions on the original interface and therefore enable the navigation of some segment of the learned plan. The first step is to identify the starting screen for each form. The abstract user-interface generator assumes that the value of each output type of information that has been identified previously is essential to inferring the set of values of the required input information occurring after it. Thus, Mathaino starts a new form as soon as it encounters any screen that contains a required input-information field, preceded by a previously identified output information field.

After Mathaino has created the list of starting screens for the various forms according to the previous heuristic, the next step is to normalize this list. The factors that must be accounted for are:

- The first screen of the trace must be the starting screen for the first form. In case it has not already been included into the list it is added now.
- To cleanly exit the legacy system, it is necessary that the last screen of the trace be the terminating screen for the last form. Thus, in case it has not already been included into the list, it is added now.

Also Mathaino ensures that all types of information that are output by information-acquisition interactions are displayed on some form in the new UI. Thus, if any screens containing output fields have been ignored, Mathaino creates a new form to accommodate their presentation.

2.2.2 Selecting the Abstract Widgets

After the original legacy screen navigation has been decomposed into a set of abstract forms, the issue becomes first, to select the appropriate widgets for receiving user input and displaying the legacy, and second, to decide the relative layout of the widgets on the form. Mathaino, based on a set of heuristics [14], proposes a widget for each input and output information field. For example, for fields with an enumerated range of values Mathaino chooses the combo box if the number of possible choices is more than two and a set of radio buttons otherwise. Similarly fields with values in open-ended domains are assigned a simple text box widget by default. However, the user can override these settings and choose another widget for the input field if he so desires. For example, a very common task is to replace the simple input box widget with a password widget for password fields. The run-time interpreters will supply a widget in the target platform that most closely matches the abstract input widget selected by the user. This way, the actual interface front-end presented to the user of each platform will have the same look-and-feel as all other applications in that platform, making it easy to learn and to use.

Mathaino proposes a tabular layout by default, and the user is able to customize this layout pattern as follows:

- The user can change the number of layout columns. Mathaino automatically rearranges the input widgets in accordance with the new layout columns.
- For output fields, the user can change the wrap length for each output field. All the data for that field are then wrapped at the new wrap length. This is helpful as many text based legacy systems rely on a particular wrap length to generate a tabular layout of data. However, Mathaino might forsake this setting for devices whose physical screen is not capable of showing the requisite number for characters per line.
- The user can customize the labels for both output fields and input widgets, and can also choose various alignments, relative to the input and output fields, for this text.

After the user is satisfied with the abstract user interface, i.e., the selected widgets and their layout, Mathaino generates an XML representation for its specification. Mathaino's run-time interpreters are responsible for interpreting this XML specification of the abstract user interface into the actual platform-specific target user interface. The idea of a declarative XML specification of the user interface is related to efforts of developing languages for user-interface specification, such as XUL [16] and UIML [1], however, Mathaino focuses on modeling existing user interfaces as opposed to designing new ones. As the basic Mathaino subsystems are platform independent, the interpreters are also responsible for interpreting platform-specific messages received via the new user interface back into a platform independent form that can be understood by the back-end Mathaino navigation subsystems. In this manner, the user can create a single, unified user-interface specification for a task in the legacy system, which can then be implemented simultaneously on multiple platforms.

3. AN ILLUSTRATIVE EXAMPLE

Let us now illustrate Mathaino's process with an example from an actual legacy system of an insurance company. The interaction of the user with the legacy interface is diagrammatically depicted in Fig. 1 below. Ovals correspond to unique system screens; the labels on the screen ovals are distinguishing names corresponding to the screens' signatures. Edges between ovals are annotated with the specification of the interactions that enable the transition between the corresponding screens.

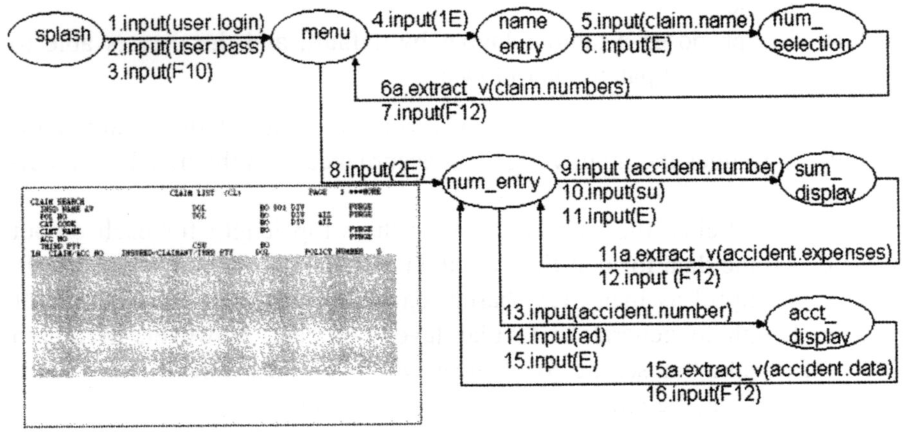

Figure 1. A diagrammatic representation of the Accident Report task.

The task performed on this legacy system involves retrieving an accident-claim report. The user has to provide her login and password to the system "splash" screen, select an option from the main "menu" screen, enter the name of the claimant ("name_entry" screen), select the specific accident-claim number ("num_selection"), and then enter this number twice on the same "num_entry" screen followed by a different function name ("su" and "ad") to retrieve the summary of expenses incurred by the accident ("sum_display") and the accident description ("acct_display"). In this scenario, the user visits 10 screens and inputs 16 pieces of information (including function key presses), some of them, such as the accident number for example, repeatedly.

We used four examples of this task performed by the expert user as input to Mathaino. In these examples, the user navigates through the same screen sequence but provides and retrieves different data, specific to each individual problem.

The first step of Mathaino is to construct the set of screen signatures for all the screens encountered in the trace (state modeling step, section 2.1.1). One of the most dynamic screens in this trace is the "num_selection" screen that shows the accident claim numbers resulting from the user entering a "claim.name", shown in the bottom left of Fig. 1. Most of the information on the (the grayed out) bottom part of the screen is problem specific, however, this screen several keywords in its header and footer like the screen title, screen ID and other constant navigation information. Mathaino's screen recognizer constructed a distinguishing signature consisting of these keywords (with their screen locations) for this screen.

The next step is to learn the syntax of the actions performed on each distinct screen, at each point in the process (action modeling, section 2.1.2). The input actions performed in this task involve entering *unpredictable*, *constant* and *redundant* pieces of information. For example, the "user.login" and "user.password" as well as the "claim.name" and "accident.number" are *unpredictable*, since they are different in every task execution. However, the "accident.number" is input twice at the "num_entry" screen, and the second instance is *redundant*. Furthermore, the strings that the user" has to type to select function names, such as "ad" and "su" input at the "num_entry" screen and all function key-presses are *constant*. The extraction actions performed in this task involve all the extraction of pieces of information from *variant* locations, namely "claim.numbers", "accident.data" and "accident.expenses", i.e., information that appears in different absolute locations in the screen, which however can be located relative to screen "landmark" keywords.

Constant, *derived* and *redundant* input actions are performed automatically on behalf of the user at run-time. In this example, the number of information-input interactions is reduced from 16 to 4, i.e., the "user.login" and "user.password" and the "claim.name" and "claim.number". The rest of the user input in the legacy interface is navigational information (constant fields) and redundant input.

The next step in the process is to organize the forms of the new interface front-end (abstract form identification, section 2.2.1). The forms of this example must present the input widgets necessary for the user to provide these four pieces of information, and receive the information of interest, i.e., the list of claim numbers from which to select the accident number of interest, the summary of expenses and the accident description.

Mathaino aggregates all input in one form, as long there is no intermediate output required. This means that the widgets for the user login and password and the claimant name are all contained in the first form of the new interface (Form 1 of Fig. 2). The next form contains a widget to display the list of claim numbers produced by the legacy interface in response to the claimant-name query and an input widget in which to enter the selected accident number from this list (Form 2 of Fig. 2).

Finally, all the rest of the information output by the legacy system, i.e., accident data and expense summary, is contained in the third form of the new interface front-end (Form 3 of Fig. 2). For this trace, Mathaino chooses simple edit boxes as the input widgets. One of the fields is the first form, however, is a password and thus the user has to substitute one of the edit boxes with an appropriate password input. Mathaino then produces an abstract interface that can be executed on both XHTML (shown in Fig. 2) and WML platforms by the corresponding interpreters.

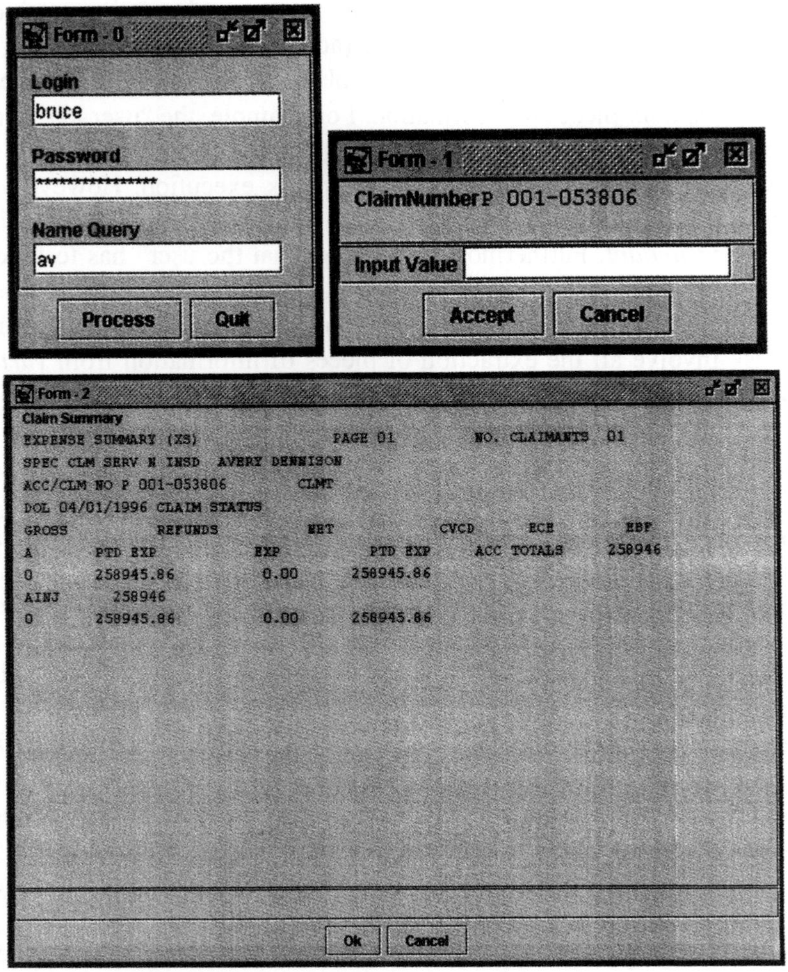

Figure 2. The XHTML interface produced by Mathaino for the Accident Report task.

4. THE RUN-TIME ENVIRONMENT

The Mathaino run-time environment consists of two subsystems. The *front-end interpreters* are responsible for interpreting the abstract user interface specification on the new platform and interacting with the user, displaying and receiving information. The *back-end remote system navigator* is responsible for enacting the navigation on the legacy interface, i.e., forwarding the user input, as received by the front-end interface, to the appropriate screens and fields of the legacy interface and retrieving the expected user output from the legacy interface to forward it to the front-end.

The back-end remote system navigator has been built on top of the Celware Legacy Connector, a sophisticated terminal emulator that supports emulation of the majority of legacy mainframe protocols, including IBM 3270, VT100 and HLLAPI, developed by Celcorp, the industrial sponsor of the CelLEST project. The remote system navigator of Mathaino includes a basic navigation API that forms a higher layer of abstraction over this API. Further, it includes a form navigator component that has been built on top of this basic navigation API. The form navigator can execute the navigation plan for any abstract form that has been produced by the abstract, user-interface generator. Any component, such as the platform-specific abstract user interface interpreters, that uses the form navigator is required to communicate the plan data to and from it in a platform independent manner. Therefore, the user-interface interpreters need to retranslate the platform specific messages into a form understandable by the back-end form navigator.

To date, we have developed two front-end interpreters: one for XHTML enabled browsers and one for WAP devices. Mathaino's XHTML interpreter maps the abstract user interface forms to appropriate XHTML CGI forms. The interpreters executes as a servlet on the web server. It dynamically parses the abstract forms and translates them into XHTML at run-time. It also parses the CGI response produced by the client web browser into the platform independent form required by the form navigator. The XHTML interpreter maps the abstract user interface widgets into appropriate CGI widgets. For example, the range fields are mapped to either a combo box widget or a set of radio buttons. The interpreter also uses XHTML tables to layout the web page in a format that closely resembles the format chosen by the user for the abstract UI. In this way, the XHTML interpreter can execute the interface, specified by the design-time abstract, user-interface generator, on web browsers in a manner transparent to the end user. Web pages produced by Mathaino's XHTML interpreter have been validated by W3C as being 100% XHTML 1.0 compliant. The WML interpreter is constructed similarly, and behaves similarly, with the difference that it parses the abstract forms and translates them into WML decks, which have a much more restricted set of widgets than XHTML.

5. EVALUATION, CONCLUSIONS AND FUTURE WORK

To date, we have evaluated the effectiveness of Mathaino with several different applications, running on vt100 and tn3270 systems. The first case study was the HOLLIS library system. Mathaino was used to generate a GUI for searching top five books on any given subject. The second example was a legacy system owned by an insurance company, collaborating with our sponsors; the example of this paper is from this system. The problem in the context of this system was to wrap a claim-report task. In our third example, we utilized Mathaino to generate a complete email reader package for cell phones. For this example we used the PINE email reader as our legacy system. Finally, we used Mathaino to wrap a job-search application. Our experiments with all these systems were successful, which leads us to believe that the approach implemented in Mathaino is quite general and robust.

Mathaino is a system that can learn by example "how to interact" with a legacy system for the purpose of accomplishing a specific task. The result of Mathaino's learning is a plan, represented in a PDDL-like language, of the user's interface-navigation and information-exchange on the legacy interface. The Mathaino run-time environment is a "shell", which, given the learned plan, can produce working interface front-ends on many new platforms simultaneously. These front-ends are effectively "wrappers" of the legacy system that enable the accessibility of the legacy system, originally developed on a proprietary platform, from the Web. Mathaino's task-specific wrappers are

- abstract: they specify the system-user interaction in terms of interface navigation and information exchange, not in terms of interface widgets;
- platform-independent: they do not assume any particular technology of the target platform, except for XML support;
- optimized: they eliminate data entry of constants and duplicate data entry; and
- reflective: they monitor the user activity and produce a record of it to be forwarded to the mediator of the aggregate consortium for further processing.

Our work on Mathaino [6] is still in early stages; however our initial experimentation results provide some evidence that the overall approach is effective and potentially applicable to real-world legacy migration problems. The CelLEST project is a close partnership between academic research and industry practice, we are have always been concerned with the issue of incorporating the methods developed in the context of CelLEST in the context of the Celcorp toolkit. At this point, we are examining specific opportunities for the integration of Mathaino capabilities into the Celware toolkit, and we expect to have results of an initial deployment in early 2002. Furthermore, we are interested in extending Mathaino in two dimensions: first, in terms of the complexity of the tasks that it can model and second in terms of its abstract widget toolkit, possibly using models imported by widget toolkits such as Swing for example or such as the models incorporated in XUL or UIML.

ACKNOWLEDGEMENTS

This work was supported by a generous contribution from Celcorp, a CRD grant by NSERC 215451-98, and ASERC. Furthermore, the authors wish to acknowledge the input of Bruce Matichuk in numerous CelLEST and Mathaino discussions that helped shape the work described here.

REFERENCES

[1] Abrams, M., Phanouriou, C., Batongbacal, A. and Shuster, J., *UIML: An Appliance-Independent XML User Interface Language*, in Proc. of 8th World Wide Web Conference WWW'8 (Toronto, 11-14 May 1999), Computer Networks, Vol. 31, No. 11-16, pp. 1695-1708, accessible at http://www.harmonia.com/resources/papers/www8_0599/index.htm or at http://www8.org/w8-papers/5b-hypertext-media/uiml/uiml.html

[2] Bisbal, J., Lawless, D., Wu, B., and Grimson, J., *Legacy Information System Migration: A Brief Review of Problems, Solutions and Research Issues*, IEEE Software, Vol. 16, No. 5, 1999, pp. 103-111.

[3] El-Ramly, M., Iglinski, P., Stroulia, E., and Matichuk, B., *Modeling the System-User Dialog Using Interaction Traces*, in Proceedings of IEEE 8th Working Conference on Reverse Engineering WCRE'2001 (Stuttgart, 2-5 October 2001), IEEE Computer Society Press, Los Alamitos, 2001, pp. 208-217.

[4] Frank, M.R. and Szekely, P., *Adaptive Forms: An interaction technique for entering structured data*, Knowledge-Based Systems Journal, Vol. 11, No. 1, 1998, pp. 37-45.

[5] Ghallab, M., Howe, A., Knoblock, G., McDermott, D., Ram, A., Veloso, M., Weld, D., and Wilkins, D., *The PDDL Planning Domain Definition Language*, The AIPS-98 Planning Competition Committee, CVC TR-98-003/DCS TR-1165, 1998.

[6] Kapoor, R., *Device Retargetable User Interface Re-engineering using XML*, Technical Report, TR-01-11, Computing Science Dept., University of Alberta, Alberta, 2001, accessible at http://web.cs.ualberta.ca/~kapoor/images/Thesis.pdf

[7] Kapoor, R. and Stroulia, E., *Mathaino: Simultaneous Legacy Interface Migration to Multiple Platforms,* in M.J. Smith, G. Salvendy, D. Harris, and R.J. Koubek (eds.), Usability Evaluation and Interface Design – Cognitive Engineering, Intelligent Agents and Virtual Reality, Proceedings of the 9th Int. Conf. on Human-Computer Interaction HCI International'2001 (New Orleans, 5-10 August 2001), Vol. 1, Lawrence Erlbaum Associates, Mahwah, 2001, pp. 51-55.

[8] Kong, L., Stroulia, E., and Matichuk, B., *Legacy Interface Migration: A Task-Centered Approach*, in Proceedings of the 8th Intern. Conf. on Human-Computer Interaction HCI International'99 (Munich, 22-27 August 1999), Lawrence Erlbaum Associates, Mahwah, 1999, pp. 1167-1171, accessible at http://www.cs.ualberta.ca/~stroulia/Papers/hci99.pdf

[9] Lehman, M.M., Perry, D.E., Ramil, J.F., Turski, W.M., and Wernick, P., *Metrics and laws of software evolution – the nineties view*, in Proceedings of the 4th International Symposium on Software Metrics METRICS'97 (Albuquerque, 5-7 November 2000), IEEE Press, Los Alamitos, 2000, pp. 20-32.

[10] Merlo, E., Gagne, P. Y., Girard, J.F., Kontogiannis, K., Hendren, L., Panangaden, P., DeMori, R., *Reengineering User Interfaces*, IEEE Software, Vol. 12, No. 1, 1995, pp. 64-73.

[11] Moore, M., *Representation Issues for Reengineering Interactive Systems*, ACM Computing Surveys, Vol. 28, No. 4es, Article No. 199, 1996.

[12] Puerta, A.R., *A Model-Based Interface Development Environment*, IEEE Software, Vol. 14, No. 4, 1997, pp. 41-47.

[13] Stroulia, E., El-Ramly, M., Kong, L., Sorenson, P., and Matichuk, B., *Reverse Engineering Legacy Interfaces: An Interaction-Driven Approach*, in Proceedings of the 6th Working Conf. on Reverse Engineering WCRE'99 (Atlanta, 6-8 October 1999), IEEE Press, Los Alamitos, 1999, pp. 292-302.

[14] Vanderdonckt, J., *A Corpus of Selection Rules for Choosing Interaction Objects*, Technical Report TR 93/3, University of Namur, Namur, 1993.

[15] Vanderdonckt, J. and Puerta, A.R. (eds.), *Computer-Aided Design of User Interfaces* II, Proceedings of the 3rd Int. Conf. on Computer-Aided Design of User Interfaces CADUI'99 (Louvain-la-Neuve, 21-23 October 1999), Kluwer Academic Publishers, Dordrecht, 1999. Description accessible at http://www.kap.nl/prod/b/0-7923-6078-8

[16] XUL, accessible at http://www.mozilla.org/xpfe/xptoolkit/xulintro.html

Chapter 27

RECOVERING ALTERNATIVE PRESENTATION MODELS OF A WEB PAGE WITH VAQUITA

Laurent Bouillon, Jean Vanderdonckt, and Nathalie Souchon
Université catholique de Louvain, Institut d'Administration et de Gestion,
Belgian Laboratory of Computer-Human Interaction (BCHI)
Place des Doyens, 1 – B-1348 Louvain-la-Neuve (Belgium)
E-mail: {bouillon, vanderdonckt, souchon}@isys.ucl.ac.be
URL: http://www.isys.ucl.ac.be/bchi/members/{lbo, jva, nsa}
Tel.: +32-10-47 {8349, 8525, 8377} – Fax: +32-10-47 83 24

Abstract VAQUITA allows developers to reverse engineer a presentation model of a web page according to multiple reverse engineering options. The alternative models offered by these options not only widen the spectrum of possible presentation models but also encourage developers in exploring multiple reverse engineering strategies. The options provide filtering capabilities in a static analysis of HTML code that are targeted either at multiple widgets simultaneously or at single widgets at a time, for their attributes and other manipulations. This flexibility is particularly important when the presentation model is itself used to migrate the presentation of the web page to other types of user interfaces, possibly written in different languages, in different computing platforms.

Keywords: Design recovery, Forward engineering, Heuristics, Interface migration, Model-based approach, Presentation model, Reverse engineering, Static analysis, Web page, XIML, XML.

1. INTRODUCTION

The technological push of newly marketed access devices—such as Personal Digital Assistants (PDAs) and Wireless Access Protocol (WAP)-enabled cellular phones—has exacerbated the need to access the same web site, from different access devices. With the demand for Internet access increasing for e-mail, electronic commerce, current events, and quick information, the need for Internet-capable access devices has extended beyond

C. Kolski and J. Vanderdonckt (eds.), Computer-Aided Design of User Interfaces III, 311–322.
© 2002 *Kluwer Academic Publishers.*

the professional desktop to the home office, the other rooms of the house, and beyond. To address these demands. ad hoc development is no longer believed acceptable in terms of the cost and time required for software engineering, development and maintenance. *Model-based approaches* [13,15,22, 25] can produce a user interface (UI) for a web site in a forward or reverse engineering manner by exploiting knowledge [16] captured in various models, such as task [8], domain [5], presentation [15] and dialog [10] models. However, most existing web sites have been developed without any model-based approaches. The goal of this paper is to address this problem by examining how a presentation model of a web page can be reverse engineered to migrate it to another environment. The remainder of this paper is structured as follows: section 2 provides a state of the art of techniques used to access an HTML page from other devices than a browser; section 3 poses the working hypotheses and specifies the goals and aims assigned to this work; section 4 defines concepts and techniques used in the VAQUITA software; section 5 discusses implementation issues and section 6 concludes the paper by reporting on progress made with VAQUITA and some identified shortcomings.

2. RELATED WORK

Many research and development have already been conducted to address the problem of making a web site accessible in multiple contexts of use. By *context of use*, we hereby refer to as a set of environment parameters (native language, computing platform, operating system, etc.) describing a given context in which a particular user (or a stereotype of user population) is carrying out a particular interactive task.

When a web site only needs to be accessed in a single context of use, a single conceptual UI model, leading to a single UI, is satisfying. When supporting multiple contexts of use is requested in the software requirements, two basic approaches can be followed:

1. *Single UI model-based approach*: although multiple contexts are to be supported, the developer still remains with one comprehensive UI model which may or may not include variation in its modeling. For instance, a HTML code may incorporate a Java script detecting the computing platform, the browser name, and the screen resolution to tailor the presentation depending on these parameters (e.g., for compatibility with different browsers). Without variation included, three sub-cases are found:

- By *generation*: when the starting model initiates many UIs for different contexts of use. For instance, UIML [1] captures presentation and dialog specification in a XML-based vocabulary which can be in turn used to generate Java code for Windows platforms, VoiceXML for telephones, WML for WAP-compliant cellular phones, and PalmOS for PalmPilots with appropriate renderers.

- By *conversion*: when the starting model initiates a UI to be converted at design-time or run-time to make it compatible with another context of use. For example, [7] describes a web proxy server that converting HTML into WML by using transformation heuristics of HTML tags and elements into WML objects. These heuristics are hard-coded, but the conversion is transparent for the end-user.
- By *adaptation*: when the starting model initiates a single UI that is adapted to a specified context of use. For example, [9] restructure HTML, XHTML and XML pages/documents into PalmPilot screens by classification of original elements and adaptation according to a device and a user model.

2. *Multiple UI model-based approach*: the developer captures into different models the peculiarities of the different contexts of use to consider. The different models may or may not share parts that are common to different contexts of use. For example, Atomica (www.atomica.com) developed three separate models to support its service on Windows Personal Computer, Pocket Computer, and HTML browser. In contrast, a context-sensitive task model [25] identifies sub-tasks that are common to all different contexts of use and isolates the rest for other contexts which are selected according to a decision tree. This gives rise to multiple UIs that are tailored at design-time.

3. HYPOTHESES, AIMS AND GOALS

Transformation techniques outlined in section 2 can be classified according to three orthogonal dimensions:

1. *Consistency* vs *variability*: some techniques are aimed at reproducing the same UI for the different contexts of use, whatever their constraints are. In contrast, variability attempts to meet the contexts' constraints, while preserving some consistency, sometimes with no consistency at all.
2. *Design-time* vs *run-time*: transformation from one context to another can be expressed and operated at design-time (before executing the interactive application as in [6]) or at run-time (when executing the interactive application). The first may be interpreted a smarter approach if local constraints are addressed at a higher-level than simply the syntactic code level of the run-time.
3. *Partial* vs *total*: transformation can be targeted to support only some sub-

tasks in the new context (e.g., due to local constraints and limited interaction capabilities, it is impossible to maintain the same level of usability [23]) or all sub-tasks.

Our work is situated in circumstances where an organization already developed a web site, but did not consider multiple contexts of use when designing the web site. Yet, this organization does not want to start again from scratch the next version for another context of use and does not want to lose the development momentum gained in the first design. Therefore, our goal in this paper is not to reverse engineer a whole web site to migrate it to another context of use or to make it accessible for a non-compatible computing platform. Indeed, interactive applications and web sites only share limited common characteristics. Rather, our goal is to migrate highly-interactive parts (e.g., input forms) of a web page to other context by combining a reverse engineering approach first and a forward engineering approach after (Fig. 4).

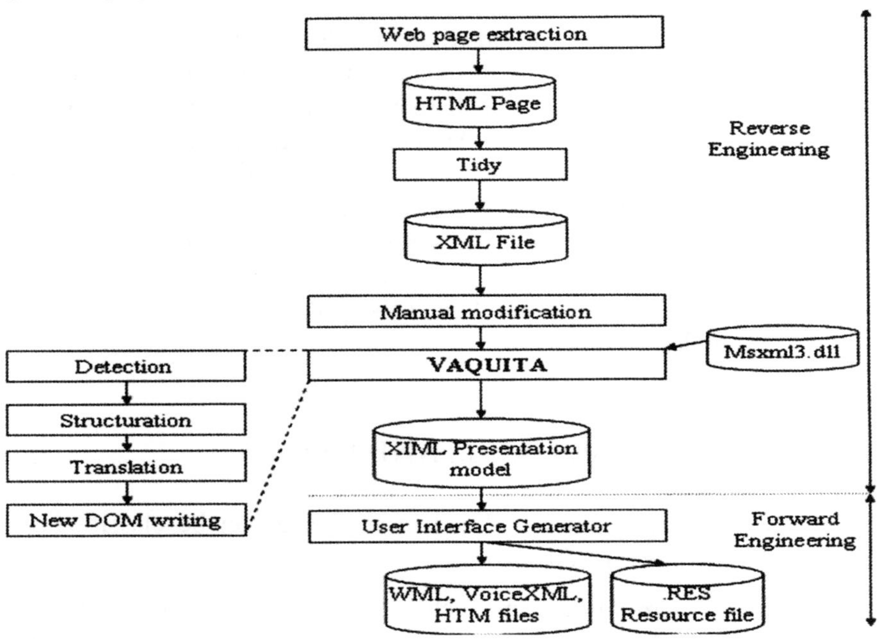

Figure 1. The complete process envisioned with VAQUITA.

VAQUITA (reVerse engineering of Applications by Questions, Information Selection, and Transformation Alternatives – See http://www.isys.ucl.ac.be/bchi/research/vaquita.htm) is a software covering the user interface reverse engineering by recovering a presentation model from a single HTML page at a time based on mapping rules (between HTML elements and presentation elements). This process should support transformation with:

- *Variability* to explicitly address local constraints, while maximizing consistency.

- At *design-time* because the process should obtain a model that is high-level enough to warrant any future potential redesigning for migration, even the unforeseen. For this purpose, the presentation model should be stored in an easily manipulable format where applying redesigning options remains as flexible as possible.
- As *total* as possible to factoring out parts of the UI which may be shared across several contexts of use.

The major requirement of VAQUITA is that it should support the reverse engineering in such an intelligent way that is flexible and developer-controllable enough to maximize the predictability of the reverse engineered model and to encourage the exploration of multiple reverse engineering options. After reviewing the state of the art, we observed that allowing only one single transformation technique, even the more elaborate, does not address this requirement. Multiple techniques should be available to the developer to render both the reverse and the forward engineering more flexible. This is not possible with built-in capabilities offered by generation, conversion, or adaptation.

The presentation model is then used in a model editor where the developer can drag and drop elements of the previous presentation and tailor it to another context. Some software already support the second part of Fig. 1. For instance, SEGUIA automatically generates a Windows UI from a presentation model by allowing the developer to explore several layouts [25]. In this second part, many redesign options may occur to tailor the presentation to a specific context, such as widget resizing, reallocation of widgets throughout windows [6], change of widget [14], graceful usability degradation [23], and layout rearrangement [25].

4. REVERSE ENGINEERING PROCESS IN VAQUITA

Any web page written in HTML 4.0 is submitted to a static analysis. This technique consists in scanning the HTML code to understand it without executing it [4,17]. This scanning activity results in identifying types of HTML tags, elements, and possible attached values.

4.1 The Target: a Presentation Model

A *presentation model* [19,20,22] is a representation of the visual, haptic, and auditory elements provided by a UI to its users. For example, a presentation element may be a window that contains additional elements such as widgets that appear in that window. This model also includes static presentation attributes, such as font styles and orientation of button groups. Presentation of web pages is progressively abstracted using four concepts, the hierarchy of which is depicted in Fig. 2:

1. *Concrete Interaction Object* (CIO): this is a real object belonging to the UI world that any user can see (e.g., text, image, animation) or manipulate such as a check box. A CIO is said to be *simple* if it cannot be decomposed into smaller CIOs. In the other case, it is said to be *composite.* Two categories are distinguished: *presentation CIO,* which is any static CIO allowing no user interaction, and *control CIO,* which support some interaction or UI control by the user.
2. *Abstract Interaction Object* (AIO): this consists of an abstraction of all CIOs from both presentation and behavioral viewpoints that is independent of any given computing platform. AIOs have been used successfully for both forward [24] and reverse engineering [10,14,15]. By definition, an AIO does not have any graphical appearance, but each AIO is connected to 0, 1 or many CIOs having different names and presentations in various computing platforms.
3. *Logical Window* (LW): this root window can be considered either as a logical container for AIOs or as a physical window, a dialog box or a panel. Every window is itself a composite AIO as it is composed of other simple or composite AIOs. All LWs are supposed to be physically constrained by the user's screen.
4. *Presentation Unit* (PU): a PU is assumed to be the complete presentation environment required for carrying out a particular interactive task. Each PU can be decomposed into one or many LWs, which may or may not be all displayed on the screen simultaneously. Each PU is composed of at least one window called the *basic window,* from which it is possible to navigate to the other windows.

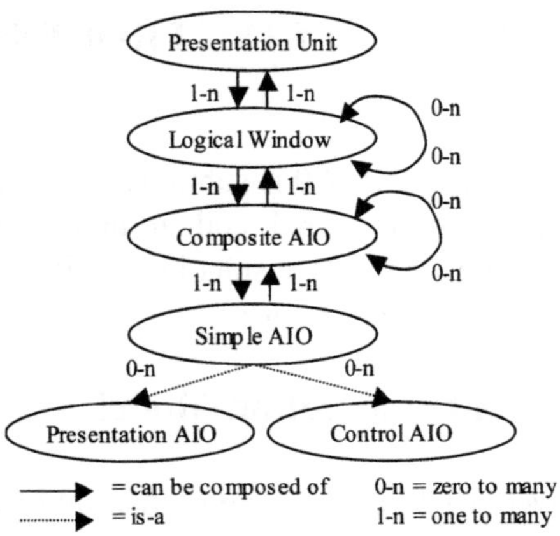

Figure 2. Hierarchy of presentation concepts.

The concepts of AIO, whether simple of composite, LW, and PU all belong to the presentation model as presentation element. Therefore, any presentation model is organized as a hierarchy of presentation elements, any of them potentially being itself decomposed into other presentation elements iteratively. GUIs traditionally incorporate widgets such as controls, windows, dialog boxes, and panels. On the one hand, some of these widgets are also found in web pages, basically the web pages holding some interaction with the end user and, on the other hand, web pages also add new types of presentation elements that are not necessarily found in traditional UIs (e.g., as in [14]). Therefore, AIOs which were pretty classic for these traditional UIs may need to be revisited for web pages in two ways: new AIO definition (links, lists, etc.) and existing AIO enhancing (expanding the definition of an attribute with new values, adding new attributes, events, etc.)

4.2 The Means: Reverse Engineering Options

The transformation of statically analyzed HTML tags, elements, and associated values into instances of presentation elements is established through mapping tables. As shown in the related work section, many systems are using more or less similar pattern matching techniques. In VAQUITA, the difference relies in its flexible usage of these mapping tables through reverse engineering options, which are classified in the following categories:

- *Single-object options* are dedicated to one and only one presentation element at a time. For example, it can govern the reverse engineering of any occurrences of a given AIO type. These options are subdivided into two sub-categories:
  1. *Attributes options*: The developer can specify that any elements (and values of HTML tags) should be taken into account by checking a check box in the option box corresponding to the AIO type.
  2. *Alternative heuristic options*: as many techniques, rules, and heuristics can be used to drive the reverse engineering, the specification of which technique, rule or heuristic based on matching tables is left to the appreciation of the developer. The developer can specify any default alternative heuristic through the alternative option box. Here are some examples:
     - *Text folding*: A folding option may be specified to tell VAQUITA to consider any series of subsequent lines as one presentation element (a label). Conversely, the unfolding option specifies that any such series should be reverse engineered into several instances of a label AIO with a relationship between to keep their sequence.

  - *Table mapping*: This option allows the developer to drive any reverse engineering of a table by generating a presentation element for each line or each column, possible with a header. Each line or column is then recursively decomposed into a series of presentation elements representing the table cells. Again, each cell can be reverse engineered into many different AIO types, depending on its contents. If each cell is occupied by a widget, then the corresponding AIO may be selected. If not, the cell AIO might be preferred.
  - *Cell span*: An option may be specified to have a cell covering several columns in a line or to keep the line as a sequence of presentation elements if the layout is not considered important.
- *Multiple-objects options* are defined with a scope of several presentations elements simultaneously, possibly widespread in the HTML page or possible of different AIO types. A representative example is the FORM tag in HTML which can hold several other types of presentation elements. HTML forms can be reverse engineered to different instances of different AIO types. When transforming HTML to WML for instance, a multiple-object option may specify which AIO type to use to perform the reverse engineering: a simple table, an indexed sub-tree or a list [7].

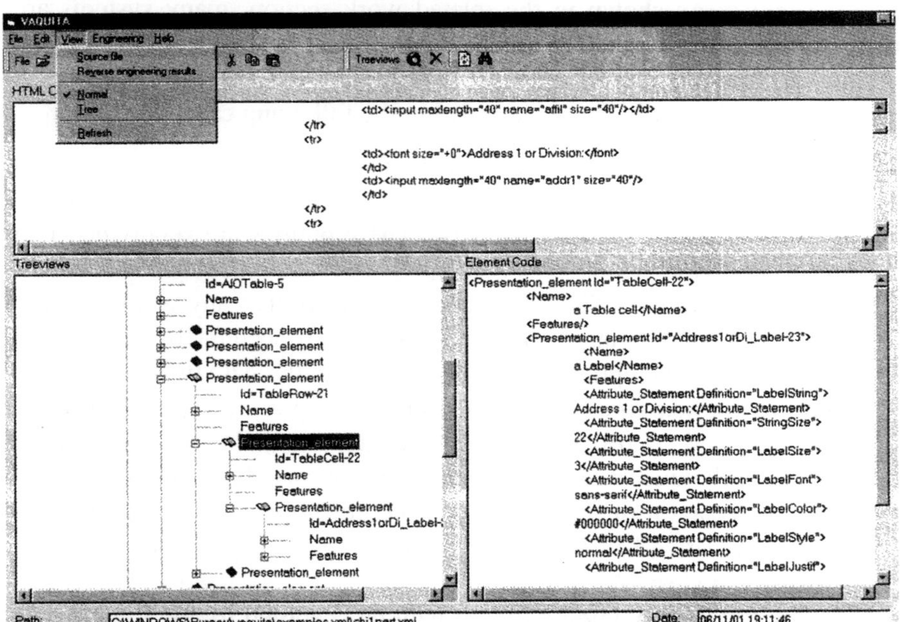

Figure 3. Three views of a VAQUITA interactive session.

The presentation model is then stored in XIML [21], a XML-based vocabulary for specifying models involved in any model-based approach for designing UI. XIML is the XML-compliant version of MIMIC, a meta-language for UI modeling [18]. XIML holds two types of relationships in the presentation model: a hierarchical relationship between nested presentation elements to reflect the hierarchical decomposition of the whole presentation into presentation elements, and spatial presentation relationships between the elements themselves (e.g., alignment). Fig. 3 illustrates a typical interactive session with VAQUITA. Three views are displayed: a tree view in which the developer can see the hierarchical decomposition of presentation elements, a source code –view where the HTML code is displayed, and a XIML view where the specifications of the presentation model are displayed. Clicking on any presentation element in the tree view automatically highlights the corresponding sections in both the HTML code and the XIML reversed presentation model.

5. IMPLEMENTATION ISSUES

To support the reverse engineering process outlined in section 4, several implementation alternatives were carefully considered: the Tidy tool, The Document Object Model (DOM), The World-Wide-Web Factory (W4F), and the HTML to XHTML conversion. All of these solutions were not considered flexible enough to meet the requirements defined in the beginning. Thus, a custom application was preferred.

Due to the above reasons, the most important being the lack of flexibility in selecting matching tables (or rules) of these tools, it was decided to implement Vaquita in a separate development environment: Microsoft Visual Basic. However, this implementation greatly benefits from the MSXML. DLL dynamic link library (http://msdn.microsoft.com/xml/artciles/msxml cabfile.asp). This library provides us with a large set of built-in functions to manipulate any XML-compliant document. Therefore, functions such as detection of a tag, of an element, retrieving of an associated value, etc. significantly reduced the development effort.

6. CONCLUSION

This work only covers the presentation model, not the navigation within a web page or within a same web site. This navigation, which is specific to web, could however be also reverse engineered to come up with a dialogue model [8,18,20] in which links can be exploited. This is a future work. The current state of the work allowed us to identify some benefits and shortcomings:

- The reverse engineering process presented here can be used as a loop for redesigning a web page: an existing web page can be abstracted in its presentation model, which can be edited and used for HTML generation. This loop may improve the usability of a web page namely by considering other models, such as dialogue, user, and platform models.
- Static analysis is easy to manipulate, cheap to use, and quick to conduct, provided that the reverse engineering options are well-founded, well structured, and organized enough to structure the process properly.
- The technique presented here does not support non-HTML code such as JavaScript, Perl, CGI scripts, and embedded objects developed in a foreign environment (e.g., Flash).
- The reverse analysis is limited to a static analysis. A dynamic analysis may improve the redesign of a web page for another context of use. By enlarging the understanding of how end user interact with an interactive web page, it is likely that a redesign may be improved based on this experience.
- The static analysis is also limited in internationalization cases: web pages developed in foreign countries, in other languages and cultures, may be not interpreted correctly. Beyond the technical problem of accessing international character sets (e.g., Japanese, Korean, and Greek), potentially different options may be needed.

REFERENCES

[1] Abrams, M., Phanouriou, C., Batongbacal, A. and Shuster, J., *UIML: An Appliance-Independent XML User Interface Language*, in Proc. of 8th World Wide Web Conference WWW'8 (Toronto, 11-14 May 1999), Computer Networks, Vol. 31, No. 11-16, pp. 1695-1708, accessible at http://www.harmonia.com/resources/papers/www8_0599/index.htm or at http://www8.org/w8-papers/5b-hypertext-media/uiml/uiml.html

[2] Bickmore, T.W. and Schilit, B.N., *Digestor: Device-Independent Access to the World-Wide-Web*, in Proc. of 6th World-Wide-Web Conf. WWW'6 (Santa Clara, 7-11 April 1997), Elsevier, Amsterdam, 1997, accessible at http://www.sco pe.gmd.de/info/www6/technical/paper177/paper177.html

[3] Buyukkokten, O., Garcia-Molina, H., and Paepcke, A., *Accordion Summarization for End-Game Browsing on PDAs and Cellular Phones*, in Proc. of ACM Conf. on Human Aspects in Computing Systems CHI'2001 (Seattle, 30 March-5 April 2001), ACM Press, New York, 2001, pp. 213-220.

[4] Chikofsky, E.J. and Cross, J.H., *Reverse Engineering and Design Recovery: A Taxonomy*, IEEE Software, Vol. 1, No. 7, January 1990, pp. 13-17.

[5] De Baud, J.-M. and Rugaber, S., *A Software Re-engineering Method Using Domain Models*, Proc. of Int. Conf. on Software Maintenance (October 1995), pp. 204-213.

[6] Eisenstein, J., Vanderdonckt, J., and Puerta, A.R., *Adapting to Mobile Contexts with User-Interface Modeling*, Proc. of 3rd IEEE Workshop on Mobile Computing Systems and Applications WMCSA'2000 (Monterey, December 7-8, 2000), IEEE Press, Los Alamitos, 2000, pp. 83-92.

[7] Kaasinen, E., Aaltonen, M., Kolari, J., Melakoski, S., Laakko, T., *Two Approaches to*

Bringing Internet Services to WAP Devices, in Proc. of 9th World-Wide-Web Conf. WWW'9 (Amsterdam, 15-19 May 2000), pp. 231-246, accessible at http://www9.org/w9cdrom/228/228.html

[8] Kong, L, Stroulia, E, and Matichuk, B., *Legacy Interface Migration: A Task-Centered Approach*, in H.-J. Bullinger and J. Ziegler (eds.), Proc. of 8th Int. Conf. on Human-Computer Interaction HCI International'99 (Munich, 22-27 August 1999), Lawrence Erlbaum Associates, Mahwah/London, 1999, pp. 1167-1171, accessible at http://www.cs.ualberta.ca/~stroulia/Papers/hci99.ps

[9] Lopez, J. and Szekely, P., *Automatic Web Page Adaptation*, Proc. of CHI'2001 Workshop on Transforming the UI for Anyone, Anywhere (Seattle, 1-2 April 2001).

[10] Merlo, E., Girard, J.F., Kontogiannis, K., Panangaden, P. and De Mori, R., *Reverse Engineering of User Interfaces*, in R.C. Waters, E.J. Chikofsky (eds.), Proc. of 1st Working Conference on Reverse Engineering WCRE'93 (Baltimore, 21-23 May 1993), IEEE Computer Society Press, Los Alamitos, 1993, pp. 171-179.

[11] Merlo, E., Gagné, P.-Y., and Thiboutôt, A., *Inference of graphical AUIDL specifications for the reverse engineering of user interfaces*, in Proc. of Int. Conf. on Software Maintenance (19-23 September 1994), IEEE Computer Society Press, Los Alamitos, 1994, pp. 80-88.

[12] Merlo, E., Gagné, P.-Y., Girard, J.-F., Kontogiannis, K., Hendren, L., Panagaden, P. and De Mori, R., *Reengineering User Interfaces*, IEEE Software, Vol. 12, No. 1, January 1995, pp. 64-73.

[13] Moore, M.M. and Rugaber, S., *Issues in User Interface Migration*, Proc. of 3rd Int. Software Engineering Research Forum (Orlando, 10 November 1993).

[14] Moore, M.M., *Rule-Based Detection for Reverse Engineering User Interfaces*, in L. Wills, I. Baxter, E. Chikofsky (eds.), Proc. of 3rd Working Conf. on Reverse Engineering WCRE'96 (Monterey, 8-10 November 1996), IEEE Computer Society Press, Los Alamitos, 1996, pp. 42-48, accessible at http://www.cc.gatech.edu/fac/Melody.Moore/papers/WCRE96.ps

[15] Moore, M.M., *Representation Issues for Reengineering Interactive Systems*, ACM Computing Surveys, Vol. 28, No. 4, December 1996, article # 199, accessible at http://www.acm.org/pubs/articles/journals/surveys/1996-28-4es/ a199-moore/a199-moore.html

[16] Moore, M.M. and Rugaber, S., *Using Knowledge Representation to Understand Interactive Systems*, in Proc. of the Fifth International Workshop on Program Comprehension IWPC'97 (Dearborn, 28-30 May 1997), IEEE Computer Society Press, Los Alamitos, 1997, accessible at http:// www.cc.gatech.edu/fac/Melody.Moore/papers/WPC97.ps

[17] Moore, M.M. and Rugaber, S., *Domain Analysis for Transformational Reuse*, in Proc. of 4th Working Conf. on Reverse Engineering WCRE'97 (6-8 October 1997), IEEE Computer Society Press, Los Alamitos, 1997.

[18] Puerta, A.R. , *The MECANO Project: Comprehensive and Integrated Support for Model-Based Interface Development*, in J. Vanderdonckt (ed.), Proc. of 2nd Int. Workshop on Computer-Aided Design of User Interfaces CADUI'96 (Namur, 5-7 June 1996), Presses Universitaires de Namur, Namur, 1996, pp. 19-35.

[19] Paternò, F., *Model-based Design and Evaluation of Interactive Applications*, Springer Verlag, Berlin, 1999.

[20] Puerta, A.R. and Eisenstein, J., *Towards a General Computational Framework for Model-Based Interface Development Systems*, in Proc. of ACM Conf. on Int. User Interfaces IUI'99, ACM Press, New York, 1999, pp. 171-178.

[21] Puerta, A.R. and Eisenstein, J., *Representational Basis for User Interface Transformations*, in Proc. of ACM CHI'2001 Workshop on Transforming the UI for Anyone. Anywhere (Seattle, 1-2 April 2001).

[22] Szekely, P., *Retrospective and Challenges for Model-Based Interface Development*, in J. Vanderdonckt (ed.), Proc. of 2rd Int. Workshop on Computer-Aided Design of User In-

terfaces CADUI'96 (Namur, 5-7 June 1996), Presses Universitaires de Namur, Namur, 1996, pp. xxi-xliv.
[23] Thevenin, D. and Coutaz, J., *Plasticity of User Interfaces: Framework and Research Agenda*, Proc. of IFIP Conf. on Human-Computer Interaction Interact'99 (Edimburgh, September 1999), IOS Press, 1999, pp. 110-117.
[24] Vanderdonckt, J. and Bodart, F., *Encapsulating Knowledge for Intelligent Interaction Objects Selection*, Proc. of InterCHI'93, ACM Press, New York, 1993, pp. 424-429.
[25] Vanderdonckt, J. and Berquin, P., *Towards a Very Large Model-based Approach for User Interface Development*, Proc. of 1st Int. Workshop on User Interfaces to Data Intensive Systems UIDIS'99, IEEE Computer Society Press, Los Alamitos, 1999, pp. 76-85.

Chapter 28

EVIDENCE-BASED USABILITY ENGINEERING

Eduard Metzker[1], Harald Reiterer[2]
[1]DaimlerChrysler Research and Technology Centre, Software Technology Lab, HCI Research Group, P.O.Box 2360, D-89011 Ulm (Germany)
E-mail: eduard.metzker@daimlerchrysler.com
[2]University of Konstanz, Department of Computer and Information Science, P.O.Box D 73, D-78457 Konstanz (Germany)
E-mail: harald.reiterer@uni-konstanz.de
Tel: +49-7531-88-3704 – Fax: +49-7531-88-2048

Abstract In this paper we propose an approach for the systematic integration of human-centered design (HCD) methods throughout the whole software development process called evidence-based usability engineering. We derive our approach from six claims that emphasize shortcomings and urgent requirements of current HCD practice. Instead of clinging to a fixed process model of the usability engineering process our approach advocates a paradigm of situated decision making. It enables software development teams to select optimal sets of HCD methods that match the engineering task at hand based on the cumulated experience of the software development organization. Qualitative and quantitative feedback on the efficiency of HCD methods is collected and integrated across project boundaries. Our approach is connected to existing process improvement frameworks such as UMM (Usability Maturity Model) via a meta-model. We present a first prototype of a novel kind of computer-aided usability engineering environment called ProUSE, that supports our evidence-based usability engineering approach.

Keywords: Computer-aided usability engineering environment, Human-centred design methods, Process improvement, Usability maturity.

1. INTRODUCTION

The relevance of usability as a quality factor is continually increasing for software engineering organizations: usability and user acceptance are about to become the ultimate measurement for the quality of today's telematics applications, e-commerce web sites, mobile services and tomorrow's proactive

C. Kolski and J. Vanderdonckt (eds.), Computer-Aided Design of User Interfaces III, 323–336.
© 2002 *Kluwer Academic Publishers.*

assistance technology. Taking these circumstances into account human-centered design (HCD) methods for developing interactive systems are changing from a last minute add-on to a crucial part of the software engineering lifecycle.

It is well accepted both among software practitioners and in the human-computer interaction research community that structured approaches are required to build interactive systems with high usability. On the other hand specific knowledge about exactly how to most efficiently and smoothly integrate HCD methods into established software development processes is still missing [6]. While approaches such as the usability maturity model (UMM) [4] or the DATech-Model [3] provide means to assess an organization's capability to perform HCD processes they lack guidance on how to actually implement process improvement in HCD. It often remains unclear to users of HCD methods if and why certain tools and methods are better suited in a certain development context than others [11]. We need strategies and tools that support engineering organizations in evaluating and selecting an optimal HCD method for a given development context and perform systematic process improvement in HCD. Little research has been done on integrating methods and tools of HCD in the development process and gathering knowledge about HCD activities in a form that can capture relationships between specific development contexts, applicable methods and tools and their impact on the engineering process [5].

In this paper we propose six claims that point out shortcomings and requirements of current HCD practice. First we take a look at existing HCD process models, trying to identify the organizational obstacles that hamper the establishment of these models in mainstream software development processes. Next we present results of a survey which examined how exactly HCD methods are applied in real projects and derive implications for tools to support process improvement in HCD. Finally we present a first prototype of an evidence-based computer-aided usability engineering environment (CAUSE) that we propose to address the shortcomings and requirements we have come across.

2. EXISTING HCD PROCESS MODELS: THEORY AND PRACTICE

A review on existing literature and case studies of some of the HCD approaches most applied revealed a number of organizational obstacles encountered in establishing HCD methods in mainstream software development processes [7]. We summarized these problems in claims 1-3.

Claim 1 – *Existing HCD process models are decoupled from the overall software development process.*
Claim 2 – *Most of the HCD approaches do not cover a strategy how to perform HCD methods and process models depending on the usability maturity of the software development organization.*
Claim 3 – *Integrating UE Methods into mainstream software development process must be understood as an organizational learning task.*

To learn more about the way that HCD methods are actually used in software development organizations we conducted a study with software developers who are working on design of interactive systems in a variety of domains [8]. The study revealed that the organizations examined are practicing highly diverse individual development processes, however none of the UE development models proposed by [1,2,6,10] are exactly used. Furthermore, the persons who are entrusted with the ergonomic analysis and evaluation of interactive systems are primarily the developers of the products. External usability or human factors experts or a separate in-house usability department are seldom available. Furthermore, few of the participants were familiar with methods like *user profile analysis* or *cognitive walkthroughs* which are regarded as fundamental from a usability engineer's point of view.

The UE methods that are considered to be reasonable to apply by the developers are often not used for the following interrelated reasons:

- There is no time allocated for UE activities: they are neither integrated in the development process nor in the project schedule.
- Knowledge needed for the performance of UE tasks is not available within the development team.
- The effort for the application of the UE tasks is estimated to be too high because they are regarded as time consuming.

From the analysis of the interviews we derived high level requirements for a software tool to support the improvement of UE processes. These high level requirements are summarized in claims 4-6.

Claim 4 – *Support flexible UE process models.*
Claim 5 – *Support evolutionary development and reuse of UE experience.*
Claim 6 – *Provide means to trace the application context of UE knowledge.*

3. THE EVIDENCE-BASED USABILITY ENGINEERING APPROACH

To address the shortcomings and to meet the requirements described in our claims we advocate an evidence-based approach to the improvement of HCD processes. We define evidence-based usability engineering as follows:

- **Evidence** – Something, such as a fact, sign, or object that gives proof or reasons to believe or agree with something.
- **Usability engineering** – (1) The application of systematic, disciplined, quantifiable methods to the development of interactive software systems to achieve a high quality in use; (2) The study of approaches as in (1).
- **Evidence-based usability engineering** – An approach for establishing HCD methods in mainstream software development processes, that uses: (1) qualitative and quantitative feedback on the efficiency of HCD methods collected in projects and integrates this data across project boundaries for controlling and improving the quality and productivity of HCD activities.
  (2) concepts of organizational learning for integrating HCD knowledge, gathered as in (1), into software development processes.

The essence of the evidence-based approach is that we do not cling to a fixed process model of the usability engineering process, but instead follow a paradigm of situated decision making. In this approach HCD methods are selected for a given engineering task, e.g. *contextual task analysis*, based on the available evidence that they will match to the development context at hand.

After performing a method it should be evaluated if the method was useful for the development context or if it must be modified or discarded. The modification of the method should be recorded and stored for later reuse. Once a certain body of HCD knowledge is accumulated in that way, we have sound evidence for selecting an optimal set of HCD best practices for given development contexts. By continuously applying this procedure of conducting, evaluating and adapting HCD methods in a number of projects, an organization gradually adapts a set of HCD base practices to a wide variety of development contexts. This directly contributes to the general idea of software maturity models such as UMM [4]. According to these models organizations are highly ranked on a maturity scale, if they are capable to tailor a set of base practices according to a set of constraints such as available resources or project characteristics to solve a defined engineering problem. So far we argue that the evidence-based approach requires four ingredients:

- A process meta-model, which guides the selection of HCD methods for a given development context and their integration in an overall software development process in a flexible, decision-oriented manner. The model must as well provide a strategy for evaluating, refining and capturing experiences for new development contexts thus promoting continuous process improvement and organizational learning in HCD.

- A semi-formal notation for structuring knowledge relating to HCD activities allowing to save it in an experience base. The experience base allows to keep track of documented best practices and their application context even if the underlying context factors such as processes, technologies, domains and quality standards are still evolving, A model is needed to formally relate the best practices of the experience base to a development context.
- A CAUSE for managing the experience base and allowing to predict optimal sets of HCD methods based on the available evidence and the experience of the development organization.
- An organizational concept for deploying, maintaining and evolving the experience base.

3.1 The Evidence-Based Meta-Model

Our evidence-based model comprises a set of organizational tasks to support the introduction, establishment and continuous improvement of HCD methods throughout the whole software engineering lifecycle. It helps to manage and tailor the HCD base practices defined in usability maturity models such as UMM [4] and the related methods practiced by the development organization according to specific constraints of the respective project and the experiences collected by the organization. The meta-model is based on our findings of experience-based improvement of user interface development processes [7]. We refined the model to the extent that we now use a formal model to relate a defined development context to a set of best practices. So the selection of an optimal set of HCD methods is guided by a model of the development context and the evaluation results of the HCD methods in real projects within the organization. In more detail the model consists of the following four logical steps:

- **Step 1: Define, revise and extend the reference model** – In the first step the reference model for the organization's HCD approach must be defined. If no reference model exists in the organization, one of the existing frameworks such as the process descriptions of UMM [4] or the DATech Prüfbaustein [3] could be used as a starting point for a reference model. After performing one or more projects, the reference model, should be revised based on the experience collected in the projects.
- **Step 2: Select suitable HCD base practices and the related methods and integrate them into the software development process practiced–**

In this step base practices are selected from the reference model to be integrated in the overall software development process. However, further important factors have to be considered, e.g. the type of system to be developed and project constraints like budget and schedules. This information must be mapped into a context model and guides the selection of appropriate HCD methods for the selected base practices. The HCD methods which have been selected for the improvement of the development process have to be integrated in the model of the practiced software development lifecycle and the project plan and complement the overall engineering process used in the project.

- **Step 3: Support effective performance of the defined HCD methods** – Generally, at this step in the model resources have already been allocated for HCD activities, e.g., a usability engineer was nominated, who is responsible for coordinating and supporting the execution of the various HCD activities of the new process. However, the efficiency and impact of the proposed HCD methods must be increased by providing the development team with best practices, tools and reusable deliverables of past projects (e.g. templates for usability test questionnaires, results of conceptual task analysis or user interface mockups) which facilitate effective performance of the selected HCD methods. This set of information should be easily accessible for all participants of HCD activities.
- **Step 4: Collect and disseminate best practices and artifacts concerning HCD tasks** – The HCD methods applied in a project should be rated by the project team members. These ratings form the rationale for following projects to adopt or reject HCD methods. Methods poorly rated by project team members in a project have a low likelihood of being reused in later projects.

During the execution of HCD activities, artifacts with a high value for reuse are generated by the participants of HCD activities, for example, templates for usability tests, reusable code fragments, or an experience on how to most efficiently conduct a user profile analysis for assistance systems. Observations like these comprise HCD experience that have to be captured and organized in best practices along with the development context in which they apply to allow for easy reuse in the same or subsequent projects.

3.2 USEPACKs and the HCD Experience Base

To capture and evolve HCD knowledge for reuse and process improvement, we need a semi-formal notation for structuring process knowledge relating to HCD methods. For this purpose we have developed the concepts of USEPACKs (Usability Engineering Experience Package) and a context model (see section 4.3). While USEPACKs are used to capture HCD methods the context model is used to formally relate these methods to a development context.

A USEPACK encapsulates best practices on how to most effectively perform certain HCD activities and includes the related artifacts like documents, code fragments or templates that facilitate the compliance with the best practice described. A USEPACK is structured into four logical sections:

1. The *core information* permits authors to describe the main message of a USEPACK. It is organized according to the pyramid principle for structuring information [9]. The information first presented to the reader has a low level of complexity, allowing the reader to quickly decide if the USEPACK is worth further exploration. With further reading, the degree of complexity rises, introducing the reader to the experience described. The core information section includes the *fields title, keywords, abstract, description and comments*.
2. The *context situation* describes the development context related to the experience in question. The context situation is generated by using the context model, allowing the authors and readers of USEPACKs to utilize a shared vocabulary for contextualizing and accessing USEPACKs.
3. A set of *artifacts and links*. Artifacts such as checklists for user profile analysis or templates for usability test questionnaires, facilitate the efficient compliance with the best practice. They represent an added value to the readers of a USEPACK. Artifacts allow readers to regain time spent on exploring the package by using the supplied artifacts to simplify their work. Links are pointing to related resources that should be considered by the reader of a USEPACK.
4. The USEPACK *rating scheme* allows engineering teams to assess the quality of a USEPACK along a defined set of dimensions. The ratings collected will be evaluated and form the rationale for selecting optimal USEPACKs for future projects.

3.3 The Context Model

The context model serves as a template to construct the *context situation* for USEPACKs – a semi-formal description of the development context in which the experience described by a USEPACK can be applied. It is organized in a hierarchical structure, divided into sections which contain groups of *context factors*. On the one hand, authors of USEPACKs can use the context model to easily construct a description of the context in which the information of a USEPACK can be applied by selecting appropriate context factors from the model. On the other hand, readers of USEPACKs can use the context model for retrieval of USEPACKs by specifying a context situation which reflects the development context for which they need support. Currently a context model containing the following four sections is used:

- The *process context* section provides context factors to describe to which base practices of the UMM reference model a best practice is related.
- The *project context* section provides context factors to describe project constraints like the size of the development team, budget or project duration which are related to the experience cited.
- The *domain context* section provides context factors to describe elements of the domain related to the experience described. Top-level context factors of this section specify domains in terms like 'home entertainment systems' or 'car driver assistance systems', which can be subsequently refined to capture more detailed domain attributes.
- The *technology context* section provides context factors to describe features of technologies related to the experience such as 'gesture recognition' or 'speech input'.

3.4 A Computer-Aided Usability Engineering Environment

To increase the impact of the evidence-based usability engineering approach tool support is needed. In the BMBF (German Ministry of Education and Research) lead project EMBASSI (Electronic Multimedia Operating and Service Assistance) we currently develop a prototypical CAUSE called ProUSE (Process centred Usability Engineering Environment). ProUSE consists of an HCD experience base and three logical components for planning, selecting, applying, evolving and assessing HCD methods and reusable artifacts.

The experience base is seeded with an initial set of best practices in form of USEPACKs. In our case we have adopted a variety of usability engineering methods from Nielsen and Mayhew [6,10] but in general any HCD approach should be appropriate. The REUSE (Repository for Usability Engineering Experience) [8] component is used to capture, manage and evolve best practices related to HCD activities. It assists in documenting best practices using the USEPACK concept and relating them to a formal development context using a context model and storing them in the experience base.

SATUP (Setup Assistant for Usability Engineering Processes) is used to plan HCD activities for a software development project. Given all available context information on the process (e.g. which HCD base practices should be performed), project (e.g. duration, budget, team size), domain and technology context factors, SATUP will propose optimal HCD methods and reusable artifacts based on the accumulated experience of the development organization stored in the experience base. If there are alternative USEPACKs available for a defined context situation, SATUP will compare the available ratings for all USEPACKs using a fuzzy multi-criteria decision making approach and propose the optimal USEPACK.

Once an optimal HCD process was planned, CUES (Cooperative Usability Engineering Workspace) can be used by a distributed development team to access, perform and assess the HCD methods selected. The ProUSE prototype is based on Java technologies and integrated via a web portal concept which makes the modules available through intranet and web browser.

4. DEPLOYMENT OF PROUSE IN AN INDUSTRIAL SETTING

Before the ProUSE environment is deployed in a development organization for the first time, the systems experience base should be seeded as described in section 3.4. After this first step, the experience base contains a set of USEPACKs that describe methods for each base practice of the reference model used. These USEPACKs will usually have a poor context situation. Imagine now that a large software development organization is developing assistive, interactive home entertainment components and has recognized that usability aspects will play a major role in a new project. In that project an intelligent avatar for assisting users in programming their video recorders should be created. The organization decides that the overall development process should be supplemented with usability engineering activities. One usability engineer is available for the project but the rest of the development team is inexperienced in usability engineering.

When the project is planned, the usability engineer logs in to the ProUSE system and starts the SATUP component. The usability engineer uses SATUP to create a new project and roughly describes the projects usability aspects in textual form. After this first rough textual description, the usability engineer uses the context model to map the projects usability constraints to the context factors of the context model thereby creating a context situation for the project. After the usability engineer modelled the development context, the project is accessible to the development team.

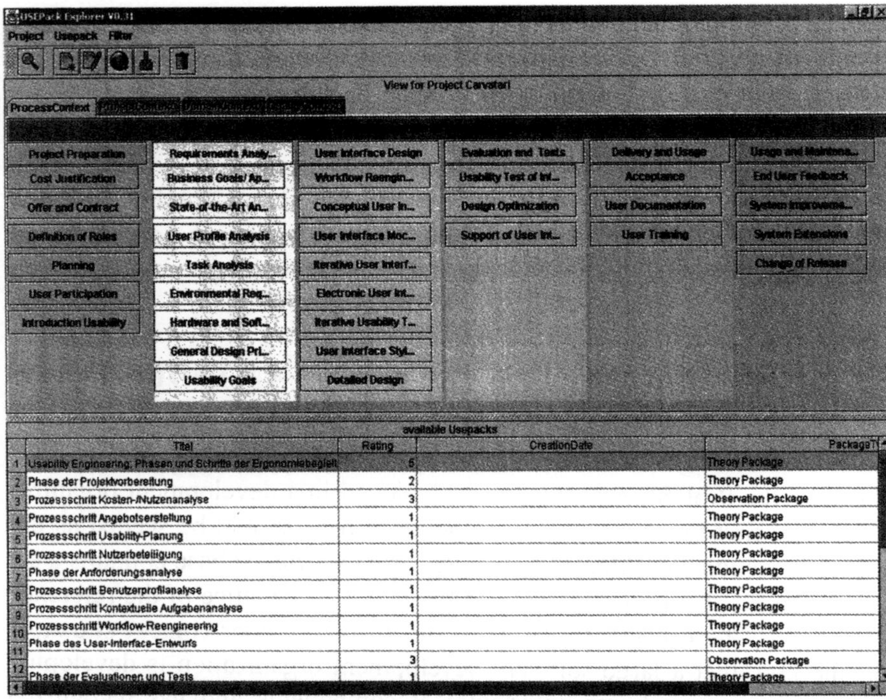

Figure 1. Browsing project related experiences with CUES.

Members of the development team can now access the new project via CUES. CUES creates a workspace where the USEPACKs relevant for the defined context situation can be accessed by the development team to support their usability engineering activities. CUES provides the development team with a tailored view on the experience base, shielding them from irrelevant information (Fig. 1).

If a certain method was not useful to the development team, the team members can assign a poor rating to the respective USEPACK. This will reduce the likelihood for the USEPACK to be selected in subsequent projects with the same context situation. On the other hand team members can assign high ratings to USEPACKs which had a positive impact on their work thus increasing the likelihood that the respective USEPACK will be reused in subsequent projects. By applying the best practices described in a USEPACK members of the development team will make valuable experiences. These experiences can be captured as extensions or comments of an existing USEPACK or can be captured in a new USEPACK.

Assume that the development team used the USEPACK "Contextual Task Analysis" to perform the contextual task activity. Though they found the general guideline useful, they soon discovered that the contextual task analysis for designing an intelligent avatar is fundamentally different from the general method they found in the USEPACK. To capture the modifications to the general method they create a new USEPACK 'Contextual Task Analysis for Intelligent Assistants' using REUSE. They enter their experiences in the USEPACK and attach documents and templates that can be reused when performing a contextual task analysis for an intelligent assistant. Fig. 2 shows how a USEPACK is created using REUSE.

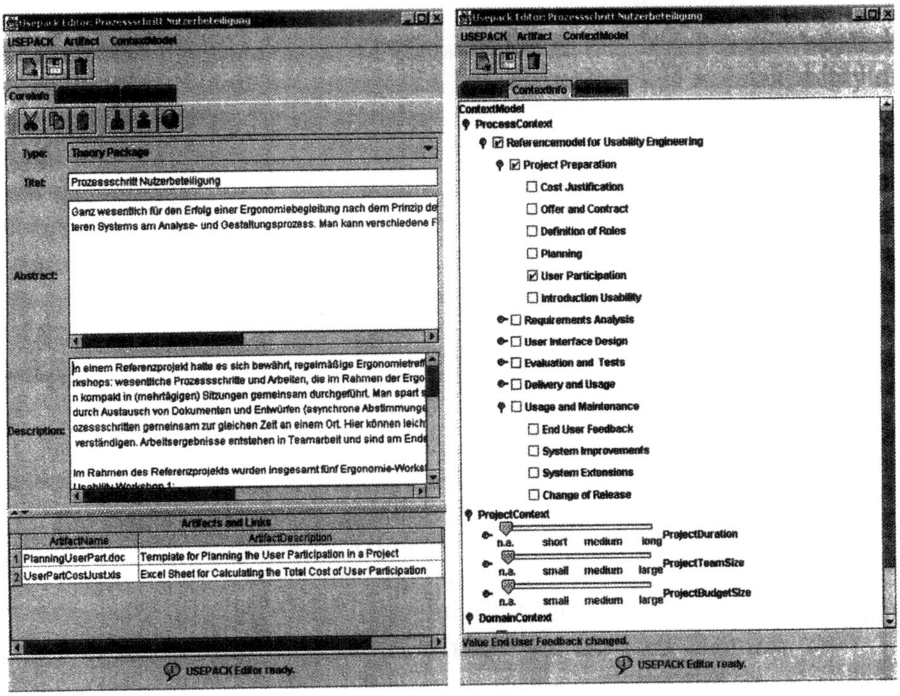

Figure 2. Capturing experiences with REUSE.

On the left side you see how the core information and reusable artefacts of a USEPACK are captured by using the USEPACK template. On the right side you see how the context situation for a USEPACK is captured by using the context model. The user can easily relate the experience described in a USEPACK to a context situation by selecting appropriate context factors from the context model.

The next time a project team has to design an intelligent assistant, it will have access to the improved contextual task analysis method and the reusable artifacts. These improvement activities will prevent subsequent development teams to encounter similar problems and will enable them to perform the task more efficiently.

How the tool support provided by ProUSE is related to our evidence-based usability engineering approach is depicted in Fig. 3. On the left side you see the steps of the evidence based meat-model as described in section 3.1. On the right side you see which component of ProUSE supports the respective step.

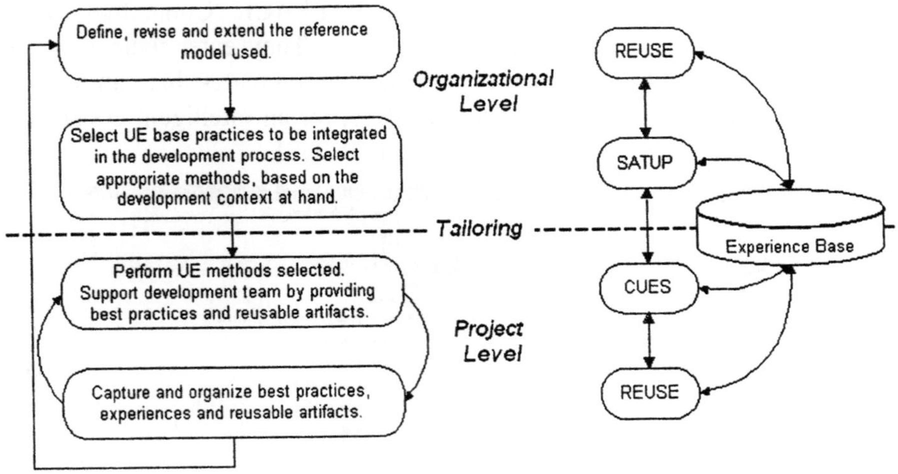

Figure 3. Tool Support for Evidence-Based Usability Engineering.

5. DISCUSSION

Evidence-based usability engineering provides a multidisciplinary approach for integrating usability engineering activities into software development processes. In fact the approach has its foundations in the intersection of three disciplines: usability engineering, software process improvement and organizational learning. This interdisciplinarity is directly caused by our practical goal: to support the introduction, establishment and continuous improvement of usability engineering activities in software engineering processes. We want to integrate usability engineering activities into software development processes to improve the engineering process for interactive software systems. As a tool to achieve process improvement we use concepts of organizational learning.

It has often been claimed that there is a gap between the need for structured approaches in HCD on the one side and creativity in the process on the other side. The evidence-based usability engineering approaches tries to balance these needs. It does not force development organizations to run a second usability engineering lifecycle in parallel to the actual development lifecycle nor does it force engineering organizations to discard their established processes and replace them by a completely usability centered approach. Following our approach usability engineering activities are not linked together in a fixed process model. Instead they are arranged in a construction-set-like reference model linked by a context model. The reference model and its base practices describe what should be done. The best practices together with their context situation describe how it should be done in a defined context situation. Engineering teams can select, evaluate, refine and extend base practices to meet their needs. By continuously evolving base practices to contextualized best practices (USEPACKs) engineering organizations compile a set of optimized methods which they can dynamically link into their development process.

Recently the idea of process maturity was introduced to the field of usability engineering [3,4]. The rationale behind usability maturity models is that there are direct dependencies between an organization's capability to tailor its HCD processes according to various constraints, the quality of the development process performed and the quality in use of the interactive software system. Our approach is geared to support software engineering organizations in reaching high usability maturity levels. At a low usability maturity development organizations can use the experience base as a repository for base practices which are found in the initial set of USEPACKs (seed of the experience base) and which enable the engineering teams to perform those base practices. By applying the base practices in various projects, the development organization is able to derive USEPACKs for each base practice which capture project constraints such as 'size of development team' or 'available budget'. Thus the organization develops a set of more contextualized methods for each base practice, which will enable the organization to control its usability engineering activities.

ACKNOWLEDGEMENTS

Special thanks go to Michael Plichta, Ingo Gruell, Gerhard Reuss and Christoph Ballhause from the DaimlerChrysler Research Center Ulm for the great job they did in implementing the ProUSE system.

REFERENCES

1. Beyer, H. and Holtzblatt, K., *Contextual Design: Defining Customer-Centered Systems*, Morgan Kaufmann Publishers, San Francisco, 1998.
2. Constantine, L.L. and Lockwood, L.A.D., *Software for Use: A Practical Guide to the Models and Methods of Usage-Centered Design*, Addison-Wesley, New York, 1999.
3. DATech Frankfurt/Main, *DATech Prüfbaustein: Qualität des Usability Engineering Prozesses*, Deutsche Akkreditierungsstelle Technik e.V., 2001
4. Earthy, J., *Human Centred Processes, their Maturity and their Improvement*, in Proc. of IFIP TC.13 International Conference on Human-Computer Interaction Interact'99, IOS Press, 1999, pp. 117-118, accessible at http://info.lboro.ac.uk/research/husat/eusc/guide/tr_ump_c.doc.
5. Henninger, S., *A Methodology and Tools for Applying Context-Specific Usability Guidelines to Interface Design*, Interacting with Computers, Vol. 12, No. 3, 2000, pp. 225-243.

6. Mayhew, D.J., *The Usability Engineering Lifecycle: A Practioner's Handbook for User Interface Design*, Morgan Kaufman Publishers, San Francisco, 1999.
7. Metzker, E. and Offergeld, M., *An Interdisciplinary Approach for Successfully Integrating Human-Centered Design Methods Into Development Processes Practiced by Industrial Software Development Organizations*, in Proc. of IFIP TC2/TC13 WG2.7/WG13.4 Eight Conference on Engineering for Human Computer Interaction EHCI'01 (Toronto, 2001), Springer-Verlag, Berlin, 2001, pp. 21-36.
8. Metzker, E. and Offergeld, M., *REUSE: Computer-Aided Improvement of Human-Centered Design Processes*, in Mensch und Computer, 1. Fachübergreifende Konferenz des German Chapter of the ACM MC'2001 (Bad Honnef, 2001), Teubner Verlag, 2001, pp. 375-384.
9. Minto, B., *The Pyramid Principle - Logic in Writing and Thinking*, 3rd ed., Minto International Inc., London, 1987.
10. Nielsen, J., *Usability Engineering*, Morgan Kaufman Publishers, San Francisco, 1994.
11. Van Welie, M., *Breaking Down Usability*, in Proc. IFIP TC.13 International Conference on Human-Computer Interaction Interact'99 (Edinburgh, August 1999), IOS Press, 1999, pp. 613-620.

Chapter 29

A FRAMEWORK AND A LANGUAGE FOR USABILITY AUTOMATIC EVALUATION OF WEB SITES BY STATIC ANALYSIS OF HTML SOURCE CODE

Abdo Beirekdar[1,2], Jean Vanderdonckt[2], and Monique Noirhomme-Fraiture[1]
[1]Institut d'Informatique, Facultés Universitaires Notre-Dame de la Paix
rue Grandgagnage, 21 – B-5000 Namur (Belgium)
E-mail: {abe,mno}@info.fundp.ac.be
[2]Institut d'Administration et de Gestion, Université Catholique de Louvain
Belgian Lab. of Computer-Human Interaction (BCHI)
Place des Doyens, 1 – B-1348 Louvain-la-Neuve (Belgium)
E-mail:{beirekdar,vanderdonckt}@isys.ucl.ac.be
URL: http://www.isys.ucl.ac.be/bchi/members/ abe, jva /index.htm
Tel.: +32-10-47 {8349, 8525} – Fax: +32-10-478324

Abstract Usability guidelines are supposed to help web designers to design usable sites. Unfortunately, studies carried out that applying these guidelines by designers is difficult, essentially because of the way of structuring or formulating them. One possible way to help designers in their task is to provide them with tools that evaluate the designed site (during or after design) and alerts them about usability errors. Ideally, these tools would support an appropriate guidelines definition language that enables structuring any guideline in an evaluation-oriented form. In this paper we propose a framework and guideline definition language for usability (automatic) evaluation.

Keywords: Automatic evaluation, Guideline Definition Language, Usability guidelines.

1. INTRODUCTION

In recent years, there has been very increasing interest in using internet as a universal show room for almost every kind of information (commercial, educational, personal, etc.). As a result, the number of web sites is increasing exponentially. Although most of these sites try to be distinguished using all

C. Kolski and J. Vanderdonckt (eds.), Computer-Aided Design of User Interfaces III, 337–348.
© 2002 *Kluwer Academic Publishers.*

possible means: design technology, presentation, interactivity, etc., they all have at least one common objective: be usable by everyone (and everywhere). This obvious objective is not always reached for many reasons:

- In many cases, site designers have little or no experience in ergonomic web design; all their attention is focused on publishing their sites, generally using web design tools that do not integrate any kind of assistance concerning designing usable sites.
- The compatibility problem between different web technologies (editors, browsers, platforms, etc.) makes it difficult and time and effort consuming to design sites compatible with multiple browsers.
- Web browsers do not immediately support new publishing technologies, and obviously, old browsers that are still used by many users do not support them.
- Many sites change their content continuously by adding, removing or updating web pages. These changes could be done by different persons and are generally a main source of usability problems, especially for very large web sites.

To help designers to reach this objective, web usability guidelines were proposed by usability and web experts, and many evaluation tools like Bobby [2], A-Prompt [1], WebSat [17], and 508 Accessibility Suite [19] that were developed to enable designers and evaluators verify the (non) respect of a page or a web site to one or many of these guidelines. A comparison of some of these tools is provided in [4].

The efficiency of these tools varies according to their scope (one element, one page, entire site) and to the evaluated guidelines set. They all have the same functioning principle: to detect usability problems by analysing the HTML code of the target page to verify some predefined evaluation conditions.

The main inconvenience of such tools is that the guidelines' evàluation logic is hard coded in the evaluation engine. This leads to many limitations:

1. Web guidelines are evolving with the continuing technology evolution; so, adding new guidelines or modifying the existing evaluation logic becomes difficult and requires modifying and recompiling the evaluation engine even for minor code modification.
2. The variety of web users stereotypes, their navigation purposes, their navigation tools, etc. makes it very probable that they do not have the same usability constraints. Thus, for many of them a site could be considered satisfying a guideline even if it does some partial checkpoint are fulfilled. Hard coding makes it impossible to specify such evaluation constraints.

3. It is sometimes desired to evaluate a site against multiple guideline sets coming from different sources. Hard coding each of these sets in a separate tool complicates this task.

2. OBJECTIVES

Automated usability evaluation of web sites, although largely underexplored, shows promises to complement traditional usability evaluation for very large web sites, or when guidelines need interpretation [5,9].

Our ultimate goal is to develop a language, a framework and a prototype to automatically evaluate the usability of web sites and to show that this combination can solve unprecedented testing issues and can break the barrier of 44% of possibly automatable guidelines [6]. For this purpose, some web design usability guidelines are formalized in a flexible high-level definition language exploited in a structured step-wise method and automatically tested in a prototype showing the feasibility and the validity of this approach.

Guidelines are numerous and distributed among different sources: recommendation papers [15], design standards (e.g., [7]), style guides that are specific to a particular environment (e.g., [8]), design guides (e.g., [12,16]) and algorithms for ergonomic design (e.g., [3]). They vary in format, level of confidence, and expressiveness, they need to be re-expressed according to a canonical common organization scheme. For this purpose, the EvalWeb [13] scheme was selected and used.

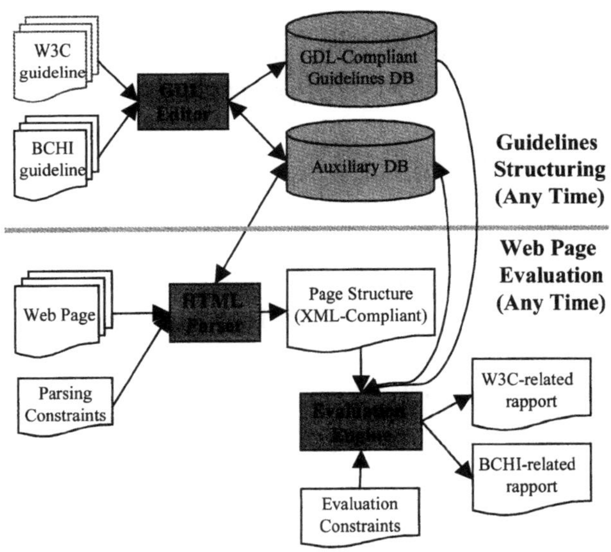

Figure 1. Architecture of a GDL-Based Evaluation Tool;

This natural language scheme will lead to a potentially expressive, yet formal expression of the guideline in Guideline Definition Language (GDL). This language is able to express guideline information in a sufficiently rich enough manner to enable an evaluation engine to perform an automated evaluation of any GDL-compliant guideline by static analysis of the HTML code. Fig. 1 shows the architecture of a web evaluation tool supporting the proposed GDL.

The next section of the paper presents an intuitive framework that an evaluator would use to structure a guideline for automatic evaluation. Some interesting concepts emerging from the framework are then underlined and completed with some others to form the set of our GDL concepts. The ERA schema of the GDL is presented and described in section 3. We conclude by discussing the interests and the scope of the language.

3. THE FRAMEWORK

In order for an artefact to be usable, it must be designed according to the way users use it [11], thus this framework organises guidelines according to evaluator's use. Here we use the framework to introduce the GDL concepts, but it is also recommended to follow this framework for future structuring of a guideline with the GDL-based evaluation tool.

The framework is defined as a sequence of six steps and is intended to help the evaluator to:

- Identify the theoretical and practical levels of automation of the guideline evaluation. Applying the framework will allow the user to see if the automation of a guideline will be theoretically or practically possible or not, total or partial (Table 1), and perhaps underline any reason why it is not automatable.
- Systematically and consistently structure each guideline.
- Optimise the guideline structuring by identifying and optionally eliminating any elements redundant in the evaluation-oriented structuring.

The framework is criteria-oriented: for all steps, some criteria guide the user in selecting appropriate concepts, in defining its automation level, and in defining evaluation conditions.

The framework's steps are exemplified on the guideline "*Never have a link that points right back to the same page*" [10]. We chose this guideline because it is reasonably simple for our understanding purpose, yet often violated, especially in home pages.

3.1 Step 1: Determining Interesting Elements

The first step consists of identifying and isolating the *HTML elements* on which the automated evaluation will be performed. Then, the guideline is said to be *theoretically possible*, respectively *impossible*, to evaluate if there is at least one, respectively no, HTML element on which the evaluation can be conducted. The evaluation is said to be *total* if all identified HTML elements are expressive enough to evaluate the complete guideline. If this is not the case, i.e. at least one part of the general guideline cannot be evaluated on identified HTML elements, it is said to be *partial*. The resulting set of HTML elements could be different from one user to another according to the HTML experience, interpretation, and understanding of the guideline's aims.

In our example, we found the following HTML elements:

1. The A element, which defines an anchor:
   - The A element's *content* defines the position of the anchor.
   - The name attribute names the anchor so that it may be the destination of zero or more links.
   - The href attribute makes this anchor the source anchor of exactly one link.

   Authors may also create an A element that specifies no anchors, i.e., that does not specify href, name or id. Values for these attributes may be set at a later time through scripts.
2. The id attribute: it may be used to create an anchor at the start tag of any element (including the A element).
3. The LINK element: it defines a link. Unlike A, it may only appear in the HEAD section of a document, although it may appear any number of times. Although LINK has no content, it conveys relationship information that may be rendered by user agents in a variety of ways (e.g., a toolbar with a drop-down menu of links).

Table 1. Examples of guidelines and their (estimated) evaluation characteristics.

Guideline	Automation level	Reason
Do not rely on color alone [11]	- Theoretically: possible, total - Practically: not possible	There are HTML color-related elements Evaluation conditions difficult to formalize
Never have a link that points right back to the same page [10]	- Theoretically: possible, total - Practically: possible, total	There are HTML needed elements Evaluation conditions can be formalized and easily realized
Provide equivalent alternatives to auditory and visual content [11]	- Theoretically: possible, partial - Practically: possible, partial	There are HTML elements but not for all desired aspects of the guideline

3.2 Step 2: Classifying Selected Elements into Evaluation Sets

After identifying the HTML elements which are important for the guideline' scope, we determine if they could be grouped into *evaluation sets* in some way. For this purpose, grouping principles need to be defined, such as: group elements by similar semantics. Some of these sets could be more important for the guideline evaluation than others. Thus, each set is assigned to a priority level to express its importance in conformance with W3C specification [17]:

1. *Priority 1*: A web content developer must satisfy the conditions for positive evaluation of this set. Satisfying this set is a basic requirement for the web content to respect the guideline.
2. *Priority 2*: A web content developer should satisfy the conditions for positive evaluation of this set. Satisfying this set will remove significant barriers for the web content to respect the guideline.
3. *Priority 3*: A web content developer may address this set. Satisfying this set will improve respect of the web content to the guideline.

Some sets have a priority level that may change under certain conditions. In our example, we could group the selected HTML elements into two sets:

1. *Set1*: Navigation links (or visible links) [Priority 1]. Links helping to navigate between any web pages. This set contains the HTML elements: A, href, name, and id.
2. *Set2*: No-navigation links (or hidden links) [Priority 2]. Links expressing other relationships between pages than simply activating a link to visit a related resource. This set contains the following HTML elements: LINK, rel, rev, and href.

3.3 Step 3: Defining Atomic Evaluation Sets

An *atomic evaluation set* is defined as a minimal set of elements that allow the evaluation of a precise objective (like "linking between two web resources"). After grouping the HTML elements as mentioned in step 2, we examine each evaluation set to find whether it contains any atomic set. Some evaluation sets could remain the same when they are already atomic. Here again grouping principles need to be defined.

In our example, the following atomic evaluation sets are derived:

1. **Atom1**: Destination anchors specified by A element (visible links). In this case, we use the name attribute of the destination A to name it. This

name will be used to designate the destination when linking it to any other source anchor. The atomic corresponding set is: A, href, and name.

2. **Atom2**: Destination anchors specified by elements other that the A element (visible links). In this case, we use the id attribute of any HTML element making it the destination anchor. The atomic corresponding set is: A, href, and id.
3. **Atom3**: Destination anchors specified by LINK and rel elements The rel attribute of a LINK element describes the relationship from the current document to the anchor specified by the href attribute. The atomic corresponding set is: LINK, href, and rel.
4. **Atom4**: Destination anchors specified by LINK and REV elements. The rev attribute of a LINK element describes reverse link from the anchor specified by the href attribute to the current document. The atomic corresponding set is: LINK, href, and rev.

3.4 Step 4: Defining Evaluation Conditions

Using elements of the atomic sets, we precise the cases or situations where the guidelines is considered respected or violated. *Evaluation conditions* are defined as triples (*HTML element, Desired value, Error ID*) or any combination of these triples. Logical operators (OR, AND, XOR, NOT) are then used to compose the full evaluation condition based on the individual element conditions. Predefined functions and values that can be typically used in some situations are available. The predefinition could be related to Java (the language used to develop our evaluation engine), or to the tool itself.

In our example, we specify the cases where the studied guideline is considered violated.

– **Guideline violation condition**: for Atom1, 2, 3, 4:

```
Href = URI of current page [link to current page] OR
Href = "#...."             [internal link]         OR
Href = URI+ "#...."        [internal link]
Error ID=1                 (the page has a link to itself)
```

In this violation condition, it is assumed that having internal navigation links (as from a table of contents to sections in the same page) are not allowed. Otherwise, we must eliminate the last two conditions, thus producing another interpreted guideline. Verifying that a web page respects a guideline suggests a rather different approach than identifying violation points. In the first case, the condition must be satisfied for all HTML elements, whereas in the second, the evaluation stops as soon as one guideline violation is detected. One or more violation/respect conditions are defined without caring if the violation or the respect of the guideline will be preferred. This choice is done at step 6.

3.5 Step 5: Cleaning Up Evaluation Sets

It is likely that after step 4 some information may become unnecessary for the evaluation. Thus, they will be eliminated. Under certain circumstances, this could lead to eliminating an entire set or atomic set.

In our example, if we do not consider other verification (like if the element in href is really in the courant page), the following elements are not needed: Atom1 (name), Atom2 (id), Atom3 (rel) and Atom4 (rev). If we consider that the normal use of the LINK element is to link to external resources, we could eliminate Set1 entirely, and so on for its atomic sub-sets (Atom3, 4).

3.6 Step 6: Defining Guideline Evaluation Interpretations (Algorithm)

A guideline could be evaluated differently from one evaluation context to another. The same guideline could have more than one *interpretation*, depending on the interpreter. Verifying a guideline may also change from one context to another. In some situations, it may turn out that evaluating a guideline, although theoretically possible, is not *practically possible* for various reasons: too many evaluation sets, a lot of code to perform the evaluation, many possible evaluation cases, etc.). Therefore, we suggest that a guideline evaluation algorithm must be defined using the sets of step 2:

1. The order of testing the evaluation sets. In some cases, according to the experience or to some statistics, we can predict the evaluation sets the most possible to be encountered in an evaluated page(s). To optimize the evaluation process, we would test these sets first, especially if we want to see if our main concern is to see if the guideline is violated or not.
2. The evaluation sets considered sufficient to evaluate the guideline at a given acceptance level. Priority levels assigned to evaluation sets are normally determined according to some considerations (priorities definition). This means that, in some contexts, we can ignore some of them without dramatically influencing mean guideline's ergonomic value.

Fig. 2 summarizes the steps of the framework and underlines the interesting concepts.

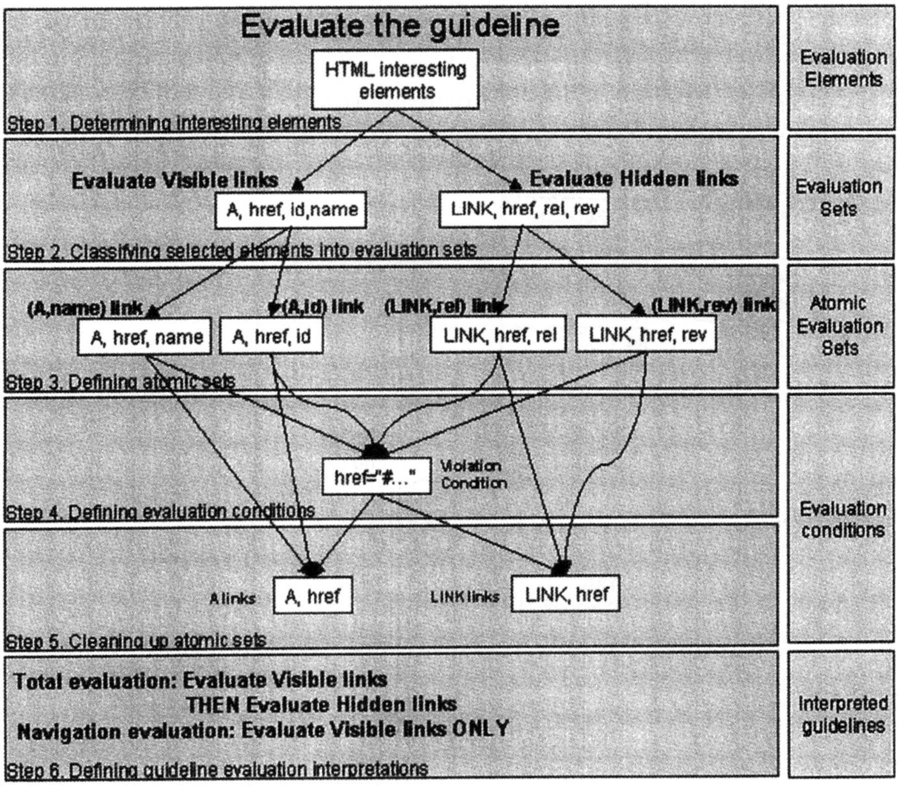

Figure 2. Illustration of the framework steps and the interesting evaluation concepts.

4. THE GUIDELINE DEFINITION LANGUAGE

A key component of any software for automated web usability evaluation is the language structuring the evaluated guideline. This language must trade-off between the richness of structuring definition and the ease with which this definition can be built [9].

As we mentioned above, the framework allows us to underline the main concepts needed by an evaluator **to structure** a guideline towards (automatic) evaluation. The ERA schema of Fig. 3 shows these concepts and the relationships among them. According to this schema, the evaluation of a *guideline* may engender one or many *interpreted guidelines* according the evaluation context. The interpretation is defined as an algorithm that organises the execution of the evaluation sets. Each set consists of at least one HTML element that the evaluator specifies as helpful to evaluate the respect or violation of the guideline. An evaluation set could be divided into smaller sets by applying some grouping criteria until we reach atomic evaluation sets witch focus on one precise HTML element (step 3 of Fig. 2). The condition of (non) respecting a guideline is expressed as mentioned in step 4 of the framework. The evaluated value could be a string, a Boolean value, a number, etc. Every condition is associated with an Error ID that will be generated if the condition value is false.

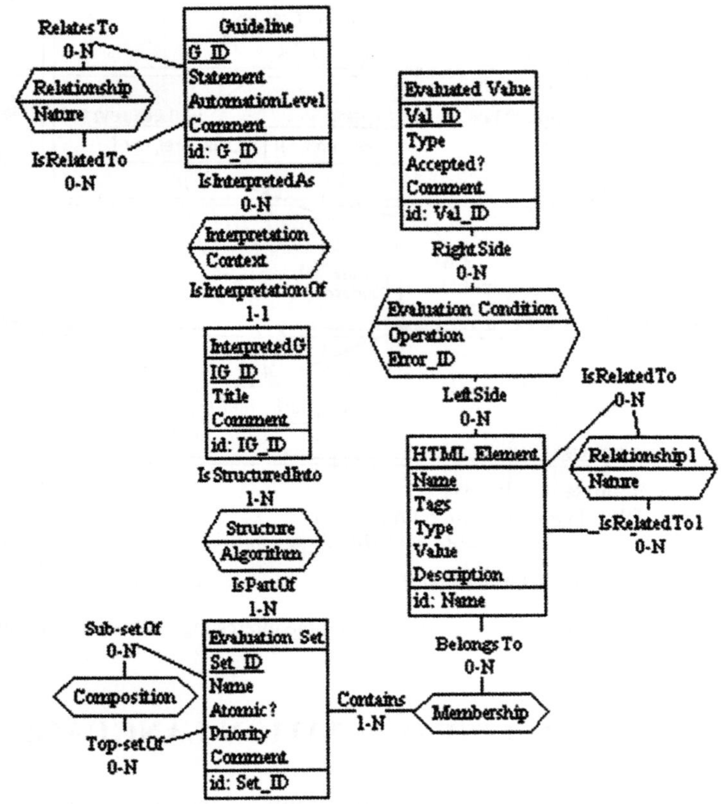

Figure 3. ERA Schema of GDL main concepts.

The GDL editor of Fig. 1 will allow the evaluator to structure a guideline, then, to save it in a XML-compliant format respecting the GDL-based DTD.

5. CONCLUSION

A framework and a GDL that enable an evaluator to structure guidelines towards automated evaluation are given. Structuring guidelines with our GDL would have the following advantages:

- Decomposing guidelines into evaluation sets enables the evaluator to re-use common sets to optimise the evaluation execution.
- Identifying guidelines that are semantically close by identifying common structuring elements (HTML elements, evaluation sets).
- Possibility of evaluating guidelines in multiple evaluation contexts
- Possibility of evaluating many interpretations of a guideline in the same evaluation context.
- Possibility of calculating the automation level and the automation feasibility of a guideline by model checking techniques.
- Putting structured guidelines under XML-compliant format enables us to realize mathematical proof of properties (such as completeness, consistency) and to benefit from the existing XML audience and tools suite (e.g., theorem prover, model checker, syntax validator).

The example of Fig. 2 and other simple ones showed that our approach is promising, but we are working on more complex guidelines to get more accurate results.

ACKNOWLEDGMENTS

The research of Abdo Beirekdar in Belgium is funded by the Atomic Energy Commission of Syria.

REFERENCES

[1] *A-Prompt Accessibility Toolkit Project*, Adaptive Technology Resource Center (University of Toronto) and Trade Center (University of Wisconsin), Canada & USA, April 1999, accessible at http://aprompt.snow.utoronto.ca/.

[2] *Bobby Version 2.0*, HTML Web analyser, Center for Applied Special Technology (CAST), National Universal Design Laboratory, Peabody, Massachusetts, 2002, Accessible at http://www.cast.org/bobby.

[3] Bodart, F. and Vanderdonckt, J., *On the Problem of Selecting Interaction Objects*, in Proceedings of HCI'94 (Glasgow, 23-26 August 1994), Cambridge University Press, Cambridge, 1994, pp. 163-178.

[4] Brajnik, G., *Automatic web usability evaluation: where is the limit?*, in Ph. Kortum and E. Kudzinger (eds.), Proc. of 6th Conf. on Human Factors and the Web HFWeb'2000 (Austin, 19 June 2000), University of Texas, Austin, 2000.

[5] Cooper, M., *Evaluating Accessibility and Usability of Web Sites*, in J. Vanderdonckt and A.R. Puerta (eds.), Computer-Aided Design of User Interfaces II, Proc. of 3rd Int. Conf. on Computer-Aided Design of User Interfaces CADUI'99 (Louvain-la-Neuve, 21-23 October 1999), Kluwer Academics, Dordrecht, 1999, pp. 33-42.

[6] Farenc, Ch., Liberati, L., Barthet, M.-F., *Automatic Ergonomic Evaluation: What are the Limits?*, in J. Vanderdonckt (ed.), Computer-Aided Design of User Interfaces, Proc. of 2nd Int. Workshop on Computer-Aided Design of User Interfaces CADUI'96 (Namur, 5-

7 June 1996), Presses Universitaires de Namur, Namur, 1996, pp. 159-170, accessible at http://lis.univ-tlse1.fr/~farenc/papers/cadui96-cf.ps.

[7] ISO/WD 9241, *Ergonomic requirements for Office Work with Visual Displays Units*, International Standard Organization, 1992.

[8] *IBM Common User Access Guidelines*, Object-Oriented Interface Design, Document SC34-4399, IBM Corp. Publisher, 1993.

[9] Ivory, M.Y., Sinha, R.R., and Hearst, M.A., *Empirically Validated Web Pages Design Metrics*, in Proc. of ACM Conf. on Human Aspects in Comp. Systems CHI'2001 (Seattle, 31 March-5 April 2001), ACM Press, New York, pp. 61-68.

[10] Nielsen, J., Website accessible at http://www.useit.com/.

[11] Norman, D.A., *The psychology of everyday things*, Harper and Collins, 1988.

[12] Scapin, D.L., *Guide ergonomique de conception des interfaces homme-ordinateur*, Research report INRIA N°77, INRIA, Le Chesnay, 1986.

[13] Scapin, D.L., Leulier, C., Vanderdonckt, J., Mariage, C., Bastien, Ch., Farenc, Ch., Palanque, Ph., and Bastide, R., *A Framework for Organizing Web Usability Guidelines*, in Ph. Kortum and E. Kudzinger (eds.), Proc. of 6th Conf. on Human Factors and the Web HFWeb'2000 (Austin, 19 June 2000), University of Texas, Austin, 2000, accessible at http://www.tri.sbc.com/hfweb/scapin/Scapin.html .

[14] Smith, G.B. and Howes, A., *Constraints on a representation language for automated evaluation*, in Ch. Johnson (ed.), Proceedings of 8th International Workshop on Design, Specification and Verification of Interactive Systems DSV-IS'2001 (Glasgow, 13-15 June 2001), Glasgow, 2001, accessible at http://www.dcs.gla.ac.uk/~johnson/papers/dsvis_2001/smith/

[15] Smith, S.L., *Standards Versus Guidelines for Designing User Interface Software*, in M. Helander (ed.), Handbook of Human-Computer Interaction, North-Holland, Amsterdam, 1988, pp. 877-889.

[16] Vanderdonckt, J., *Guide ergonomique des interfaces homme-machine*, Presses Universitaires de Namur, Namur, 1994, ISBN 2-87037-189-6.

[17] *WebMetric Tools*, National Institute for Standards and Technology, 1999, accessible at http://zing.ncsl.nist.gov/webmet.

[18] *W3C Web Content Accessibility Guidelines 1.0*, accessible at http://www.w3.org/TR/WCAG10/.

[19] *508 Accessibility Suite*, Program to test websites accessibility, UsableNet Inc., New York, 2001, accessible at http://508as.usablenet.com/508AS/1.0/help/Help.html.

Chapter 30

FIRST STEPS TOWARDS TASK-RELATED WEB USER INTERFACES

Birgit Bomsdorf
University Hagen, Praktische Informatik I
Feithstraße 142, D-58084 Hagen (Germany)
E-mail: birgit.bomsdorf@fernuni-hagen.de – Tel.: +49-2331-987 2962

Abstract A task-based approach for developing UI's of web applications is presented. Refinements of task model concepts are shown by means of examples. Task-related components are proposed as enhancements of the presentation layer of web server applications. Starting from a task model the development of the UI and the application functionality can be separated more effectively and, in addition, is based on the user-oriented view.

Keywords: Architecture, Executable task model, Task-based design, Web applications.

1. INTRODUCTION

Designing and maintaining user interfaces of web applications is still a challenge for the developers within the community of software engineering and HCI. Programming the UI is often solution-driven based on ad-hoc implementations of HTML prototypes. In large projects this is criticised for being too unstructured. To face this problem different approaches were developed, e.g. [1,3,3,4]. These approaches, however, suffer from the fact that the realisation of the UI is based on models reflecting a system-centred view, i.e. on models designed describing implementation aspects of the software and underlying databases.

Within the established three-tier architecture (as described for instance in [4]) the three components *business logic, data storage,* and *presentation* are separated. The presentation component represents the UI shown to the user on the web, i.e. the web pages returned to him as a response to a request. This might be a simple link following operation, or the return of an interac-

C. Kolski and J. Vanderdonckt (eds.), Computer-Aided Design of User Interfaces III, 349–356.
© 2002 *Kluwer Academic Publishers.*

tive web page with fields filled in by the user. We refer to a UI like this as *web UI* throughout this paper.

Although the three-tier architecture separates out presentation concerns, the UI design in these approaches is driven by technical aspects and not by a user-oriented view describing how users can fulfil their tasks when interacting with the application. Knowing the user's goals and tasks is essential for the designer to construct interactive systems which adequately reflect the tasks' properties. Hence, the importance of task models has increased in UI design. The feasibility of integrating an explicit task model into the design of GUIs has been demonstrated by different approaches in the field of HCI [6,7]. However, within the development of web UI's these results are not yet sufficiently taken into account.

This paper presents an ongoing work on a task-based approach for the development of web UI's, in which concepts of task models are refined and task-based components are integrated into the server-side architecture, i.e. in the presentation layer of a three-tier architecture. As a consequence, we impose additional structure on the presentation layer of a web server application while at the same time the implementation model of the system is based tighter on a user-oriented view. Starting from a task model the development of the UI and the application functionality can be separated more effectively as in a pure three-tier architecture.

2. TASK-BASED CONSTRUCTION OF WEB SITES

In task based development the design of a UI is based on an envisioned task model [7]. This model describes a future situation where the user performs his tasks under the assumption that the target system is in operation. It documents among other information the new task structure and data to be presented to the user in the context of each task. Hence, it comprises information relevant to UI design. The order of task execution, for example, imposes constraints on the sequencing of user interactions – and on the sequencing and construction of web pages.

To realise a task-based presentation layer of web applications within the three-tier architecture we developed a task-related *presentation component* in conjunction with a *task processing manager* (Fig. 1). The runtime system of the manager is derived from an envisioned task model by means of a technique stemming from our previous work on simulating task models [2]. Based on such an executable task model the task processing manager determines all tasks for each role which can be performed in a current situation, according to all temporal relations and conditions specified influencing the situation (see below).

Such information is used by the *task-related presentation component* to dynamically compose web pages to be presented to users. Depending on a task description and state information as determined by the task processing manager a page comprises content as well as active elements the user can interact with to fulfil the task. Depending on such interactions and invoked domain rules (also named business logic in web applications) the processing manager determines the next state of all tasks concerned. Subsequent views are composed based on the new state information. Both the task-related presentation component and the task processing manager are enhanced by descriptions dealing directly with the presentation of the user interface (UI description in Fig. 1), e.g. HTML statements describing a table.

A first prototype of both the processing manager and the presentation component are currently under development within the project ALVA (German acronym for: Adaptierbarer LehrVeranstaltungsAssistent – in English: adaptable course administration assistant), the objective of which is to realise a web-based course administration tool in an environment for distance teaching. Within the next sections we casually refer to examples from the web-based teaching environment developed in this project.

3. TASK MODEL CONCEPTS

In general, a task model is defined in terms of the following core concepts: *tasks* the user has to perform; *hierarchical structures* describing the decomposition of tasks into sub-tasks; *temporal relations* specifying the order of task execution, such as sequential, parallel, or iterated execution; *conditions*, such as pre- and post-conditions for starting and ending tasks; *task objects* describing the objects involved in task execution; and *roles* users take while performing a task.

In our approach we have refined these concepts in two directions: On one hand the concepts are adapted to concerns of web interfaces. On the other hand additional attributes and rules are introduced to realise the task-related presentation component and the task processing manager.

3.1 Adaptation to Concerns of Web Interfaces

As an example of adapting task models to the domain of web applications let us consider the concept *task object*. In our approach, similar to [6], the task objects contained in the task model represent entities, their properties and semantic interrelations, which are meaningful to the user. An individual tutor, for example, assigned for coaching a course is *contained in* the list of all course tutors. In task models describing web applications we currently distinguish three classes of task objects: *domain objects, web units,* and *internet services*. Within our practical work we found that task objects of these specialized types are frequently used – they show up during modelling and necessitate specialized treatment during task model execution.

Domain objects represent parts of the business objects stored in a database. On purpose, we explicitly distinguish the domain objects and the business objects from the database. By doing so, we represent the user's view on the system in the system development. Hence, composition of web pages is not based on design decisions for realising a database, but on information from a user-centred task model instead. If web applications and the underlying database are developed simultaneously, the structures of the domain and the database object model are identical or close to identical. If, however, a new application is developed using an existing database, the structure of the associated task-related domain object model may be very different, e.g. attributes of a task object may comprise fields from diverse entities or relations between entities stored in a database.

Web units are pre-defined pages or web-forms. In our project, for instance, a typical web unit is a registration form for students to enrol for a course. Of course there exist specialised specification mechanisms (such as JSP, Servlets, HTML) to define web units, rather than using concepts for describing general task objects.

Task objects representing **internet services** encapsulate functionality of internet services, such as ftp, newsgroups, and e-mail, and the necessary interactions to invoke them. These components need not be described within the envisioned task model because their functionality and interaction possibilities are generally well-known.

3.2 Additions to Support the Implementation of the Concept

A task is defined by its name (an acronym symbolising the task) and its relation to other model elements, e.g. by describing the decomposition of the task into its sub-tasks as well as the objects involved and the agents allowed to perform the task. To realise the executable task model, we introduced, among others, additional attributes describing the processing state of a task at each point in time and events (*task events*) to trigger state transitions. The user can, for example, start to perform a task (e.g. "register for a course") only if the software object representing the task is in the state start_possible. This state is reached as soon as the temporal relations and conditions defined in the envisioned task model are fulfilled. After sending a start event the state changes to started.

In general, both kinds of attributes – attributes derived from the envisioned task model as well as those added for the purpose of managing task processing are also stored in a database. This database may be physically the same as the business object database, but conceptually it is a separate, task-specific database. This persistent data is used by the task-related presentation component to compose the different parts of web pages as outlined in the next section.

4. "ACTIVE" TASK MODELS

Fig. 1 gives an overview of the proposed enhancement of constructing web UI's, which is based on a three-tier architecture as realised within our first prototype. The three-tier architecture consists of the three components: business logic, data storage, and presentation. The code realising the interface on the server side is referred to as the presentation layer, which is to be distinguished from the browser at the client side. The task-related presentation component is part of the presentation layer consisting of a *task oriented controller* and a *task view composer*.

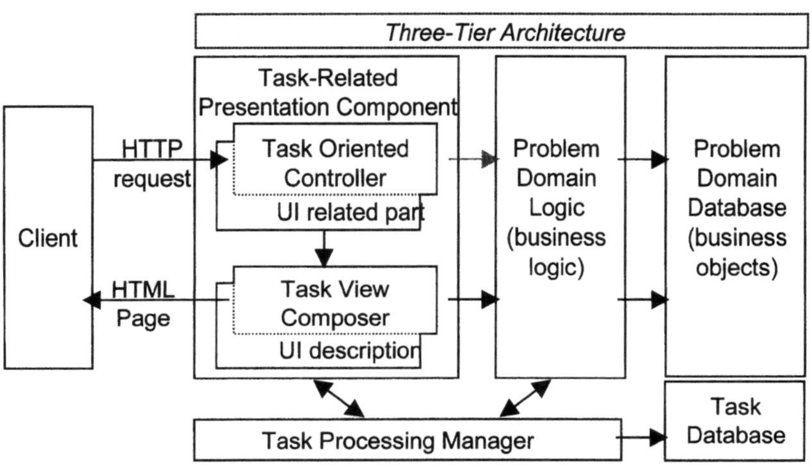

Figure 1. Three-tier architecture comprising task-based components.

Each of them is complemented with code concerning pure UI aspects, such as visualisation styles. The task processing manager spans the presentation and the problem domain layers interacting with both the presentation component and the business logic. The functionality of the executable task model is implemented primary by the task processing manager, while task information is stored in the task database. We will discuss the task related construction of the web UI in more detail in the following, Fig. 2 depicts the relations of the task components introduced.

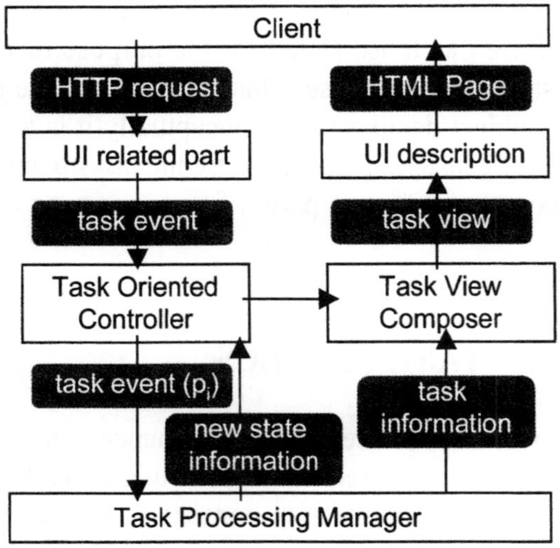

Figure 2. Relations of task components.

4.1 Incoming User Request

The UI related part of the controller is responsible for incoming HTTP requests. Apart from parameter parsing, session-tracking, and similar activities this comprises the translation of the user interaction events into task events. As described in section 3.2, the processing of a task is represented within the executable system by means of state changes triggered by task events. The task event start, for example, indicates that the user wants to start working on a task. While realising the presentation component the designer defines corresponding user interaction events for the task events. This relation, referred to as mapping rules, defines the events to be triggered within the system for the different incoming HTTP requests.

If a student, for example, wants to enrol for a course he has to "press" a simulated button presented to him within the course announcement web page. As a result of this user interaction a request is sent to the web server to provide an appropriate page for performing the task "register for a course". The request is mapped to the start event of the software object representing the task and sent together with additional information (indicated by p_i in Fig. 2), e.g. the students identification, to the task oriented controller. Based on the session information the event is sent to the task processing manager, which determines the next state as a function of the current task state information.

The task processing manager comprises the executable task model, which is and has to be separated from single user sessions. Although many state transitions are triggered by user events, there also are cases, where task state transitions may occur without incoming user requests. In our course registration example the form should not be available longer if the maximum number of allowed attendees is reached. This constraint is defined by a precondition of the registration task and evaluated by the task processing manager based on the enrolled students stored in the database. In other cases a task has to be performed completely independently from user requests, such as sending a message automatically to students as soon as a predefined point in time is reached. To be independent from the existence of a current user session the task processing manger has to be implemented as a separated component, which receives events from the system.

In some cases the controller, on the other hand, may also directly invoke application functionality to evaluate incoming requests. Within the architecture it is the component which informs the task view composer that a new page (or frame) is to be sent to the client.

4.2 Page Composition

The task view composer is responsible for generating and sending an output stream to the client. Information on how to compose an HTML page is received from the task processing manager (Fig. 2) and from the problem domain data storage (Fig. 1). Hence, depending on the user role and the current state of task processing a task view is derived. Such a task view describes *which* objects, e.g. business data or hyperlinks, have to be presented to the user in the context of the current task (in our implementation using XML). The UI description, on the other hand, defines *how* the objects should be presented within a web page.

In the example of enrolling for a course, besides other task objects, a list of already registered students is defined as being relevant for performing the task. As this domain object is mapped to business objects stored in the problem domain database (in this case course, student, and the participate-relation between them) the appropriate entities are selected resulting in a set. For representation purposes detailed UI descriptions are added to visualise the set, e.g. as a table within the web page returned to the client.

Considering our example again, let us now assume that the number of allowed attendees is reached. Thus, the precondition of the registration task is no longer fulfilled, which changes its state to not_possible. Hence, the view composer does not activate the button for enrolling in the course announcement web page.

In the case of task objects defined as internet services or web units the related links are inserted into the page. Input parameters, similar to OOHDM [3], are provided by the task context, e.g. a course author will see only the tutors of the course he selected before.

5. CONCLUSION

In the presented approach a task-based view is introduced into web UI's. In many model-based approaches the envisioned task model is used to generate parts of a GUI or even the entire interface, or it is used to inform the designers while they are developing the UI. In contrast to that, in our work we make direct use of the information described within a task model to define the task processing manager, the task oriented controller, and the task view composer. Thereby, the development of the UI and the application functionality is separated more effectively. Furthermore, the coding of the presentation gains more structure and, in addition, is based on the user-oriented view.

In single approaches to generating web applications (e.g. in Areanus [1]) a page composition model is considered, representing a domain oriented view, which is, however, still technique-driven.

Like in WebMVC [4] we have introduced a controller and a view component into the presentation layer but in contrast to the above system we distinguish task and pure UI relevant aspects. In both approaches, state information is stored in a database. However, in contrast to WebMVC, in the approach presented here a state can be changed without any user request as the task processing manager can be invoked by internal "demon" processes.

Our current work aims at enhancing the UI specific part of the presentation component and at implementing a task management system, which is based on the task processing manager.

ACKNOWLEDGEMENT

The author would like to thank Gerd Szwillus, Inga Saatz, and Christian Neumann for helpful discussions and the reviewers for their comments.

REFERENCES

1. Areanus, accessible at http://www.dia.uniroma3.it/Areanus.
2. Biere, M., Bomsdorf, B., and Szwillus, G., *Visual Task Model Builder*, in J. Vanderdonckt and A.R. Puerta (eds.), *Computer-Aided Design of User Interfaces II*, Proceedings of CADUI'99, Kluwer Academic Publishers, Dordrecht, 1999, pp. 245-256.
3. Rossi, R., Schwabe, D., and Lyardet, F., *Web application models are more than conceptual models*, in Proc. of ER'99, 1999, pp. 239-252.
4. Server-Side MVC Architecture, accessible at http://www.uidesign.net/1999/papers/webmvc_part1.html
5. Strudel, accessible at http://www.research.att.com/sw/tools/strudel.
6. van der Veer, G., Lenting, B., and Bergevoet, B., *Groupware Task Analysis - Modelling Complexity*, Acta Psychologica, Vol. 91, No. 3, 1996, pp. 297-322.

Chapter 31

CO-OPERATIVE AGENT DESIGN IN A TECHNOLOGICAL WATCH CONTEXT

Ludivine Jonnequin, Emmanuel Adam, Christophe Kolski, and René Mandiau
LAMIH - UMR CNRS 8530, Université de Valenciennes et du Hainaut Cambrésis, F–59313 Valenciennes Cedex 9 (France)
E-mail: {emmanuel.adam, christophe.kolski, rene.mandiau}@univ-valenciennes.fr
URL: http://www.univ-valenciennes.fr/LAMIH/
Tel.: +33-3-27 51 {1411, 1499, 1469, 1438} - Fax: +33-3-27 51 13 16

Abstract Internet technologies and company networks have contributed towards the boom in electronic documents which are often accessible to all internet users. For most companies, an essential objective is now to be the first to find the information required. It has become extremely important to own a rapid information search and distribution tool. Admittedly, tools have already been suggested, such as search engines, meta-engines, and, more recently, information agents, capable of searching for, sorting and filtering information. But teams of human actors searching for information need teams of agents which act in a co-operative manner. In this paper, we present a system integrating co-operative information agents for co-operative technological watch. A first prototype has been designed and is currently being used in a large company.

Keywords: Human-Agent Interaction, Information Agents, Multi-Agent System (MAS), Technological Watch.

1. INTRODUCTION

Generally, the watch is the faculty that we have to perceive our environment; a kind of state of mind oriented towards the outside. In practical terms, the watch is a technique including three main actions: the gathering of information; the analysis and synthesis of the information gathered; the diffusion of relevant information. The term 'relevant information' means that the data gathered has to be subjected to several treatments. So, a first phase of validation consists in checking the validity and the relevance of gathered in-

C. Kolski and J. Vanderdonckt (eds.), Computer-Aided Design of User Interfaces III, 357–366.
© 2002 *Kluwer Academic Publishers.*

formation, a second phase of elaboration and synthesis means extracting the relevant information from the gathered information and grouping it by theme in order to send it to the right person. This part is essential because even if a piece of information is relevant, it must be diffused to the person who is able to process it. The information must be used as a decision support tool. There are several stages of evolution in the watch: (1) a first degree of the watch concerns above all papers and data bases (documentation is a general term that groups together press, books, research work and data banks; information watch is characterised by a work specialisation of information officers and an optimal monitoring of the information search topic); (2) a second and more recent stage is composed of specialised watch, strategic watch, and economic intelligence (called technological watch).

The technological watch's domain is "the observation and analysis of the scientific, technical, technological environment, followed by the properly targeted diffusion to the relevant persons of selected and useful information necessary to make a strategic decision" [8]. In this paper, we will begin by briefly describing several existing works on information agents and Multi-Agents Systems (MAS). Then, we will propose an agent-based architecture for technological watch and finally, an application within the watch cell in a large firm.

2. RELATED WORK

An Information Multi-Agents System (IMAS) is composed of information agents that search for information from databases (local or distributed) or from Internet sites, on the basis of requests that are sent to them (directly or indirectly through a database). It is often useful to co-ordinate agents' activities using co-ordinator agents. These agents possess knowledge concerning the information agents (such as an address or their search domain, for instance) to which they send requests either in targeted way (if they have knowledge on the competence of the information agents) or in a general way (by broadcast techniques). Then, the co-ordinator agents have to gather this information, to check it if necessary, to compare it or to filter it. Most of IMAS are directly in touch with the user, upstream (to integrate new requests) and/or downstream (during the presentation of search results). The principle that recommends a separation between interface and treatment is also guaranteed by the design of agent based systems. In order to have an interface which is reactive and distributed at the level of various users, some IMAS propose the use of interface agents which act as an interface between the users and the system.

Fig. 1 shows an example of IMAS architecture. Actors can interrogate the system about the presence or the content of a piece of information thanks to interface agents. These agents can distribute the request to several coordinator agents which are in charge of co-ordinating their activities. Information agents can search for information on the Internet, in databases or with other information agents (if these information agents have knowledge about data). The figure presents an IMAS, its agents and the communication between the various agents. But in the case of a technological watch department, each actor needs an IMAS; furthermore, in order to avoid redundancy of information between the IMAS, each IMAS has to communicate with the others. This is why we propose a cooperative IMAS.

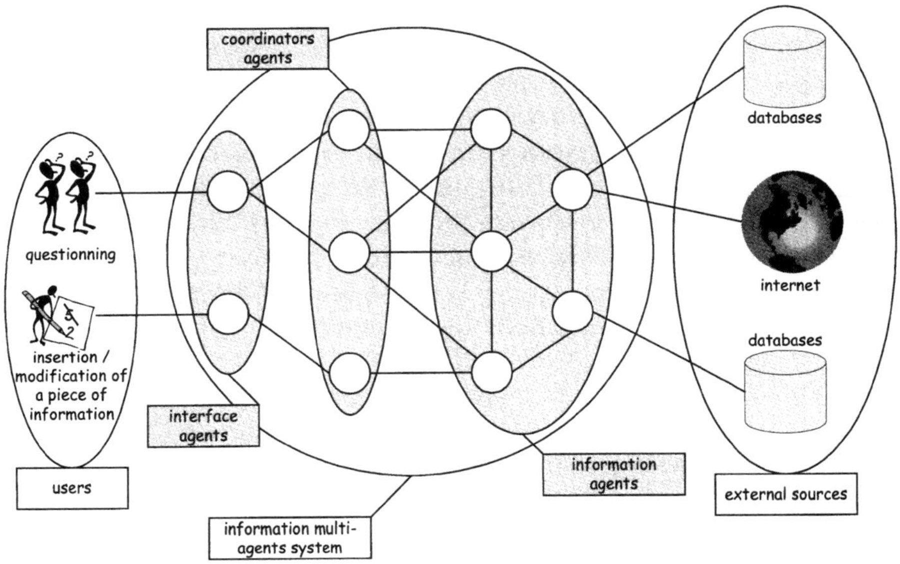

Figure 1. A typist's work environment.

3. PROPOSITION OF INFORMATION AGENT ARCHITECTURE FOR CO-OPERATIVE WATCH

By considering the general study concerning MAS described above, we have defined a MAS whose goal is to lead watch actions within a team. The CIASCOTEWA architecture (Co-operative Information Agents' System for Co-operative Technological Watch) is based on a set of autonomous entities. The main elements of this system are information agents. In the architecture, we associate an information agent system (a CIASTEWA, for Co-operative Information Agents' System for Technological Watch) to each actor of the watch cell. Indeed, it is better for each watchman to have his/her own subsystem on his/her computer. It allows greater flexibility at the system level and a larger degree of autonomy for each watchman. In fact, it is easier to integrate a new watchman if an appropriate sub-system is on his/her own computer. On the other hand, if we choose to use a server system, we must reinitialise the system upon each arrival or departure of an actor.

In order to design this architecture, we re-used a methodology which we developed in order to design Holonic MAS (called Holomas) [3] to help actors in a cooperative process. Such systems are based on the holonic principles.

3.1 Holonic Systems

Holonic systems were proposed by Arthur Koestler around 30 years ago [9]. The underlying principle is the fact that, in real life, an entity must be considered both as a whole made up of other entities, and as being part of a set. Koestler's ideas have already been applied in various fields, notably in an international project named "Intelligent Manufacturing Systems" [12], in order to form one of the models on which the factory of the future could be built. These ideas are also applied in the field of robotics [4], as well as in the field of cognitive psychology [13]. The work of Siekmann [7] on the formal description of holonic agents and his proposals for application in the fields of transport planning, flexible production systems and Robocups (a Robocup is the simulation of a football tournament in which the teams are made up of robot or software agents) should also be mentioned.

A Holon is defined by Koestler as being a part of a whole or of a larger organisation, rigorously meeting three conditions: to be stable, to have a capacity for autonomy and to be capable of co-operating (in fact, Koestler proposes 65 rules describing the architecture of a holonic system and the communication rules between entities of the system):

- Stability means that a Holon is able to cope and react when it is subjected to high demand or to major disturbances,
- Autonomy suggests that a Holon is capable of managing itself when subjected to demands in order to achieve its own aims,
- The capacity to co-operate means that the holons are able to coexist with other holons or other layers of holons, and are capable of working on common aims and projects.

Here we can find at least two of the characteristics of the agents in a MAS sense: autonomy and co-operation [10]. The third characteristic, the capacity to adapt itself to an environment is suggested by stability. Between each part of a holonic system (each Holon), a relation of responsibility exists. So, a Holonic MAS (Holomas) is a MAS which has a hierarchical structure in which each agent is responsible for a sub-holonic MAS which is working. This notion of recursivity is very interesting in the design of Holomas. In fact, each part of the holonic system, globally, has the same working manner as the global system (it can, of course, have specialities).

We therefore specified our CIASCOTEWA according to a Holomas architecture and re-used a methodology that was built in order to set up a Holomas intended for administrative processes [3].

3.2 Description of a CIASTEWA (Co-operative Information Agents' System for Technological Watch)

Each sub-system goal is to search for information, to gather it, to sort and to communicate relevant information. The sub-system may be considered as an IMAS; so it must be made up of a *co-ordinator agent*, an *interface agent* and *information agents* whose actions are co-ordinated, in our case, by an *agent responsible for information* (Fig. 2).

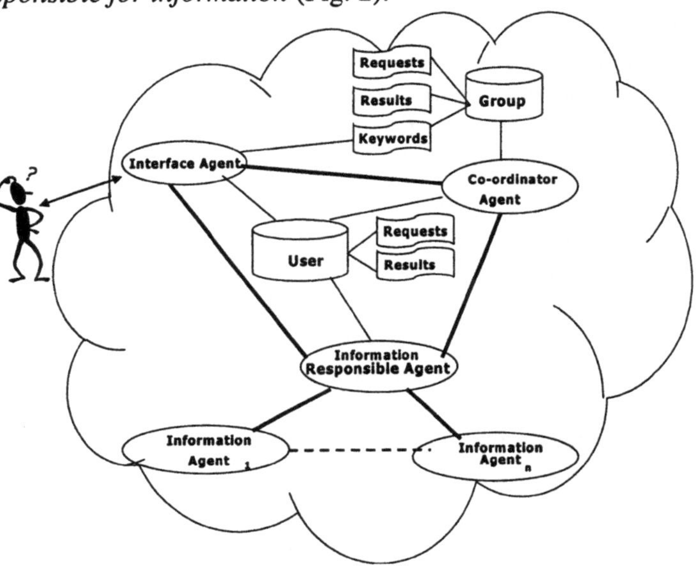

Figure 2. Architecture of a CIASTEWA

In order to manage all the work, the search (according to requests) and the return of results, these agents have to co-operate through a shared database associated to the user [5,11]. This user database is made up of a database concerning requests and a database relating to results. So, the hierarchy is organised around these bases: the co-ordinator agent is the only one which is authorised to change their content whereas the other agents only have access for consultation purposes. A CIASTEWA, shown in Fig. 2, also has a group database. This is intended for collecting all the knowledge of the group to which the user belongs, that is to say the requests of the group, results of these requests and the list of keywords generally used in the requests. The user database only records data adapted to the user.

We describe the co-operative functioning of the different agents following the description of their function.

3.2.1 Roles of CIASTEWA Agents

The *interface agent* serves as a link between the user and the system. It assists the users to express their requests by permitting the consultation of the base of requests as well as the list of keywords. It allows interaction between the users and results provided by information agents (i.e. the selection, consultation, deletion, and sending of information) or between the different users of the group (for the exchange of information).

The *coordinator agent* has the task of coordinating the actions of other agents of the CIASTEWA. So, it can be considered as the manager of interface and information search agents. It fixes the communication of information (requests and results) with the other CIASTEWA of the global system.

The *agent responsible for information* executes requests recorded in the request database. For that, it distributes the request to the information agent according to a search strategy. This strategy depends on what the user wants. For example, if the user wants to obtain information quickly, the agent responsible for information chooses a strategy by invitation to tender (where the first results are selected), rather than a strategy by broadcast (where the agent responsible for information compares all the results).

The *information agents* have to get information according to the request sent by the agent responsible for information, and then send the information found back to it.

In order to describe the general characteristics of the various types of agent (the procedure manager, the station managers and the executing agents), we use a grid adapted from Ferber [6]. This grid enables us to define the functions for each holonic agent relating to: knowledge (the representational function also describes the non-procedural knowledge); action planning (the organisational function); interactions; regeneration (the preservation function) and actions specific to the role of the agent (the productive function). These functions are described in relation to the agent's environment, the other agents and the agent itself. Table 1 shows the behaviour of the co-ordinator agent. The roles of the interface agent, the agent responsible for information and the information agents are described as the same way.

As regards the agent responsible for information, it should be able to organise the work of the information agent by itself (among several strategies such as work delegation, or specialisation, for example).

Table 1. Definition of the work co-ordinator agent.

Dimensions/ Function	*Social*	*Environmental*	*Personal*
Representational	Knows the information search agent, interface agent and all the other co-ordinator agents.	Knows the requests and results of the user, the keywords the requests and the results of the group.	Knows its name, capacity to reorganise itself.
Organisational	Watches over the co-ordination of actions of the group of agents of CIASTEWA.	Manages the databases of the user and the group.	Checks that the request doesn't exist.
Interactional	Is the superior of interface agent and information search agent.	Interacts with coordinator agents of the CIASTEWA.	Ø
Productive	Feeds databases with results provided by information agents.	Sends requests and results to coordinator agents.	Modifications of knowledge, of its role.
Re-generation	Checks if its contacts (co-ordinator agents) are active...	Requests (databases of the user and the group).	Refers to its contacts.

3.2.2 Co-operative Functioning of CIASTEWA

After having described the individual role of the agents which make up a CIASTEWA, we will now explain the cooperative functioning within it. For this, we used a method especially suitable when we have to model flows (of communication or of data) among entities, where there is a hierarchical capacity between these entities. This method is called AMOMCASYS (meaning the Adaptable Modelling Method for Complex Administrative Systems, it is completely described in [1]). This method has already been used for the modelling and design of MAS intended to help actors in human organizations [2].

An extract of the treatment model resulting from this method is given in Fig. 3. It shows an extract of a cooperative activity within a CIASTEWA. The user defines a request to its CIASTEWA through the interface agent. The interface agent forwards the request to the coordinator agent which checks if the request exists in the group request database. If the request does not exist, it is recorded in the user's request database and a message is sent to the agent responsible for information. This message asks it to execute the requests which have not yet been carried out. For that, the agent creates or forwards the request to the information agent. If the request exists and has been defined by another user, a message is sent to the CIASTEWA of this user in order to get the information.

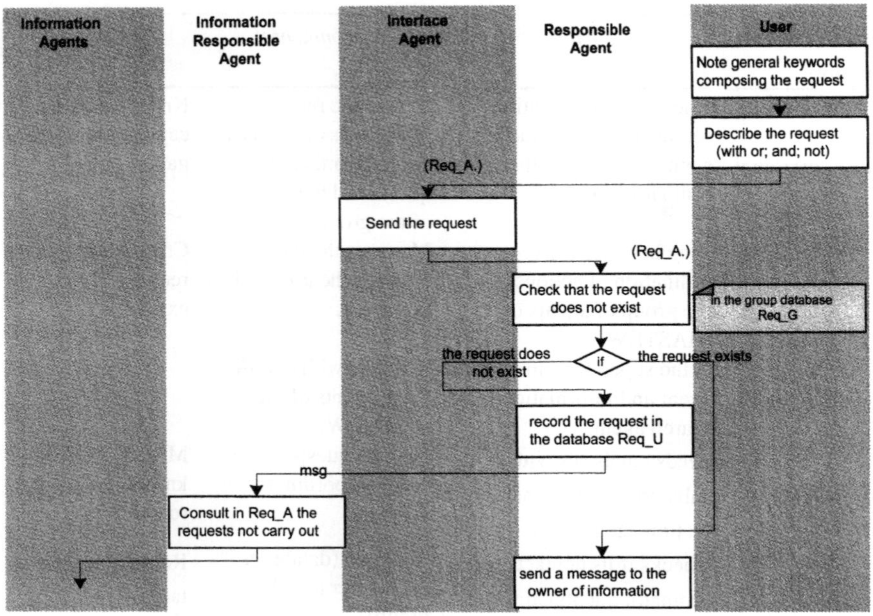

Figure 3. Extract of a cooperative activity of a CIASTEWA

So the AMOMCASYS method is interesting because it allows the integration of users in the specification phase, not only on the model, but also practically during the setting up of the system. Actually, the models used were chosen for their accessibility to a wide "public", that is to say, not only to the computer scientist. So, future users will be able to give their opinions and make comments on the future working of the system. Thanks to the AMOMCASYS, we have defined other interactions between users and agents of the Cooperative Information Agents System for Cooperative Technological Watch, such as the automatic search for information and its management by each actor (which implies an interaction between users by the sending of mail) for example.

4. APPLICATION

Our work is applied in watch cells composed of a restricted number of actors (about five watchmen). Their goal is to make relevant information available to the decision makers in order to guide them in the decision-making process. Actors of these cells have to search for and gather "rough" information coming from different sources (company personnel, the Internet, the media, a personal network...). They then have to classify the information according to topics (market, product, competition) suitable for the company in order to make this information available to a targeted public. In agreement with the watchmen, it was decided to place information agents at the head of the watch procedure. The goal of these agents is to carry out search, gathering and primary filtering operations. In order to obtain a prototype rapidly, all the components of the CIASTEWA were merged into one agent with three roles (Fig. 4): the role of user interface; the role of coordinator and the role of agent responsible for information.

The search engines play the role of the information agents queried by the main agent. A first prototype, built in visual basic, is currently being used in a small competitive intelligence service of a large company. It allows the automatic search and comparison of results and makes the communication of information between users easier. Personally, we use a Java version of this prototype that is currently being set up in the department with the help of a small computer company.

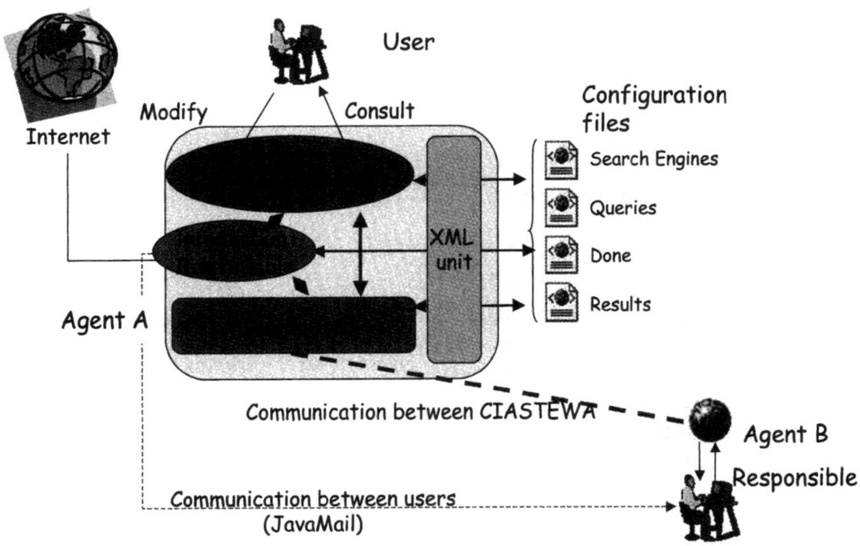

Figure 4. Architecture of our prototype.

5. CONCLUSION AND PERSPECTIVES

In order to specify a co-operative information agent system for co-operative technological watch, we re-used a particular organisational approach: holonic systems. This approach enabled us to obtain a distribution of knowledge and roles providing a good compromise between the reactivity of the information search system and the management of coherence in the results given. Thanks to the AMOMCASYS method, which was built to model complex administrative systems (in which actors have different levels of responsibility, and exchange information), we have modelled interactions between agents and between users and agents. In our prototype, which is currently being used in a small competitive intelligence service, the functionality proposed in this article has not been totally developed. So, we are developing a more complete CIASCOTEWA using Java language in order to obtain a system able to adapt itself to the user and to the result obtained by the information agent. In order to obtain a better degree of reactivity, the CIASCOTEWA should be composed of a set of agents according to the holonic concept we have described.

REFERENCES

[1] Adam, E., *Modèle d'organisation multi-agent pour l'aide au travail coopératif dans les processus d'entreprise : application aux systèmes administratifs complexes*, Ph.D. thesis, Université de Valenciennes et du Hainaut-Cambrésis, 2000.

[2] Adam, E., *Specifications of intelligent human-machine interfaces for helping cooperation in human-organizations*, in H.-J. Bullinger and J. Ziegler (eds.), Ergonomics and user interfaces,Proc. of HCI International'99, Vol. 1, Lawrence Erlbaum Associates, Mahwah, 1999, pp. 311-315.

[3] Adam, E., Mandiau, R., and Kolski, C., *Application of a holonic multi-agent system for cooperative work to administrative processes*, Journal of Applied Systems Studies, Vol. 2, No. 1, 2001, pp. 100-115.

[4] Arai, T., Aiyama, Y., and Sasaki, Y., *Holonic Storage: an assembly and storage cell by manipulation using environment*, in New Manufacturing Era - Adaptation to Environment, Culture, Intelligence and Complexity, Proceedings of the 29th CIRP International Seminar on Manufacturing Systems (Osaka, 1997), 1997, pp. 221-226.

[5] Brajnik, G., Guida, G., Tasso, C., *User Modeling in Expert Man-Machine Interfaces: a Case Study in Intelligent Information Retrieval*, IEEE Transactions on SMC, Vol. 20, No. 1, 1990, pp. 166-185.

[6] Ferber, J., *Les systèmes multi-agents, Vers une intelligence collective*, InterEditions, Paris, 1995.

[7] Gerber, C., Siekmann, J., and Vierke, G., *Holonic Multi-Agent Systems*, Research report RR-99-03, DFKI GmbH, March 1999.

[8] Jakobiak, F., *L'information scientifique et technique*, PUF, Paris, 1995.

[9] Koestler, A., *The Ghost in the Machine*, Arkana Books, London, 1969.

[10] Nwana, H.S., *Software Agent: an overview*, Knowledge Engineering Review, Vol. 11, No. 3, 1996, pp. 205-244.

[11] Shardanand, U. and Maes, P., *Social information filtering: algorithms for automating word of mouth*, in Proceedings of ACM Conf. on Human factors in computing systems CHI'95 (Denver, 7-11 May 1995), ACM Press, New York, 1995, pp. 210-217.

[12] Van Brussel, H., Valckenaers, P., Wyns J., Bongaerts, L., and Detand, J., *Holonic Manufacturing Systems and IMS*, in J. Browne *et al.* (eds.), IT and Manufacturing Partnerships, IOS Press, 1996, pp. 185-196.

[13] Young, M.J., *Human Error and the holon cognitive architecture*, in Proc. of 6th Symposium on analysis, design and evaluation of Man-Machine systems, MIT Press, Cambridge, 1995.

Chapter 32

A MULTI-AGENT APPROACH TO CO-OPERATIVE WORK

Jean-Christophe Routier and Philippe Mathieu
Laboratoire d'Informatique Fondamentale de Lille, CNRS UPRESA 8022 – Bâtiment M3
Cité Scientifique, F-59655 Villeneuve d'Ascq Cedex (France)
E-mail: {routier, mathieu}@lifl.fr – URL: http://www.lifl.fr/~ {routier,mathieu}
Tel.: +33-3-20 43 45 04 – Fax: +33-3-20 43 65 66

Abstract This paper presents a multi-agent approach for user interface design of co-operative applications. We show here that this approach provides advantages from multi-agent researches about intelligence and modeling. It allows the designer to develop more easily the user interface of his application. Two different aspects are improved: first, the management of the interactions between components of the interface and second, the interactions between the user and the application, in particular thanks to intelligent assistants. Moreover, an agent oriented analysis of the problem highlights the different role and skills and thus eases the programmer task and the evolution capacity of the application. To illustrate our purpose, we present a co-operative work application built with our multi-agent development framework, called MAGIQUE. The main goal of this article is not really to present a groupware application but rather to show how it can be easily developed, maintained and extended thanks to MAGIQUE and its multi-agent approach.

Keywords: Agent based design, Collaboration, Co-operative work, Interaction of humans and agents, User-interface applications design.

1. INTRODUCTION

For many years, many researchers and industrials have worked on working group applications [1,2,4,5]. It is indeed more and more necessary to provide tools that give to physically remote people the possibility to work together, to communicate, to exchange documents and to present their information to the other members of the distributed team. Now, we must re-

C. Kolski and J. Vanderdonckt (eds.), Computer-Aided Design of User Interfaces III, 367–380.
© 2002 *Kluwer Academic Publishers.*

mark that the few available tools offer only some of these functions. This is probably due to the fact that the existing tools are difficult to apprehend and moreover difficult to extend, mainly because of the diversity of the new idea to be added to the software. Simultaneously these last years, works on multi-agent model [6,8] have been put into concrete form through the realization of development platforms [7,9]. These platforms offer tools specially fitted to the modular conception of multi-skilled applications as those previously mentioned. Indeed, the properties of reactivity and proactivity of agents allow a slender and evolutive development of such applications. Moreover, the interpretation in terms of roles and skills of the capabilities of agents eases the analysis work and its decomposition.

This article presents a co-operative application based on the multi-agent platform called MAGIQUE (read [11] for another example of the use of multi-agent in groupware). The objective of this application is to provide to the user the possibility to exchange slide-like information, to all its collaborators. The analysis highlights two kinds of role: the teacher or *speaker* and the students or *listeners*. The difference between these roles is determined by the fact that the *speaker* holds the unique remote control. This allows him to spread slides to listeners and listeners can claim to the remote control. At a given moment there is only one speaker, but holder of this role can change during the conference in order to allow a former listener to show his slides. Some other tools, useful to documents manipulation, are provided too.

The building of this application is based on the multi-agent system (MAS) development platform called MAGIQUE. MAGIQUE is primarily a system to build MAS distributed on a heterogeneous network. MAGIQUE uses the skill notion, and in MAGIQUE, everything is a skill [9]. Then, to be (ie. play the role of) a listener is a skill, as well as the remote control. MAGIQUE offers some important features to manage and exchange these skills, then it is very easy to give the remote control from a user to another through the skill exchange. That means that the changes in the roles of the agents is not a trivial flag placed in source code but there is an effective dynamic evolution of the agents capabilities and then of the roles. Moreover, since an agent can have as many skills as it wants, it is easy to add new functions to the system to adapt it to some new required features. For example, we will present in the following an *assistant* skill to the user agents, this was not present in the first version but had been added with no impact on what was existing, only by creating the new skills and plugging them to the agents. This assistant is a proactive and reactive "intelligent" entity that helps the user in its management of the co-operative work and then allows him to better contribute to the conference. This assistant provides also a model of the other members of the conferences since it determines their expertise fields.

The main goal of this article is not really to present a groupware application but overall to show how this, thanks to multi-agent approach and the MAGIQUE platform, can be easily designed, maintained and extend. In a first part we will present the application and its functions, and particularly the assistant. Then after a brief presentation of MAGIQUE, we will describe the principles of the design of such an application using MAGIQUE.

2. THE SLIDE-CONFERENCE APPLICATION

The aim of this co-operative work application is to provide a framework that gives the possibility of a conference between geographically remote people.

Each of the members has a set of document resources ("*slides*") that he wants to spread to the others. He can do that if and only if he is the owner of the (unique) *remote control* which is associated to the application. This control allows him to browse and spread his resources. Moreover, it plays also the role of a "pointer" that the speaker can use to attract the other users attention on a particular point of the currently displayed document.

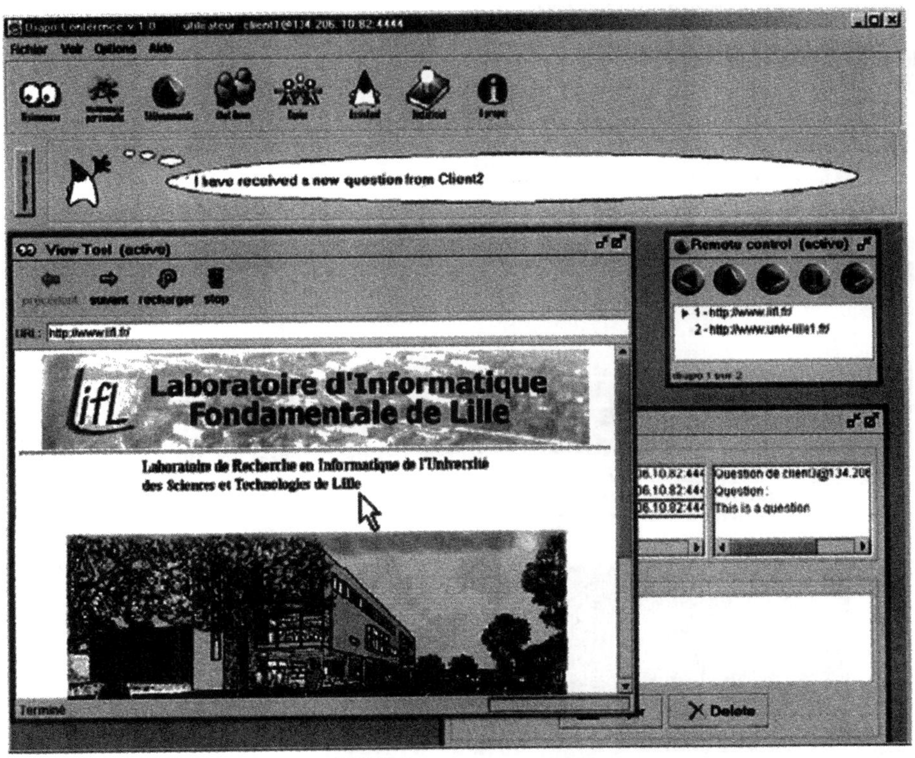

Figure 1. A speaker side view...

This pointer can be seen in real time simultaneously by every users. Two *roles* can be distinguished in this application: the one of *speaker*, plaid by the control holder, and the one of *listener*, for the all other members. Like in a real conference (we mean where all the audience is gathered in the same place), the speaker can, at any time, give the control to one of the listeners and then the respective roles of the two users evolved dynamically. We have particularly bring attention to the similarity with real conferences, since this should ease the user to apprehend such an application.

Fig. 1 and 2 give a look on the application from the speaker and listener points of view. It is possible to distinguish different tools on the two images: the view tool on the left side of the screens (you can notice that the dimensions are the same in the two views), the mouse pointer that can be viewed in the speaker window is represented by a large dot in the listener one (In the two screenshot figures pointers have been enlarged to highlight them). Some other tools such as the remote control (which is "active" for the speaker and "passive" for the listener), the team management and messages windows, and the assistant (here it makes an announce in the speaker window and you can notice the two different kind of presentations, the top one with an animated character and the bottom one with a most recent messages list.) at the top of each screen are visible too.

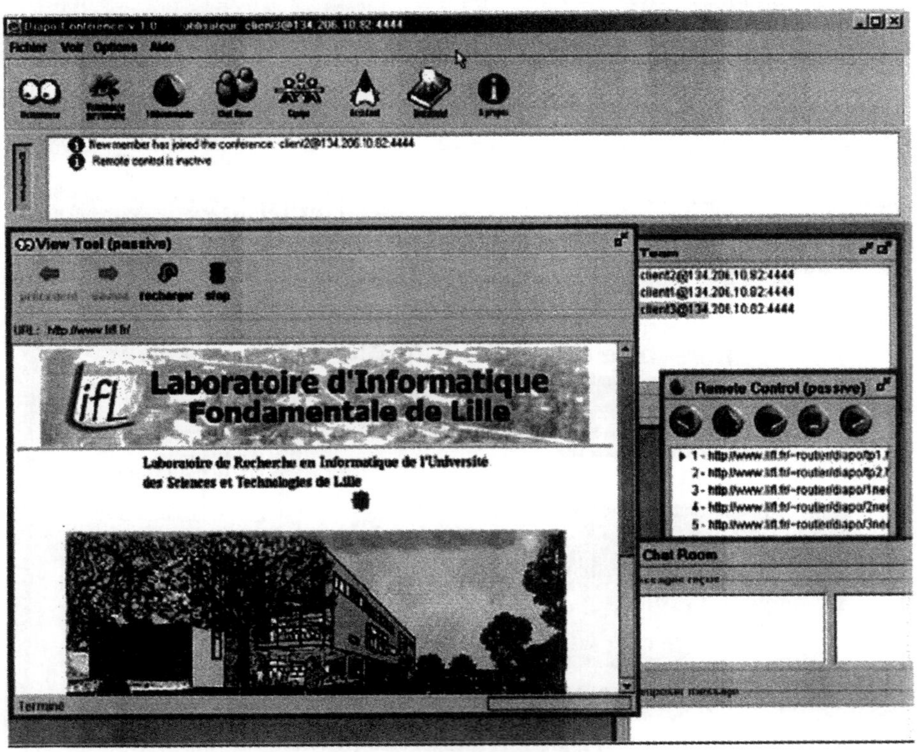

Figure 2. … and the corresponding listener side view.

2.1 Basic Functions

In the prototype, resources are designed by URL. The advantage of such a format is clear. It allows to represent different kinds of documents (texts, images, sounds, video, etc.). Moreover, it allows to benefit of the browsing capabilities due to hyperlinks, as well as to dispose of dynamic document thanks to applet for example. Each user has his own resources and he can gather and organize them in order to build a structured lecture. In order to afford the conference, the two essential tools are the *view tool* and the *remote control*.

The view tool. Each participant has a medium to view resources (in our case it is a URL browser). The speaker has the control over the interactions of this tool for all the audience. The views in the different tools are fully synchronized with his own and the WYSIWIS [10] principle is applied here. Thus, the mouse pointer in his browser can be seen by all the listeners, so he can insist on some particular point of the slide (Fig. 1 and 2). In the same way, the speaker controls the size of and the scrolling in all the viewer tools.

The remote control. The second essential function is of course the remote control. It is active for the speaker and passive for the listeners. At any moment, a listener can ask for the control, and this is the speaker who has the choice to give it or not to him. Its first role, when it is active, is to allow to spread a document to all the audience or to automatically browse a slides sequence. In reality, the speaker side transmits to the members the URL address of the document that he proposes. The view tool of each listeners is responsible of the downloading of the applications and of its interpretation. The remote control provides also some tools that allow to gather and to organize documents.

2.2 Tools that Help Co-operation

Adding to the minimal functions presented above, the application offers some other tools that promote the co-operation and the awareness of the other listeners. Let us cite three of them: the audience "visualization", an assistant and a message system. We will present them briefly.

2.2.1 The Members Window

The first tool goal is to highlight for the user the fact that he is not alone. The list of the members can be seen in a window where the current speaker is clearly identified. The need to concretize a "global awareness" is a well known problem in CSCW [3]. The request for the control can be done from this tool. The different requests made by the different listeners, as well as their “oldness”, can be viewed by all. The names of the requesters are highlighted and this effect vanishes slowly with time. Interest is twofold. First, the speaker can directly see from how long a request has been made, and he can, for example, consider that a request is too old and then is no more appropriate. Second, from the listener point of view, he can hesitate to make a request when he sees that a lot of requests have already been made (this is like the number of raised fingers in an assembly).

2.2.2 The Assistant

A second tool is provided to allow to everyone to bring a better contribution to the co-operation. It is an *assistant* who, obviously, must ease the use of the tool by the user. It is possible to cite three main roles for this assistant: highlighting of events, helping to participate to the co-operation, modeling the other members for future collaborations.

Highlighting Events The distributed nature of the application implies that it is necessary to emphasize some events that would have been more easily detected in a real conference. As an example we can cite the incoming/outcoming of members, the change of the speaker, the sent messages (Fig. 3),... The contextualization, according to the mentioned events, of the graphical interface of the assistant helps the user by leading him to the concerned tool. Thus this function contributes to ease the use of the application.

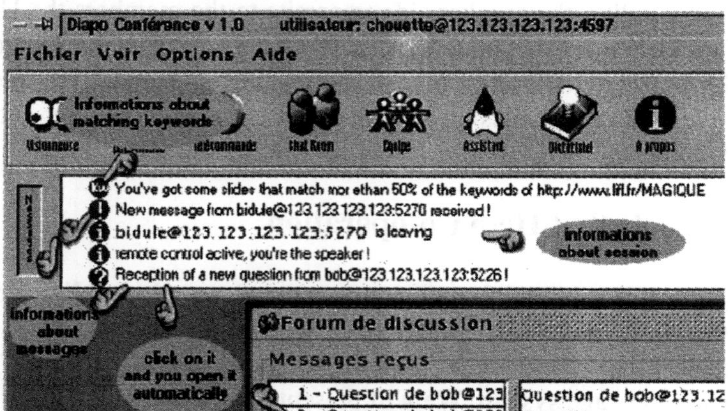

Figure 3. Events mentioned by the assistant.

Helping Co-operation “reactions”, one of them provides an help to the cooperation emergence. Indeed, during a slide-conference, the assistant will help the listener user to bring its tribute to the conference. Each time a new slides is proposed by the speaker, the assistant warns the listener if it has in its resource base, a document which is correlated to the currently diffused one. Then the assistant proposes to the user to preview this (or these) selected document(s) so that he can judge by himself of the pertinence to propose it. Then the listener can ask the control to become the speaker, but it can also simply ask to his assistant to transmit this document to the current speaker assistant. Thus the speaker assistant warns its user that a listener has proposed a document and this one can chose to spread it or not. In the current version, the decision process of the assistant is based on keywords that must have been given in the resources. The assistant explores the user resource base and wakes up each time there is sufficient matching keywords. The correlation criteria can be changed by the user.

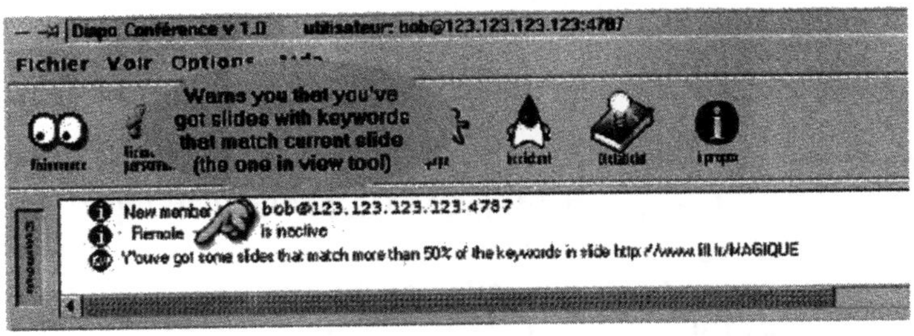

Figure 4. The assistant warns me that I have correlated resources.

Modeling other members can have another use and be exploited differently by the assistant user. It is indeed possible, for every proposed resource, to note the keywords and thus to build step by step an image of the expertise domains of the speaker, but also of the domains of interest of the listeners. Thus from conference to conference, a model of the members can be done. This knowledge can then be used to facilitate the creation of new conferences: experts can be invited to bring their contribution and interested listeners to attend it. This information could be used outside of the conference context too, when the user needs an information on a particular domain, then he can ask to its assistant if a skilled person is known.

2.2.3 The Message System

At last, a message system allows the listener to ask question to the speaker (and only to him). This last can broadcast a message (an announce or the answer to a question) to all the audience.

3. REALIZATION

We have briefly presented in the previous section the offered functions of this slide conference application. The problem of the well fitted tools that can be used to develop such an application arises. We claim that the use of a multiagent development framework, and as an example of the MAGIQUE platform,

form, eases the realization of such applications. The advantages of a multi-agent development environment like MAGIQUE is that it provides all the functions for the distribution and all the mechanisms for the communications between agents. This allows the programmer to get rid of all these problems and thus to concentrate on the purely applicative problems. In this case, it consists of the delegation to the agents of the management of the different parts of the application, thus several agents can be used for one client.

We will present *quickly* the MAGIQUE multi-agent platform before to show how it can be used to develop the conference application.

3.1 MAS: MAGIQUE

MAGIQUE means "hierarchical multi-agent" ("Multi-AGent hiérarchIQUE" in French, see http://www.lifl.fr/SMAC, MAGIQUE topic). MAGIQUE proposes a hierarchical organization of multi-agent systems (MAS). This structure provides a mechanism to delegate the exploitation of the skills of the other agents, and thus eases the programming task. MAGIQUE has been put into concrete form through an API JAVA that allows to develop hierarchical distributed MAS. Thus MAGIQUE is a framework that frees the programmer from the distribution and agent communication problems. MAGIQUE can be used to do different kinds of multi-agent applications: auction system with buyer agents with different strategies and one seller agent, exploration of a unknown territory by several agents, multi-player games with one referee agent and several player agents, etc.

3.2 Agents, Skills and Hierarchies

In MAGIQUE, an agent is an entity gifted with some skills. These skills give to the agent the possibility to play a *role* in a multi-agent application. The skills of an agent can dynamically evolved (through exchange with other agents) while the agent lives. This implies that the roles that it can play in a MAS, can evolve too. In fact, an agent is dynamically build from an atomic "empty" agent through the learning of its skills. From the programming point of view, a skill can be seen as a software component that groups a coherent set of functions. The skills can thus be developed independently from any agent. Once the skills are created, the building of a MAGIQUE agent is simply made by a "plugging" like mechanism of these skills (this the agent education phase). Thus it is easy to add new functions to a MAS application.

All the agents are grouped into a MAS which is organized according to a hierarchical structure that constitutes the default acquaintance links between the agents. Thus a hierarchical link means that there is bi-directional communication channel between the two agents. Thus when two agents from the same hierarchy communicate, the path, followed by the message they exchange, maps to the hierarchy. The organization of the agents can evolved dynamically if a re-organization of the MAS structure is required during the use. This hierarchical organization provides an easy mechanism of delegation between agents inside a given MAS. An agent has a task to achieve, this task requires the exploitation of some skills that the agent can or cannot own. In the both cases, but the "invocation" of the skills by the agent will be done in the same way in MAGIQUE. That the realization of some subtask will be delegated to some other agent will be hidden and taken into account by the hierarchy. The consequence is that, an agent that must delegate some skill realization, does not need to explicitly known the agent who will perform it, the organization has the responsibility to find it for him. It is a main difference with the "distributed objects" approach: the receiver of a message is not necessarily named and "who does what" is not necessarily known, the MAS takes this in charge. Thus, interactions between skills is automatically performed, when one skill S_1 needs to interact with another skill S_2, whether S_2 is or not known by the agent that has "invoked" S_1 is transparently managed by MAGIQUE. Even if the set of skills known by the agent evolved, this evolution is taken into account.

One advantage of this delegation is from the programming point of view. It is not required to explicitly know the (name of the) agents that will be present in the application. The references are located at the skill level, and it suffices for the programmer to know that a skill will be present in the MAS, without necessarily knowing the skilled agent. A consequence is, that when designing a MAS, the important point is not really the agents themselves but the skills. Therefore it is more easy to reuse the code. Moreover, the MAS application is more robust since the skilled agent not being necessarily defined, it is possible that for a given skill, this agent changes with time (if an agent disappear from MAS, or becomes unavailable or overloaded for example).

3.3 The Realization

To design a MAS, we need to determinate the implied agents and the skills of each, then to define the organization (or structure) of the MAS and the possible interactions.

3.3.1 Analysis

In a first step, the required roles must be clearly identified as well as the skills corresponding to these roles. The definition of a multi-agent methodology based on the skill/role/interaction principles is the purpose of one of our current project. Nevertheless, a methodology like the one presented in [12] can be used.

The Roles. We have already clearly identified two of these roles for our conference application: the *speaker* and the *listener* roles. However there exists a third roles that we have not yet explicitly named. Indeed, it is necessary for the conference to happen, that the members can join (and leave) it. Therefore an entity is required to make the link between all the participants. We will name "*co-ordinator*" this role. But it can be seen as the *environment*, classical in MAS, since it constitutes the support for the interactions and since it gives a shape to the co-presence of the members of the conference.

The Skills. For the *co-ordinator* role, the corresponding skills are rather limited. It suffices to provide to the other agents an entry point to the conference and to maintain the coherence in case of departure (particularly if the speaker is leaving the session, it is necessary to find a new speaker and to give him the remote control). The skills are quite the same for the speaker and listener roles. They correspond to the functions described in the first part of the article. To describe them quickly: the view skill is used to download, to interpret and to display the resources, to manage the pointer and the mouse event on the windows; the members window allows to manage the control request as well as its exchange; the message system contributes to allow the exchange between the members with the respect of the status of speaker and listener, thus this skill must be sensible to the role context; theassistant provides the functions to help the co-operation and to model the other members as mentioned above.

Last, for the two roles, we still have to treat the case of the skill that manages the *remote control*. This skill must provide the possibility: for the *speaker*: to lead the conference (document presentation, pointer management and the visualization area); and for both roles: to manage the resources and to organize document sequences. The case of this skill is particularly interesting, since it creates the difference between the two main roles. The dynamic evolution of roles during a session (from *speaker* to *listener* and conversely) implies a dynamic evolution of the skill known by agents. It is indeed necessary to give to a new speaker the functions to lead a conference, and to take them out from the former speaker.

3.3.2 The Choice of the MAS Organization

As it has been mentioned, the MAGIQUE multi-agent framework has been used to develop the prototype. Each member of the conference is defined by an agent that represents him, one of this agent will have the *speaker* role and the others will be the *listeners* (Fig. 5). We have decided to create an additional particular agent to play the *co-ordinate* role (even if this role could have plaid by some other agent, the initiator of the conference for example, or could even dynamically change).

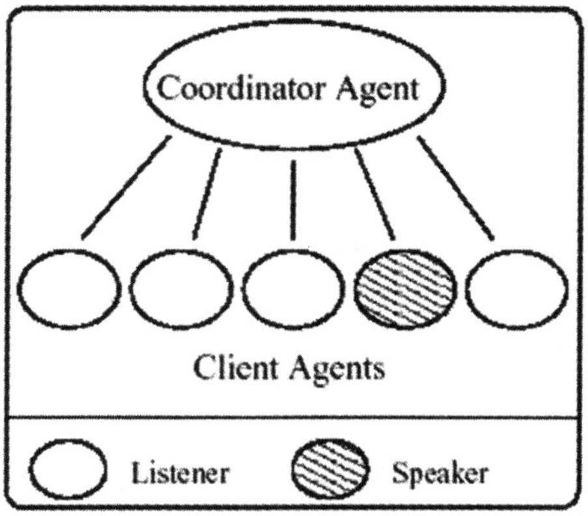

Figure 5. Hierarchical organization of the MAS.

We have explained that MAS in MAGIQUE are hierarchically organized. In this case, we have chosen to locate the *co-ordinate* agent at the root of the hierarchy and all the other agents at the lower level. Let us note that it would have been possible to locate the *speaker* agent at the root, this would have implied a reorganization of the hierarchy when roles change. This can be one with MAGIQUE. The dynamical evolution of the roles *speakerlistener* is easily managed with MAGIQUE. Indeed, this platform offers the advantage to allow the dynamic evolution of the skills of the agents, through exchange. In MAGIQUE, the agents learn and forget effectively their skills. The exchanges of skills are effective, independently of any assumption on the code of the skills and of the distribution of the agents over the network. The *speaker* agent will then be able, as the microphone is physically given during a real conference, to give the remote control skill to the new *speaker* and therefore to lose it (Fig. 6).

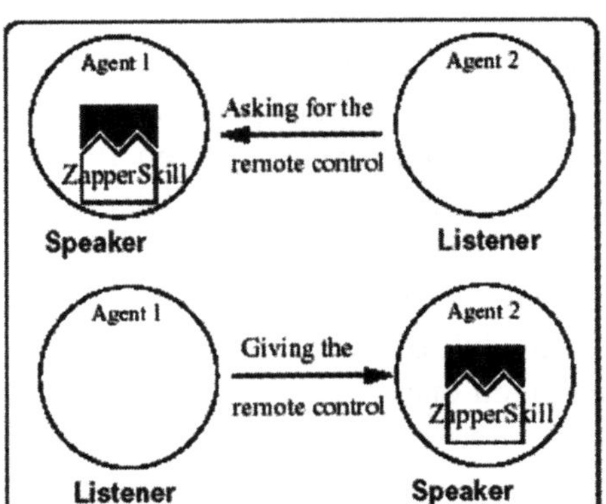

Figure 6. Dynamical evolution of roles through skill exchange.

And it is not here a simple modification in the value of an attribute but of a real concrete alteration of the agent and of the role it plays, and therefore in a way of its right over the application.

3.3.3 The Programming

To realize this application with MAGIQUE, it "suffices" to develop the different skills mentioned previously. Each represents a component. Once the interface of the skill has been defined, it must be implemented by JAVA objects, the sole difference that must be taken into account is the need to do interactions with the agents and the different other skills. We have already seen previously that this is easily done thanks to the delegation mechanism and primitive for delegation are provided.

The independence between skills provides independence between the different components. The possibility with MAGIQUE to make unnamed requests allows to have a more functional view of the different aspects of the applications.

The roles/skills interact without needing to have an explicit knowledge of each other. This eases development and possibility of evolutions. Once you have the skills, the agent building is very easy. You just have to "teach" to the atomic agent the required skills one by one.

Then the MAGIQUE layer manages the connection of agents and the communications due to interactions between agents. These communications do not explicitly appear in the code since they are implied by the skill invocations and interactions and thus taken in charge by MAGIQUE.

3.4 Evolution and Adaptivity

The skill notion eases the evolution of the application and its adaptation to different contexts. Thus it is possible to easily extend the offered functions through the creation of new skills that you just have to "teach" to the agents.

Thus it is possible to consider an incremental building of the applications. For example, a skill allowing to transport the voice could thus have been added to ease the information exchange, and this would have no consequence over the rest of the application. The adaptation to different supports or different kind of resources can also be easily obtained. For example, if one of the listeners want to use the application on a personal assistant, he can adapt the visualization skill by "teaching" to his agent the correct view tool skill instead of the default one.

To give one last example to illustrate that such an application developed with MAGIQUE is open, it is easy to consider to adapt the assistant for each of the users. For example, different strategies to determinate the correlation of the resources can be considered, or even different criteria to model the other members of the conference.

4. CONCLUSION

Through the presentation of an application for distributed conference, we have shown how the use of a multi-agent framework like MAGIQUE eases the development of a co-operative application and its user interface. The use of such a platform allows to get rid of the problems due to the distribution and to the communications, thanks to the "normal" interactions of agents. Moreover, the incremental building of the agents in MAGIQUE, through dynamical skill learning, eases the programming and the evolutivity of the application. The prototype application provides the support for co-operation and tools to help it. These are tools essential like the view tool and the remote control. This last is the central tool since its possession defines the role of each member and its exchange implies the dynamic evolution of the roles. Some additional tools are provided also. They are essential too: the team management, the capability to organize resources, or the message system. Last, the assistant allows a better exploitation of the resources when they are correlated to the current one. This assistant allows to model the co-members of the conferences and thus eases future co-operation. This prototype, and a tutorial, can be downloaded at: http://www.lifl.fr/SMAC topic MAGIQUE

ACKNOWLEDGMENTS

We would like to thank the anonymous referees for their helpful comments.

REFERENCES

[1] Baecker, R. (ed.), *Readings in groupware and computer supported cooperative work.* Morgan Kaufman, San Francisco, 1993.

[2] Beaudouin-Lafon, M. (ed.), *Computer-Supported Cooperative Work*, John Wiley Sons Ltd., New York, 1998.

[3] Brinck, T. and McDaniel, S., *CHI'97 Workshop on awareness in collaborative systems,* in Proc. of ACM Conf. on Human Factors in Computing Systems CHI'97, position papers accesible http://www.usabilityfirst.com/groupware/awareness/

[4] Derycke, A. and Hoogstoel, F., *Le travail coopératif assisté par ordinateur : quels enjeux pour les concepteurs,* in Actes du XIIIme Congrès INFORSID (INFormatique des ORganisations et Systèmes d'Information et de Décision), Grenoble, 1995.

[5] Ellis, C., Gibbs, S., and Rein, G., *Groupware: some issues and experiences*, Communications of the ACM, Vol. 34, No. 1, 1991, pp. 38-58.

[6] Ferber, J. and Gutknecht, O., *A meta-model for the analysis and design of organizations in multi-agent systems*, in Proceedings of ICMAS'98, IEEE Computer Society Press, Los Alamitos, 1998.

[7] Gutknecht, O., Ferber, J., and Michel, F., *Madkit: une plateforme multi-agent générique*, Technical report, FIPA, 2000.

[8] Jennings, N., Sycara, K., and Woolridge, M., *A roadmap of agent research and development*, Journal of Autonomous Agents and Multi-Agent Systems, Vol. 1, 1998, pp. 275-306.

[9] Routier, J., Mathieu, P., and Secq, Y., *Dynamic skill learning: A support to agent evolution*, in Proceedings of the AISB'01 Symposium, 2001, pp. 25-32.

[10] Stefik, M., Bobrow, D., Foster, G., Lanning, S., and Tatar, D., *Wysiwis revised: Early experiences with multi-user interfaces*, ACM Transactions on Office Information Systems, Vol. 5, No. 2, 1987, pp. 147-167.

[11] Tarpin-Bernard, F. and David, B., *Amf: un modèle d'architecture multi-agents multi-facettes*, Techniques et Sciences Informatiques, Hermès, Vol. 18, No. 5, 1999, pp. 555-586.

[12] Wooldridge, M., Jennings, N., and Kinny, D., *The gaia methodology for agent-oriented analysis and design*, Journal of Autonomous Agents and Multi-Agent Systems, Vol. 3, No. 3, 2000, pp. 285-312.

Chapter 33

AGENT ORIENTED SPECIFICATION OF INTERACTIVE SYSTEMS: BASIC PRINCIPLES AND INDUSTRIAL CASE STUDY

Francois Cartegnie, Houcine Ezzedine, and Christophe Kolski
LAMIH - UMR CNRS 8530, Université de Valenciennes et du Hainaut Cambrésis, F–59313 Valenciennes Cedex 9 (France)
E-mail: {francois.cartegnie, houcine.ezzedine, christophe.kolski}@univ-valenciennes.fr
URL: http://www.univ-valenciennes.fr/LAMIH/
Tel.: +33-3-27 51 {1262, 1469} - Fax: +33-3-27 51 13 16

Abstract Several methods and models for interactive system specification can be found in research literature. An agent-oriented approach inspired by Multi-Agent Systems (MAS) is proposed and discussed in relation to its value for UI design. This approach is currently being tested as part of a project which aims to design a supervision system used by regulators of a public transport system.

Keywords: Agent oriented specification, Multi-Agent Systems (MAS), Supervision system, UI specification.

1. INTRODUCTION

Common specification approaches often do not fulfil the needs of designers as regards the architectural aspects; UI specification in a multi-agent perspective can bring some answers in this field. Current methods and models offer different ways to describe a system, each applying different focuses and scopes: cognitive methods and models provide an abstract representation level which identifies modules, describes the actions used in the interaction with the user and their location in the main interactive process; at the architectural level, other models describe the way of implementing the UI on the target system. Despite the fact that they are well-known in research literature, it is useful to summarise their basic principles in order to gain a better comprehension of the proposed agent-based specification.

C. Kolski and J. Vanderdonckt (eds.), Computer-Aided Design of User Interfaces III, 381–389.
© 2002 *Kluwer Academic Publishers.*

1.1 Cognitive Methods and Models

Cognitive methods and models build a specification from determined user tasks. They are used to identify action sequences based upon user strategies and alternatives. The dialogue required between UI and user can then be determined. For instance, the CLG Model [11] offers a multi-layer abstract view of the user task model: three main layers (Conceptual, Dialog and Physical), each one divided in sub-layers. Other approaches are based on a break-down of the task from global strategies to atomic actions, opposed to the vertical decomposition of the CLG model, such as the GOMS model and the MAD and DIANE methods. GOMS [3] describes tasks, from the identified goals to the operators (actions) in their methods, through alternatives. DIANE [1] is a method derived from the MERISE software engineering method, which also describes tasks following a model with different layers (organization, procedure description, task description). These methods and models show that user dialog can be layered and that a minimal, invariant task-relative action sequence can be determined. Furthermore, new languages are appearing, such as XML-based languages applied to UI in order to provide flexibility and portability in the description: see, for instance, UIML (User Interface Mark-up Language) [10] and XUL (XML-based User Interface Language [13]). By the use of style-sheets, integrated scripting language and integrated UI data, they successfully provide a platform non-dependant UI, in which syntactic and lexical levels can be dealt with independently by the designers.

1.2 Architectural Models

These models are used to specify the software structuring which will be used in order to implement the UI. Specification concepts are applied at this point, and these depend on the characteristics of the model chosen. The most common way to proceed, offering modularity, extendibility and maintainability is using modules. Seeheim [14] and ARCH [2] are well-known models. The Seeheim principles consist in separating the UI into three levels (presentation, dialogue controller, application). The ARCH model develops Seeheim by adding intermediate levels which are used as adaptation components for the implementation language. One weakness of these models is that they are unable to describe parallelism which can occur in the UI [5]. Using a model based on agents, such as PAC, PAC-Amodeus and MVC, solves this problem. For instance, PAC [4] and PAC-Amodeus [12] are based on a hierarchical separation of the system into autonomous entities. Each entity is based on three components: the *Presentation* contains the interactive elements; the *Abstraction* contains data and methods for accessing the application; the *Control* is used for passing data through other entities, for conversions, communications and synchronisations. PAC-Amodeus uses the PAC architecture in the ARCH dialogue controller and aims to offer the same modularity and parallelism as with PAC. Domain adapters are present to make uniform concepts, which previously brought inconsistency because of their distribution. These models show that a layered UI structure is needed and PAC integrates this principle into a modular construction. Current UI architectures are built on a hierarchical relation between components, which are to be found in current object-oriented toolboxes. Another fact is that the PAC architecture does not use the potential of agents to the full. Modularity is not really conserved in the control components which still have to rely on the other components of the same family. Our approach uses a MAS to build an UI, using the agent properties and abilities to the full.

2. AGENT ORIENTED SPECIFICATION

There is no unique definition of the agent [9,15]. Besides the agent definition applied to UI architectures in [4,5,12], we will also consider the definition provided in [15] which identifies 4 key properties: (1) autonomy in relation to the user and the environment, (2) collaborative ability, negotiation and communication with other agents, (3) reactivity in relation to the environment, and (4) proactive behaviour influenced by own specific goals. The common principle of MAS consists of the coordination of cooperative entities in order to reach a common goal. In an UI, a simple common objective would be to allow the users to perform their task, i.e. allowing them to carry out their action sequence and returning information when necessary.

2.1 Agent Organisation

Taking our inspiration from the PAC agent layering, we can define three types of agents: firstly, the *application agent*, which handles application data and methods, which are only accessible to other UI agents. They will capture events from the application and dispatch them to other agents in such a way as to give the information required in the cooperative work of the UI agents. This information will relate the context of the process controlled by the application. Secondly, we define *interactive agents* which are directly in contact with the user. Each interactive agent has its own interaction mode: i.e. it sends data and/or capture commands. These interaction modes can be graphical UI with dialog boxes, windows, bar graphs, or they can be audio and voice recognition modules, and so on. Finally, we define *control agents*.

They are the link between application and interactive agents. Their role consists in synchronizing dialogue elements. Data conversion and command translation in communications are performed, along with the dispatching of roles to agents related to current events. With the aim of obtaining an interactive MAS, we can also define the users viewed as agents: they have their own interaction modes, cooperative ability, knowledge and needs.

2.2 Agent Coordination

Agent coordination must be carried out in such a way so as to obtain a behaviour similar to a traditionally implemented UI. This is done by extracting the user action sequences, with which the agents can cooperatively find the current user task and/or strategy, from the identified tasks. It is possible to extract a minimal action sequence, composed of invariant actions. Agent local knowledge is not sufficient and environmental knowledge is required.

Two types of agent behaviour can be identified: behaviour with *global* objectives, intended for the cooperative execution of goals; behaviour with *local* objectives, which for interactive agents is the local interaction resulting from the user action and for application agents is the calling of application methods, event handling and data exchange; the various knowledge levels (cooperative or local) will be defined by analysing the user tasks and extracting the invariants in these schemes.

2.3 Multi-Agent Architecture

It is often useful to select a UI architecture model which will offer a higher modularity level in order to avoid the software dependencies that could be engendered. Our approach uses the functional and structural principles of the MAS and the PAC architecture.

An agent will be composed of the following components: from the PAC architecture, a decomposition into layers (Abstraction, Control, Presentation); from the MAS domain, communication ability based on the control layer, coordination, negotiation, reactivity, autonomy, and proactive behaviour resulting from its own goals.

Considering a single window as an agent with interactive components such as buttons and text areas, we can define this set as PAC architecture, built over the interactive agent. Button side-effects (sending text content) only need to be specified in the interactive agent. The abstraction components may correspond to local data (button text) or data accessed by methods. UIML and other portable notations can be useful in this architecture model.

2.4 User Integration

Considering a user as an agent part of the system, the interactions can be specified into the cooperative properties of the interactive agents. These interactions are specified as communication resources between the user and interactive agents. The presentation components can be adapted to user preferences and behaviour. This functionality is part of the negotiation and communication competences of the agent. An interactive agent will deal with intra- and extra-individual differences in adapting syntactic and lexical layers to a user. As this treatment is local, it is necessary to be coherent along all the UI components, along all interactive agents. This capacity is part of their negotiation ability and will allow a presentation type only after a negotiation process intended to coordinate all the presentation layers. The final objective is to provide a dynamic system able to handle resource and user complexity.

2.5 Distribution

Goal oriented behaviour makes it possible to duplicate interactive agents without worrying about spatial disposition. This offers advantages in UI customisation, revision and evolution. The UI can be modelled with no consideration of the interactions between components and thus can avoid code modification. This spatial disposition (on the screen) can be extended to the host localization, building a distributed UI. Replicated agents used on a different UI have to be distinct from their copy in another location in order to react with their own UI agents and not with all agents without distinction. This is done by adding the notion in agents of belonging to a group. Groups represent the UI or UI components and depend on the designers. Agent-based UI specification offers distributivity, user-adaptivity, evolutivity and maintainability prospects. Nevertheless, more complex codes are needed and the newer agent-based development platforms may then be adapted and used to make the design stage easier. Our multi-agent UI specification application to process supervision is described in the next section.

3. CASE STUDY

The proposed approach is currently being used as part of a GRRT (Groupement Régional de Recherche sur les Transports) research project. Our partners are the Semurval company which runs an urban public transport system, and the laboratories Inrets, Lail, I3D. The urban network is currently composed of coaches and tramways. Our work consists in a revision of the regulator's present UI with an aim to providing better customer-targeted information. The regulators are the users of this system, regarded as being as an Information System (IS). The customers are the users of coaches and tramways.

The IS is composed of assistance tools for the regulators (located in a regulation room); it is divided in three separate subsystems (Fig. 1): the exploitation help system (EHS) manages all information relating to exploitation variables (schedules, alerts, messages…); the decision help system (DHS) provides the regulators with strategy-based answers; forecasted events on the urban network are dealt with here; the information help system (IHS), on which we are working, is responsible for all information (schedules, delays, alerts…) given to the customers. The information broadcast should ideally provide the customers with useful information while considering marketing strategies and the regulator's choices. The HIS UI must also provide the regulators with all information relating to their tasks [7,8].

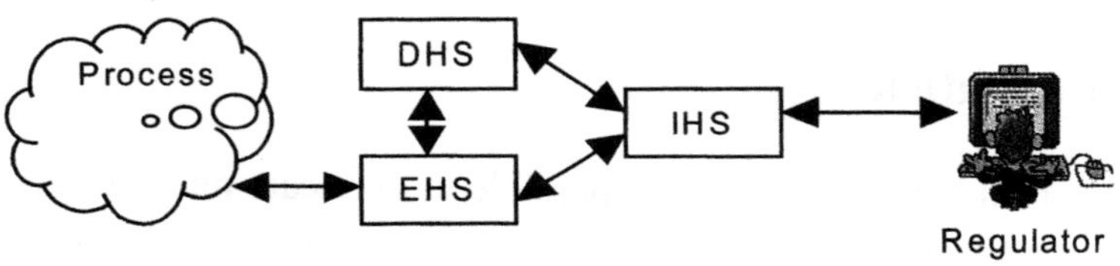

Figure 1. Global overview.

The UI decomposition is directed by the following constraints: a large number of agents increase the complexity; many UI components built on agents help prototyping; agent components make it possible not to consider the final number of views; the UI must be autonomous and should not care about protocols and communication architecture. Structuration choices are described in Fig. 2 in which the EHS and the DHS are seen as application agents implemented for our needs as a simulator sending, receiving and treating the events and data in the same manner.

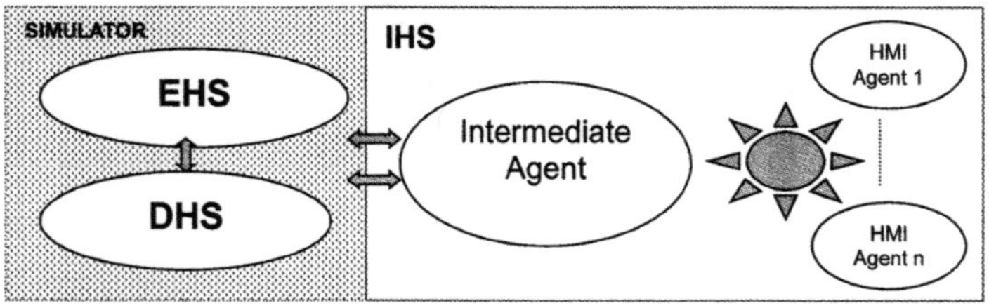

Figure 2. The HIS composed with agents.

The IHS is composed of several agents. Interactive HMI agents are synchronized and send data and commands to the application through an intermediate control agent. This agent assumes the role of (1) referee between interactive agents, (2) translator between the IHS environment and the simulator. It also acts as a data filter by only keeping useful information and considering useful events, and as buffer by keeping a local representation of the process by the way of events and data structures, thus lowering the system load engendered by interface calls.

The interactive (also called HMI) agents are based on the functional decomposition of the human task and its corresponding needs. Five HMI agents have been identified and are currently being designed and tested:

1. a first agent concerning the delays (i.e. dysfunctions) and states of the traffic (coaches and tramways);
2. a second one dealing with the different traffic lines and also showing their characteristics and the potential delays (Fig. 3);
3. a third one provides the regulators with useful information about the stations (characteristics, alerts…);
4. a fourth one allows the description of each vehicle (type, forecast scheduled stops, alerts…);
5. a fifth one allows the regulators to edit and send messages to any vehicle, station or line, and to monitor all the messages currently shown to customers.

All these HMI agents written in Java can communicate with other HMI agents but the intermediate control agent deals with synchronization. Synchronization is performed when a message is sent to the application agents and the effects need to be applied to the UI. In the case of multiple UI, the intermediate agents can be replicated with their interactive agents, but will communicate with other control agents in order to synchronize themselves and coordinate cooperative work between regulators.

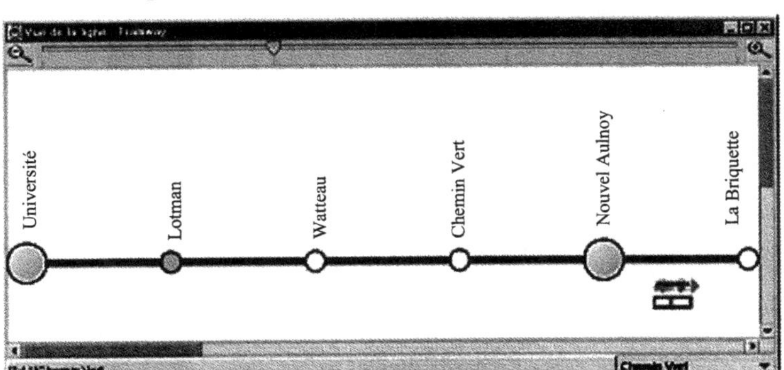

Figure 3. Extract of the interface managed by the second HMI agent.

4. CONCLUSION AND PERSPECTIVES

After a critical description of models and methods which can be used for UI design, we have explained our agent based approach. Using such an approach requires a functional decomposition, with modularisation of the functionalities based on the user needs. Each module (interactive component) is specified separately, which allows its UI to be designed at a second level, while a functional level is still operational and can be tested with simple interactive elements. Such a modularisation brings 3 main levels of independence: (1) about the application, by the use of application agents (in our case, we have simulated them), (2) about the global UI organization, by the use of control agents able to communicate between themselves, (3) about the presentation, by the use of HMI agents which can be designed progressively and independently from the other ones. The UI is not yet finished, several modules are being developed. Furthermore, with the objective of evaluation, we are building scenarios which will be played by the simulator and supervised by real regulators. Data collection will be done using the following methods: (1) eye tracking, (2) monitoring, (3) questionnaire, and (4) verbal confrontations, like in [6]. It will be very interesting to assess the user-agent interactions. Other research perspectives concern the cooperative abilities and learning capacities of agents.

ACKNOWLEDGMENTS

The GRRT (Groupement Régional de Recherche sur les Transports) research project gratefully acknowledges the support of the FEDER funding programme.

REFERENCES

[1] Barthet, M.-F., *Logiciels interactifs et ergonomie*, Dunod informatique, Paris, 1988.

[2] Bass, L., Pellegrino, R., Reed, S., Sheppard, S. and Szczur, M., *A Metamodel for the Runtime Architecture of an Interactive System*, The UIMS Workshop Tool Developers, SIGCHI Bulletin, Vol. 24, No. 1, 1992, pp. 32-37.

[3] Card, S.K., Moran, T.P., and Newell, A., *The psychology of Human Computer Interaction*, Lawrence Erlbaum Associates, Hillsdale, 1983.

[4] Coutaz J., *PAC, an implementation model for dialog design*, in H.-J. Bullinger and B. Shackel (eds.), Proceedings of 2nd IFIP International Conference on Human-Computer Interaction INTERACT'87 (Stuttgart, 1-4 September 1987), North-Holland, Amsterdam, 1987, pp. 431-436.

[5] Coutaz, J. and Nigay, L., *Architecture logicielle conceptuelle des systèmes interactifs*, in Ch. Kolski (ed.), Analyse et conception de l'IHM-Interaction homme-machine pour les SI, Vol. 1, Hermes, Paris, 2001, pp. 207-246.
[6] Ezzedine, H. and Abed, M., Une méthode d'évaluation d'Interface Homme-Machine de supervision d'un procédé industriel, Revue JESA, Vol. 31, No. 7, 1997, pp. 1078-1110.
[7] Ezzedine, H., Cartegnie, C., Peninou, A., Maoudji, H., and Kolski, C., *Amélioration de la qualité des correspondances dans les réseaux de transports urbains*, Rapport d'étude, projet coopératif GRRT, LAMIH, Université de Valenciennes et du Hainaut-Cambrésis, France, 2001.
[8] Ezzedine, H., Peninou, A., and Maoudji, H., *Towards agent oriented specification of human-machine interface: application to the transport systems*, in Proc. 8th IFAC/IFIP/IFORS/IEA Symposium on Human-Machine Systems (Kassel, September 2001).
[9] Ferber, J., *Multi-Agent Systems: Introduction to DAI*, Addison-Wesley, New York, 1995.
[10] Harmonia, *UIML 2.0 spécification*, Harmonia Inc., 1999, accessible at http://www.uiml.org/specs.
[11] Moran, T.P., *The Command Language Grammar: a representation of the user interface of interactive computer system*, Int. Journal of Man-Machine Studies, Vol. 15, 1981, pp. 3-50.
[12] Nigay, L., *Conception et modélisation logicielles des systèmes interactifs: application aux interfaces multimodales*, Ph.D. thesis, Université Grenoble 1, France, 1994.
[13] Oeschger I., *XUL1.0, XML Based User Interface Language*, Fifth Draft, part of XP Toolkit Project, 2001, accessible at http://www.mozilla.org/xulref
[14] Pfaff, G.E., *User interface management system*. Springer-Verlag, Berlin, 1985.
[15] Woolridge, M. and Jennings, N.R., *Intelligent Agents: Theory and Practice*, The Knowledge Engineering Review, Vol. 10, No. 2, 1995, pp. 115-152.